To Edmond

ith my respect T

a professional

Rev Koly

5/23/99.

Clayment Cant

P.E.P.

Providing Executive Protection

Volume II

edited by

Dr. Richard W. Kobetz

Published by

EXECUTIVE PROTECTION INSTITUTE
Berryville, Virginia

Library of Congress Catalog Card Number: 94-061208

ISBN: 0-9628411-1-0

Kobetz, Richard W.
    Providing Executive Protection - Volume II/Richard W. Kobetz
    Includes bibliographical references.
    1. Executive Protection   2. Bodyguards
    3. Dignitary Protection   4. Personal Protection
    5. Providing Protective Services 6. VIP Protection

Printed by
WINCHESTER PRINTERS, INC.
Winchester, Virginia

Printed on acid-free paper

Dedicated To:

Those Personal Protection Specialists who perform pro-
fessionally everyday throughout the world. . . and to the
memory of our departed members of the Nine Lives
Associates. May the remembrance of their contributions
to our lives remain with us, as shall the lessons con-
tained herein. . .

Table of Contents

PART I: HANDS-ON TECHNIQUES IN PERSONAL PROTECTION

administrative-type questions that can be asked to give you a better picture of the applicant's ability.

with these incidents; but of great importance also is the prevention of incidents and reduction of exposure to serious litigation.

protection specialists might be able to employ when dealing with persons who pose danger to a principal. This chapter provides an introduction to that particular area of training by examining the basic functions of the Ego. Understanding these functions can be extremely helpful when trying to assess a possible psychological abnormality.

PART IV: PRACTICAL MATTERS

The Contributors

William M. Besse

William M. Besse is the Director, Protective Services, Mary Kay Corporation, Dallas, Texas. Mr. Besse began his varied career in Special Operations and Counterintelligence assignments with the U.S. Military. His experience includes service with the Dallas Police Department where he received numerous commendations. Mr. Besse developed the Executive Protection program for the Mary Kay organization and has traveled extensively on protective assignments. During his career at Mary Kay, Mr. Besse has been responsible for large Special Event security and contingency planning for groups up to 40,000 attendees. Mr. Besse has provided protective consulting services to private families, and the U.S. Government, as well as guest lecturers at St. Edwards University and The University of Texas at Dallas. He is a certified Emergency Care Attendant and holds membership in the International Security Management Association; the American Society for Industrial Security; the Computer Security Institute; the Society of Competitive Intelligence Professionals and the National Fire Protection Association.

Charles H. Blennerhassett

Mr. Blennerhassett was a former security specialist with James River Corporation. His background included the planning and implementation of executive security in over 60 foreign countries, as well as throughout the U.S. He had been responsible for the protection of corporate executives, entertainers and prominent individuals. He served as Senior Security Agent to Dr. Henry A. Kissinger, Former Secretary of State and Chairman of Kissinger Associates. He also served as Chief of Security for a prominent family in the U.S. His attention to detail and specific arrangements and concerns brought him recognition for his creativity and specialization in the field of providing advance work.

Roch D. Brousseau

Roch D. Brousseau is a very experienced professional in performing personal protection for high profile dignitaries, their families and business operations. He has performed independently on short term assignments as well as in the role of team leader for full-time assignments. His experience includes the position of Executive Director of Security Operations for a group of hotels and conducting investigations for several major corporations on internal theft problems. He has formed, trained and managed protective personnel for corporate, family and residential assignments. Mr. Brousseau is a strong proponent of Personal Protection Specialists performing their role with a concern for a high level of care and attention toward their protectee. He has been frequently referred to as the best "Butler with a gun," in the protection field.

Peter J. Brown

Peter J. Brown is a freelance writer, and his chapter on team dynamics appears in the first volume of *Providing Executive Protection*. He is a graduate of both basic and advanced executive protection courses at the Executive Protection Institute. He has been a guest instructor at both the Institute and at law enforcement seminars at the University of Maryland. He assisted the U.S. Secret Service when foreign heads of state visited

Maine, serving as a driver and events coordinator. As a writer, he specializes in the international satellite TV industry, while at the same time, his articles on national security issues have appeared in publications such as the *Proceedings of the U.S. Naval Institute*. He has been interviewed by the *Wall Street Journal* and the *Washington Times*. He is a former volunteer emergency medical technician (EMT), and he served on ambulance/rescue squads in Camden and Bar Harbor, Maine. He graduated with distinction in Asian Studies from Connecticut College in 1976, after working briefly in Laos.

H.H.A. Cooper

Dr. Cooper is President of Nuevevidas International, Inc., a Texas corporation specializing in safety, survival techniques and conflict resolution. He was the Staff Director of the National Advisory Committee Task Force on Disorders and Terrorism and is a prolific author whose writings on various aspects of extraordinary violence have been widely disseminated. His background includes chairman, United Nations Alliance for the Control and Prevention of Crime and Her Majesty's Civil Service. He currently lectures on terrorism and espionage at the University of Texas at Dallas and Southern Methodist University. His books include: *Catching Spies, Making Spies* and *On Assassination*.

Bruce L. Danto

Dr. Danto is a practicing psychiatrist and most active as a researcher, author and lecturer in security and law enforcement. He has the unique distinction of being the only man in his profession who has completed police recruit training school and was a sworn officer in the State of Michigan and an advisor to several law enforcement agencies. As a forensic and police psychiatrist he has specialized in characteristics of criminal behavior and aspects of dangerousness for those who deal with violent persons and who expose themselves to life threatening situations. His books include *Crisis Behind Bars: The Suicidal Inmate; So You Want To Be A Psychiatrist; Identification and*

Control of Dangerous and Mentally Disordered Offenders; and *Prime Target, Security Measures for the Executive at Home and Abroad.*

Susan A. DiGiacomo

Ms. DiGiacomo earned a B.A. at the University of Toronto. She is a media consultant. Formerly Production Coordinator for Canada A.M., Canada's premier television, coast-to-coast morning news and current events program, she has been employed in various capacities in the investment community for the past ten years. She is, presently, a Technical Systems Engineer and Certified Novell Instructor (CNI). She studied at the Royal Academy of Dramatic Art and worked for the United Nations in Geneva, Switzerland. In her spare time, she is a bilingual guide for the Royal Ontario Museum.

George Duet
Karen Freeman Duet

George and Karen Duet own and operate Kingsden's Kennel and K-9 Companions Dog Training Co. They specialize in training dogs of sound temperament in the art of personal protection and home and business security. K-9 Companions has branches in Los Angeles, Orange County, Riverside, and San Diego, California. The Duets' backgrounds include experience in American Kennel Club Obedience Trials and conformation shows, German Schutzhund and French Ring Sport training. George Duet retired from the Army after 20 years' service, and spent time as Kennel Master in Fort Benning, Georgia, and now also teaches the use of firearms. He is a distinguished pistol shot and was the Chief Sniper Instructor for the U.S. Army in Vietnam as well as the coach of the U.S. Army Shooting team, pistol Division. The Duets also provide protective services for VIPs in the form of handler-dog teams or protective agents on an on-call basis. They are pioneering the field of K-9 security in the role of executive protection and estate protection. The Duets are working with trainers and breeders to educate the public in K-9 management and training.

Jerome H. Glazebrook

Jerome H. Glazebrook, director of Security and Special Assistant to Dr. Henry A Kissinger (Chairman of Kissinger Associates, Inc. and former Secretary of State and National Security Advisor) began his career in the Military Special Operations Command U.S.M.C. and later as Principal Security Escort and Chief of Detail for the Ambassador's Personal Security Unit in the Republic of Vietnam. During the final days of the war, he assisted in the evacuation of Saigon. Following Vietnam, he provided protective services in Asia, Africa, Europe and South America. Subsequently, Mr. Glazebrook became Senior Security Specialist and Corporate Officer for several prominent families and their estates. As a specialist in executive and VIP protection, he is frequently asked to provide training and protective services for a wide range of clients. They have included several personalities from the entertainment industry as well as one of the major television networks during the 1992 Olympics in Barcelona. His book, *Executive Protection Specialist Handbook* is used by security professionals throughout the world. Mr. Glazebrook is a member of: American Society for Industrial Security; Association of Former Intelligence Officers; Force Recon Associate; F.O. of UDT/Seal; and Tactical Response Association.

Craig Fox Huber

Mr. Craig Huber is Director of Security Services for H&H Arms International, an outdoor writer, ballistician and gunsmith who specializes in combat handguns and sniper rifles. His career in security began in the Marine Corps during the Viet Nam era, and in executive protection over twenty five years ago with a southwestern sheriff's department. Mr. Huber worked on witness and VIP protection details and did investigative work for several departments before moving into the private sector. He then did investigative work for Pinkertons and Burns, was Chief Investigator for Superior Protection Service and the Arkansas Bureau of Investigation before concentrating his efforts on executive protection. His clientele include members of royal families, top ranking executives, wealthy heirs and law enforcement agencies. He co-authored *Secure From Crime—How To Be Your Own Bodyguard* and is the author of *Always a Victor—Never a Victim.*

Dr. Richard W. Kobetz

Dr. Kobetz is a recognized Consultant and Trainer for major corporations and government agencies on matters of security, counter-terrorism and executive protection. He is a former Assistant Director of the International Association of Chiefs of Police (IACP) and has served as an appointed member of the U.S. Task Force on Disorders and Terrorism. He was a delegate to INTERPOL on issues of hostage rescue operations; and for over a decade, he directed the U.S. Attorney General's International Conference on Narcotics and Smuggling Intelligence. Dr. Kobetz retired as a Commanding Officer with the Chicago Police Department and has served in a variety of practical experience positions from patrolman to Chief of Police and special agent to Director of Security. He is an accomplished author and lecturer and serves as President of The Academy of Security Educators and Trainers (A.S.E.T.). His corporation provides a variety of security services for public and private clients, and Dr. Kobetz is the Executive Secretary of the Nine Lives Associates (N.L.A.), a worldwide fraternity of Personal Protection Specialists involved in executive and VIP protection.

John I. Kostanoski

Professor John I. Kostanoski, Chair, Department of Criminal Justice, State University of New York, College of Technology at Farmingdale is a noted authority on security and loss control and an expert on principal protection. He is a member of the International Facility Management Association and has been appointed to IFMA's Educators Council. His is currently Vice President of the Academy of Security Educators and Trainers, has served as president, and holds the highest honor the Academy can bestow on an individual, that of Distinguished Fellow. Prof.

Kostanoski is coauthor of *Security And Loss Control*, Macmillan; *Introduction To Security And Loss Control*, Prentice-Hall, and has recently completed, "An Analysis of the Hallcrest Report II: Private Security Trends, 1970 to 2000," for the National Institute of Justice. He has also been selected as a Consultant to provide technical assistance under contract to the National Institute of Justice.

W. Greg Light

W. Greg Light, a veteran law enforcement officer, is currently a consultant and trainer for private industry and government agencies. A number of his training programs have been featured on the Law Enforcement Television Network. He is a certified Hazardous Device Specialist and instructs Explosive and Booby Trap Detection programs throughout the State of Virginia. He is also responsible for developing the High Risk Warrant Service Program and Chemical Agent/Riot Control Program of the Virginia Criminal Justice Training Council. He is a graduate of the F.B.I. Chemical Agent Instructor and Firearms Instructor Training Programs and their Hostage Negotiator School. He is a staff lecturer at the Rappahannock and Central Shenandoah Criminal Justice Academies and serves as a United and World Airways Security Consultant. He has provided personal protection for government leaders and celebrities and served on the Protection Detail of the 1989 Presidential Elections for Candidate Dukakas. He was selected "Police Officer of the Year" by the Fraternal Order of Police in Virginia for 1989.

F. C. Miller

F. C. Miller is Sr. Vice President and Director of Intelligence Operations for Pro-Files Threat Assessment Group, Inc., and well known lecturer and writer on the topic of propaganda techniques and psychological warfare. F.C. is a published author, quoted in international publications and newspapers regarding Travel and Hotel Security/ Safety, and an authority on the subject of Intelligence Operations. F.C. is a professional member of the Tactical Response Association International (TRA), International Association of Counterterrorism and Security Professionals (IACSP), National Association of Investigative Specialists (NAIS) and the Academy of Security Educators and Trainers (ASET).

Michael C. Miller

Mr. Miller is President and Director of Risk & Threat Assessment Operations for Pro-Files Threat Assessment Group, Inc. He has spent the past twenty-four years in private, civil and corporate law enforcement as field operative, investigator consultant, and various positions in management and administration for Fortune 100 and 500 companies. Mr. Miller is a member of: the Tactical Response Association International; the International Association of Counterterrorism and Security Professionals (IACSP); National Association of Investigative Specialists (NAIS); and the Academy of Security Educators and Trainers. He has been guest speaker at the American Society for Industrial Security (ASIS) Training Seminars, Tactical Response Association (TRA) International Seminars, Tactical Response Exposition (TREXPO) Seminars and the Academy for Security Educators and Trainers (ASET) Annual Symposium on Corporate Intelligence. He has published articles on Methodology for Intelligence Operations, Risk and Threat Analysis and the Use of "High Tech" in law enforcement and protective services.

Raymond L. Mirabile

Mr. Raymond L. Mirabile is Principal of the Lawrence Group, a specialized firm offering consultation and training in executive protection, surveillance/ counter surveillance, and investigative techniques, to law enforcement and investigative agencies. He has been a licensed private detective, Director of Security for an international retailer, a Police Officer and an undercover Special Agent with the Metropolitan Narcotics & Dangerous Drugs Enforcement Group (M.E.G.). His background also includes employment as a Special Agent for the

Santa Fe Railroad and service with the U.S. Marine Corps as a sergeant in the Criminal Investigations Division (C.I.D.) conducting special investigations during the Viet Nam era. Mr. Mirabile's expertise is in personal protection assignments, surveillance and counter-surveillance activities, and he holds the rank of 2nd degree black belt in Okinawan Karate.

Tobie L. Naumann

Tobie L. Naumann has been a student of defensive tactics for over 23 years and has served as an instructor for 20 years. She is a member of Defenders Incorporated Tactical Team and is an authority in Kenpo and Chin-Na styles of control techniques, pressure points and grappling styles. Tobie Naumann has routinely trained law enforcement, military, correctional and security officers in the tactics of "street survival," compliance, take down and walk away methods of defensive tactics. She conducts weekly classes for groups and has been involved in individual tutoring for over a decade. Her present activities include investigative and executive protection services. She is an advanced member of the Nine Lives Association (N.L.A.) and serves on the Board of Directors of the Academy of Security Educators and Trainers (A.S.E.T.).

Alan E. Minnick

Alan E. Minnick is currently the Assistant Director of the Central Shenandoah Criminal Justice Training Center in Waynesboro, Virginia. Mr. Minnick is certified to teach all facets of criminal justice, as well as, defensive tactics, firearms, and driving. He was recently certified as a Smith and Wesson semi-auto armorer. His ten year service with the Waynesboro, Va. Police Department include: assistant platoon commander, field training officer, accident investigation specialist and color guard commander. He also served as adjunct faculty member of the Regional Police Academy for eight years. A graduate of the Blue Ridge Community College with an Associates Degree in Criminal Justice, he is currently attending James Madison University pursuing a degree in Human Resources Devel-

opment. A graduate of the Scotti School of Defensive Driving, Mr. Minnick also serves as a Scotti instructor and member of the adjunct faculty at Blue Ridge Community College in the Administration of Justice Department. He is a member of the American Criminal Justice Association, and the International Association of Law Enforcement Firearms Instructors.

Robert L. Oatman

Robert L. Oatman is the President of R. L. Oatman & Associates, Towson, Maryland. He is the former Chief of Detectives of the Baltimore County, Maryland, Police Department. As a career officer he served in a variety of ranks from Patrolman to Major. He was the originator of the special operations response teams within his department and participated in training exercises and served as the department's hostage advisor. He personally negotiated over 100 hostage-taking incidents. His duties also included providing protection to visiting VIP's within his jurisdictional area. Mr. Oatman is a most experienced and accomplished provider of corporate and private family protection. His international experience includes routine travel with corporate principals, family members and assignments during the past two Olympic Games in Korea and Spain. He holds a B.A. in Criminal Justice from the University of Baltimore and is a graduate of the F.B.I. National Academy. He is the co-author of *You're The Target, Coping with Terrorism and Crime.*

Anthony J. Scotti

Tony Scotti is an internationally recognized authority on instruction in safe driving and protective techniques involving vehicles. His driving school started operations over a decade and a half ago and he has been progressively improving defensive driving skills and instructional techniques. He has taught security personnel in 20 nations, police officers in 35 states and worked with numerous federal agencies. His students have been from 70 nations on 5 continents and he has trained personnel from over half of the U.S. Fortune 100 companies. He is the author of *Emergency Driving for*

Police Officers and *Executive Safety and International Terrorism*, both published by Prentice-Hall Company. He holds a B.A. degree in electrical engineering from Northeastern University.

Elmer L. Snow, III

Elmer L. Snow, III is President of Snow and Associates, Inc., a company that specializes in "Security Ground Transportation" of key executives for several major corporations. Based in Jupiter, Florida, the company provides services in several major U.S. cities. From 1985-1987, Mr. Snow was the elected Mayor of Delaware City, Delaware. During his term of office, he was also employed by a Fortune 25 Corporation in Delaware where his responsibilities involved protecting key executives. He traveled extensively, both nationally, and internationally, while escorting key executives in numerous high risk areas. He retired as Sergeant from the Prince George's County, Maryland, Police Department, and is a graduate of numerous training schools. He is a certified Personal Protection Specialist with an advanced rating. He has been awarded various commendations throughout his career, including an editorial note in *Law Officer Magazine* for bravery exhibited in a gun battle with armed robbery suspects, during which he was shot several times. He formed Snow and Associates, Inc., in 1988, and is proud to say his company has never lost a client due to inferior performance.

Patrick L. Spatafore

Patrick L. Spatafore is the President and Chief Executive Officer of Secure Communications Services, Inc., located in the New York Metropolitan area. His corporation specializes in Technical Security Counter Measure Surveys and Armored Vehicles. Prior to establishing Secure Communications Services, Inc., Mr. Spatafore served in the U.S. Navy as a Communications Technician and has been employed by the Federal Bureau of Investigation and U.S. Secret Service in both the electronics and communication sections for over ten years. He holds a B.S. Degree in Criminal Justice and is working on his Master's Degree.

Michael R. Tucker

Michael R. Tucker is a Registered Pharmacist and owner of Trident Arms in Dallas, Texas. He is an advanced member of Nine Lives Associates and has provided advance and personal protective services for SONY Corp., J. M. McNamara Advertising and has assisted H.H.A. Cooper, President of Nuevevidas International, Inc., with security matters. He has had articles published concerning health and travel for the Executive Protection Specialist.

Dennis Van Deventer

Dennis Van Deventer is Director of Security for the Worldwide Church of God and Ambassador Foundation at its headquarters in Pasadena, California where he has been employed for the past 20 years. He has experience in organizing and training security units of various types and sizes, including special operations groups. He is a member of the Police Marksman Association, the Southern California Campus Police and Security Association, and the American Society of Safety Engineers, where he currently serves as president-elect for the Los Angeles chapter. He also serves on the executive board of the Southern California Industrial Safety Society. As a much sought after speaker, he has traveled extensively both in the United States and abroad. In addition to his numerous other responsibilities, he also provides consultant services to private business and industry.

Oliver O. Wainwright

Oliver O. Wainwright is the Director of Corporate Security for the Sony Corporation of America. He is responsible for advising and directing all security operations. Mr. Wainwright previously served as Director of Corporate Security for American International Group, Inc. (AIG). He also held corporate security positions with Mobil Corporation and SCM Corporation. His experience in the assets protection field began as a career officer in the US Army with specialties in Intelligence, Investigations, Training, Operations, and Counterterrorism. Mr. Wainwright has earned certifications as:

a certified Security Trainer from the Academy of Security Educators and Trainers, and Certified Protection Professional from ASIS. He holds certificates of appreciation from the U.S. Department of State for service on the "Overseas Security Advisory Council" (OSAC); and the U.S. Department of Justice for serving as reviewer of the Hallcrest II Report. Mr. Wainwright earned a Masters Degree in Communications from Wm. Patterson College and Industrial Management from Central Michigan University. He received a Doctorate in Administration from Nova University with his research dissertation on "Developing Security Programs In A Complex Organization." He has lectured at schools and universities, including Jackson State, John Jay College of Criminal Justice and Long Island University. He is a graduate of the US Army Command and General Staff College.

Nine Lives Associates

WHAT IS N.L.A.? Nine Lives Associates (N.L.A.) is a select group of professionals who have shared a unique training experience through their attendance and participation in the program entitled Providing Executive Protection. These special programs, emphasizing personal survival and advanced techniques for the protection of others, are provided by The Executive Protection Institute. The common understanding, skills and fellowships developed under conditions of stressful realism have been translated into a permanent and exclusive professional association. Members recognize each other worldwide by a distinct Black Cat lapel pin, symbolizing the group's striving for a special kind of professional excellence.

Members of N.L.A.
- Are certified as Personal Protection Specialists (P.P.S.).
- Benefit from membership in an exclusive fraternity.
- Exchange and obtain information through a worldwide network.
- Have access to exclusive placement services.
- Maintain communications through a secretariat office.
- May purchase items of wearing apparel with membership logo.
- Obtain discounts on training programs and book purchases.
- Participate in annual training conferences and advance programs.
- Receive special newsletters and announcements.
- Secure opportunities for part-time assignments in providing protective services.

EXECUTIVE PROTECTION INSTITUTE
Clarke County, Virginia

P.E.P.

Preface

by Dr. Richard W. Kobetz

AS EDITOR OF THIS WORK I tried to serve as both architect and builder—first, planning the direction and expected material contributions, then pounding, polishing and removing "rough spots," replacing them with the appropriate connections to achieve the final product. All chapters contribute to, and are an integral part of the whole. Each is able to stand on its own merit, yet each has been placed with the others in a building block style in order to achieve a worthwhile "collection." As such, I believe we have created another significant contribution to the protective services literature currently available.

The use of the B-word (Bodyguard) has now become synonymous with Executive Protection Agent (E.P.A.) and Personal Protection Specailist (P.P.S.) in this career field. They are all used throughout this book, however we have at times emphasized the dimensional differences between them for clarity and understanding. The changing contemporary view being put forth in this industry is that anyone can protect anyone else. Or at least, claim that they can protect anyone else. This view follows the belief that all you need to be able to do is: walk and chew gum at the same time; and be able to stand in an intimidating manner with your arms folded, staring straight ahead while wearing an expensive pair of sunglasses. Since this image appears to suffice for many consumers of protective services as well as the providers, perhaps this shall remain for years to come as the total understanding of the needed qualifications. If so, indeed then anyone can protect anyone else.

However, we believe, and have believed for the past two decades, that the total depth of knowledge required for protecting principals continues to expand. Although exceptional individual skill levels must be achieved with weapons, vehicles and defensive tactics, these skills are only necessary when proper advance work, pre-planning and preventive measures have been inadequate or have failed. Many believe that only those men and women who have been police officers, served in the military or have been in security positions are qualified and suitable to enter this new career field of personal protection. Myths die hard and the truth is that many professionals are entering this new discipline from previous careers in medicine, teaching, business, computers and law along with former security or police officers and military personnel.

Successful candidates are intelligent, trainable and focused upon current steps toward success. Prior experience has limited value if improperly focused. **Re-active** training for responses to emergencies is not related to the more important **pro-active** concerns of advance work and pre-planned protective measures. Salvageable traits from previous police, military and security careers generally include discipline, personal appearance, team work and obedience to orders.

The concerns for the protection of a principal have moved far beyond merely responding to direct attacks with fists, feet or weapons and kidnap attempts. Although these actions remain as primary focus, they have been expanded with preventive methods of proper vehicle entrance and exit; transportation planning; proper protective foot movements (choreography) of the principal, and control of the arrival and departure environment. Active considerations have expanded to include: possibility of accidents; medical concerns of an on-going or emergency nature; evacuations from smoke and fire events in restaurants, hotels or public places; and a continuous awareness of embarrassments caused frequently by the protective team members through misunderstanding of the total concept of "low profile" protection.

The depth and variety of the contents of this text should serve to prepare the experienced provider of protection, along with the novice, for the performance of "other duties as assigned."

A sincere thank you to all of my colleagues who responded with their chapters to make this book a reality. A special thank you to Jane Ashby for her very dedicated secretarial assistance both on this project and others over the years, to Melanie R. Crawford for her professional editing and Clare Hendrix of Winchester Printers for her lay-out and graphic skills. My deepest appreciation to each and everyone for their advice and assistance in producing this text.

Dr. Richard W. Kobetz
Arcadia Manor and Farms
Clarke County, Virginia

P.E.P.

Introduction

by H. H. A. Cooper

"The last thing one discovers in writing a book is what to put first."
Blaise Pascal

IN PENNING THE INTRODUCTION to a new work, there is a distinct advantage in having authored the introduction to the old. One has a certain sense of what to expect whether as a reader or contributor to a sequel. There is, nevertheless, always a sense of adventure, of expectation to these things. Otherwise, why embark upon such voyages of discovery? This is all the more so when it falls to one's lot to introduce the work of others. There is so much that is fresh and at times, unexpected, even where the work of those others has become familiar over the years. This book, a true sequel to the highly successful volume of instruction published in 1991 under the title, *Providing Executive Protection*, has a well-established lineage. Its roots go deep into a rich soil of knowledge tilled and worked over by a small band of dedicated professionals some of whom, sadly, are no longer with us. In a very real sense, their work lives on in this new offering and their contribution is noted here both as a tribute to their memory and an exhortation to those who have taken, in turn, the mantle upon their own shoulders. For the present work contains new voices, intoning after their own fashion, some of the earlier themes, while adding distinctive flourishes of their own. The torch is passing into confident hands and it casts its illumination upon new problem areas, while yet shedding its glow upon some of the patches still calling for enlightenment. In some ways, an introduction to a work such as this is less an exercise in whetting the appetite for the reader with respect to what is in store than a rather subjective review of what has gone before—and how much remains to be done even after the present volume has been written, bound, and published.

The watchword, for those who provide protective services, is, eternally, *Vigilance*. The bodyguard can never afford to rest upon his or her laurels. An impeccable, professional career, attested by the years, can be destroyed in a heartbeat by a moment's inattention, or the cruel, inexorable swiftness of the assassin's bullet, bomb, or slashing blade. Over the years, we have insisted on the need to *Expect the Unexpected*. It is the kinetic energy by which the profession of bodyguarding is driven. This is a stressful business and, once again, that subject finds, in a practical way, further, insightful expression in these pages. There is a special kind of tension that informs this kind of professionalism. While it is common to many vocations where danger lurks, constantly, and as a steady theme, it is of particular importance for those who serve to protect the lives and physical integrity of others. While we have not sought to dwell, overly, upon human frailties, the present book seeks to deal, sensibly, with some of them, so far as they affect performance and the ability to get the job done. Providing protective services is not for everyone, no matter how well endowed physically; there are important issues of temperament, attitude, and ethics that must also be taken into account. Those who would presume to serve others, in so responsible and potentially dangerous a field, have an obligation to explore some of the more difficult regions of the self. For the true bodyguard is closer to those whom he or she undertakes to protect than many others and, assuredly, than those from whom harm is traditionally feared, and against whose activities these services have been sought in the first place. It is a terrible tragedy when the bodyguard dies along with the principal, by reason of an inability to ward off the destructive harm directed at the target figure from the outside. It is the rankest of treason when the attack comes from within, from the very individual engaged to protect against such harm.

While our original *Providing Executive Protection* was directed, primarily at those in the business of undertaking, professionally, the protection of others; it contained many, unsubtle hints directed toward the consumer, the purchaser of protective services. It was our not immodest belief that some of those, in the market for such services, might benefit greatly from a reading of this text. The present volume is, if anything, directed even more pointedly at this other, hardly secondary audience. There is no *Consumers' Guide* for the purchase of protective services. In the nature of things, it would be very difficult to produce one. But the principles which should guide the consumer are not too difficult to state. If there were one thing, in our opinion, which should be given pride of place in this introduction, it is the need for this special class of reader, the consumer of protective services, to extract these guiding principles to his or her own advantage. We have tried, without blatant commercialism, to provide as much guidance as possible in the interests of purchasers and vendors alike. The market for protective services is expanding. There are new threats, new dimensions of criminality and, as elsewhere in these hard economic times, there is a developing interest in what might be termed, "do-it-yourself applications." This poses new challenges for those who provide training, which, if it is authentic, and of real utility to those for whom it is intended, must take prudent account of the difference between those who, professionally in the truest sense of the word, provide protection for a living and those who, as confessed amateurs, seek to do what they can on their own account. Any training text must be posited upon the obvious: these are two different markets, and the merchandise has to be appropriate to each and packaged accordingly.

It remains a continuing source of disappointment and frustration to us that some of the best potential instruction is not to be found within these covers. An old adage has it that those who can, do, while those who cannot, teach. While this is unkind and certainly unfair to many who have achieved great distinction in the field of instruction, it remains the case that busy practitioners, those who, perhaps, have more to impart than most, share the greatest reluctance to impart their knowledge in written form. We are anxious, here, to dispel any misperceptions that may arise on this account. Some who are currently engaged in the provision of protective services are inhibited, by reason of confidentiality considerations, from writing about those subjects with which they have the greatest familiarity and concerning which they have the most instructive of things to say. We must be patient until they are in a position to give us in their own words, the benefit of their experiences. In the meantime, their associates have made the fullest use of this ever-active network, to act as their surrogate mouthpieces. A unique fraternity of protective service providers now exists. All have shared the same training, and much the same professional aspirations. The original *Providing Executive Protection* was designed as a text for their instruction and inspiration. That, and its sequel, stand as a kind of monument to this growing band of professionals whose work and experience translate into what is now offered here. We have come a long way since the Black Cat lapel pin worn, with pride, by a select few, excited curiosity in airports and professional meetings; it has been earned (for it can only be earned) by more and more with each passing year. It has come to be recognized by those who demand quality in much the same way as the Good Housekeeping Seal. The Black Cat stalks through these pages with a confident step and unmistakable feline grace. Its tracks are manifest to the eye of the knowledgeable stalkers.

And speaking of stalkers, in another context, the menace of these obsessed creatures has greatly extended the range and scope of the provision of protective services beyond their traditional boundaries. While many states now have anti-stalking laws, in one form or another, on the books, the economics of the matter dictate that fewer public resources are available for the protection of potential victims and the lengthy investigation, surveillance and analyzes necessary to prosecute these cases effectively. More and more those who are threatened in this way are finding themselves cast back on their own resources. There is a need for discrimination in the purchase of protective services in this delicate area; not every bodyguard is equipped with the right skills for the job. Coping with the serious, persistent stalkers has become a very specialized business, in which very fine judgements as to the risk involved have to be made. This is no field for tyros or amateurs; besides the harassment, stalkers do regularly injure and kill the objects of their morbid attentions. The publicity generated by the more notorious of these cases tends to incite and encourage others rather than the reverse; there is a real danger of contagion. To the careful, serious shopper for protective services to cope with this problem, we have a few short words of advice: Buy from a reputable vendor with a good track record. For those, with such problems, for whom the acquisition, privately, of protective services is, economically, out of the question, we hope some of the guidance offered in this present book may yet prove to be of personal value, if to no other purpose than to define, with greater precision, what may be needed in the case at hand.

Yet withal, this book is concerned with the providing of protective services, for those who need them, and can afford them. It is not concerned with their substitution by other means or dispensing with them altogether where they are clearly required. There are those who, on deeper analysis, are seen to have purchased protective services from which they benefit not at all. Either they have taken on the wrong kinds of services, from the wrong people, or their personal circumstances are such that they simply have no need for the services they have been led to engage; why walk on crutches when you can walk perfectly well without them? It remains of concern to us that there are those who, on any objective evaluation, have a need for protective services of the kind which form the subject matter of this book but who are simply unable to afford them. Their personal safety would be enhanced by the services of a Personal Protection Specialist but, practically, this is out the question. We might all benefit greatly from the safety provided in the automobile field by Mercedes engineering, but most of us have to get around as best we can in whatever we can afford. Will the paladins of the legal profession eventually turn their professional attentions to this field? Will those who employ others to undertake dangerous work or go into dangerous areas on their account eventually be obliged to provide adequate personal protection to those engaged about this business? We have in mind the health care professionals and social workers who daily go about their work in some of the most dangerous areas of our inner cities, unescorted, and without the slightest training in how to protect themselves from the more obvious dangers they have to face. They are truly on their own and must do the best they can to protect themselves if they are to get the job done. These are known dangers, which can be fairly accurately appraised. As our system for controlling the source of illegal drugs moves ever away from interdiction and punishment towards treatment and prevention, the class of persons providing such services, and thus at risk, will be greatly enlarged. Will failure to provide a Personal Protection Specialist, one trained as such at that, lead to a law suit for negligence if death or injury result? Only time will tell, but we think it quite likely, in which event, some of what is to be found in these pages will take on a new meaning and relevance.

As we have stressed, this book is not a do-it-yourself manual for amateurs or laypersons. It does, however, provide the ordinary, non-specialist reader with an idea of how the professionals in this field go about their business. We feel it appropriate, here, to paraphrase the warning affixed to some films and T.V. presentations: These stunts are performed by specially trained and equipped personnel. They are not to be imitated at home. We have tried to make this book useful and accessible to the lay reader. All we ask in return is that it be used sensibly and with a clear understanding of its limitations; it may help you to dance better, but it will not turn you into Fred Astaire or Mikhail Baryshnikov. It is, like its predecessor a training aid, not a substitute for that training, but a supplement to it. There are few who cannot benefit from training so as to be better able to protect themselves in times of danger. That charming canine, McGruff tells us that, "Although statistics are not yet available, *carjacking* has every appearance of becoming the growth crime of the 90's." A defensive driving course from a respected school, might well make you less liable to be victimized by this novel form of criminality, and for those who cannot have the benefit of the services of a Personal Protectional Specialist, it is highly recommended on that account. Such a course will not, however, make you an instant expert on carjacking nor license you to hold out yourself as qualified thereby to protect others. It is still better than reading this, or any other book, for there are some things you cannot learn by just reading about them and defensive driving is one of them. Much the same might be said, equally aptly, of most of the other subjects treated in this book.

When all is said and done, an introduction is not a book review, though the two do share some things in common. Both, if properly executed, should convey to the reader something of the flavor of the book into which he or she is being invited to delve. Both have a tendency to stray, on occasion, from the task at hand, so as to permit the author to take a personal position upon his or her own literary soapbox with respect to the issues addressed between the book's covers, rather than confining the exercise to a mere recitation of contributors, titles, and synopses better suited to a table of contents. Confessedly, such license has been taken, without apology, here, in the interests of laying some foundation for what is to follow and by way of explaining how the present work differs from its predecessor and why, rather than viewing it as a sequel to it, this book might, more properly, be considered a companion volume to it. While this book does stand, and was intended to stand on its own, the reader, who is already familiar with the original *Providing Executive Protection,* will feel much more comfortable with this new offering. We have tried to set down in the present work, a few of the things for which there was simply not room in the earlier text, or which required more extended treatment to do them justice. Or, alternatively, those matters whose time had not yet come when the earlier offering went to press. In truth, the subject of providing protective services is not easily exhausted, and the respective lengths of the chapters herein are no real guide to what might yet be said about the subject matter with which they deal. There is little likelihood that what we have presented here will soon be overtaken by *The Compleat Executive Protection Handbook* à la Izaak Walton. All too soon, God willing, we shall be considering what should be put first in the sequel to the present sequel. We would greatly welcome suggestions from those who have been so kind to accompany us on the voyage of discovery so far.

PART I

Hands On Techniques
For Personal Protection

ONE

Theory of Defensive Combat:
Unarmed Close Quarter Third Party Defense

by Raymond L. Mirabile

Ode to THE PROTECTORS
On their shoulders life could depend
Against those that threaten they defend
The place they stand is in harm's way
That's the sum of things they do. . . .
For pay. . . .
— *R.L. Mirabile 1/21/94*
(inspired by some works of A.H. Houseman circa 1935)

IN ORDER TO RESPOND in a correct and timely manner to a situation, it is necessary not only to have speed but the response must be the correct one. This leads us to the dilemma that dictates haste makes waste — we must, in situations of life and death especially, not allow that axiom to prevail. To do this we must develop a "conditioned response." A reaction is relatively slow, we must go through a clumsy mental check list then determine the proper action and then implement it. Although it may take only a second or two, it is much too long a time in a life threatening scenario.

On the other hand a reflex, especially a conditioned reflex of the type striven for by the martial artist, is extremely fast; it is a conditioned reflex action that has been imbedded in the nervous system and muscle memory of the individual. This kind of reflex action is the result of years of hard and diligent training and the repetitive exercise of the techniques taught. But, is it always the correct response? In the martial arts there are many techniques, once imbedded in the martial artist's memory and internalized they become systematic, in other words one technique is not counted on alone, it is a series of movements designed to attain the intended results at any given point in the conflict. One failed technique sets the stage for another technique and so on until the desired result is achieved. This is not possible in the profession of personal protection. A response must be the right one, there is no time for secondary follow-up techniques. The attack MUST BE THWARTED ON THE FIRST TRY — no other result is acceptable.

So the question now becomes how do we accomplish this, one time effective, response? Although some in our profession have studied the martial arts and have become proficient and even earned their black belts, it is truly unrealistic, given the demands of the job, that one in this business can maintain the high level of proficiency that can only come through constant diligent daily practice. In addition, many in this profession do not have the time nor the inclination to take up the serious study of the martial arts. (I would like to deviate for a moment at this point to state that this chapter is about 'third party protection.' Remember once you have thwarted the attack, you may have to defend yourself, against the attacker! For this reason I recommend that some training in SELF DEFENSE be undertaken by anyone considering this field of endeavor as their livelihood.)

Over the years I have had the experience of being quickly trained in a few basic techniques, with the intensity of purpose, that would enable me to confront a potentially dangerous situation unarmed, and have the tools to give me a fighting chance. I am not speaking here of the serious study of the martial arts which came many years later. I am speaking of the training received while with the U.S. Marines, at the Chicago Police Academy and even during a summer Judo course at a YMCA when I was fifteen years old. The common denominator of all these training experiences was that they were limited in time and thus the instructors taught the basics of a few techniques that could be incorporated into a personal response to a variety of situations. This therefore, is what the intent of this work is all about. Developing a personal response that the professional can incorporate and use within the individual's range of perception to the threat and their personal background and abilities.

It is therefore more important that the "Theory of Defensive Combat" be internalized, than the actual techniques themselves be memorized to rote. The concept of defensive combat as applied to third party protection is that you, as the protective specialist, will be either in front of, to the side of, or behind the attacker. No matter what position you find yourself in regarding the attacker, the basics of third party protection remain as outlined in the book by Dr. Richard W. Kobetz, *Providing Executive Protection:* ***Deflect, Adhere, Ground.*** From this basic concept, I will draw the analogy of the game of football. This is, with minor differences, the basic tenet of the game. The defenders attempt to deflect a pass or a touchdown by adhering to the person who has possession of the ball and to eventually (and as expeditiously as possible) "ground" that individual. In like manner the protection specialist must do the same. I believe that the "Theory of Third Party Defense" is parallel to the game of football. If you know how to block, tackle and HANG ON! you have the concept. Now we can break this idea down into 'types of response.' There is obviously a different 'type' of response based on the situation you find yourself in at the time.

THE ARMED ASSAULT

Responding to the Frontal Attack:

At times you may find yourself face to face with an individual running or walking toward your principal. He or she may be disregarding barriers, police lines, or warnings; on other occasions there will be no barrier or police line. This is the time for calm professional risk assessment — on the spot. A person walking toward your principal is obviously not going to require the quick reaction that a running individual would require. But nevertheless, an appropriate response is required. (Remember, this chapter is not on executive protection, it is a chapter on third party defense and all scenarios depicted here are assumed to be hostile to the principal.) The main consideration at this point is the question of a weapon. The type of weapon and the ability of that weapon in terms of inflicting damage to your principal and also to others that may be in the area. [Let me state right here that you have chosen a profession in which YOU ARE REQUIRED TO PUT YOURSELF IN HARM'S WAY to insure the safety of others and that includes bystanders and others in the group with the obvious exception of your counterparts on the team, who share the same responsibility and risk as you do.] This, of course, does not mean getting yourself killed or wounded, but it does mean that you TAKE THAT RISK! This is not a profession for the faint of heart, nor is it a place for poorly trained, ill-equipped wannabees. You must be good at your job, to the point of a purist. That is the only way that you and your principals can reduce the risks inherent to those who have a need for, and those who provide protective services.

While on assignment in the Republic of Vietnam at the height of the war in 1969, I spoke with an army warrant officer that I had attended C.I.D. school with the year before. He had been assigned to the protection detail of a very prominent General serving at headquarters in Saigon. He told me that it was understood among the team, that if the General were attacked by assassins several of the team would be killed during the attack in the course of protecting him. That's the bottom line! But it need not be so, if the professional has prepared himself and the team AND has kept his principal out of high risk situations. [Of course during a war this is impossible as in the case I mentioned above.] Now we have a frontal attack. We must break this down further — weapon? Gun! A frontal attack with a gun. (All positions depicted are from the standpoint of the protection specialist not the principal.) Response: Concentrate first on the weapon; it must be neutralized. The first move is to deflect the gun (when there is no danger of persons being shot by doing so.) Seize control of the weapon whether semi-automatic pistol, revolver or automatic weapon. A body block is then accomplished by thrusting your entire weight into the attacker. Holding firm, wrap your leg (any leg) around and behind the attacker and continue to push your body into his/her torso, causing the attacker to trip or stumble thus facilitating the 'grounding' movement. At all times concentrate on the direction that the weapon is pointing. Use ANY MEANS NECESSARY to get your opponent off his feet. Push, trip, twist, use one arm around the neck, push into the face, both hands on the weapon arm, whatever presents itself, do it with all of your might! DO NOT LIMIT YOURSELF TO ANY TECHNIQUE, IF IT WORKS DO IT! Thinking on your feet is a necessity for the professional; you must continually respond to the situation as it is unfolding, you must adapt, persevere and overcome! Once grounded hopefully you will have assistance, but don't count on it! You may, as I said earlier, now have to defend yourself!

In responding to the frontal attack the principle of "blinding" may prove useful. By blinding I mean obscuring the view of the attacker. This could be accomplished in many ways. A coat flung in the face, keys, hat anything that would help distract the attacker from his goal. This could also assist you in the three stages of close quarter defense — **deflect, adhere** and **ground.** The principles remain he same, grasp the concept!

Responding to the attack from the side:

This scenario is set in which the attacker comes at the principal and you find yourself facing the attacker's profile as he/she attempts to skirt past you. Here again we will assume the weapon is a firearm. As you begin your response and close in on the attacker, the weapon may not be within your reach to grasp and control as in the frontal attack scenario. It is most important to deflect the weapon, a push or sharp shove may do nicely, but you must follow up immediately with an adhere technique. Wrap your arms around the attacker's upper body attempting to lock the 'gun arm' to his/her torso. Gain control of the weapon as in the frontal attack by any means! Slide around behind, step in front, leap over the attacker's head but get to the 'gun arm'! Continue your forward movement causing the attacker to move sideways keeping him/her off balance, advance without restraint! Trip, pull or twist to the ground! The 'blinding' principle may be used if the opportunity presents itself. NEVER LIMIT YOUR OPTIONS!

Responding from the rear:

You may at one time or another find yourself 'behind' the attacker. For whatever reason this has happened, the fact is, it HAS HAPPENED! Once again we will assume the weapon to be a firearm of some type. There are several methods by which you may accomplish your three objectives of **deflect, adhere** and **ground.**

You may grab the back of the clothing, jerking the attacker backwards and accomplishing the defection, you must then quickly grab the 'gun arm' by using any technique—possibly an arm bar, or you may find that trapping (pressing the 'gun arm' to the body) may be more expedient. In any case, as with any situation, do what is necessary to control the 'gun arm.' Then by wrapping a free arm around the attacker's head (possibly covering the eyes) or neck, bend him/her to the rear, once again pull, twist, push or trip, but get the attacker to the ground.

Grabbing the clothes, especially in the summer when light tearable clothes may be worn, may not be feasible, you may have to grab the upper torso or the head and neck area, but remember, get the job done! That is what's important, NOT the technique used. These methods are not supposed to look 'pretty.' You

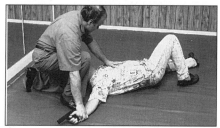 

Clockwise from top left: **The subject has pointed a gun at your principal. As you approach from the rear, quickly grab the 'gun arm' deflecting the gun away from the principal. At the same instant, blind the subject by striking across the face with the opposite hand, continue the movement by straightening the subject's arm across your body and at the same time force your forearm under the subject's jaw or chin. While maintaining the "arm bar," forcing the subject's head to the rear and downward, step back and effect the grounding phase.**

may look awkward, and to the uninitiated, foolish, but this is "down and dirty" and it's real life not Hollywood, remember that! Your job is to protect life not mug for the news media!

RESPONDING TO THE UNARMED ATTACK

Although armed attacks upon your principal are more dangerous and require a higher level of response, the unarmed attack is no less serious. An attack upon your principal is an attack, period! The difference is not in the speed and ability with which you respond. The difference is in the method or approach.

In cases in which an individual begins with verbal insults while walking toward your principal, you may simply place yourself in-between and speak calmly but firmly to the subject. If he/she continues, place yourself in a position that will force the subject to make physical contact with you before he/she can continue toward the principal. This serves two purposes. One, you are now on better footing legally as you personally have been subjected to the threat of physical harm, and two, the subject is within your grasp, and that is right where you want him. As stated earlier, a knowledge of self defense is desirable in this business, and now is the opportunity to turn the situation into a one-on-one self defense response. The use of grappling techniques, not unlike those discussed for the response to an armed attacker would be an appropriate response at this time.

TECHNIQUES

"Unbalancing"

Once the attacker has placed his/her hands on you in a threatening manner several responses present themselves. You may be able to push the subject at the shoulder with either hand in an open hand move. This will turn the subject enough that you should be able to step behind the attacker and bring your arm across his/her neck in such a manner as to facilitate a rear choke and/or takedown by simply stepping to your rear and pulling downward. You will note that this as well as other techniques discussed apply the basic *deflect, adhere, ground* principles discussed earlier.

Another technique can be accomplished by placing one hand behind the subjects head and the other hand cupped to his/her chin. By pulling toward your body with the hand at the rear of the subject's head and pushing away from your body with the cupped chin hand and stepping to your rear the subject will be pulled off balance, and continuing the motion will force the subject to the ground. This technique must be done quickly and followed through until grounding is accomplished. Grabbing the hair with the rear hand may in some cases facilitate the maneuver. Remember the body likes to keep itself in one piece, especially the head. Where the head goes the body will surely follow. By forcing the head down and keeping downward pressure on it throughout the maneuver you will also force the body toward the ground.

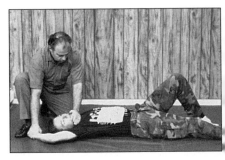

The subject is heckling your principal and makes an overt move toward his position. You approach from behind cupping one hand under the chin and the other at the small of the back, pull the subject's head to the rear and side thus redirecting the subject's movement away from your principal. Ground if necessary.

Utilize your body weight. You must apply your entire weight to an individual sector of the subject's body. This is essential because you weigh more than the subject's arm, head, leg, etc. You have a distinct advantage once you have unbalanced your opponent. Your weight, no matter how light you may be, is normally enough to ground an opponent once they have been put off-balance. But as stated earlier, you must do it with all your might. If you're going to take someone down, take them down fast and hard! Anything less can get someone hurt or killed.

Arm Bars

Arm bar techniques are easy to apply and when properly employed they are very effective. They are simple to master and therefore lend themselves nicely to this business.

"Arm bar" is a description as well as a technique. Basically you straighten your opponent's arm into a 'bar' configuration and apply pressure. It works like this. . . .

The elbow is designed to bend in only one direction. Any other movement dislocates or breaks the elbow. This is simple enough and it is the foundation of arm bar techniques. In any given situation when it is possible to straighten your opponent's arm, pressure applied in the opposite direction in which the elbow normally bends, produces pain. Pain is a control mechanism. The mind and body react to alleviate the pain and to prevent injury. The reaction to an arm bar is to follow the source of the pressure with the arm and retreat from the pressure with the body. Example: You are behind an individual. Their arm is extended as if pointing a gun. You grab the wrist with one hand and apply pressure to the rear of the elbow with the other while pulling back on the wrist. A push/pull action. The subject will instinctively turn toward the arm and bend forward in an attempt to alleviate the pressure. In so doing he/she has become unbalanced to the extent that you can now, by continuing the push/pull combination and stepping to the rear, force the subject to the ground. They must submit at this point or risk breaking their arm at the elbow. Any part of your body can act as the fulcrum for the elbow.

Should you find yourself grappling with an individual and you have an opportunity to grab the wrist, you can initiate a very effective arm bar technique. The main idea here is: remember which way the elbow is designed to bend and find a way to force it in the opposite direction; the individual must submit or break their own arm.

Wrist locks, finger grabs and infighting

I once had an experienced martial artist and ranking black belt who is also a Chicago Police Detective tell me that the easiest way to remember joint locking techniques is simply to bend the joint in a direction it is not supposed to go! That is good advice and I feel, more than adequate to explain the process. A wrist lock like the arm bar is done by forcing the wrist into a position that causes discomfort and pain. By twisting the wrist in either direction you will cause the subject to react as in the arm bar—turning away from the pain. Locking the elbow in place increases the pain and your control. Finger grabs are similar. Bend the fingers back far enough (except in double jointed individuals, and this holds for wrist locks also) and you cause great pain and the subject once again will move in a direction away from the pain, i.e., force the fingers back and down and the subject will go back and down. Simple. One or two fingers are best as it gives you more control than if you grab all four.

Infighting is what you do when you've closed-in on your opponent and it has deteriorated into an in-tight, grappling, wrestling, down and dirty, kicking, scratching, biting, spit-in-your-eye kind of situation that we all prefer to avoid.

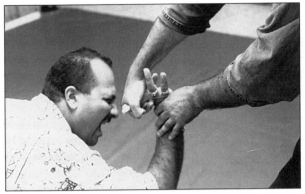

The Finger Grab: By bending the fingers to the rear and forcing them toward the back of the wrist, great pain can be easily generated in the subject. This is very helpful in facilitating the grounding phase, as explained in the chapter.

Your best weapons in these situations are your head, elbows and fingers. You don't need to have a lot of room to be effective with these weapons.

An elbow brought swiftly upward or swung horizontally can be quite effective. A head butt to the nose is a nice touch, as well as a finger in the eye. Keep moving and get your opponent off balance, snap your head up at your opponent's face, scratching and biting are also allowed. And remember the skin is the body's largest organ. It is just chock full or nerve endings, vis-a-vis aunt Harriet pinching your little cheeks or grandma taking you by the ear! They knew how to get your attention! Improvise, fight hard, win! The other choice in our business is unacceptable. But. . . winning in the professional sense is NOT the same as winning a fight. That is not what we are after, this is not personal! Winning is protecting your principal and neutralizing the attack, that is it! Making it personal and going beyond that is unprofessional and not acceptable conduct. Self control is essential, if you do not have that the kind of discipline, you do not belong in this business!

I would like to add that relying on techniques and locks can be foolhardy, most techniques cannot be applied to a subject who is stronger than you are unless he/she is diverted in some way. You must have the element of surprise. You may have to begin a technique with a diversionary kick or punch, and remember if it isn't working go to another tactic, do not limit yourself to any one idea or technique. A fight is dynamic and constantly changing, look for opportunities at all times. React to your opponent, don't try to anticipate the next move, that is how you can be faked out. Use pain control to steer your opponent and take his/her mind off of their intended purpose. PAIN OVERRIDES MENTAL COMMAND. To prove it, try and touch a very hot iron, as soon as you feel pain the reaction is to pull away from the source of the pain, no matter what your intention was. Oh yes, there are some individuals who have trained themselves to overcome this reaction and follow through, disregarding pain or fear of injury and death. Well, if you run up against one of these, you're in a world of trouble, no matter how tough you are. But for the most part these people are professional assassins and your intelligence apparatus and risk assessment should have prepared you for them. And that brings me to an axiomatic truth in this business: If you have need to use any of the techniques or philosophies of unarmed defensive combat enumerated in this chapter, then you have blown your assignment and led your principal into harm's way. Somewhere, somehow, someone goofed. That is why in essence this should be the least used chapter in this book.

Knives, liquids, etc.

Assailants with knives, dangerous liquids, etc., may have to be handled somewhat differently than the unarmed attacks or those in which a gun is employed. I would like once again to mention that it is not technique that counts, it is the aggressive pursuit of completing the grounding phase during the encounter, that you should concentrate on. You must use "ingenuity" — good old-fashioned American ingenuity. If it can work DO IT! REMEMBER YOU'VE ONLY GOT ONE SHOT!

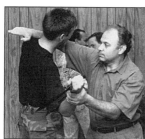

Left to right: **The subject attacks with a machete or other edged weapon. Secure the "weapon arm," once deflected, using your forearm powerfully into the attacker's jaw and chin area, step behind the attacker and force the grounding phase.**

For instance, if an attacker is coming at your principal with a vial or can containing an unknown substance, you may possibly throw your coat over the container, trapping the attacker's hand, and then follow up with a takedown. On the other hand, deflecting a knife attack may be a simple matter of getting 'in the way,' not in the sense of getting knifed yourself, rather, by putting yourself in the attacker's path, other team members will have time to get your principal out of the area. Once done, several methods of knife defense can be used.

In most cases kicking at the attacker's legs, groin and in some cases the arm, are effective measures of keeping a knife wielding attacker at bay. Use objects such as trash cans, briefcases, chairs, etc., to keep the distance. This is very important. Unlike firearms in which case you must get close with the attacker and 'pin' or 'trap' the weapon, with knives or other edged instruments "distance" is the key.

However, simply putting yourself in the path of the attacker may not solve the problem. The attacker may come at your principal fast and without warning from close proximity. In this case you must go for the weapon hand, and immediately force a takedown. You must continue to follow up with strikes, gouges and pain inducing techniques in order to neutralize the attacker. Arm bar techniques work well in these cases, as do wrist locks.

Strikes

One basic axiom to remember in most cases is that striking with the fist in close quarter combat, is usually ineffective, and can easily cause injury to your hand. Military and police agencies have for years (since WW II) taught strikes that did not include the use of fists. The two best, and in my opinion, most effective strikes are the 'knife edge' and 'palm heel'. Injury to the hand is negligible and the effectiveness of the blows can be devastatingly effective. Knife edge strikes are accomplished with the fingers forcefully extended and the hand flat. The fleshy outer portion of the hand is used. Quick, snapping, forceful strikes can be effectively delivered to the back of the neck, side of the neck, forearm, biceps, solar plexus, groin, floating ribs, bridge of the nose, upper lip and side of the face and jaw. (These are usually considered non-lethal strikes, although enough power can turn any blow into a deathblow, USE CAUTION!)

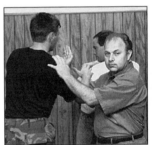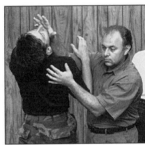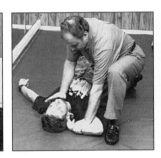

Left to right: **The subject attempts to attack your principal from the front and there is no weapon involved. Step between the principal and the subject and using the "palm heel strike" drive the subject to the ground.**

The 'palm heel' utilizes the fleshy lower part of the heel of the hand with the wrist bent to the rear, fingers slightly bent and spread. The strike can be delivered to almost any part of the body with little risk of injury to the striking hand. However, tremendous force can be put behind this strike in a thrusting movement, that can severely jar an opponent. One of the best known uses of this strike is under the chin; this is usually followed with a rear tripping technique to accomplish the grounding effect. It can also result in a knockout.

Other strikes that may be utilized are one-knuckle jabs to the eye or cheekbone. Fingertips flicked across or into the eyes, a flat palm slap across the face or snapped into the ear. This can be a dangerous strike as it could result in inner ear damage or worse. It is not for the kibitzer in the crowd, it is for a serious attack. Remember you are morally and legally accountable for the amount of force you use in defending your principal! Excessive use of force will put you out of this business FAST! And could also put you in jail. Only **reasonable force** can be used in any situation that requires defensive combat techniques. The **reasonable force** doctrine generally means, that force to which a "reasonable" man can rely in order to protect himself or another. Anything more is AGAINST THE LAW!

Kicks

In general only a few kicks are suitable for close quarter combat. They are low and fast, difficult to see and block, and effective in distracting or neutralizing an attacker. Kicks are NOT the first line of defense however. They are useful only in combination with strong counterattacks that utilize the principles already set forth in this chapter. The specific kicking techniques that I will discuss here, although certainly not all inclusive, should suffice for any close quarter encounter. Save the fancy high techniques for the gym, or better yet, Hollywood. I would like to point out a few facts about high kicking. The higher you raise your leg, (a) the more vulnerable you are, (b) the more off balance you are, (c) the less power you have, (d) the less prepared you are for a follow-up move, (e) you lose the element of surprise because a trained person will sense the beginning of the technique and an untrained person will probably see it before it is completed, (f) if thrown to the head you are aiming at a small moveable target, easily missed, (g) you are overly committed, therefore a missed technique slows recovery time, and finally (h) high kicks are environment and terrain sensitive. Just try being effective in street clothes on an icy sidewalk!!

Now in response to those who are screaming foul, I will say only that there may be a few Masters of the Martial Arts that could pull it off, but I venture to say, they are not in this business and that if you are reading this chapter as a professional, you are not one of them. (As I stated earlier, this business does not lend itself to that kind of training regimen.) I would also say that only a few of the Martial disciplines stress high kicking and then it is mostly for the aesthetics of training and competition. In conclusion, I remind the reader that in WW II our G.I.'s and the British (even the commandos) were trained in the art of dirty fighting called DEFENDU; it was simple, effective and could be taught quickly and easily. The Japanese have a long history of disciplined Martial Arts traditions. . . we won the war. Enough said.

The first kicking technique I will discuss is the **oblique.** This is a fast technique, almost impossible to see or block. Its simplicity makes it one of my favorite "distracting" moves. The foot is brought up from the ground in a whipping motion across the opposite knee and snapped into the inside of the attacker's knee in a sweeping-type motion. This technique can be effectively used when responding to the frontal attack and may assist in the grounding phase.

The second technique is a **joint breaker.** This kick can be used from any direction. The leg is lifted off of the ground as if to stomp and then is quickly and forcefully slammed into the attacker's knee at a slight angle. You may pivot on the supporting leg for more power or you may simply drive forward. This can be very effective when taking someone to the ground from behind. To do this, grab the attacker from behind by the hair or back of the shirt/coat and pull sharply to the attacker's rear, at the same time snapping the side of your foot into the back of the knee from the position mentioned above, this should unbalance the attacker and facilitate the grounding phase.

The third technique is a **thrust kick.** This kick is most effective when delivered to the front, and is an excellent method of stopping forward movement in the attacker. In some cases it may be used (and is more effective) when

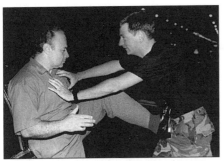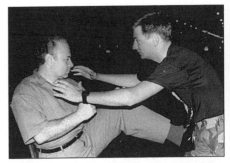

Left to right: **An attacker attempts to assault your principal as he/she is entering or leaving the vehicle. You quickly close the door protecting your principal by keeping them inside the vehicle. You place yourself between the attacker and the car and using the vehicle as a brace utilize a "front thrust kick" to push the subject away from the car.**

your back is braced against a wall or even a vehicle. To accomplish the kick simply raise your knee as high as possible and thrust straight out into the attacker's midsection or chest area, extend your leg forcefully and fully, keeping it tense so that the attacker runs into a "human pole." Timing is important here. If you put it up too soon the attacker will not be caught off guard and will avoid the kick. However, if you are a little slow, simply turn the kick into a 'push-away' technique and force your opponent backward.

In conclusion, the techniques addressed in this chapter are easy to perform, versatile, varied enough to be adapted to most defensive situations, and therefore fulfill the requirements for unarmed close quarter combat. The rest is all in the mind of the defender. Remember, innovation is the key. The protective service business is dynamic, never static. You must "expect the unexpected." You must be innovative and always aware of what is going on around you. If an attack occurs you must THINK, RESPOND, PROTECT, SURVIVE! THAT IS OUR BOTTOM LINE!

TWO

Executive Transportation—
The Right Way

by Elmer L. Snow, III

THERE IS NO GREATER COMPLIMENT or honor, than for a transportation vendor, or individual driver to develop a new corporate client. It's only after the client development phase is over that you begin to ask yourself, how do I keep this client forever? The answer is really simple. You become a part of the client—their likes, dislikes, expectations. Then, you design your services specifically for that client. You design a custom service for your client that is based on individual needs. The generic approach is left for your competitors. After all, someday you'll have their clients, also.

With the soaring increase of criminal activity directed at the traveling public, a professional driver should simplify his/her task by approaching the assignment in stages. There are really three phases of offensive/defensive driving:

1) Learning what to do

2) Learning how to let the car drive you

3) Learning how to drive the car.

Almost everyone with a driver's licenses is aware of 'how to let the car drive you.' The vehicle does the work, and you occasionally exert a little influence on the vehicle so it will continue to drive you. Most drivers let the car drive them. Unfortunately, 'most drivers' also includes professional chauffeurs, cab drivers, and police officers. However, there are two other phases of driving that merit consideration—learning what to do, and how to do it. In short learning 'how to drive the car.'

First, and foremost, let's put the vehicle in its proper perspective. If used properly it's one of the most lethal weapons in the world. Just ask anyone who's encountered a drunk driver. But, this article isn't about drunk drivers, it's designed for the professional driver who's involved in personal protection, or at the very least, who wants their client to remain safe.

Statistics throughout the years have proved an important point: An executive in transit is more at risk than at any other time. Political figures have been assassinated in their vehicles, corporate executives have been kidnapped from their vehicles or assassinated, and entertainers have been mobbed while inside their vehicle, not to mention all of the problems that occurred while politicians, or V.I.P.'s, were entering or exiting their cars. Could these incidents have been prevented? Most assuredly many of them could have been. "Pro-active Planning" would have saved many lives, injuries, and the associated grief. But, what is "Pro-active Planning?"

A pro-active approach to any situation means considering the possibilities of problems, and taking the necessary steps, or procedures to avoid those problems. Pro-active planning can be something as simple as gassing a vehicle before travel begins to ensure that you won't run out of gas during the trip, or something as complex as advancing routes of travel in order to find the best, and safest route to travel, as well as a series of alternate routes in the event the primary route presents a problem. Pro-active planning is knowing what has to be accomplished, and then planning how you're going to proceed to accomplish it.

The worst part of corporate travel may be the limousine or security company responsible for meeting executives at an airport, and escorting them to various functions. A top quality executive transportation service is a rare find in today's business world.

Of all the support services available to upper management in national and international corporations, perhaps none is more important than the ground transportation vendor. Traveling executives know how the wrong vendor can ruin a business trip if they have ever lost valuable time, and stockholders' money, by waiting in an airport for a limousine, or sedan.

During the past several years, the security industry has seen several new terms surface. Perhaps the term most closely associated with ground transportation services is "Pro-active Planning." This is appropriate in that there is no other segment of travel that demands more of a pro-active approach, than in the field of ground transportation. "Pro-active" doesn't have to begin, or end with a security service. By utilizing good judgment, and placing emphasis on the word *service*, any ground transportation vendor can add emphasis to a security approach—through "service."

Ground transportation should be viewed as part of a perfect circle. A circle, which is divided only in theory, because a circle has no beginning, or ending. The circle could be viewed as a "round trip" travel plan. For instance, a client leaves home, goes on a business trip, and returns home. This circle, or round trip, should be smooth, perfect, and incident free. If ground transportation breaks down, air/train travel breaks down, hotel accommodations break down, then the circle has not been executed perfectly. The circle should represent incident free travel which is never-ending. If there is a break down in any part of the circle, then all of the elements involved in the travel procedure will suffer. For this reason, the vendor who provides ground transportation should be viewed as one element, part of an overall team, who must perform their service correctly the first time, and every time. Ideally, support staff, flight crews, hotel management, will also see themselves as part of the team. They too, are an integral part of the circle. When an executive returns home, and every stage of the travel program was blemish free, then the "Team" has succeeded. Unfortunately, all too often, when one element of the circle breaks down, then everyone suffers. How can we, the ground transportation providers, ensure that our link in the circle isn't broken?

We, in the ground transportation phase of travel must recognize the fact that we need certain, and specific information, in order to provide our services. We need to know who the client is, when they're scheduled to arrive, where they're arriving, and hopefully, where they're going. This is the minimum information needed to start our "pro-active planning." Most companies don't think enough of their clients, security, or their own revenues, to plan further. What would happen if they did?

1. An arrival time is normally an estimate. However, what happens if a plane has a tail wind? The actual time of pick up may be moved ahead. Forget the delays, because we know in the service industry that it's better to be an hour early, rather than one minute late. There is nothing more re-assuring to a traveling client, than to have the ground transportation in place when they arrive earlier than anticipated. In all cases, a client is willing to pay for the extra time spent in waiting for a late arrival. You'll find that in most cases, they're also willing to pay for their earlier than expected arrival. For this reason, vendors should expand their "window of arrival, or departure." In short, maintain a comfort zone between clients to ensure there isn't a conflict in a late departure for one client, and an early arrival for another.

2. Know, and practice alternate routes. There is only one prescription for delays caused from traffic, and that's knowing a series of alternate routes to take. The same theory applies in personal security. If there is a situation on one route which could be harmful to a client, then use an alternate route. In most situations, good security or good service, lead to the same excellent results.

3. Another situation in which a professional security specialist, or professional chauffeur can avoid problems, is by avoiding known areas of criminal activity. Just as one wouldn't take his/her family into a high crime area, that same person should never knowingly take a client into that area. Once again, knowing a route is basic, knowing alternate routes is service par excellence.

4. Pre-registration of the client at their hotel is another step in pro-active planning. Many corporate executives earn salaries well beyond what a ground transportation vendor charges. Isn't it practical for a driver to pre-register their client at their hotel? The cost for an executive to stand in line while waiting to check-in is pale in comparison to paying a driver to handle these seemingly mundane tasks, at a fraction of the cost. Pre-registration allows the driver to check a room to ensure it's ready to accommodate the client. It also allows the client to proceed directly to his/her room on arrival at the hotel. Through co-ordination with the support personnel who arranged the travel itinerary, you may find that a corporation is more than happy to compensate the vendor for attending to this task.

5. Conducting an "Advance Survey" is the most effective way of handling travel. After all, how can you really know where a client is going, if you've never been there yourself? Driving to the correct door, every time, reflects the professionalism that any "service" provider wants the client to recognize. An added bonus is the ability to direct the client to the hotel room, rest rooms, restaurants, gift shop, or the scheduled meeting locations.

6. The comfort level established by seeing the same familiar face is an excellent way of maintaining the allegiance of a client. Familiarity doesn't always breed contempt. Especially when a client knows the face of the driver who is waiting to transport him/her. By assigning the same driver with the same client on an on-going basis, the client is left with the feeling that they have their own personal driver. It also allows the driver to think in terms of security because of the bond that has been established.

7. Another area in which a vendor can gain client approval is by instructing drivers to notify flight crews of corporate aircraft when their passenger will arrive for departure. This courtesy call allows the flight crew to begin their preparations for travel. It also shows the client that the circle is working, and all parties involved are coordinating their efforts. In almost all situations, a few minutes of advanced notice to the flight crew will save departure delays. Once again, those delays reflect a savings to your corporate client.

8. After the client departs there's yet another area in which the ground transportation vendor can reflect professionalism. By calling ahead to let the driver at the next stop know that a client is enroute. Or, by calling the flight department of the client's corporation to inform them that their executive has departed. Once a vendor does either of these acts, almost always in the future they will be requested to repeat the service. This is then a billable service.

9. Since most businesses are in a cost cutting mode of operation, the use of a smaller, luxury car is a viable alternative to stretch limousines. Through the use of a luxury sedan, a client can travel unobtrusively to the destination. A conservative, comfortable image can be maintained for economy, and for business profile.

In the past several years of involvement in executive transportation, I have seen numerous situations where management of a ground transportation service will become intimidated when a client repeatedly asks for the same driver by name. Too often, management becomes wary that if that driver is terminated, or quits, then they will "steal" the client. To restore peace of mind management may resort to saying the particular driver is on another assignment, thus assigning another driver, and eventually facing the prospect of the loss of a client.

Through a "pro-active approach" to client service, the transportation vendor shows that the driver is a product of the company's attitude toward their clients. You may lose a driver for long term, you may lose a client for short term, but if you've dealt pro-actively with your client, then they'll be back. After all, it's you, and your immediate office staff who ensure that security is a by-product of service. You're accepting the assignments, providing the peace of mind to the proper people, and getting the task done through your direction. When there's a glitch in the plan, who do they call to fix it? The driver, or you?

PRO-ACTIVE INFORMATION NEEDED:

A transportation assignment actually begins when an assignment is received in the office of the transportation vendor. This is the most important of what becomes several phone calls regarding the scheduling process. Ideally, the vendor will have all of the following information prior to the day of assignment.

I. Scheduling process
- a. Date of arrival
- b. Time of arrival
- c. Name of client or company
- d. Arrival location
- e. Tail # (Plane)/ Flight #/ Train #
- f. Itinerary (times, addresses)
- g. Departure information
- h. If staying overnight, does the client wish to be pre-registered at their hotel/motel?
- i. Member of flight crew who can be contacted when returning to the airport.
- j. Does the requesting agent wish to be advised when the client has departed your area?
- k. Is the vendor aware of parades, demonstrations, road construction, weather conditions, etc., of which the client should be informed? Delay in travel causes lateness of appointments.
- l. Has a name, car phone number, or pager number been provided to the corporate agent to ensure that the driver is accessible?
- m. If a client requests to be pre-registered, do they understand that it is necessary for them to transfer the billing to their own credit card at the time of check out; or, is there a procedure which has been established to direct bill the client. (A nominal service charge would be appropriate if a "known" client prefers that the billing be handled through the transportation vendor.)
- n. Have you received all the necessary information that your driver must have, in order to make your company look good.

II. Driver
- a. Do you have all of the information which is listed above?
- b. Do you know the route? Alternate routes?
- c. Have you advanced the route? Alternate routes?
- d. Are you aware of the nearest hospitals, police stations, fire departments, and any well populated location that could be considered a "safe haven" in time of crisis?
- e. Are you dressed conservatively? Shoes shined? Haircut?

f. Are you proceeding to the pick-up location ahead of the scheduled pick-up?
g. Is your vehicle clean, gassed, in excellent condition?
h. Have you picked up a copy of the daily newspaper?
i. Do you have a credit card to pre-register the client at his/her hotel?
j. Do you have petty cash for tips, parking, client necessities?
k. Have you planned your assignment through "proactive planning"?
l. Do you have necessary names, phone numbers, etc. for notification of flight crews?
m. Are you mentally prepared to provide the necessary service that translates into good security?
n. Have you protected the identity, itinerary, and all information on your client?
o. Are you aware of high crime areas which should be avoided?
p. Are you aware that good security is maintained through the execution of excellent service?

Whether you're an Executive Protection Specialist, or a Professional Chauffeur, you should always remember that whenever you're escorting a client, driving a client, or performing any aspect of travel preparation, your task is to reduce all risks to the lowest acceptable level. Your task is to provide security through service, and relax only after the job is complete. Additionally, prior assignments you've undertaken, and completed successfully, don't have any bearing on the assignment you do today. In short, you're only as good as the assignment you perform today.

III. Management of Ground Transportation Companies

There could never be enough emphasis placed on the role of a manager whose company is charged with the transportation of corporate personnel. You are in the "Service" industry. By that very title you, and those who work through you are engaged in providing service. Security is also service. Therefore, being intimidated by phrases such as executive protection should never be considered. If you insist that a driver locks the car doors so a client won't fall out, then you've also established a security procedure that makes it more difficult for a "carjacker" to get in. If you authorize a driver to give a gratuity to a doorman to ensure the car is closer, and the client has less distance to walk, then you've also provided a security function by shortening the passengers' vulnerability to crime.

As a manager, owner, or supervisor, it falls on the shoulders of the decision makers in ground transportation services to ensure safety, not merely for the client, but for your drivers. By adapting procedures which enhance the safety of your clients you're going to receive a clear message that your efforts have been successful. It will probably be in the form of, "I need a car for my executive."

THREE

Handguns—The Primary Weapon
of the Security Specialist

by Craig Fox Huber

SAFETY FIRST

THE GREATEST TRAGEDY for a security specialist might not be the loss of his client or a team member to an assault; it could be his seriously injuring or killing a client or a member of his team by accident, with a firearm. There are four simple rules which, if followed, can guarantee this won't happen.

1. Treat every gun as if it were loaded, all the time!

2. Do not cover anything with the muzzle you are not willing to destroy.

3. Do not touch the trigger until your sights are aligned on the target you wish to hit.

4. Be sure of your target.

WHICH IS BEST?

Want to start a real argument? Make the following statement to any gathering of people whose profession requires them to go armed, especially Personal Security Specialists: "The very best handgun for a bodyguard to carry is the _____." It doesn't make much difference what you fill in the blank with, 90% of the people in any such group are going to disagree with you.

Nowhere in this profession does the personality and personal preference of the PPS come into play more than in the choice of his or her handgun. Were you to listen to any group discussion on the subject of executive security, you would likely find the professionals present to be in general agreement on most key issues, until the subject of weapons was raised.

Ex-military types often opt for a large frame semi-automatic, such as the venerable Colt Government Model chambered for the .45 ACP cartridge, or the newer Beretta Model 92 in 9mm. Older, retired police officers might choose a .38 Special or .357 Magnum revolver while a younger officer, who left the force to enter the private sector, or one who is only moonlighting, might carry a Sigarms Model 229 in .40 S&W. A small framed operative might favor one of the compact semi-autos such as the Walther PPK in .380 ACP, or a snub nose revolver like the Smith & Wesson model 60s chambered for the 38 Special cartridge. About the only thing everyone will agree on is:

> **"WHEN a situation deteriorates to the point that a handgun offers the only viable solution, then any handgun is better than none."**

One well known bodyguard and author, swears by the 9mm Browning Hi-Power, another favors the Sigarms 220 45 ACP and yet another feels if you aren't carrying a Colt Government Model chambered for its original cartridge, you are unarmed. One gentleman I have worked with several times carries an older Smith & Wesson Model 39 and swears by it. Another carries a CZ-75 and says he'd rather carry a pointed stick than a Model 39. Neither of them likes the Glock, the choice of one of their younger partners. One female PPS carries a Walther P88 in 9mm, another carries an antique FN .25 ACP and another carries a customized Colt Officers Model in 45 ACP. The man I trust more than anyone else in the world, to cover my "6," is a former Navy Seal who now carries a stainless "L" frame Smith & Wesson chambered for the .357 magnum cartridge. These people are all active in the industry and have been for some time. All are highly thought of by their clients and peers.

There is no viable argument against any of these choices as long as they work for the person choosing them. The measure of whether or not they work is simple: Has the bodyguard ever lost a client or a gunfight because of his or her choice of weapon?

The fact they might not have been in a gunfight to date is not germane to the discussion. This only shows that they have been doing their job properly and (or) are lucky.

The fact is: There isn't a "perfect" handgun for the bodyguard. What is just right for everyday carry on the estate, or in the limo, may be way out of line for the formal dinner or the trip to the beach. What is just right for a large person with big hands might not be worth beans to the small handed operative.

It's not my job to decide what the perfect security handgun is, which is fortunate because that item just doesn't exist. You must choose a manufacturer, type, model and chambering, finish and options that work for you. Given any set of circumstances, there are probably dozens of sound choices of weapon and as many ways to carry and feed it. I will discuss some of the viable options as they exist today. (Tomorrow someone may come up with a new weapon that does it all, but I doubt it.)

There was an old time saying to the effect one should beware of the man with only one gun. The idea was, if he only had the one he probably knew how

to use it, and use it well. Today I would say, "Beware of the bodyguard who will only use one gun, he is probably hardheaded and a bit of a fool."

There are those who say it is better to choose one weapon, and to carry this one all the time, than it is to carry different weapons in different situations. Some of those people go so far as to say it is better to carry a small gun, in a minor caliber, which you can conceal anywhere, than to choose a larger, more effective weapon which might be inconvenient to carry in some circumstances. Those who opt for the one gun approach say it is better to have only one gun to learn to shoot well, one gun to maintain and one gun to keep track of. In truth there is something to be said for this approach; but I think I can argue against each of these points effectively, and will try to do so.

There are others who carry a veritable arsenal on their persons, and advise others to do likewise. In the early seventies I knew an old pro who worked very high risk clients, always worked alone, and toted as many as four handguns at one time. He was big himself and could easily conceal this much hardware. He survived in the field for over thirty years. I had no intention of telling him he was wrong in his personal choice of armament. I did ask him once if he had ever needed all "that iron." His response was noteworthy. "Not yet, but if I ever do, I'll have it handy."

There is a middle ground and, as in many other things, the middle ground might be the soundest sod to trod. Flexibility, which many experienced operatives think is the key to success in the personal security business, is an excellent concept to apply to one's arsenal. Since there is no one weapon perfect for all situations we should consider having more than one handgun available when we work.

Keeping in mind always, our job is: **To keep the client out of trouble, not to get the client out of trouble.** There are two things to think about: First, the fact is, our chances of getting into a gun fight in this profession, if we are doing our job properly, are probably somewhat less than if we were clerking in a twenty-four hour convenience store. Second, if we do get into a shooting situation we will probably be dealing with a well armed and dedicated adversary, most likely more than one, not some desperate druggy armed with a pot-metal pistol. We may not have any effective backup until well after the shooting is over. (Another point in favor of carrying a second weapon.)

Like most police officers, the vast majority of people in this industry will never have to draw a weapon of any kind, much less have to shoot anyone, during their entire career. However, to be a Personal Protection Specialist and not be prepared for that possibility, through training and the acquisition of the proper equipment, makes as much sense as an inner city police officer going nude, unarmed and untrained.

On some jobs the decision about weapons may be taken out of your hands. Some clients have a real interest in weapons and want their "security" armed to the teeth with the latest offerings. Some clients may insist on purchasing and maintaining ownership of the security weapons. (A good reason to be familiar with and competent in the use of many types of handguns.) Other clients don't like guns at all and don't ever want to know what you are carrying or have any of their friends or associates see you armed. This increases the handiness of the compact items.

I'm not a "one gun for everything" person myself. I am a hunter and a gun enthusiast. Some might say this affects my decision in the matter of multiple working handguns. They could be right. My belief is: While the right rifle for dealing with the deadly Cape Buffalo, in heavy cover, will most certainly handle the diminutive Bush Duiker, the converse does not hold true. I feel pretty much the same way about working handguns. What is just right for one situation may be dead wrong in another.

Here are some possible situations which might cause you to adopt the multiple gun arsenal, and in some cases the two gun carry:

You are working, one on one, with a client who travels extensively, works and plays with equal devotion, is in good physical condition and is not a stranger to firearms. You are a one gun operator and your weapon is a large frame revolver or semi-automatic pistol chambered for the .45 ACP.

A. *Your client decides to spend a weekend at the beach. Do you wear a jacket to cover your sidearms, stick out like a sore thumb on the beach and draw attention to yourself and your client? Do you try to hide the weapon in your bathing suit, and risk having it drop onto the beach, or carry it in a beach bag or one of the new fanny packs? What happens when your client goes for a swim, do you carry the bag with you or wear the pack into the water? Or do you leave the gun in the condo or hotel room where it might be seen by the staff, stolen or draw attention to you and your client?* **Alternative:** *have a small frame auto, like the stainless steel Walther TPH, in a zip-loc plastic bag in your jockstrap. Ladies have alternative carry options. Keep your* *main weapon wrapped in a towel in the beach bag or in a zip-loc bag in a small cooler.*

B. *You accompany your client to a formal dinner, a limo is sent by the host and you don't know the driver. The driver takes a route you are unfamiliar with. A disturbance on the sidewalk has traffic stopped. A couple of suspicious looking characters approach your vehicle. Do you watch them or the driver?* **Alternative:** *slip your client your back up gun and let him know his job is to watch the driver while you observe the more likely threat approaching.*

C. *Your client likes the Baretta Model 92 and wants you armed with one. you don't like it and don't shoot it well. Do you carry a gun you are uncomfortable with or do you quit and seek other employment.* **Alternative:** *carry the Beretta as a back up, maybe in a shoulder holster, and keep your personal favorite on your hip or vice versa.*

D. *Your choice of weapons is illegal to own and or carry in the country you are working. Do you: a. Break the law; b. Go un-armed; or c. Adopt a weapon that is legal for the duration of the stay. Another reason for proficiency with a variety of weapons—FLEXIBILITY.*

My personal choices for carry aren't important at this point, but the numbers might be of interest. I generally have three handguns on a job, though not necessarily all on my person at one time. I choose one of several large frame semi-automatics chambered for either the 9mm or the 45 ACP or a medium frame revolver in .357 magnum. This is my primary weapon. My stature does not lend itself well to the concealment of large frame revolvers, like most .41's and 44's, unless I wear an overcoat. I don't think there is much need for those cannons in this line of work anyway. Sorry Harry. I also carry a compact semi-auto such as the Walther PPK or the Sigarms 230 in .380 ACP, the newer Firestar in 9mm, or a small frame revolver, such as the S&W Model 36 or 60 chambered for .38 Special. My third handgun is a small frame semi-auto such as the Walther TPH or the Beretta 950 in either 22 LR or 25 ACP.

Under normal circumstances, going about the day to day business, I carry the larger weapon, my primary piece. I will often carry the small automatic as well. Going to a formal dinner where concealment is more critical or the perceived threat lower or level of security higher, I might carry the compact weapon and the little auto. In some rare cases I will carry the little auto alone. Not often.

There are literally hundreds of makes and models of handguns in various calibers to choose from today. Twenty-five short years ago it seemed like only a tenth that many. There are so many things to consider when choosing a personal weapon, I often wonder how someone new to the business goes about it.

Some take the advice of an older more experienced associate. Great if he or she chose for the right reasons. Some choose on the basis of something they have read in a book or seen in a movie. This is chancy, at best. Others may choose solely on the basis of cost. Usually a mistake.

Let's take a look at some choices we have to make as we come to a decision. When I am in the market for a new handgun I generally make a decision about caliber first. This will somewhat limit the choices as to type and model and even manufacturer. Still, the choice must be made between revolver (the double action is the only viable choice here) and automatic (double action, single action, double action only, de-cocking lever or no), domestic or foreign made, single stack magazine or staggered box. And on and on and on. The only way to decide which weapon is right for you is to try several.

I don't know anyone in the business who carries a primary weapon chambered for the .45 Winchester Magnum, the .44 or .41 Remington Magnum, the .357 Maximum or any of the wildcat cartridges. Doesn't mean nobody does, just means I don't know them and haven't heard of them. There used to be a well known Austrian bodyguard who was fond of the .30 Mauser, and a former Legionnaire who favored a 7.65mm MAS. One of the more interesting characters I worked with carried a pair of Smith & Wesson Model 51 Kit Guns chambered for the .22 Magnum round. The most exotic round I've ever had a working gun chambered for is the .38 Super. The gent who bought that piece from me is still carrying it to work in Central and South America on a daily basis, and has done so for eleven years.

Despite all the new caliber offerings available, most of the specialists I know of are still carrying weapons chambered for old standards such as the 9mm Parabellum, the 45 ACP, the .38 Special or the .357 Magnum. There are some .40 S&W's showing up, a few 10's, fewer of the old .44 Specials. I know of at least one person who carries one of the following as either their primary or only handgun: .22 LR, .25 ACP, .32 ACP, .380 AP and .38 Super.

The consensus of opinion is that your best choice for a primary weapon should be in one of only seven or eight calibers. Deciding to go with a revolver or semi-automatic will cut that number nearly in half. If you choose the wheel gun your choices are limited to .38 Special, .357 Magnum, .44 Special or .45 ACP. The semi-auto choices include the same .45 ACP, the .38 Super, the 9mm Parabellum, the .40 S&W or the 10mm Auto. There are some small frame revolvers chambered for the 9mm; however, since the only advantage that cartridge has is its availability in large capacity weapons, there is no practical use for adopting such a piece in this line of work.

A case can be made for any one of at least as many chamberings for a backup weapon.

A person having a large frame pistol chambered in .45 ACP, another in 9mm or .38 Super, a revolver chambered for the .357 Magnum or the .44 Special, a small frame auto in .380 and a five shot revolver in .38 Special, plus both a small frame revolver and a semi-auto in .22 Long Rifle, would have just about all the bases covered. Hold on, I'm not saying you need seven guns to work this job. But, if you did have those seven, you would have a handgun for any situation that might come up. You would be covered for any dress code, most international prohibitions (except those that prohibit all handguns), and most, if not all, tactical requirements, as far as handguns are concerned.

No matter what weapon you choose, the weapon should be proven reliable in so far as function is concerned. The only way this can be done is by firing several hundred rounds though it, under a variety of conditions. It is not imperative that you have a weapon which produces the most "stopping power." No one can define "stopping power" in scientific terms anyway. If you can't control the weapon, no amount of stopping power is going to do you any good. Nor is it necessarily important for you to have an ultra high capacity firearm. Most situations are settled with one or two well placed shots rather than the spraying of the landscape with lead. What is most important is for you to have a weapon you are comfortable with, one which is mechanically reliable and with which you can produce consistently accurate fire. The old boy who said, "I'd rather be missed by a .45 than hit with a .22," knew of what he was speaking.

Ideally, one would carry the most powerful of the viable choices he or she was able to handle well, was comfortable with and was of the best quality obtainable. Remember, the chances are excellent, if gun play becomes necessary, you won't be able to use two hands on the weapon. You will probably be breaking a fall, moving your client or fending off an attack with your weak hand. Your strong hand may be out of action due to injury. Be sure the weapon you choose is one you can fire effectively with one hand and remember, that hand may be your weak one. Practice firing one handed, weak-handed and from a variety of positions in relationship to the target, cover and mother earth.

In any given set of circumstances, carry the weapon, or weapons, you are most comfortable with, carry them the way you are most comfortable carrying them and load them with premium ammunition you have tested in the weapon for reliability of function and accuracy and which you know to be effective. Practice! Practice More!

My personal choice for a primary weapon is a single action semi-auto in .45 ACP, like the Colt, in a compact and lightweight form such as the Light Weight Commander, or a double action semi-auto such as the SIGARMS 220 or the EAA Witness in the same caliber. I'm not fond of the double action only automatics. If I need to make a long range shot, or a precision short range shot, I want the option to fire from the single action mode. I've never had it happen to me but have been told, occasionally a de-cock weapon will fire on the de-cocking stroke. Embarrassing and possibly fatal, to someone. There are times when a revolver is mandated and in that case I pack an old and dear Smith & Wesson Model 66 with a 4" barrel.

My secondary or backup gun is usually a Walther PPK in .380 ACP. I like the stainless version because this weapon is often carried next to my skin and exposed to perspiration. I sometimes carry a Smith & Wesson Model 60, in .38 Special, with a 3" barrel and Pachmayer grips. This weapon is also stainless steel. My particular piece is equipped with adjustable sights, which it does not need, and night sights from IWI, which it does need.

The third handgun I carry is the little Walther TPH, mine is the U.S. made stainless version chambered for the 22 LR cartridge. I've never been in a situation where I couldn't carry this tiny backup, perfectly concealed but still handy to get to if need be. Loaded with High Speed Remington Hollow Points, this piece beats being un-armed all hollow.

There are dozens of good weapons available. Some of the better choices, in my opinion, are listed here by category:

MANUFACTURER	MODEL	CALIBER
Primary		
Colt (and clones)	Government Model	.45 ACP
Colt (and clones)	LW Commander/Compact	.45 ACP
Sigarms	Model 220	.45 ACP
EAA	Witness	.45 ACP
Glock	Compact	.45 ACP
Walther	P88	9mm Parabellum
Glock	Compact	9mm Parabellum
CZ	75	9mm Parabellum
Browning	Hi-Power	9mm Parabellum
Sigarms	225, 226, 228	9mm Parabellum
Taurus	PT-91/92/99	9mm Parabellum
Star	Model 30M/30PK	9mm Parabellum
Smith & Wesson	3rd Generation Autos	9mm & 40 S&W
Sigarms	229	40 S&W
Smith & Wesson	19, 65, 66, 586, 686	357 Magnum
Colt	Python	357 Magnum
Colt	King Cobra	357 Magnum
Ruger	GP-100/Security Six	357 Magnum
Backup		
Star	Firestar	9mm Parabellum
Smith & Wesson	469/669	9mm Parabellum
Taurus	PT 908	9mm Parabellum
Walther	PP or PPK	380 ACP
Sigarms	230	380 ACP
Beretta	85F/86	380 ACP
Smith & Wesson	36, 38, 49, 60, 649	38 Special
Colt	Det. Special/Agent	38 Special
Ruger	SP-101	38 Special
Hideout		
Walther	TPH	22 LR/25 ACP
Beretta	Model 21	22 LR/25 ACP
Hi-Standard	Derringer	22 Magnum
Browning	FN (Baby Browning)	25 ACP
Davis	P-32	32 ACP
Wilkinson	"Sherry"	22 LR
Colt	Mustang	380 ACP
AMT	Backup	380 ACP
Taurus	PT-22/PT-25	22 LR/25 ACP

As has been stated, there are dozens of good models available. Just because yours doesn't appear on this list is no reason for concern. It is much more important for you to choose a weapon that you are comfortable with, can hit consistently with, and one that functions perfectly and can get the job done, than it is for you to choose a weapon from my list, or anyone else's list for that matter.

Whatever handgun you choose can be altered or customized to fit you better, be more comfortable, more reliable and/or easier to conceal. Good gunsmiths, who specialize in this type of work, can be found in most areas of the country. One of the very best for work on the big autos and revolvers is the Gunsmithy at Gunsite near Paulden, Arizona. These folks also do practical modifications to fighting shotguns and other longarms.

Remember, some weapons are precluded from use by law and some are precluded from use by client dictum.

AMMUNITION

My advice is to carry only factory ammunition in a work gun. There are reliability, liability and other legalistic reasons for this advice. Always follow the manufacturers instructions

regarding ammunition. Some makers will not honor the warranty if a weapon has been fired with handloads or with certain factory or military surplus loads.

Winchester, Remington, Norma and Federal all offer excellent defense rounds for all of the major calibers listed above. There are some specialty houses that produce first class loads as well but I still recommend products from the majors. All three of the major domestic manufacturers offer several options in each of the calibers discussed here. Federal Premium, Remington Golden Saver and Winchester Black Talon are all first class choices for working loads as are the offerings from Norma. Remington's "Plus P" (+P) loads and Winchester's Supreme ammo are also viable choices for the professional shooter. Experiment until you find which load works best in your particular weapon.

You may find that your weapon functions better with one of the standard loads, offered by all of these manufacturers, than it does with premium loads. I have one much used Colt Government Model in 45 ACP that does magic with standard military ball loads and won't shine at all with the premium offerings. Remember, function and reliability are more important than accuracy and power. In any serious social function, I much prefer to score a hit with a bullet that is "plain Jane roundnose" traveling at a snail's pace than have miss with a state of the art projectile traveling at "Warp Speed," not to mention having a malfunction.

HOLSTERS & ACCESSORIES

There is almost as much discussion amongst professionals regarding choice of holsters as there is about choice of handguns. Some folks swear by the cross draw, others like a high hip carry. Some favor the inside the pants rig and others think the shoulder holster is the only way to go. One associate doesn't like holsters at all and uses the waistband carry exclusively. Leather and nylon both have their ardent supporters.

A good holster can make your day, and a bad one can ruin it. In this business it is not unusual to spend 20 hours, or more, in the same shirt,

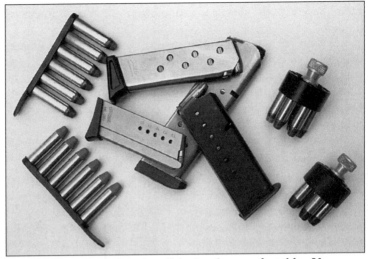

shoes and holster. All three had damn well better be comfortable. You may have been lucky enough to find a source of well made and comfortable "cheap" shoes. I haven't. There are no well made and comfortable "cheap" holsters, so don't bother looking.

When shopping for a new carrying rig for a handgun look for quality first, then comfort, concealability, security and speed in that order. There will be very few times when speed alone is the key to survival but several times when the security of your weapon, during a less than lethal confrontation, will be very important. Remember, you can't miss fast enough to win a gunfight. Concealability and comfort are always important to the security specialist.

There are a number of good houses in this market. Safariland and Bianchi are possibly the best known names and both have good working models in their lines for the person in this business. DeSantis also makes great products, specializing in high quality concealment holsters for "special ops" groups. Milt Sparks is another source of excellent concealment holsters. My favorite leather holsters are produced by GALCO and Mitchell Leatherworks. Michael's of Oregon and Eagle Industries are my favorite sources for nylon holsters and accessories. Eagle's new "HIGH RIDE BODYGUARD" is an excellent choice. Both Galco and DeSantis also offer excellent nylon models.

I have at least two holsters for each of my carry guns. I like to have a leather and a nylon rig for each handgun. I'm not too fond of shoulder holsters as a general rule but there are times when nothing else will work as well. As a result I have several shoulder rigs; the most used of these is a Galco offering for the Walther PPK. This is a great way to carry in a Tux or other formal wear. I do like the new fanny pack holsters for casual wear and Eagle, Galco, Michael's and DeSantis all offer workable models of these, as do Bianchi and others.

The best carry for the female agent may well be one of the purses specially designed to secure a weapon in an easy to get to "kangaroo" pouch with Velcro closure. "Feminine Protection by Sarah" is the best known of these but there are several good models available now including models from "Lady B

Safe" and Guardian Leather, Inc. The thigh holster is also an option for the female specialist and there are holsters being made now which take into consideration the anatomical differences between the sexes. This allows for a concealed high hip carry that wasn't practical before. Galco also makes a holster designed to ride in the small of the back (Model SOB) which is an extremely comfortable way to carry a small handgun and works equally well for both men and women.

It is very important that you have clothing, especially dress clothing, tailored to help conceal your armament.

MAINTENANCE

If you aren't going to take care of a weapon, don't buy one or carry one. If you don't perform proper maintenance on a weapon there is a good chance that the one time in your life when you have a real need for the weapon it won't function properly. Why carry something that is heavy, uncomfortable and always in the way if it isn't going to work when you need it? Some people have bought stainless steel firearms because they are under the impression that stainless steel weapons are maintenance free. Wrong! At best they are low maintenance compared to weapons constructed of tool steel but they are far from maintenance free.

Weapons should be kept dry and free of dirt and rust. They should be very lightly lubricated on a regular basis and wiped down with a clean, soft cloth daily. Weapons should be thoroughly cleaned after each practice session.

It is a good idea to keep a small service kit packed with your travel gear. The best I have found is called the "KIT AND CABOODLE" and contains everything you will need to properly care for all your carry guns. The kit comes in a case the size of a can of shoe polish.

Unless you know what you are doing, take gun problems to a competent gunsmith.

PRACTICE

Where handguns for professionals are concerned, there simply is no such thing as too much practice. At a minimum you should plan to spend at least two hours of live fire practice on the range each month. More is better, a lot more is a lot better! It is not unusual for my associates to fire in excess of 5000 practice rounds each per year. Most years I will expend closer to 10,000 rounds.

If you consider your handgun to be your insurance policy then consider your practice sessions to be the premiums you have to pay to maintain the effectiveness of that policy. Practice gives one confidence in his or her own abilities as well as confidence in the weapon with which you are practicing.

At least part of each practice session should involve firing the exact same ammunition that one carries in the weapon while working and also draw and fire drills using the various carry rigs one employs on the job. I also like to do several live fire drills with my weak hand during each practice session.

TRAINING

Every person who carries a firearm for protection, should avail themselves of a good training course in practical shooting concepts. If you carry a handgun for a living you should take as many training courses as your time and money allow. The best course I have attended so far was put on by GUNSIGHT Training Center in Paulden, Arizona. Each student fired over 1000 rounds during the six day course and the training and practice was of a very practical nature.

WARNING

Finally, never draw a handgun unless you are prepared to use it as it was intended to be used. The firearm is not useful in a bluff. Anyone who represents a serious threat to yourself or your client will not be bluffed by a display of weapons. All modern handguns, including those constructed of light weight alloys and polymers, are totally indigestible and make very uncomfortable suppositories. If you draw one and aren't prepared to use it, you will find out what I mean.

SUPPLIERS

Ammunition

Federal Cartridge Company
900 Ehlen Dr.
Anoka, MN 55303

Norma Precision/Paul Company
RR 1, Box 177A
Wellsville, KS 66092

Remington Arms Co., Inc.
1007 Market St.
Wilmington, DE 19898

Olin/Winchester
427 North Shamrock
East Alton, IL 62024

Holsters

Bianchi International
100 Calle Cortez
Temecula, CA 92590

DeSantis
P.O. Box 2039
New Hyde Park, NY 11040

Eagle Industries Unlimited, Inc.
400 Biltmore Drive, Suite 530
Fenton, MO 63026

Feminine Protection by Sarah
10514 Shady Trail
Dallas, TX 75220

Galco International Ltd.
2019 West Quail Ave.
Phoenix, AZ 85027

Guardian Leather, Inc.
P.O. Box 277
Newton Centre, MA 02159

Michaels of Oregon, Inc.
P.O. Box 13010
Portland, OR 97213

Mitchell Leatherworks
1220 Black Brook Road
Dunbarton, NH 03045

Safariland
3120 E. Mission Blvd.
Ontario, CA 91761

Milt Sparks
605 E. 44th #2
Boise, ID 83714

OTIS Gun Cleaning Kit Company
"Kit And Caboodle"
Route 12-D P.O. Box 454
Boonville, NY 13309

Training

Gunsite Training Center
P.O. Box 700
Paulden, AZ 86334

Gunsmithing

The Gunsmithy at Gunsite
P.O. Box 700
Paulden, AZ 86334

FOUR

Driving and Shooting

by Anthony J. Scotti

THERE ARE CERTAIN THINGS in life that you never mix.

Drinking and driving.

Wife and girlfriend.

Driving and shooting.

Although it's not an easy subject to discuss, this chapter will cover driving and shooting. We don't think about it too much because it's only done when all hell has broken loose. But there is an art and a science to shooting from either a stationary or moving vehicle. We feel we can discuss shooting from a vehicle with some authority. Over the past 20 years, we have conducted training programs in the garden spots of the world; places like Columbia, Peru, and Kuwait, to name a few. These are places where vehicle ambushes have been raised to an art form. Out of necessity, we have had to address the issue of shooting from a vehicle. Shooting from the vehicle being defined as:

1. Shooting from a moving vehicle.

2. Shooting from inside the vehicle when it is stopped.

Through the assistance of John Meyer of H & K, we have taken a close look at the subjects above, and will cover some basic driving techniques needed to escape a vehicle ambush. We are talking about a vehicle ambush where the sole intent of the attackers is to kill the occupants of the vehicle. When the attack happens, you have three options—remove yourself from the kill zone, return fire, or die. Shooting from a car is a final option with one basic scenario: "I am in my car, the bad guys are shooting at me, and if I don't do something quick, I'm going to die."

BASIC VEHICLE AMBUSH

No explanation of a vehicle ambush can be discussed without talking about the time-distance relationship. An ambush is simply managing time and distance. How close are the attackers? How much time do I have? When a moving vehicle is in motion, the time and distance relationship is speed. How fast is the car moving when all the problems start? The relationship between time and distance you are probably familiar with, but as a quick refresher, at 20 mph you are traveling 30 feet per second (20 mph x 1.5). If you are moving at the rate of 40 mph, which is 60 feet per second, and the attack starts 240 feet in front of your car, you have four seconds to react. When you look at it, you have a few options—drive out of the kill zone or stay in the kill zone. The only reason you would want to stay in the kill zone is because there is no other option.

REMOVING YOURSELF FROM THE KILL ZONE

Once the ambush starts, there should be one thought on your mind and one thought only—get your buns out of the kill zone, and do it as quickly as possible.

If your vehicle is stopped and there is a path of escape to the rear, along with enough distance between you and the attackers, the objective should be to exit to the rear as quickly as possible. The easiest way to do this is to put the vehicle in reverse and step on the gas pedal. The problem is that backing up at speed can be a completely unique experience. The conventional method taught in most police driving programs is valid if you want to back up slowly. In this situation, you want to navigate backwards by using the rear view mirrors. This is unconventional, but you don't want to turn around in the seat and look away from the attack. When driving in reverse, 30 mph can seem like you're driving 90 mph going forward. Although 30 mph in reverse is exciting, small movements of the steering wheel will cause the car to lose control. In fact, you can flip a car over in reverse easier than you can going forward (we speak from experience). But if caught in the kill zone, backing up fast is a necessary skill. The quicker you go in reverse, the further you are from the attackers. At 30 mph, in 4 seconds, you would be 180 feet away from the attacker.

There are two other maneuvers that are often talked about, and are valid if caught in the kill zone—the J-Turn and the Bootlegger Turn. The J-Turn is used if the vehicle is stopped and you want to reverse direction. The objective is to take a vehicle from a stopped position and reserve its direction in a minimum amount of time and space. This is accomplished by putting the car in reverse, backing up at speed, and sharply turning the steering wheel. When this is done, the car will spin 180 degrees. As it's spinning, put the car in drive and drive off into the sunset. The Bootlegger Turn is used if you are moving forward and want to reverse direction. To perform the Bootlegger Turn, you step on the emergency brake as the car is moving forward, and sharply turn the steering wheel. When this is done, the car will spin 180 degrees. When the car is pointed in the opposite direction, drive off. Both are aggressive maneuvers and require a world of caution. Don't practice this unless you are instructed by a qualified instructor. There is a lot more to doing a Bootlegger and a J-Turn than is mentioned above. You can't believe the disaster you can create if you try to do this unsupervised.

If you do not have time to do a Bootlegger or a J-Turn, and there is no escape to the rear, the only option may be to ram through the blockade.

POSITIONING THE VEHICLE

If all hell breaks loose, and you can't escape the kill zone, your only option may be to position the vehicle in a manner that achieves maximum cover. If the car is moving, the objective is to put the car at a 90 degree angle from the threat. You must put as much metal between you and them as possible. This is a simple maneuver to accomplish. Just press on the emergency brake and turn the steering wheel. It requires a little practice to get the car positioned where you want it. If you turn the steering wheel too much, you will spin the car 180 degrees. You need to be gentle and accurate with the steering wheel. Figure One demonstrates how you can practice 90 degree turns. What we

Figure One

do is drive up to a series of cones laid out in a semicircle. As you drive into the semicircle, someone calls out a number that represents one of the cones. You must spin the car and get as close as possible to the cone at a ninety degree angle.

RETURNING FIRE FROM A STOPPED VEHICLE

If you are caught in the kill zone, you must immediately return fire. It is vital that you do all that is possible to disrupt the ambush. Why your car is stopped and why you can't get out of the kill zone can be the subject of a book. For our purposes, we will assume all else has failed. There you are and here they come. You are in a car, under fire with the folks rushing you. At this point, it's not a good idea to get out of the car. No matter how quick you are, if you get out of the car, they can be on top of you in seconds. This leaves one alternative—shooting at the bad guys from the comfort of your vehicle.

SHOOTING THROUGH THE WINDSHIELD

Shooting from inside the car will require doing things that may be considered an unnatural act. Things like shooting through the windshield from inside the car. This is not something that most people get to practice. It can get expensive. But it's something that is a necessary skill to combat a vehicle ambush. Keep in mind that the only time you would use this is when there is no other option.

Your weapon needs to be where you can get to it quickly. Brace yourself in the seat and put the muzzle close to the glass. Putting the muzzle close to the glass reduces the possibility of glass coming into your face. The muzzle blast pushes the glass away from you. Double taps are used. The first round breaks the windshield and the second round goes through. This is not an easy skill to acquire and requires practice. When practicing, wear ear and eye protection. This is an extreme measure, but in the final option scenario, there are few alternatives.

We also need to look at shooting through the side windows which requires practice as well. The side glass is made of different material than a windshield. Once the round hits the side window, it simply evaporates. With the limited field of vision, it's a lot harder to shoot through the side windows. You should practice shooting from the driver's side out the passenger window, and from the passenger side out of driver's side window. Keep in mind that this is the worst possible case scenario; you shoot from inside the car or you die.

seconds at 10 mph	0	1	2	3	4	5	6	7	8	9	10
distance to the target	212	202	192	183	175	168	162	157	153	151	150

Table 1

SHOOTING FROM A MOVING VEHICLE

Shooting from a moving vehicle is also unique. The first thing you need to understand is that shooting from a vehicle requires a reverse lead, meaning that you shoot behind the target. Shooting at a stationary target from a moving vehicle is, at best, difficult.

Look at Table One. If you were driving at 10 mph (which is slow), and were approaching a target that was 150 feet away from your front bumper and 150 feet away from your door (look at Figure Two), every second you would be getting closer to the target, and the angle of the target would also be changing (Table Two). What's interesting, and makes shooting from a moving vehicle difficult, is that the rate you close in on the target is not linear. From Table One we see that when you start shooting, you are 212 feet away from the target; two seconds later you are 192 feet away from the target, but notice that the closer you get to the target, the less effect the speed of the vehicle has on the distance from the target. In the first two seconds, the change in distance from the target is 20 feet and in the last two seconds it is 3 feet.

Also, the angle the weapon is pointed is changing in relationship to the speed. As Table Two shows, the closer you get to the target, the angle at which the weapon is pointing also changes.

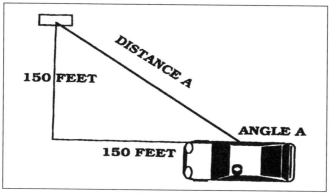

Figure Two

seconds at 10 mph	0	1	2	3	4	5	6	7	8	9	10
angle from the target	45	48	51	55	59	63	67	72	77	83	90

Table 2

The faster you go, the harder it is. Look at Table Three. At 30 mph, in three seconds, the distance from the target has changed 50 feet, and the angle (Table Four) has changed 20 degrees.

seconds at 30 mph	0	1	2	3	3.3
distance to the target	212	183	162	151	150

Table Three

seconds at 30 mph	0	1	2	3	3.3
angle from the target	45	55	67	85	90

Table Four

Therefore, distance and angle change rapidly as you approach the target. In the scenarios we mentioned above, the speed was constant. If you change the speed, accelerate or slow down, then things get even worse. Shooting from a moving vehicle is another last option tool, but if you feel the need may arise to use these techniques, you should spend time practicing. Again, do not attempt this unless you have an experienced instructor with you.

SHOOTING AT A CAR

Although it may sound strange, it is a good idea to shoot at a car and measure the results. There are videos available that show the effects of rounds on a vehicle. But it is better to do your own research on a vehicle that resembles the car you drive. Keep in mind that all cars are slightly different, and how one round affects one vehicle may not be the same as how it affects another.

You need to determine the relationship between a round's penetration and the distance from the vehicle. The issue is—how far do you have to get away from the kill zone? If you know how distance affects the round's ability to penetrate the vehicle, then you know how far back you need to move away from the kill zone. This is not easy to do; there are a lot of complications involved, and it is time consuming.

FIVE

The Use of K-9s in Executive Security

by George and Karen Duet

ONE OF THE LEAST UNDERSTOOD assets at the Personal Protection Specialist's disposal is the properly trained K-9. K-9s have numerous possible uses for the protection specialist who is looking for an additional deterrent, an early warning system, explosives detection, or a man stopper.

When we harness the abilities of the K-9 for our own use, we gain the asset of his heightened instincts. For example, the dog's hearing is at least ten times better than ours. Likewise, his sense of smell can be compared to a microscope in that he can identify scent by the elements that make up a particular scent.

The dog's natural drives (specifically the defense and prey drives) are of use to us in security work. The defense drive is the dog's natural drive to protect himself, his home, his pack (family), his food, etc. Prey drive is the drive to chase and catch prey. In the wild, this drive is used in hunting for food. We use the drive to teach the dog to apprehend a person.

The two drives must be balanced in the dog. The best security patrol dogs have 60% defense and 40% prey drives. The proper balance for a European sport dog (see page 44) is 60% prey and 40% defense. A Security or police dog who is higher in prey than defense will not be sus-

Snarling and showing teeth. This German Shepherd dog displays the <u>defense drive</u>.

Focusing intensely, poised to leap and bite the subject, this Rottweiller displays the <u>prey drive.</u>

picious enough to react properly in a real situation. On the other hand, if the dog is too high in defense (70% or more), the dog will be difficult to control and so low in prey drive that the bite work will be difficult to control.

THE BLACK TIE K-9

Most people think of the security K-9 as a snarly mouth full of teeth waiting to attack. While this may be true of the antisocial fence dog, there is no place for the antisocial dog in executive protection.

The black tie K-9 (as his title reflects) is a gentleman. This dog is calm, well-mannered and totally voiced controlled. It takes a very special dog to be a black tie K-9. He is typically 3-5 years of age, is very social by nature, but very effective when he is called into action. The black tie K-9 is perfectly balanced in temperament, with 50% defense and 50% prey drives.

ESTATE SECURITY

The first, and most likely, use for the security K-9 is in estate protection. In order to be highly visible, dogs can be posted at gates and entrances. They also can be used to patrol with an agent at set intervals. In either case, K-9s are an excellent visual deterrent, particularly when a deterrent is desired to harden the target. Hardening of the target is the process of making the target harder to attack. In addition to being a visual deterrent, the dog aids the handler in remaining awake and alert, especially at night. His keen hearing and sense of smell are excellent aids to the agent in darkness. The dog tends to boost the morale of the agents. He adds an element of friendship to his handler and the

Whether handled by the principal or the security agent, the K-9 is an excellent deterrent when used in estate security.

team. The K-9 and handler checking the alertness of the posted agents in the early morning hours in a good way to keep the agents awake and alert.

In addition to fixed posts or roving patrols for particularly high risk situations, the K-9 can be used in close proximity to the principal. A good example of a high risk VIP protection scenario would be when the deposed and exiled Shah of Iran came to the U.S. As Dr. Richard W. Kobetz explains:

> "The Iranians had put out a death notice on him saying anyone responsible for his death would sit at the right hand of Allah. This represents the heaviest possible of threats."

In a case such as this, you may use explosives detection K-9s and multiple man-dog teams both inside and outside of the estate, as well as other agents and security measures.

In some cases, the explosives detection dog is the highest priority. This was the case when a bomb was left in an executive washroom. The intended victim was not hurt; however, another bomb was then thrown in this person's backyard. Luckily, the bomb rolled into the swimming pool. When security was arranged for in this situation, an explosives detection K-9 was an essential tool.

The K-9 that is utilized in the principal's residence must be calm and well-mannered. He must not be excessively vocal by nature and should not whine or fidget. He should be very social with people, not overly defensive, and totally voice controlled. The Rottweiler is a good choice for this role, as this breed is of the mastiff type and is therefore comfortable on a down/stay for extended periods. On the other hand, the patrol dog generally needs to be leaner, more active, and possess greater endurance. The German Shepherd Dog or Belgian Malinois would be more suitable for this type of work.

ADVANCE WORK

The K-9 is also of use in advance work. Advance work is the process of checking in advance on the security of the area where the principal is due to arrive, as well as preparing the accommodations and making sure that everything is in working order. Explosives detection K-9s are a valuable addition to an advance if the principal is assessed as a high risk or he/she is to speak in public or to attend functions that have been announced in the media. The K-9's exceptional sense of smell cuts the time it takes to clear an area to a minimum. The Labrador Retriever is excellent performing this type of work.

Movement with a K-9 can be as high/low profile as the principal desires.

MOVEMENT

Movement brings up another potential opportunity for the use of the K-9. K-9s can be brought along in a follow car when desired. Automatic door and window openers are available if the K-9 is not to be outside of the vehicle unless needed. Vehicles of choice when utilizing the K-9 would be enclosed trucks, such as the Jeep Cherokee, or a station wagon or van. If a car is used, K-9 containers may be purchased for long term use. One country utilizes a limousine that is specially fitted with a K-9 compartment in the trunk area, where the dog rests out of the way unless called into action.

Movement with a K-9 can look as low profile as a stroll in the park with a dog, or as complex as the use of dogs to perform a diamond pattern or crowd control line to keep people from crowding the principal. In order to prevent accidental bites in crowd situations, a muzzle can be worn with a quick release drawstring designed to release only when the handler deems necessary. A muzzle is worn in a crowd situation because people may try to reach out and pet the dog, pull his tail or ears, etc.

LANDING ZONES

Aircraft and Helicopter Landing Zones

Landing zones—or any area that needs to be secured for the comings and goings of the principal—are another area of possible use for the K-9. Man-dog teams can fan out in either a diamond or pyramid formation (see diagrams). Formations are determined by the area size, terrain, strength of the team, and threat assessment. It would, of course, be determined by the mode of transportation, such as private aircraft or helicopter, and whether or not the airstrip is private or there are other aircraft operating in the area. (X=agents, K-9=man-dog teams.)

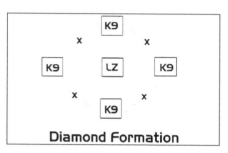

Diamond Formation

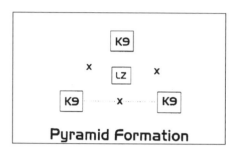

Pyramid Formation

K-9 HANDLERS AND ASSISTANTS

Man-dog teams never work alone. There should always be an agent without a dog who can assist the handler when necessary. There are several reasons for this, the primary one being that the handler may need assistance in dealing with the dog and an unwanted visitor. An agent who is not schooled in the handling of a K-9 is not a good backup for the man-dog team. If the K-9 handler should become injured, the second agent may be required to step in and take control of the K-9.

It does not take as much training for an agent to learn how to back up a K-9 team or to be an assistant as it does to be a K-9 handler. As long as the agent doesn't have a fear of K-9s, he can learn how to assist a team by attending a seminar.

The backup handler must understand how the K-9 thinks, how K-9 training is handled, and how the dog is likely to respond to various commands and situations. Safety measures such as, "never get between the K-9 and the bad guy," help to keep accidental bites from happening.

Familiarity with the K-9 keeps the backup agent from being overly nervous in handling him. If he has a rapport with the K-9, has petted him, and gotten close, the K-9 will be more comfortable with him as well.

Another reason the agent should be schooled with the K-9 for backup is the need for a spotter or A.T. (Assistant Trainer). This person works as an assistant to the handler in providing training to the dog by using aids and giving rewards at appropriate times.

It would be more typical to see the K-9 used in a less dramatic fashion. Some principals desire to have their own K-9s for protection AND companionship. The ideal situation occurs when the principal is a dog lover and desires to be trained as a handler for his or her own dog.

There is an allowance for great flexibility when the principal agents are trained handlers as well. The principal can freely move about, enjoying the company of his own K-9, while having the convenience of handing the responsibility of the K-9 over to his agent at any time.

K-9s USED IN STALKER CASES

An excellent situation for a K-9 is in a stalker case, especially when the principal is a female. An agent in the residence in the evening can be a little intrusive. The K-9, however, can be at the principal's side regardless of the room she is occupying or what she is doing.

Cost is another factor. The K-9 costs less than an agent, especially in a long-term protective assignment. The principal purchases the dog and is given basic handling instructions. At the end of the assignment, there is the option of keeping the dog or turning it back to the trainer.

K-9s are very visual and high profile. This high visibility allows them to be used as deterrents or diversions. A stalker may determine

In a stalker case involving a woman, the K-9 makes an excellent equalizer.

that the K-9 is too difficult to get past and choose an easier target. On the other hand, the stalker may be convinced that the principal may enter or exit at the doors where the highly visible K-9s are posted. This could, in fact, be a diversion so that the principal can use another entrance.

WHAT QUALITIES DO YOU LOOK FOR IN A K-9?

When searching the right K-9 for the purpose of executive security, one must be mindful of several points.

1. Breed of Dog

Not every dog is a suitable candidate. The dog must be of the correct breed, type, and temperament. There are about a dozen possible breed candidates. Of these, the top three choices generally are regarded as the Rottweiler, German Shepherd Dog, and Belgian Malinois (not necessarily in that order). Other possibilities are the Doberman Pinscher, Dutch Shepherd, Akita, Bullmastiff, Dogue de Bordeaux, Belgian Shepherd, etc.

2. Temperament

The dog's temperament is the key to success. Just as the Personal Protection Specialist needs a balanced temperament, good nerves, stamina and courage, so does the K-9.

A lack of good temperament could put the agent or principal at risk. This risk is not limited to the over-aggressive dog, but also to the dog who does not respond when called upon. This is the dog handler's worst nightmare. In order to prevent disaster due to over-estimation of the dog's abilities, situation set-ups should be a regular part of the K-9's training maintenance.

3. Prior Training

This is where many well-intended trainers and directors of training programs often break down. Many believe that dogs who have previously been worked in or titled in Schutzhund (a German protection sport where obedience, tracking and protection are taught) are the best protection candidates. It is easy to understand why they believe this concept. Schutzhund is a sport used as a breeder's tool in Germany.

It stands to reason, to most educated individuals who purchase 2 to 3-year-old K-9s schooled in Schutzhund, that this would be a wise investment. While there is some credence to this theory, there is also a built-in flaw to this view. Dogs are easily conditioned creatures. Whatever the dog spends the majority of his early life learning is what he is likely to follow as an example the duration of his life.

The Schutzhund dog has learned a sport that requires a emphasis on equipment. For example, the Schutzhund dog will bite the equipment if it is thrown to the ground. The reason for this is that, when the dog was a pup, he was taught to focus on the equipment rather than the man. The dog also was typically taught on a field with jumps and blinds for props. Now, as an adult, he is expected to deal with a number of changes. He is expected to be defensive to the man. In general, this is a drive that the K-9 hasn't spent much time working on. Oftentimes, a soft dog is the result.

FOUNDATION TRAINING

A Schutzhund dog is rarely, if ever, stressed in his defense drive. Being stressed while in the defense drive is exactly what a good patrol dog is subject to. Executive security is not a game (such as Schutzhund), but reality. Many Schutzhund dogs cannot handle the stress of police work.

You are much better off to purchase a dog who has been trained from the beginning for police or security work. This will be a dog that is high in defense and has been worked in defense from the onset of his protection training. His focus has always been on the man rather than the equipment.

Ideally, the dog should be trained in and around the surroundings that he will be expected to work. This will eliminate the problem of the estate protection dog that tries to chase down and kill the principal's prize Arabian Stallion, etc.

Training the dog from the ground up is not always possible. The reason behind this is that most K-9 handlers have no idea how to "create" a K-9. They purchase one already trained. A similar analogy would be the driver who drives his car, but did not build it.

CONVERSION TRAINING THE EUROPEAN SPORT DOG

A working Security K-9 needs to know that he can bite anywhere on the body to apprehend the suspect.

Conversion training is the act of converting the dog from the training he is used to (such as Schutzhund) to security or police work.

This is done often and with mixed results. There is no doubt that there are some excellent working K-9s who have been converted from Schutzhund. In most cases when it works well, the dog was always high in defense, even when working in Schutzhund. A dog who is higher in defense than in prey drive can still qualify in Schutzhund. This dog will need a lot of work in defense. He will need to work without obvious equipment present. Muzzle attacks and hidden sleeve work will help this dog to get past his equipment orientation.

THE DOG HANDLER

The handler is the most important part of the training equation. In order to be effective, it makes no sense to teach a dog for two years and then give the agent two months of training instruction. Both require ongoing (maintenance) training. Just as an agent has a regular fitness program, attends marital arts training, driver's training and goes to the range to stay proficient in shooting, the K-9 and his handler need regular training practice.

The K-9's usefulness, in terms of health and reliability, is about 5-7 years. The best K-9 protection programs are self-generating. This means that as the handler's K-9 ages, youngsters of six months of age are brought in to begin their foundation training. With a self-generating program, each K-9 handler has a youngster to train with 30 minutes per day toward his end goal of replacing the aging K-9. K-9 trainers teach handlers how to train the dogs in each phase and then the training director spot checks every few months to ensure the K-9s are coming along as planned. On an estate, agents may be taught to decoy for each other's dogs to keep them sharp, thus avoiding the expense of an outside trainer coming on a weekly basis.

The advantage gained here, with the in-house training program, is that cost is cut in half and the efficiency of the dogs is doubled. Many police departments have gone to in-house training programs for two reasons. Cutting costs, of course, is one. However, the other — for "EFFICIENCY" — is far more beneficial. With an in-house training program, the agents who have been schooled in the art of K-9 training can train their own dogs at will. If circumstances and the threat level rises, they can work the dogs in the necessary fashion without having to wait for the trainer to arrive to do so.

All too often the K-9 is purchased without enough regard to the handler's education. As previously stated, the handler's role is more important than the K-9. The K-9 has no reason ability, so he is likely to make mistakes if allowed to react totally on instinct. It is the handler's job to reason for the team. The handler must know how to read the K-9 (how the animal thinks and how to predict his actions) to control his every move.

Ongoing practice with experienced decoys is necessary to maintain the dog's efficiency.

The handler must be well schooled in the use of his dog for defensive purposes. He must understand safety procedures and the law as it applies to his job. He must know how much stress his dog can handle and when his K-9 partner is tired, excited, uneasy, etc. This bonding takes place through time, training and everyday interaction.

The K-9 and handler team must be physically strong and healthy. The handler must have sufficient strength to hold his or her dog back while the K-9 lunges against the end of the leash. The handler must not be afraid of dogs and he/she must be able to discipline like a drill sergeant.

SKILLS OF THE SECURITY K-9

Although the security patrol K-9 will always be worked on the leash, the handler must have him voice controlled off the leash as well. The following are basic skills that the K-9 should be taught, both on and off the leash.

1. Alert and bark on command or when the proper situation arises.

2. Be quiet on command.

3. Apprehend an aggressor and control him.

4. Stand guard on the perpetrator.

5. Reattach if necessary.

6. Return to the handler heel position when called.

7. Check buildings for intruders and warn of their presence.

Guarding an object such as a briefcase has applications in Executive Security.

8. Escort the intruder off of the property or to the desired destination.

CONCLUSION

Among the tools that the Personal Protection Specialist may use on any given assignment (i.e., firearm, vehicle, portable alarm system, cellular phone, radio, emergency care kit, etc.) is the well trained K-9.

If it fits into the agent's lifestyle, the K-9 can also function as protection for the agent's home and family, thereby serving a dual purpose. The K-9 will not be appropriate for every job assignment the Personal Protection Specialist may encounter. It is true, however, that it is much better to have your K-9 available and be well schooled in the uses of the K-9 when called upon, than to wish you had a K-9 and the training necessary when the job requires one.

Speaking from personal experience, from estate protection to the 1992 Los Angeles riots, when the threat assessment rises, it is most comforting to know your team can be immediately strengthened with a well trained K-9.

SUGGESTED READING

Barwig, Susan, and Stewart Hilliard. *Schutzhund—Theory and Training Methods.* New York: Howell Book House, 1991.

Bamberger, Michelle, DVM. *Help! A Quick Guide to First Aid for Your Dog.* New York: Howell Book House, 1993.

Campbell, Dr. William. *Behavior Problems in Dogs.* Santa Barbara, CA: American Veterinary Publications, Inc., 1991.

Carlson, Delbert G., DVM, and James M. Giffen, MD. *Dog Owner's Home Veterinary Handbook.* New York: Howell Book House, 1992.

Duet, Karen Freeman & George. *The Home & Family Protection Dog.* New York: Howell Book House 1993. *The Business Security K-9.* New York; Howell Book House 1995.

Fox, Michael. *Understanding Your Dog.* New York: Coward, McCann, and Geoghegan, 1992.

Pfaffenberger, Clarence. *The New Knowledge of Dog Behavior.* New York: Howell Book House, 1963.

Lanting, Fred L. *Canine Hip Dysplasia.* Loveland, CO: Alpine Publications, Inc.

Saunders, Blanche. *The Complete Book of Dog Obedience.* New York: Howell Book House, 1978.

Strickland, Winifred. *Expert Obedience Training for Dogs.* New York: Macmillan Publishing, 1988.

Whitney, Leon, DVM. *Dog Psychology.* New York: Howell Book House, 1971.

SIX

The Threat of Carjacking

by Alan Minnick

ALL WHO ARE TRAINED in the profession of Personal Protection should be familiar with the risks involved in transportational movements of the principal. Security concerns become paramount anytime the principal leaves a secure environment and is exposed to the general public. Much time is spent in planning any movement of the principal and contingency plans for all situations imaginable are considered. Route planning during the "advance" stage of a movement also entails lots of planning and considerations such as time of day, traffic conditions, time constraints, detours, road construction, hospitals, and safe havens to mention a few. The increase of incidence and publicity of carjacking has prompted another look at the planning stages of a movement and how we might defend our principal and our detail from this threat, should it present itself. Some additional research which should be considered by the protective specialist would be such factors as the type of environment to be driven through, incidence of crime along the route, and more specifically, assaults on vehicles.

Carjacking is not a new crime, per se. It is another form of robbery; which commonly means the taking of property by force, or threat of force, or intimidation from a person, or the presence of another. The general intent is usually robbery with specific intents such as larceny, abduction, and assault. Carjacking is more closely associated with the violent street crimes perpetrated by street gangs and the drug subculture. The increased availability and use of handguns today is considered, by law enforcement officials, an underlying factor contributing to carjacking. Other factors considered to contribute to the increased incidence of this crime are that thieves find it easier to use force than to deal with anti-theft devices, and because they can obtain the keys and registrations for the cars. According to statistics compiled by the FBI and available through the National Institute of Justice, the primary motives appear to be transportation to or from another crime, joyriding, and to derive a quick profit from resale of the vehicle or its parts.

Law Enforcement Crime Prevention Specialists nationwide consider the criminal to be an opportunist whose goals involve three elements. These are ABILITY, DESIRE, and OPPORTUNITY. These goals reveal the obvious differences between the common criminal carjacker and the much more serious terrorist. In training we have been exposed to assaults on motorcades or the principal's vehicle by terrorists and we have been taught how they are very organized and thorough in their assaults on dignitaries and VIPs. In the *Mini-Manual Of The Urban Guerrilla* written by Carlos Marighella, the author sites four elements which must be present to ensure a successful assault during transit. These are:

1. Surprise

2. Better knowledge of the terrain

3. Greater mobility and speed than the enemy

4. Total command of the situation

Marighella states that in order for the ambush to be successful, all four elements must be present. Again this brings to light the difference between the criminal carjacker and the terrorist. As you can see the terrorist is not an opportunist; he/she is very organized and certain about a specific target under very specific and controlled circumstances. The opportunist criminal carjacker may have the desire to commit the crime but is uncertain of his ability and even more so of the opportunity. In other words, if his mind is set on a carjacking he will commit the crime on any victim who will allow him to do so. If one attempt is not successful then he will await the opportunity and try again. He's not very target specific, as you can see. Unless someone in the vehicle has been targeted as the recipient of the attack, then any attack on the vehicle would be random in nature; meaning if the carjacker does not succeed with this one, he will most likely try again on another vehicle and another victim.

Understanding the information just discussed allows us the opportunity to see the potential weaknesses inherent in carjacking, and once knowing these weaknesses, we may then consider our tactics of detecting and defending ourselves and our principals from it. Case studies nationwide suggest that most carjacking incidents are random in nature and are not usually target specific, that is to say no particular vehicle is designated as the target. It is true that certain types of vehicles are targeted by the would-be car thief but in such cases it is not important to them who is driving them. Females traveling alone, drivers of popular and expensive automobiles, and persons appearing wealthy are likely targets of carjackers. The *principal,* in many cases, appears wealthy and he/she also usually travels in attractive and expensive automobiles. These factors would be of interest to robbers and car thieves. A female principal very

likely would stir the interest of the aforementioned offenders as well as sex offenders.

There is no way of telling, with any degree of certainty, when or where an attempted carjacking might occur. It is possible at any point along your route of travel so a *constant* state of alertness *must* be maintained. This is nothing new however. Case studies do reveal that carjackings are more prevalent in urban areas. This is attributable to such factors as dense population, heavy vehicular traffic, and more potential for the vehicles to have to stop. The factor of having to stop the vehicle becomes the subject of concern in defending ourselves from a potential carjacking. In terms of carjacking we are safer when our vehicle is in motion because a successful attack requires that the vehicle be stopped, and that the criminal gain entry into the vehicle. If both of these factors are not present, it is impossible for the carjacking to be accomplished.

Common sense tells us that there will be times when we must stop the vehicle, especially in urban areas. Traffic controls such as signs and signals, congested traffic, accidents, roadway construction and repair sites, are all common reasons for stopping the vehicle. It is during these stops that we should remain alert to activities around us. Some points of consideration during these stops are:

- Always be aware of your surroundings
- Keep doors locked and windows up
- Make sure air conditioning is working
- Be suspicious of persons approaching your vehicle
- Leave distance between your vehicle and the one in front of yours
- If being approached drive away safely

By stopping the vehicle the carjacker is given one of the two crucial elements needed to accomplish his goal. Stops are necessary, but do not let them become deadly restrictions. A sign or a traffic signal is simply an indication to stop, but they are not barriers. We stop because we should. In the event of a possible threat there is no reason to remain stopped. Drive away safely!

Recently, I had the opportunity to provide training for the employees of a major newspaper, in New York City, during its labor strike. The delivery truck drivers were being attacked at stop signs and traffic lights by persons from following vehicles. While stopped at a light the attackers would run to the truck, cut the tires and then enter the vehicle and assault the driver. Had the driver been alert, and they sometimes were, and perceived the attack, they could have safely driven through the light and to a safe haven. Many thought the truck was inoperable because they had flat tires. Nonsense! During training we cut the tires on a couple of the trucks and required the drivers to drive a basic cone course—the trucks were operable. DO NOT remain at the site of a potential attack. The carjacker has a new set of obstacles when the target vehicle is moving at twenty-five miles per hour.

Now realizing that we are more vulnerable while stopped, and that we must remain keenly aware of our surroundings, our next step is to prevent an attacker from gaining entry into our vehicle.

This is done by always keeping the doors locked and the windows in the up position. Case studies reveal that a majority of successful carjackings occurred because the attacker simply walked up to the target vehicle and opened an unlocked door to gain entry. These perpetrators are opportunists and they rely on our bad habits to accomplish their crimes. More often than not, they are able to succeed. It is worthy of mention here that the air-conditioning component on the vehicle should be maintained during periods of warm weather. Equally important is maintenance of the exhaust system to prevent exhaust fumes from entering the passenger compartment. And finally do not forget that movement of the vehicle will assist you in preventing an unwanted entry into your vehicle. It should be noted here that there have been cases where carjackers have used other vehicles to bump into the rear of the target vehicle causing the driver to believe he/she has been involved in an accident. In these situations the unsuspecting driver has gotten out of the vehicle to inspect the damage only to afford the carjackers the two necessary elements to accomplish their crime. . . stopping the target vehicle. . . and access to the driver. Should this happen to you and you suspect the threat, do not get out of the vehicle and do not open the door. Stay secure in the vehicle and wait for police to arrive. If the situation warrants, drive away to a police station or other safe haven.

We have discussed the importance of safely driving away from a potential threat and it is important to realize that this ability affords us the upper hand against the carjacker on foot. Protective personnel should have been trained to maintain this advantage at all times during vehicular movements, but often they are not. A case in fact would be the violent assault in 1991, on CIA personnel reporting for work in Northern Virginia. This was unfortunate and unnecessary.

The lone gunman, wielding an AK-47 Assault Weapon, walked up to five different vehicles stopped in line at the entrance of their headquarters for a traffic light and fired numerous shots into each vehicle. Surely the victims would have wanted to escape this attack but they were bumper to bumper and could not drive away. Leaving enough distance between your vehicle and the one in front of yours will further the opportunity to drive away. In many cases it becomes a situation of not doing it, more so than not knowing. It also becomes important to realize that the escape route may be down the street ahead, and maybe it is over a curb or across a median strip. If the threat develops into an actual attack the escape maneuver may even involve your vehicle coming into contact with another or with a fixed object. My point here is, do not let habits and driving norms cloud the reality that you must do something and that you might damage your vehicle.

It becomes important to discuss the type of vehicle you are driving at this time because of the possibility of a firearm being involved. The added threat of a firearm makes it even more critical that we perceive a possible threat and that we begin our evasive response as soon as possible thereafter. Chances are that the criminal would not run two or three blocks wielding a gun out in the open, but instead would wait until they are close to the target vehicle before brandishing one. This creates a sudden decision for the driver. Only armored vehicles will repel bullets and then we have to consider the threat level for which the vehicle is equipped. Various levels of threat protection will stop only certain calibers of weapons and often times the added security (armor) is in strategic locations on the vehicle. For example only the doors and/or windows may be armored leaving the roof and the bottom plate vulnerable and maybe even the engine compartment. Armored vehicles are great, but the protective specialist must know the strengths and weaknesses. Again it becomes extremely important that you recognize a potential threat and react to it as quickly as possible. If we have been alert and have perceived the threat then gun or no gun we have thwarted the attempted attack. If in fact there was a firearm involved, time and distance become our saving grace. We are now a moving target, the criminal has a longer shot, and because we are moving away from the bullet we are weakening its ability to penetrate the vehicle.

A final thought on prevention of carjacking would be communications. Access to reliable communications is extremely important and should be maintained at all times during transportation movements. Cellular phones have opened the lines of communication dramatically during protective movements and have given protective personnel access to emergency services across the board. It is advisable that this be a part of your equipment not only in the event of carjacking but for any emergency which might occur. Also installing an external speaker on your vehicle would give you the ability to communicate with persons outside the vehicle without compromising your security. This speaker may be used for legitimate communications or to attract attention to your vehicle in the event of attack. A manually activated alarm or siren would also be useful in this case. Of course we should not forget the advice of Dr. Kobetz, which is, "Expect it to malfunction and have a contingency plan! REACT!"

In conclusion, carjacking is another trend in crime. Criminals constantly search for new ways to take advantage of people and their vulnerabilities. In this case they have simply found another way to commit those crimes which have plagued society for centuries. It therefore becomes incumbent upon the Protection Professional to stay current and educated on such trends and new threats as they develop. We never learn it all and we can never anticipate all that can happen, however, we can continue to learn and to educate ourselves. Further options may be afforded the Protective Specialist through advanced driving instruction. Better knowledge of the vehicle and its capabilities also offer new opportunities for defending the principal and the protective detail against attacks during transportational movements.

PART II

Interpersonal Aspects of Concern

SEVEN

Sex and the Single Bodyguard

by H.H.A. Cooper

*"Unfortunately, little darlings, there is no such
thing as a simple love story."*

Tom Robbins[1]

THIS IS A SERIOUS ATTEMPT to deal with a serious, difficult subject. The difficulty in treating of it is compounded by the fact that it has long remained unacknowledged. It is not freely talked about in polite, professional company. It has something of the quality ascribed by Gail Sheehy to the Male Menopause.[2] It seemed to be there all right, but until comparatively recently, no one wanted to supply the specifics. A more focused interest has been sparked by the film "Bodyguard," casting Kevin Costner in the role of a Personal Protection Specialist dancing with different kinds of wolves.[3] There is obviously nothing new about the plot; it certainly predates Hollywood in real life. As entertainment, it was fair enough, but from a professional perspective, about as useful as *Hunter* to the science of criminal investigation. It generated some interest on the talk show circuit, but this evaporated quite quickly. Perhaps its most useful contribution is that it set people thinking, if not yet actually talking about a very complex area of human relations. It is time, in a serious setting, to explore some of the complexities.

---

1 *Even Cow Girls Get the Blues,* New York: Bantam (1980), 12th Printing, Page 79. Robbins, outrageously funny, is yet one of the most profound social commentators of our times.

2 For an interesting discussion of this, see, "The Unspeakable Passage," Gail Sheehy, 56 *Vanity Fair,* No.4, page 164 *et seq.*

3 It is worth entering a lonely footnote for posterity to correct any mistaken impressions. Larry Wansley's book *FBI Undercover,* New York: Pocket Books, (1989) contains at page 258 the following: "In the summer of 1988 he took a three-month leave of absence to serve as director of security for the European tour of pop singer Whitney Houston before returning to his work with the Cowboys." Kevin Costner is simply entertaining fiction. Mr. Wansley, who now heads up corporate security for American Airlines, is very much a distinguished, factual law enforcement personality.

Sex can now be spoken and written about in the most candid of terms. Language that would once have been thought of as extremely vulgar, indelicate, unfit for use in mixed company is now commonplace in what some might feel, still, inappropriate settings. Yet, as the struggles with AIDS education have, dramatically, borne out, all this openness has not really done a great deal to improve levels of human understanding about the subject. For many, perhaps most people, the implications of sex remain a mystery scarcely less puzzling and confusing than the meaning of life itself. What is certain, is that sex, *per se*, cannot be isolated and dealt with as a discrete topic. Even where it does not dominate, it certainly permeates all other areas of human activity. It has to be factored into every undertaking.

What we are looking at here is sex as an element in a very special kind of human relationship. It is of concern to us to examine how that relationship may be affected by the sexual dynamic. This is but a particular category within the wider genre of sex and working relationships. The subject has achieved considerable recent attention through a preoccupation with what has come to be known as sexual harassment. The Anita Hill/Clarence Thomas confrontation, in many ways, did for sexual harassment what the English trial of *Lady Chatterley's Lover* did for the emancipation of language in literature. In a sense, it defined the issues without settling the matters in any definitive way. It gave us a better understanding of the true nature of the problem, even though we might not yet be prepared to deal with it in any effective way. It pointed up the prosaic, but important, fact that sex and power are a highly volatile mix. Each, by itself has extraordinary potency. Together, in certain proportions, they can be a career-stopper.

There are many relationships, in which sex and power have a potential for explosive criticality. Psychiatrist and patient, professor and student, master and servant relations (in the Jeffersonian sense), all have the makings of abuse, by the unscrupulous. Sex is a precious commodity. It can be put in play, bartered, or seized, like any others. We are not concerned, at this point, with the propriety or even the advisability of injecting sex into relationships, which have an altogether different primary purpose. What we need to notice is that, in every case, the relationship is drastically altered, deformed even, once sex enters upon the scene. Anyone who doubts this, in the kind of setting we have been considering would profit from a reading of *Genesis* 16, 1-6. Sex is a kind of transaction, in which the parties to it tend, in some way or another, to be transformed.

People are capable of forming and enhancing the strongest of relationships although separated by distances of thousands of miles, and without any direct contact of any kind. On an intellectual level, people fall in and out of—love, even though their communications be restricted to those of a written nature. Yet it remains true that by its very nature, sexual intercourse between human beings requires proximity and no amount of sophistry or ingenuity can dispense with this requirement. Sexual desire may not be generated or stimulated by physical contact, but it remains the case that the sex act cannot be completed without it; all else is simple masturbation. You can sexually harass someone by mail or by telephone; stalkers frequently do. Normal sexual relationships are premised upon narrowing the space, physically and psychologically between the parties. Working relationships provide the opportunity. The ingredients that go to make up that difficult to analyze property we call "attraction" do the rest. Whenever there is sufficient proximity plus overwhelming attraction, sex becomes a real possibility to be conjured with.

These are very uncertain waters. There are no charts, by which one might safely navigate. What are the ingredients of attraction, their blend and proportions, are highly erratic variables. What is attractive to one may be repellent to another, and even the most exhaustive of studies fails to reveal wherein the difference resides. The circles of love and hate can, at times, intersect, and some highly surprising and rapid, mutations of both can take place. That hatred can turn to love, and *vice versa,* is a not uncommon human experience. A catalyst is sometimes needed, in either case, before the process of transformation can take place. At times, the sexual spark is initiated with an immediacy and suddenness that smacks of summer lightning and a certain kind of craziness. At others, the process is slow, imperceptible, yet when it is complete, it is just as capable of stopping the parties to it by its surprise. Attraction, like charm, is difficult to describe, but we know it when we experience it.

Although there is no universal standard of attractiveness, there are undoubtedly those who attract a higher percentage of their fellow human beings than do others. Sometimes it is *who* they are. Sometimes it is a matter of status or position. With others, it is *what* they are that attracts. Some jobs have a kind of glamour quality about them that rubs off on those who are interacting with them. Other jobs are potentially of the non-glamorous variety. If you come across an attractive janitor, garbage-collector, or postal clerk, you can be pretty sure that it is the personal qualities of the individual that you find attractive rather than something conferred upon the job-holder by reason of what he or she does for a living. There is an undoubted allure about the job of bodyguarding. There is rarely a shortage of those who aspire to undertake what is involved, even in the best of economic times. It has something of the heroic about it; it is more than just a paycheck. The bodyguard is on the side of the angels. He or she protects the principal against the forces of evil. That, at least, is the way the job is perceived by those who do not actually have to do it. And perception, all too often, is reality. Think of the image of Kevin Costner as *The Bodyguard.* What gives the cinematic role its peculiar appeal?

Bodyguarding, then, is a very sexy job. When the individual doing the job is endowed with those indefinable personal qualities of attractiveness, of which we have spoken, this is an exceedingly powerful combination. It has a special allure of its own. Such a combination ought, possibly, to carry the Surgeon General's Warning! There is danger in the pull exerted by such feelings. Especially when those drawn are the very ones the Personal Protection Specialist is engaged to keep safe from harm. Defenses against the powerful feelings unleashed are difficult to erect and maintain. The morality of the matter need not detain us here. Whether we speak of love or lust, the consequences are the same. Giving in to these temptations changes forever the relationship that gave rise to them in the first place. Inevitably, the bodyguard becomes something other than a bodyguard, a protective lover, perhaps. There is, even more to the point, in some cases, a kind of awkward role reversal prompting the question: Who's the Boss?

The essence of professionalism is detachment. At best, intimacy corrodes objectivity. At worst, it leads to total confusion. The nature of the profession of Personal Protection Specialist cannot take such extreme pressures. It is founded, premised upon a certain relationship between the parties. One of its central pillars is a particular kind of mutual respect. Sex is an extremely strong acid that eats away at the base of that pillar so that it might be replaced by a structure of a very different kind. The sex act between any two human beings is, by its nature, an agent of change. It has a profound effect upon any relationship of power governing the individuals engaging in it. The relationship of protector to protectee, professionally, is not one of equality. It is governed by a delicate and often unarticulated etiquette. Any alteration, for whatever reason, has an impact upon the nature and quality of the protection provided. Sex is but rarely a transaction between equals. Where there is a substantial disparity, in terms of power, between the parties, explosive and manipulative factors come, vividly, into play. The sexual activity itself takes on the character of a power struggle. The sexual drama is a kind of shadow play between the forces of possession and submission. In the arena we are considering, it is often enough a triumph of madness over reason.

There is no effective immunization against such craziness. It can strike the most unlikely of subjects. It is no respecter of office, training, experience, or upbringing. The disease may have a long incubation period, or it may strike with the rapidity and short range of the mamba. It can simmer unnoticed or churn away at the entrails. It can, when it occurs, rarely be denied, and even more rarely resisted. What we shall call, here, the Bodyguard's Dilemma, namely what to do about it, when the symptoms are recognized, has its counterparts elsewhere, from the highest to the lowest strata of society. An English king gave up the throne for the woman he loved, an American at that! But at least he had the option open to him. Of course, principals do, on occasion, bed their bodyguards and, sometimes, bodyguards do succeed in wedding their principals, though, on the record, the prognosis for a happy and enduring union cannot be said to be a favorable one. Let us look at it from a somewhat hard-nosed perspective. In some situations, a popular analytical tool is to ask: *cui bono*, who stands to gain? More sensibly, in the situations we are considering, here, the question should be, who stands to lose? Especially in those instances where, predictably, matters turn out badly. Soberly, it must be acknowledged that the chances of the bodyguard becoming the darling of high society as a result of his or her conquest are quite slim; even mere acceptance may not be in the cards. Reviewing the ranks of bodyguards who have faced this dilemma, it is hard to point to a Grace Kelly in their midst. Or a Wallis Simpson.

It is here that the relative disparities of power and position must be most realistically taken into account. A principal entering into a sexual liaison with his or her bodyguard is unlikely to suffer socially or economically if matters go radically wrong. It is, after all, not like entering a cult. Among some, it might even be regarded as chic, or amusing. In strictly human terms, even a mere dalliance may have its price, but it is hardly likely to be exorbitant. What, on the other hand, does the bodyguard have to look forward to as a result of such a departure from the straight and narrow? A useful answer can only be given on a case by case basis and by reference to the character of the individual affected. Even on the most favorable basis, it can hardly be rated a career enhancement. It does little for one's reputation as a bodyguard that one has taken advantage of a position of trust to enjoy the body one was supposed to be guarding, or to be used and discarded by one's principal like a rented tuxedo. This is surely reducing the profession of Personal Protection Specialist to the level of some escort services advertised in the *Yellow Pages*. One's reaction to all this, in this modern age, are founded less in prudery than in personal pride and the professional standards the individual sets for him or herself. But make no mistake, the opportunities—and the temptations—are there and they must be prudently taken into account in any attempt to resolve the Bodyguard's Dilemma.

There is much more than Casting Couch politics to all this. There is, on balance, little to be gained personally or professionally from sleeping with the Boss—or his or her sons or daughters. Bodyguarding is not the royal route to fame, fortune, or the social register. The principal, any principal, literally places his or her life in the hands of the selected bodyguard. If this service were rated on any lower scale, such personal protection must be accounted an unnecessary luxury. Anything that interferes with the diligent, efficient performance of the duties involved diminishes the value of what is to be accomplished. It is like making a pet of a guard dog. The proper distances must be kept if the job is to be done properly. What the Personal Protection Specialist gives up by surrendering to his or her clamorings of a sexual nature, urged on by a complaisant principal, is no less than the ability to do the job. This must be clearly understood by the parties. If you are prepared to accept, in all its aspects, the transformation from Doberman to Pekingese, this may be for you. Just don't try snarling. To mix metaphors a trifle, you may be a tiger in bed, but is that where you are really being paid to be a tiger? And, if so, what does that make you?

The title for the present piece was selected in conscious imitation of that ground-breaking work by Helen Gurley Brown, *Sex and the Single Girl*.[4] In our context, that title ought not to be interpreted too literally; all are fair game regardless of their civil state. Rather, single should, perhaps, be read as "available" or, even more exactly, "separable." Marriage offers no protection. To some, indeed, it may constitute a provocative challenge. Again, we are not discussing common issues of morality here. What is raised, rather, is the efficacy of possible defenses against something with career-destroying potential. Love, it is popularly said, is blind. Lust is scarcely better sighted. Such defects are hardly to be recommended in one whose primary job is to protect the persons of others. Nor is this selective blindness. It distorts and hampers the vision all round. The career bodyguard can no more allow his or her vision to be affected in this

---

[4] More recently, we have had "Sex and the Single Guy", *Esquire*, June, 1993 and, on PBS, the NOVA program, "Sex and the Single Rhino."

way than Samson could afford to have his locks shorn. To borrow an illustration from another ancient culture, he who does not tie himself to the mast, so as not to heed the Siren's Song, is sure to end up wrecked on either Scylla or Charybdis. Once more, the Bodyguard's Dilemma. How to resist, gracefully, and still keep your job.

This, when it comes down to the bare bones, is the crux of the matter. The position taken, here, is quite clear: the Personal Protection Specialist who seeks to initiate a sexual relationship with his or her principal or any of those he or she is engaged to protect is either a rogue or a fool. Such individuals deserve all they get. We need waste no time or sympathy over their plight. Their case is not part of the Bodyguard's Dilemma. Here we are on different ground altogether. The sexual initiative proceeds not from the protector, but from the protectee. This is, more properly, the case of the Personal Protection Specialist as sex object. Here, momentarily, we must turn our spotlight away from the bodyguard so as to illuminate those who might bestow these attentions. It is immediately apparent that both classes are heterogeneous; bodyguards can be considered, as a class, only because of the distinctive, common service they provide within the general class. There will be many sub-categories; there will be those with considerable experience and training, and those with neither; there will be the smart and the not-so-smart; those who look the part, and those who do not; the well-paid, the over-paid, and the under-paid. Detailed analysis points up seemingly endless differences. But, when it comes down to it, they all do the same, basic thing for the same kinds of people. Their job, their *raison d'etre*, is to protect those who employ them. Anything else, such as walking the dog—or pleasing the principal in bed, or on the back seat of the Rolls Royce, is strictly an extra-curricular activity.

As individuals, those who employ bodyguards are as one writer puts it[5], "impossibly different." Such is their diversity that they seem scarcely worthy of discussion as a class. Yet, on deeper analysis, they too, can be seen to have characteristics in common relevant to the present subject. However different they might be as individuals, they are united in this single respect: they all employ bodyguards. They are sufficiently apprehensive about their personal security, or that pertaining to those about whom they care sufficiently, to engage the services of persons they hope and believe can protect them from the apprehended harm. For some, having a bodyguard goes along with the job. Whoever, ultimately, picks up the tab, much the same hopes and beliefs, with respect to the services rendered, are entertained. Providing protective services, on even the most modest scale, is a costly business. The class of those who enjoy the services of Personal Protection Specialist anywhere in the world is thus relatively small, and exclusive. The economic aspects of the matters ensure that this is the case. The class is broadly comprised of the powerful, the rich, and the famous (or the infamous). However, they might have managed to get there, these are people at the top of the social ladder. The very fact that they have chosen to have, or been persuaded to have, bodyguards indicates their

---

5   *Setting Free the Bears,* John Irving, New York: Pocket Books (1968). page 311.

consciousness of their position. They are, by and large, accustomed to what that position brings them. In consequence, they are not, as individuals, used to taking "no" for an answer from those on lower rungs of the ladder. Especially not from those in their employ.

We are considering, then, a very demanding class of people. Those who are used to wielding considerable power over others. Those who are used to issuing orders, even when those are couched in the form of requests. They have their own notions of hierarchy, where other people fit into their scheme of things. Some see themselves, not unjustifiably in some cases, as being at the head of their own universe. They do not take lightly (or even well) to the notion of placing their lives and the lives of people about whom they care, in the hands of others. It not only reminds them, uncomfortably, of their own mortality but in a certain unwelcome sense, it diminishes them in status. They are most unwilling, therefore, to concede that their loss in this respect might be another's gain. It is most unwise of the Personal Protection Specialist to give him or herself airs and graces on account of some assumed powers of life and death that the job might signify with respect to the principal. Whatever the reality of the matter, this is a sure way of being cut down to size. Whatever our station in life, we all have a need to try to control our own destiny, and never more so than when our fate has, perforce, to be entrusted, however partially, to others. Imagine a physician, in the course of a delicate procedure, announcing grandiloquently to the patient: "Your life is in my hands. If I choose to make a mess of things, you could die!" Might not the patient, if there is still time, and alternatives are available, be tempted, there and then, to get out of such a physician's care? But, then, it would be a most unwise physician who tried this on with the powerful, the rich, or the famous. Face it, there is a hierarchy, even in America's supposedly "classless" society, and he or she who handsomely pays the piper gets to call the tune.

While these may not always be particularly, or even sensibly perceived, there are practical limitations imposed on the exercise of the powers that stem from being rich and famous. Nowadays, you can be rich, famous, and relatively brainless. That does not, of course, inhibit you from the earnest pursuit of what you feel your wealth and fame entitle you to enjoy. The sad and cautionary tale of Mike Tyson is a case very much in point. Even for the rich and famous, there is always someone richer, more famous, more powerful, perhaps simply smarter, on the prowl. The world is a dangerous place, even for, or maybe especially for, the rich and famous. That is why so many of them have a need for bodyguards. The impression might be gained from this that the powerful, rich and famous are, *as a class,* dissolute, shameless and utterly unworthy in countless unnamed ways. While this may, indeed, be true of some (as it might of the members of any other artificially constructed class), it would be the greatest injustice so to characterize all, or even a majority of them. But it is undoubtedly the case, that wealth and power provide the means for indulgence in behaviors and activities that are scarcely possible for those of less generous means. They must content themselves with other vices. But power and wealth understandably produce a certain attitude towards, shall we say, entitlement.

The appeal of this is validated, in our society, by the not-so-affluent. The indigent are not poor from choice. Remember John Connolly's experienced observation, "I've been poor and I've been rich, and rich is better". Recall, too, the Golden Rule according to the Wizard of Oz: He who has the gold rules. There is nothing judgmental in this, and certainly nothing touching upon the justice of the matter. Maybe, in some cases, the gold is in the wrong hands, but that's the way the world, our world is.

It is easy, dealing in abstractions like "bodyguard" or "principal" to forget that these are merely terms of our own choosing to represent real, live human beings in a certain situational relationship. It is the human dynamic that is so unpredictable, so difficult to factor in when we treat of these relationships. To believe that it is solely the human dynamic, that makes human beings regardless of, or because of, wealth, position, power, behave as they do, is dangerous and unrealistic. People simply do not always act as they might, having regard to their situation or station in life, be expected to do. Those well versed in the arts of manipulation know that sex and greed are two of the strongest drives governing human behavior. They cause ordinary human beings sometimes to do extraordinary, even heroic things. And, others to commit the basest of crimes. When we feel a euphemism is necessary to substitute for greed, we speak of "ambition." Similarly, in the case of the sex drive, we soften the terminology by couching the matters under the more romantic rubric of "love": he or she did that wild, crazy thing for love. We need not get bogged down in semantics, here, nor in difficult definitional issues. The lessons of common experience amply demonstrate how irrationally human beings are prone to act when the powerful, for most, irresistible stimulus of sex is introduced into their lives. Middle-aged maiden ladies, with irreproachable careers in government service betray their nation's secrets to some scheming Lothario. Otherwise shrewd businessmen hardly in their sexual prime, are kidnapped while visiting young mistresses. Mafia dons are entrapped by law enforcement authorities, who have learned of some fatal infatuation for a servant. And a young lady of quality falls hopelessly for her bodyguard. How familiar it all sounds. How rarely does the tale have a "happily ever after" ending.

There is never any useful logic to love; it would not be what we know it to be if there were. It is difficult enough figuring out what attracts people to each other without trying, in specific cases, to determine the true nature of the malady that impels them to do these impulsive, and, often, highly destructive, things. With enough application, reasons can usually be teased out of even the most irrational imbroglio, but to those not immediately involved, the matter generally remains a mystery even with the most cogent of explanations. It is very true that you never know where a shoe rubs until you wear it. Sex is capable of making nonsense of social and other status barriers. Old men, who, chronologically and by reason of experience should know better, make fools of themselves over young women. Older women feel themselves rejuvenated to the point of throwing all caution to the wind for the attentions of a younger swain. Whatever the bodyguard might have been trained or trained himself to guard against, he or she is often as powerless as any other against the irresistible forces of the human sex drive. There is no known body armor that can resist, or deflect Cupid's darts. In the realm of sexuality, nothing is, perhaps, quite so intoxicating and irresistible as finding oneself, unexpectedly, miraculously, even, the object of desire of one thought, by all standards, to be beyond reach, unattainable. The personal protection business is all about coping with a certain kind of vulnerability. All training is geared to that end. What is discussed here is a different kind of vulnerability, but vulnerability nevertheless. It is all the more dangerous for its ability to affect both parties to the bodyguarding transaction simultaneously, though not always with the same intensity.

As in any other situation, arising within the exercise of this profession, it is the primary duty of the bodyguard to protect. If the bodyguard succumbs, the cause is lost. And as always, *only* the bodyguard is responsible for whatever might go wrong. He or she has not only the principal's vulnerability to take into account, but also his or her own. All this, with a difference. As we have seen, in the nature of things, the principal is likely to survive relatively unscathed. Whatever the bodyguard may suffer personally, as a result of any close encounter with his or her employer's sex drive, professionally, the damage is likely to be substantial, in some cases irreparable. An ounce of prevention is better than a peck of damage control. Very few are ever blind-sided by sex. Rather, the victims generally blunder into it head-on. A curious form of denial seems to affect those smitten. While this may be excusable in the practice of some professions, it is wholly antithetical to that of the Personal Protection Specialist. Surely, the worst of all epitaphs for the bodyguard must be: he or she saved others, him/herself he/she could not save. Let us return to basics for a moment.

The importance of advance work is drilled into every neophyte bodyguard. Even great armies do not venture far afield without scouting the territory ahead. Advance work is essential preparation for any serious undertaking, and it assumes a role of special importance in the daily routine of the Personal Protection Specialist. A good advance person is highly prized by experienced detail leaders, to the point where this vital task has become a sub-specialty of its own. Good advance work is simply sound preparation for what is to come. Small wonder that, whatever their personal preference in hotel chains, sensible Personal Protection Specialists have a singular affection for the Holiday Inns' theme: The best surprise is no surprises. The devil, as always, is in the details. What is sometimes overlooked, is that good advance work begins at home, with the very selection of the person to undertake it. That individual must have the right qualities for the job, the right attributes and attitude. He or she must have an inquiring mind, a certain kind of curiosity about what is going on around them and an ability to quickly perceive what is important to the matters in hand so as to distinguish it from what is not. The advance person should be quick, thorough, accurate and methodical, and a concise reporter of what is observed. Advance work can be taught and learned from experience, but the person chosen must be trainable in the first place. Some, with sterling qualities in other departments simply do not pass muster here; they lack the essentials for the job. You do not want a scout with a Munchhausen-like mind. You want, as detail leader, to be informed, not entertained. If there are monsters out there, you want, indeed, need to know about them. The last thing you need is to be regaled with the imaginings of a febrile, over-active mind.

In the great savannas of human sexuality, every personal protection specialist is his or her *own* advance person. And the work, as ever, begins at home. Before you can begin to evaluate the sexual potential of others, and its significance for you, you must be able to make a useful appraisal of your own. This is a task very few are, adequately, equipped to undertake unaided. It requires more energy and a higher degree of honesty than most people are prepared to commit to the project. It calls for a careful, objective scouting of one's own sexual history, with all its highs and lows, its altitudes, and its deserts. A formidable task and one certain to offer at least some embarrassment to many. The objective of this self-analysis is the same as any other kind of advance work; to see the hazards along the way so as to be able, successfully, to negotiate them. You need, in particular, to be able to recognize your own weaknesses, how others might be able to take advantage of your sexual nature. What problems have you had in the past? What are your pet aversions in sexual matters? Are you angered by miscegenation or homosexuality? Do these feelings have the potential for affecting your performance in the field of providing personal protection? Do you find yourself particularly susceptible to certain kinds of sexual overtures? Can you consciously control your responses? Are you repeatedly involved in unsatisfactory sexual relationships with the same type of person? These are just a few of the questions that might usefully start you on the road of sexual self-inquiry.

The practical importance of this exercise in self-exploration cannot be over-stressed. In the ordinary course of events, the worst that you can expect from sloppy advance work is that you lose your principal. Provided you survive the experience intact, you might well be absorbed into the employ of another and take the matter in your stride. Failure to do your sexual advance work, or to do it well enough, could well terminate *your* professional career and drastically alter your life in the bargain. The work of the Personal Protection Specialist is, essentially, defensive. Making a correct and timely appreciation of what you have to face enables you to have a handle on your own likely reactions, to be able to structure appropriate responses, and to get out of the way of what you see coming down the pike. There is always the danger with any kind of threat assessment or the type of survey that advance work entails, of missing something important or failing to attach the proper significance to it. The danger is greatly increased in the case of a delicate subject such as one's own sexual nature, which touches upon the very core of our being. Look on it as a necessary part of your professional education. After all, no one is asking you to share your finds with others! You may mark them *For Personal Use Only*.

All inter-personal relations are affected, in many cases, governed by communication. Communication, in all its different facets, is what makes human intercourse possible. The outcome of the different interactions engaged in with others, in our conscious state, is determined, in large part, by how well we have understood what others have tried to communicate to us and how well we have made ourselves understood to those others. We are probably only imperfectly understood for a greater part of the time. A lot depends not only on our own skill in expressing our meaning, but in our ability to do it in a way that is compatible with the abilities of our intended audience. When we do this well, we say that we are on the same wave-length. Whatever the chosen method of communication, opportunities for misunderstandings abound. The literature on this subject has grown enormously over the last few years; the work of Dr. Deborah Tannen is especially noteworthy.[6] And particularly relevant in the present context, for few misunderstandings of the kind that concern us here are so vexing, so potentially dangerous, and so common, as those between men and women.

The language of love is often veiled and esoteric. It has many dialects and few, with confidence, can claim proficiency in more than a handful. The language of lust can be even more convoluted and difficult to interpret correctly. The mating dance for all species is largely symbolic, ritualistic. But success in this essentially bio-cultural department depends upon a knowledge of the steps and being able to perform them acceptably for the intended audience. The mating ritual of the male African elephant is unlikely to impress the lesser bustard as being anything but clumsy and indelicate in the extreme. The dance may be short or it may be long, but it must be appropriate to convey its intended meaning and invoke the desired response. Human sexual rituals are so much more complicated than those of the animal kingdom by reason of the extraordinary range and flexibility of communication of which our own species is capable. And so, consequently, the opportunities for misunderstandings in this critical area of human interaction are greatly increased. The matter is further complicated by the expectations engendered, in any particular society in determined social epochs, by the demands of conventions, mores and the like, which are fluid and subject to change. For long enough, in our own society, the responsibility for undertaking the sexual initiative was felt to rest, broadly, with the male. Traditionally, a man who was slow on the uptake might be subtly and gently nudged in the desired direction, but it was generally the case that only "fast" women (with all that term connoted) made advances. The male led the sexual gavotte, even though the female might have been the better dancer and more in tune with the music. The Sexual Revolution of the 1970's changed all that, but as many feminist writers of the time recognized, these notions proceeded from certain assumptions about relative powers and status. The consequences of the old assumptions die exceedingly hard, but there can be little doubt about the correctness of the political analysis of the matter.

In the personal protection field, there can be no doubt, in a formal sense, about the respective positions of power and status. Whether the Personal Protection Specialist is an employee or an independent contractor, there is no mistake about who is the boss. Yet the sexual dynamic has the potential for altering, uncomfortably, the certitude of such relationships. Or, simply reinforcing, equally uncomfortably, the traditional attitudes with respect to male/female

---

6 *You Just Don't Understand: Women and Men in Conversation*, New York: Ballantine Books (1990).

relationships. More and more well-qualified women are entering the personal protection field.[7] They bring a different perspective and often, a different range of valuable skills to this demanding job. In some important situations, indeed, their services are specially sought after, where, for example, cultural imperatives dictate that only a woman might undertake the providing of personal protection for another woman, or young children, or where a woman, requiring such services, might simply feel uncomfortable with a male bodyguard. There is a definite niche for the female bodyguard and this is growing steadily larger as more and more among the client base have come to recognize, within the framework of their own personal protection needs, the value of women in this role.[8] The business of providing personal protection is, however, still very far from being an equal opportunity one. Women bodyguards, like women police officers, have had to struggle very hard for the measure of professional recognition they have, to date, achieved. There is a clear sexual dimension to this that is rarely discussed in those professional circles where its consideration is merited.

Women bodyguards are not often faulted by their male counterparts because they are felt to lack the skills and dedication that are required for this exacting job; there is not quite the same feeling, here, that has, for so long, kept women out of combat roles in the armed forces.[9] There is not felt, in the main, to be a gender deficiency that renders women less than competent in acquiring and exercising the basic skills required of a Personal Protection Specialist. Indeed, it is tacitly accepted by those in a position to know that a fit, well-trained woman is more than a match for some, at least of the sorrier male specimens who present themselves for employment in this field. Nor is there a feeling among male bodyguards that the entry of women into this profession is taking bread out of their mouths. Rather, the male disquiet, when it is felt, even when it is not articulated, is based on essentially sexual grounds. Bodyguarding, as we have observed, is perceived as a sexy profession; there is a certain glamor to it. Some of the women entering this business are extremely attractive physically and intellectually and constitute a disturbing and challenging presence to their male colleagues. Even those sufficiently in control of their own emotions to be able to view this with true professional detachment, cannot fail to feel apprehensive about the assignment of such sources of allurement and temptation to, say, powerful and wealthy male principals, who would hardly hesitate to take advantage of what was proffered, in a most unprofessional

---

7 And receiving appropriate recognition. See, for example, "Eye-Scoop," *Women's Wear Daily,* December 10, 1990, page 18. "To Avoid the Paparazzi Outside, Jackie O sneaked in through a back entrance with George Plimpton—her date for the evening—and, of course, her bodyguard, a lean, strong-looking woman dressed in dark skirt and jacket. "Watch her," marvelled one guest. "She just quietly follows her through the crowd. She's martial arts trained and everything." From the description, her friends and colleagues will recognize Katherine L. Friese of K. L. Friese * Associates, a New York City based provider of protective services.

8 See, for example, "Female bodyguards are all the rage in China," the *Dallas Morning News* (ex *Chicago Tribune*), May 6, 1993, page 44A.

9 This may be an oblique, unarticulated understanding that the real task of the Personal Protection Specialist is to avoid confrontation and certainly not to seek, aggressively to engage in combat. Those seeking to inculcate a contrary philosophy, at least in the Untied States, are rapidly being consigned to a PPS Jurassic Park.

sense. This is the special calvary of the most physically attractive of female bodyguards, who must ever wonder if they have been selected for their professional skills or their more obvious personal attributes; for who, save a Lionel Schaeffer[10], would want an Irma Griese for a bodyguard. The female bodyguard stands, therefore, in a kind of double jeopardy, of being regarded slightingly and, in some instances, fair game on a personal basis by her male colleagues, and as available for more than the usual range of extra-curricular activities by at least some of her more predatory employers. This not only makes the job extraordinarily difficult to do; it radically redefines it. It would be most unfortunate if the term "female bodyguard" were allowed to take on the same veiled, salacious connotation acquired by the title "housekeeper" in years past.

The pressures faced by the woman Personal Protection Specialist in a profession substantially defined and controlled by men cannot be underestimated. Some societies are potentially more sexist than others, which pay lip service to equal opportunity. Nowhere is it easy for a woman to break into this profession and maintain her professional standing with a reasonable volume of work without a male sponsor or mentor. The exercise of this profession is what determines whether one is or is not a Personal Protection Specialist. There is no such thing as a non-practicing bodyguard. As is recognized among thespians, it is possible, for short intervals, to be "resting", but, male or female, you had better not rest for too long if you wish to retain your professional standing. In a profession where what you are depends very much upon for whom, and with whom you work, the opportunities for sexual exploitation are rife. While the "casting-couch syndrome" is not as prevalent as in the case of the Silver Screen, its equivalent is something that cannot fail to be present in the minds of all women trying to make their mark in this business. It casts its own unfortunate pall over any success gained, especially where the woman in question is more than ordinarily good-looking. It is bad enough trying to exercise one's profession while fighting off the usual offers of advancement in return for sexual favors. It must be galling in the extreme to know that success is less likely to be attended by belated recognition than by ill-concealed insinuations as to the way in which it was achieved.

All this, it might be argued, applies equally to all women, whatever their business or profession, a fortiori if it is one largely dominated by men. The strong, where they are unconstrained by moral or ethical considerations, are ever prone to take advantage of the weak. But there is an important difference in the field we are considering. Bodyguarding is not only perceived as a sexy profession, it is also regarded, not unnaturally, as being no place for the weak. Personal Protection Specialists look after others. It follows, then, that they must not only be physically strong enough to undertake the arduous responsibilities involved, but commensurately tough-minded. There is a kind of testing process involved, here, with the ultimate accolade being the respect awarded those deemed to have passed. Sexual encounters, under these circumstances, take on the character of a power struggle; the party propositioned is in the nature of a

---

10 One of that excellent writers, Erica Jong's more unpleasant, true-to-life, fictional characters. See, *Any Woman's Blues*, New York: Harper and Row (1990).

trophy. The object of the exercise is conquest and collection, not a relationship. Obviously, this is a game that can be played by women as well as men. The trick is in recognizing the true nature of the challenge and the consequences of taking it up. In orienting strategies for response, it helps to bear in mind that the entry of women into the field of providing protective services is regarded by some, atavistically, as contrary to the course of nature. In the wild, the protection of the herd, in general, is the duty and prerogative of the dominant male. As a recompense, he enjoys the sexual favors of the females of the herd and the obeisances of his male inferiors. This is the established order of things designed for the better preservation of the species.

For all this, the physical prowess of the female is never in doubt, when, in the course of nature, there is appropriate call for its exercise. The female has a clear, if limited, protective role. A tigress, for example, will easily worst a full-grown tiger in defense of her cubs. Dragon ladies abound in nature, where there is ample evidence that, on occasion, the ". . . female of the species is more deadly than the male." An obvious residue of this lingers on into our own times. There is little enough objection to the female bodyguard protecting, say, the odd Saudi princess, or even women of lesser rank from other cultures. Female bodyguards might, without the raising of any eyebrows undertake protective responsibilities for children and the like. It is the expansion of their role into the area of protecting full-grown males, company presidents, captains of industry, national leaders and such that raises masculine hackles. Again, it is the sexual dimension that many find so disturbing. A very real apprehension arises that the woman Personal Protection Specialist will be subject to sexual advances by her male employer, which she will be unable to resist, unable to handle in a satisfactory professional manner, or which will otherwise adversely affect her in the performance of her duties. While these concerns cannot be lightly dismissed, some male colleagues, especially detail leaders, are prone to act like doting fathers anticipating the worst on their daughters' first date. It is not easy for the female Personal Protection Specialist to be taken seriously. Like Avis, she has not only to try harder, but to adjust her marketing strategies to the exigencies of the case. She ignores the sexual dynamic at her peril. She is in the unfortunate position of having to win respect twice over, once as a Personal Protection Specialist, and secondly, as a woman.

How these matters are handled in practice is dictated by individual choice, economic circumstances, and personal qualities. They are probably the most difficult a woman is likely to face in a career as a Personal Protection Specialist. Keeping the principal out of harm's way will, for the well-trained, probably prove a breeze by comparison. It requires an extraordinary amount of coolness and grace under pressure. It calls, too, for a poker player's skills at bluff and knowing when to fold. A woman needs to learn how to handle awkward situations like a man, yet without surrendering her femininity to the occasion. The key lies in the development of a calculating professional detachment. Involvement on a personal level is fatal to objectivity. A general observation, applicable to both men and women is in order here. The provision of protective services is a full-time job. It cannot be done efficiently in conjunction with other tasks. And if, in a particular case, it is felt that it can, it probably doesn't need to be done at all. Let us be quite blunt about this. A woman cannot be an efficient bodyguard and a mistress at one and the same time. Efficient bodyguarding does not, sensibly, permit of such distractions. Any principal that believes otherwise is fooling himself as to what he really needs. He should be gently but firmly set to rights on the matter. Providing protective services for a former lover requires more emotional resilience than most women bodyguards can probably muster. The ideal bodyguard is one thought to be unaffected by lust and the like. It is no accident that the women of the seraglio were protected by eunuchs. Male critics of women in the field of protective services are ever fearful that feminine emotion will take over in a crisis, especially a crisis of the heart. The corollary? Real men don't dance or eat quiche. And bodyguards don't cry. No tears on the job, please.

Both men and women face these same situations. What is different is the way in which men *believe* women respond to them. There are not only problems of perception involved here; there are problems of communication. The genders are often, to adapt Shaw's aphorism, separated by a common language. The problems are greatly accentuated when sexual matters are involved. Man's sexual banter may be salaciously innocent or designedly seductive.[11] It may start out in one vein and change course, depending upon the reception. On sexual ground, a kind of jousting goes on between men and women, a tactical probing of the defenses. We often begin with the telling of off-color jokes or the use of risqué or double-entendre expressions designed to test the understanding and receptiveness of the person at whom they are directed. Nowadays, in our own society, speech, between men and women is much freer, and consequently, this kind of verbal foreplay has come to take on a somewhat modified character. It is nevertheless, still a frequently observed precursor to a more direct sexual propositioning. There is a tendency to regard a knowledge of sexual humor as sophisticated, and ignorance is somehow unworldly or evidence of a dull and sheltered mind. As a result, there are many who feign an appreciation of such humor without really understanding its meaning, in substantive terms, or even what might or might not be funny in what is recounted. In verbal communication, there are cases of individuals, male and female, failing to recognize that they are being propositioned, sexually, while others imagine that even the most inoffensive of remarks is sexually loaded. Just as beauty is in the eye of the beholder, so too, might it be said that a sense of sexual meaning or lack thereof resides in the brain of the individual in these kinds of encounters. Security, like charity begins at home. Those who provide personal security for others would do well to make, with or without professional assistance, a profound and honest exploration of their own sexual nature. Only thus will they be able, with confidence, to adjust correctly their relations with others.

Corporeal propinquity tends to encourage familiarity of speech. Distance is difficult to maintain in relationships that extend over long periods. Barriers break down or are gradually eroded. There can be few working relationships

---

[11] For a very instructive discussion on this, see, "The Male Approach," in *The Rationale of the Dirty Joke*, G. Legman, New York: Grove Press (1968), pages 217/235.

with a potential to exceed that inherent in the relationship between the Personal Protection Specialist and the individual protected.[12] The opportunities provide for a kind of psychological conditioning of the parties, enhancing the prospects of their relating on other than a strictly work-oriented footing. Add to this potent mixture the twin spices of danger and dependency. However much they may struggle against the notion, intellectually, the rich and the powerful are still mightily dependent upon those engaged to protect them. The very notion of protection implies a state of dependency, one, moreover, in the circumstances considered here, involving matters of life and death. Erica Jong, in a different context, puts it this way.[13] "As for protection, of course I want that — don't we all?" Such feelings can act powerfully upon the emotions of those who, whether it is acknowledged or not, are already strongly attracted to the person providing the protection. The element of dependency, in the form of sudden, incongruous feelings of attraction, transcending the bounds prescribed by convention, status, and commonsense, has received some notice in connection with the phenomenon known as the Stockholm Syndrome.[14] It is not something which lasts much beyond the duration of the events giving rise to it. It cannot reasonably be expected that this parallel phenomenon might prove to be of more lengthy duration.

For some, at least, in some situations, danger may be a powerful aphrodisiac.[15] Or, more accurately, perhaps, the scent or hint of danger rather than the immediate realization of what is portended by it. The profession of a Personal Protection Specialist carries with it the subtle fragrance of danger. The bodyguard represents the forces of good versus the dark forces of evil. This, plus a shared sense of the apprehended dangers involved, lends considerable, if not always warranted, romanticism to the office. Shared danger, another ingredient of the Stockholm Syndrome, has the capacity to draw closer those who are affected by it. There are powerful sexual forces at work in these situations.[16] As they have a propensity for wreaking havoc with the established order of things, real danger paints the world in different colors. Those who survive life-threatening experiences are prone to review their lives through different eyes. Again, the duration of these reflective periods varies quite widely from case to case. Some persons recover their normal equilibrium more quickly than others. A few are so profoundly touched by a brush with violent death that they are never quite the same again. Such experiences are especially disturbing for

---

[12] The term used in the United Kingdom, so very evocative, is indeed "close protection."

[13] Op. cit. supra, note 11, at page 69.

[14] On this, generally, see "Close Encounters of an Unpleasant Kind: Preliminary Thoughts on the Stockholm Syndrome:, H.H.A. Cooper, 2 Legal Medical Quarterly, No. 2, (1978), pages 100/114.

[15] A number of studies have tested this hypothesis. See, for example, *Sexual Chemistry*, Julius Fest and Meredith Bernstein, New York: M. Evans (1983). See, also, "Some evidence for heightened sexual attraction under conditions of high anxiety," D. G. Dutton & A. P. Aron, 30 Journal of Personality and Society Psychiatry (1974), pages 510/517

[16] It might be opined that there is almost always a sexual dimension to every act of violence and there is an abundance of evidence to sustain such an opinion. A very fine novel on terrorism makes the following observation: "Violence is sexual, Walsh knew, as every soldier knows." *Blind Pilot*, Ambrose Clancy, New York, William Morrow (1980, page 117). For a pertinent discussion of sex and aggression, specifically in a homosexual context, see *Phallos*, Thorkil Vanguard, New York: International Universities Press (1972), pages 101/110.

persons of elevated status, wealth and power. They are suddenly brought to a stark realization of their own mortality, a distinctly sobering process for some. There are those who display a surprising, unanticipated strength of character, and there are others who demonstrate weaknesses of which they would rather not be reminded, should they survive.[17] There are often situations of great mental confusion, in which love and hate lie so close together as to be indistinguishable. While love may survive an episode of shame, lust is unlikely to do so. Those who find themselves in such situations ought not to be surprised by an unpleasant, emotional about-face.

We must now embark upon the most delicate and difficult passage of this sexual odyssey. If the topic of male menopause has been correctly labeled as "unspeakable," then, surely, until very recently, the subject of homosexuality was, among most men, the most "unspeakable" of all topics. Real men did not discuss such things; they probably experienced difficulty even thinking about them. Homosexuality, like cancer, bad traffic accidents, or getting fired, was something awful—which happened to other people. Obviously, nothing in the nature of strict scientific rigor is claimed for these or any of the following observations. But, even if they are labeled as merely impressionistic, they give a pretty good impression of what was certainly correct at the time. The profession of providing personal protection was, until comparatively recently, an almost exclusively male field of activity; there simply were no women and *their* sexual preferences were not, accordingly, a matter of consideration. The great tides of history that have swept over so many others, in so many different spheres of activity cannot, reasonably, be expected to have by-passed those in the profession of providing personal protection. We are now in what some are calling the Gay Nineties.[18] While muted during the first two years of the decade, coinciding with the final period of the Reagan/Bush era, the movement quickly reached a crescendo as the Clinton Administration sought, early, to make good on its campaign promises. With the furor unleashed by the demands of the gay and lesbian community and, in particular, the impact of those demands on service in the Armed Forces of the United States, it is no exaggeration to aver that "this is the thing of the 90s." Whatever one's position on the issues, the "thing" cannot be ignored. Whereas, but a short while ago, silence on this topic was the general rule, it now seems positively unfashionable not to talk about it. Such openness is particularly helpful in the context of the impact of alternative life styles on the provision of protective services.

Let is be emphatically stated from the outset that gay sex, like cigarette smoking, the Holocaust, and the right to bear arms is a topic on which strong, even extreme views are held. And, as in the case of those other topics, the expression of one's true feelings on the subject has to be mediated with a certain caution. For, whatever else may be the case, we are living, in the United States at least, in the *politically correct nineties.* However strong a feeling of revulsion may be induced in the recipient by a homosexual proposition, it is,

---

[17] Historically noteworthy, in this regard, is the experience of T. E. Lawrence, whose entire life was said to have been altered by his sexual treatment at the hands of the Turks.
[18] See, "The Gay Nineties," Luisita Lopez Torregrosa, 56 *Vanity Fair,* No. 5, pages 122 at seq.

seemingly, no longer polite or acceptable to react with violence, of even a moderate kind, against the offenders. While some sensitive new-age guys may be able, gracefully, to decline the unwelcome offer while yet conveying the impression of being flattered at having been singled out for such attention, these gestures are beyond the scope of most straight males. The more natural impulse to stomp the propositioner to death on the floor of the men's room clearly has to be restrained. Something like a happy medium has to be sought, difficult though it may be for those who, on account of this unwanted attraction for members of their own sex are persistently pestered in this way. It is clearly a problem which many women will readily recognize in connection with the fending off of unsought attention by men. It is particularly acute and the cause of a real dilemma when the person doing the propositioning is the boss, the person for whom the protective services are being provided. There has always been reason to believe that this problem was more widespread and serious than had been acknowledged. The new openness has merely tended to confirm what had long been suspected.

One healthy consequence of these new, open attitudes is that many principals and potential clients for the provision of protective services have now unequivocally declared their gay life style. It is, in some cases, notorious. This does put the bodyguard on notice so that he (or, she, for we may properly include lesbian principals, here) can make an informed decision about the advisability to taking the job. If you are disgusted by the very notion of same sex intimate relations, the job is decidedly not for you. Even though you may feel perfectly secure in the knowledge of your own sexuality, situations may well arise that could test your professionality to its limits. The job is stressful enough without adding, unnecessarily, to the burdens.[19] This should not be taken to mean that a straight bodyguard can never, or ought not to provide personal protection services for a principal who is known to be gay or lesbian. The choice should be made, in each case, on an individual, informed basis. Where necessary, it may be advisable to take appropriate professional advice on the matter. As always, the task begins with an honest, searching, self-examination of one's own sexuality and attitudes. Two general observations may usefully be offered here. Economic consideration ought never to be allowed to prevail over concerns raised by the possibilities inherent in the situation. Secondly, be guided by your doubts. Where these cannot be resolved to your own satisfaction, you ought not to take the job. These inner promptings are not to be ignored. They serve the same function for the psyche that pain does in the physiological sphere. Nor should it be inferred from the foregoing that protective services for principals who are acknowledgely gay ought only to be provided by those with similar inclinations. While this does take care of the attitudinal problem discussed above, it raises other considerations. The criterion in every instance should be: can the job be done to the standard required without the issue of sexuality getting in the way.

---

19 See, on this, "Stress and the Personal Protection Specialist," Bruce L. Danto, M.D. in *Providing Executive Protection.* Ed. Richard W. Kobetz, D.P.A. Berryville, VA: Executive Protection Institute, (1991), pages 92-101.

A single individual may often have overall responsibility for the provision of protective services for a particular principal. He or she will have powers of hiring and firing often without the assistance, welcome or otherwise, of a specialist personnel or human resources department. There is, often enough, a very limited universe of qualified applicants from among whom to choose. Personal recommendations and referrals are very important. Much of this is done on a very informal basis, among professionals who know and trust each other. There is much, understandable confidentiality in these processes and a great deal hangs upon them. A good deal of caution has to be exercised in the making of these recommendations for people will sometimes be hired on little more than a few words from the "right" source. If, as sometimes happens, the person recommended for the job turns out to be rather less than satisfactory, this does little for the reputation of the person who made the recommendation. The sexual matters we have discussed, generally, cannot, prudently, be left out of consideration. To add an attractive female, however professional and well-qualified, to an otherwise all male detail may be so distracting that the work inevitably suffers. To add such an element to a detail protecting a principal who is a known womanizer may be more fatal than failing to bring along a supply of his regular heart medication. Engaging a gay bodyguard, uncritically, to protect a principal with known sexual leanings of a similar nature, may have similar results. Known sexual preferences and proclivities should be taken into account in making assignments, in the interest of getting the job done efficiently.

Where homosexuality is declared, or, at least, acknowledged, it can be appropriately factored into the scheme of things. Many homosexuals remain, however, for a variety of reasons, figuratively in the closet. There are others who exhibit no clearly defined sexual preference, but vacillate between homosexuality and heterosexuality.[20] There is considerable potential for problems in this even where a fairly accurate knowledge of the true state of affairs is held by the provider of protective services. Individual sexual attraction, of a wholly unanticipated kind, can generate embarrassing or even ugly situations where it is inappropriately and unacceptably displayed toward the provider of protective services. These situational episodes involving concealed homosexual leanings are prompted by a variety of stimuli, but are commonly induced by the consumption of alcohol or drugs. Both of these may have the effect of releasing inhibitions, which might otherwise serve to restrain such exhibitions of behavior. The unexpectedness of these approaches, where they occur, can be particularly damaging. As in the case of some rape victims, there is sometimes a tendency, on the part of those subjected to this behavior, to blame themselves for something they might have done or said so as to give the impression that such advances might be not unwelcome. These tendencies are exacerbated where an otherwise well-respected employer has acted in an uncharacteristic fashion, seemingly on impulse, especially where the behavior in question is quickly followed by what seems to be sincere contrition.[21] The real issue in all these cases

---

[20] See, for example, "Bi Sex," Salem Alaton, *The Globe and Mail,* Section D., Focus, June 26, 1993.
[21] The damage is sometimes aggravated when this contrition is quickly followed by a rapid attempt to make inappropriate, often insulting amends perhaps in financial terms.

is how destructive is what has occurred to the delicate relationship between the protected person and the individual providing the protective services. There is almost always, in these cases a certain loss of respect. Is this, in the particular instance, so great as to impair, fatally, the relationship? There is, understandably, in even the rarest and most aberrant of cases, the apprehension of an unwelcome recurrence. In each instance, the matter must be carefully and objectively assessed to determine its effect upon satisfactory future performance of the job.

Any intimate relationship in the protective services field has the potential for compromising the ability to do the job to the standards required. Unwelcome homosexual advances are more than ordinarily corrosive, whatever the direction of the approach. Such approaches have the capacity to occasion embarrassment, disgust and, in the worst of cases, actual physical violence. In a certain sense, they may also represent an abuse of trust, the delicate bond by reason of which the very protective services relationship can be said to subsist. The bodyguard, because of the necessary closeness of the physical relationship is like some long-suffering spouses, privy to a different side of the protected individual from that ordinarily displayed in public. Some of these "street angels" have a distinctly ugly or perverted side, which they are not at any great pains to conceal from those closest to them. This can be extremely disconcerting to those who have difficulty in reconciling the conflicting sides of the individual displaying such traits. These are not likeable characteristics nor ones conducive to respect. It is always more difficult for an employee to be tolerant of such failings, however much they might be balanced by generosity and other good qualities, than it is for a family member or a spouse. Only by the most strained use of language can there be said to be any obligation to overlook such conduct. A special kind of awkwardness arises where the behavior in question is prompted by sexual urgings. The question the Personal Protection Specialist must ask in all such cases is: how does what has occurred affect my ability to do my job? It is a question that must be answered with scrupulous and thoroughgoing honesty. There is no room for equivocation here. Much more than career prospects and reputation are at stake here. It may be a matter of life and death.

The professionalization of the business of bodyguarding has coincided with two dramatic sexual revolutions. The first, that of the late 1960s/1970s, witnessed an extraordinary liberalization of sexual attitudes, bordering almost upon licensed promiscuity. The impact of this is enshrined in the arts and the language of the times. The second revolution, that of the 1980s was an outgrowth of the first, but represented an ominous kind of counterpoint to it. The AIDS epidemic has yet to run its course, but already it has had a dramatically chilling effect upon the kinds of casual sexual relationships that had sprung out of the altered mores of the earlier decade. No one can yet predict where all this is leading, but what is certain is that a pervasive climate of fear has now replaced the happy-go-lucky sexual attitudes, which had but lately come into being. Many jobs formerly done with casual abandon, now call for the routine use of surgical gloves. There is hardly any sector of the community that has not been hit by the menace of AIDS, but some have been much harder hit than others. The entertainment industry has been struck particularly hard and prominent personalities have died well-publicized deaths. The lifestyles of many of these were such that they routinely employed bodyguards. Clearly, this form of protection was, in the end, as ineffective as any other form of prophylactic that might have been utilized to ward off this dread condition. Yet even those dying of AIDS might feel a need for protection against other harms with which they might be threatened. There is a real dilemma here for the provider of protective services. More and more, in recent years, we have stressed the need for the bodyguard to be trained to minister to the medical needs of his or her principal. What if the person protected is suffering from AIDS and is in the terminal stages of some terrible illness as a consequence? There is no mere issue of sentimentality, here. For even the best informed about HIV and AIDS there is always the lingering question: Am I at risk? Once again, this goes to the very root of the ability to render, conscientiously, the quality of service for which one is engaged. Then, there is always the question of where you will go and what you would do when your principal has passed on. Regrettable though it may be, there is an understandable fear of being close to someone who has been around one who has died as a consequence of the AIDS. How will being so stigmatized affect your future career prospects?[22]

Thus far, we have been considering the problems of sex in the context of the providing of protective services, in terms of a variety of irregular relationships. Now, let us look at these matters from a different perspective. *Love and Marriage,* so goes the song, go together like a horse and carriage. Is marriage the panacea for all the ills we laid out for consideration? In the *particular* context of the providing of protective services, is marriage a bulwark against the corrosive effects of sex on professional performance? On the evidence of social patterns, generally, the prognosis is very poor. The incidence of infidelity and divorce in society, does not suggest that even in particular areas, marriage might be expected to have some special, protective value so as to commend it for the purposes we have been considering. While no general criticism of the institution of marriage is here intended, it cannot be overlooked that the providing of protective services is one of those professions that, by its nature, imposes its own peculiar strains on intimate relationships of this kind, whether formalized or otherwise. The bodyguard is of necessity, very much at the beck and call of his or her employer. On a long term basis, it is extremely difficult to manage the demands of such a career and balance them, sensibly, against the requirements of a happy and lasting marriage. Few marriage partners can, for long, tolerate being so manifestly placed second, however generous the economic benefits of the arrangement. Marriage, itself, generates considerable stresses of its own. It can hardly be expected to flourish when it is additionally burdened by the kinds of sexual tensions adumbrated above. Far from being a bulwark, then, against the ills betokened by sex in the professional life of the provider of protective services, marriage might more properly be regarded as a millstone. It is

---

22 Those interested in examining the question in more detail may refer to "Rosellini's Requiem," Ben Brantley, 56 Vanity Fair, No. 5, page 154, at pages 184-185. "He kept at least one bodyguard with him until the end of his life." He was an AIDS victim.

just one more element tending to reduce the concentration required by this exacting job. Again, it is emphasized that none of this should be seen as an attack upon or argument against marriage, but rather as a cautionary note against marriage, in this particular context, for the wrong reasons. Thus, marriage is no magic nostrum for the sexually vulnerable, single bodyguard. Rather, it may be seen as an irritant, like a grain of sand within the shell of an oyster, which, while it may yet produce something uniquely beautiful and valuable of itself, renders its host ever more vulnerable on another account.

Despite the dark, ominous shadows cast by the AIDS epidemic, many of the changes brought about by the earlier sexual revolution are here to stay; in the popular language of our times, they are irreversible. Attitudes about sex, relationships between men and women, the common language, are all looser, more relaxed. To a great extent, the place and meaning of sex in social life has changed, and attitudes towards marriage have, inevitably, changed along with it. The change has been comparatively rapid in the Untied States. The difference in public attitudes towards marital infidelity in high places between the presidential campaigns of 1988 and 1992 is quite remarkable. Adultery may never have been an absolute bar to high political office, but it has now become so commonplace as to require no apology. Nor is this laxity simply the prerogative of the privileged classes. It has come to infect the whole spectrum of society. In consequence, marriage no longer affords even the illusion of security it once did. Till death do us part has come to take on a cynically hollow ring. Even fairy-tale marriages like those of Charles and Diana, Andrew and Fergie are seen to end, spectacularly, on the rocks. Marriage is no longer a guarantee against being regarded as available; desire knows no such bounds. The issue, nowadays, is whether the party desired may be regarded as separable. All too often, the only determining factor is opportunity. Absence may, in some cases, make the heart grow fonder. Too frequent absences provide opportunity for mischief. Such aphorisms are probably as old as human society itself. The business of providing protective services often demands frequent absences, of a duration difficult to measure with exactitude and having, sometimes, an unplanned character. For the one left behind, it is easy to imagine the glamor, the excitement, the pomp and luxury, all in the company of beautiful, "available" people. The reality, which needs no description for the experienced professional, is more difficult for the uninitiated to imagine. What is not difficult to imagine is how jealousies and resentments can build. To a certain kind of mind, there are no innocent explanations. Such feelings are not wiped away by gifts of Hermés scarves and liberal doses of French perfume. Those who marry bodyguards should have a clear idea of the demands of providing protective services. Those who cannot provide the support and understanding required of a true marriage partnership, under what will often be trying circumstances, would be well advised to think long and hard before entering into it. Even monarchs have had to choose between marriage and the job. While such choices have their romantic aspects, in practice, they can be excruciating and productive of endless regrets.

Sex, then, plays a larger role in the business of providing protective services than many would concede. In the final analysis, it can determine how well or badly the job is done and even, in some cases, whether it can be done at all. Sex, like eating and sleeping, is one of the most normal of adult, human activities. As the late, great Malcolm Forbes said,[23] "What's unnatural sex? Having none." Sex and all it connotes for the great complex of human relationships, in which we are all involved, has to be sensibly factored into the business of providing protective services; it cannot be ignored. There is nothing exotic or even strange about what has been written here. Most of it is within the common experience of every provider of protective services. The real problem is that few involved in matters of the heart and loins can see these things, unaided, with sufficient objectivity. There are few others with whom such matters can safely be discussed detachedly. There are serious difficulties of confidentiality impeding such discussion. Were there no other inhibitions of a more personal nature, these alone would be a serious obstacle to full and frank discussion with others. What it comes down to in the end, is that each is thrown back on his or her own devices to solve the problem as best they can. What is offered in conclusion, here, are a few simple precepts to aid in this lonely task. While these precepts might well be thought to have more general application, it should be borne in mind that they are set down, here, specifically with the needs of those who provide protective services in mind. They apply, with equal force, to both men and women.

(1) It is unwise in the extreme to use sex for the purposes of professional advancement. Not only is it generally unethical to the point of being deceptive; in the long run, it is bound to be counter-productive. The ideal bodyguard is sexually indifferent to those he or she is assigned to protect as well as to those with whom he or she has to work.

(2) The provider of protective services should be alert to any change in his or her own feelings or behavior toward those whom he or she is charged to protect, or with whom he or she is working and, in particular, if those feelings or behavioral changes are a consequence of some sexual stimuli.

(3) In the event of being the subject of unmistakable sexual advances by those for whom the protective services are provided or by any of those with whom he or she is working to that end, the person so affected should make an immediate and sincere appraisal of the consequences of rejecting such advances. If such a rejection is considered to impair, seriously, the basis upon which the protective services relationship is considered to exist, the person concerned should withdraw at the earliest possible moment from the assignment, indicating, in the clearest possible terms, that what has occurred has so compromised the protective mission that it can no longer be effectively undertaken.

(4) The provider of protective services should never allow him or herself to be drawn into any sexual liaison, which has the potential to affect the satisfactory performance of the protective mission undertaken. The bodyguard has a primary overarching responsibility to the person protected. Any sexual relationship incompatible with the discharge of that obligation to the best of his or her

---

[23] *The Sayings of Chairman Malcolm*, New York: Harper & Row, (1978), page 111.

ability is to be avoided.

(5) The intrusion of feelings of a sexual nature into any situation involving the providing of protective services is a danger signal which must be heeded and obeyed. Sexual impulses can be enormously powerful. Do not make the mistake of believing you can keep them firmly under control and function effectively as a provider of protective services at the same time.

(6) The providing of protective services is concerned with matters of life and death. If you have lost respect for those for whom or with whom you are working, you may be putting them in peril unless you withdraw from the situation. It is dishonest to remain in post purely for other reasons, such as financial, considerations.

(7) Do not allow yourself to be drawn into or to remain in a compromising sexual situation in the belief that your non-compliance with what is sought of you will damage you professionally. If you find it difficult to resist pressures of this kind, it calls, fundamentally, into question your ability to function effectively as a provider of protective services to others.

(8) Rejecting unwelcome sexual advances must be handled with extreme delicacy, tact, and grace. Avoid, if at all possible, making enemies among those you have had to fend off in this way. Remember, the Rich and Famous, and the Powerful, are not used to being spurned. In your own professional interests as well as theirs, avoid embarrassments.

(9) Be as alert for sexual situations of the compromising kind as you would any situation touching upon the safety or security of your principal. As in matters of this kind try to avoid anything in the nature of a confrontation. Try to anticipate what might be coming, and sidestep, adroitly.

(10) Examine,carefully and honestly, your own sexual signalling apparatus. Make sure you are not giving out misleading indications of your own interest or availability. Even when you are interested, be careful that you do not display your feelings where this would be inappropriate. From a professional perspective, make sure your sexual "command center" is properly manned and under control at all times. There are those who never take 'no' for an answer, but 'maybe' in any language is a clear incitement to pursue the matter to 'yes.'

EIGHT

Media Encounters of the Non-Destructive Kind

by Susan Di Giacomo

"Tis pleasant, sure, to see one's name in print."
George Gordon
<u>Lord Byron</u>[1]

PROVIDING PERSONAL PROTECTION is a private pursuit with manifold public implications. In many ways, it is a business, but it is a business in which, contrary to received wisdom, it does not always pay to advertise. At least, not in conventionally accepted ways. Providing protective services requires, above all, a certain discretion. It took, after all, a long time before lawyers could be professionally persuaded to tout their services in the *Yellow Pages*. And there are those, even today, who regret the lowering of dignity entailed by some of the more strident displays of the attorney's skills indulged in by a few, and their copywriters. The ideal bodyguard should be self-effacing to the point of being unobtrusive, save when called upon to exercise his or her professional talents. The hallmark of this job is that it should be done without ostentation. Graven in stone should be the precept: never upstage thy principal. Especially if the person protected is a high-profile figure, a darling of the media. Yet such fame inevitably has its fallout. Those close to these public figures are often, unwittingly, illuminated by its glow. How to handle such possibilities without like the moth, too close to the candle, getting singed? The following are a few suggestions.

The secret to handling the media successfully is control.. You cannot control the media, or its intrusion upon your professional life. You can, however,

---

[1] *English Bards & Scottish Reviewers.*

control your interaction with it. In the first place, this involves a cool, professional, objective appraisal of your own abilities and attributes. Very few people, even media personalities themselves, are capable of undertaking such an awesome review without professional assistance. "I can handle the press," should find a place, somewhere, in an anthology of *famous last words*. Along with, "I was misquoted," and "I was quoted out of context." After such experiences, many are tempted to expostulate, "I should have just kept my damned mouth shut." Remember: words uttered cannot be re-called. Nor usefully amended. In serious cases, in print journalism, a retraction may be in order, but what appeared on page 1, is rarely corrected with any usefulness if the retraction appears later in some remote corner of page 11. And if the perils and pitfalls of tangling with those who consume printer's ink by the barrel are not fearsome enough, consider the dangers of the new all-pervasive electronic journalism, which has the capacity to catch us all, instantly, unaware, and often enough, with our worst side to the camera. No time for retractions here. Nor the Andy Warhol fifteen minutes in history's limelight. If you are accorded a fifteen second sound byte, generosity on the part of the show's producer or a low news night rather than any recognition of your natural talent are probably the cause. Are you ready to say something in fifteen seconds that doesn't sound completely inane?

An old Yorkshire saying that was probably directed at college professors or putative criminals is useful counsel on these occasions: when in doubt, say nowt. But who can resist the lure of unexpected publicity, of appearing on camera? Look at any sporting event and note how many among the ranks of the spectators cannot resist the urge to wave to family and friends as the cameras are pointed in their direction. People consciously preen for the camera; they change, visibly, before its cruel, unwinking eye. Before succumbing to such indulgences, recall this: such casual advertisement does few very much good, in a professional sense, and it may do them a great deal of harm. Unless you have a real flair for uttering the memorable spontaneously before the mini-cam, you would be wise to forego the temptations of competing for instant stardom. Leave such opportunism to those whose business might be enhanced by such appearances. It is flattering to be told by acquaintances, "Caught you on the six o'clock news," but there is also the possibility that the relentless camera will also have caught other things you might rather have wished remained concealed. Such as that odd bulge in your right-hand jacket pocket.

Casual media encounters are hard to avoid, and harder still to control. Those whose principals are constantly in the public eye are particularly prone to meet the press in some, not always congenial, form or forum. Such interactions are all in the day's work. Controlling one's own reactions is fundamental. Journalists after a story can be aggravating creatures. Even the nicest among them appear to turn into selfish monsters when a Pulitzer seems to beckon. From their own perspective, even the most over-zealous of journalists, whatever their media, are *just doing their job*. There is, obviously, great potential for a conflict of interest when you are just doing yours. Whatever the cost, whatever the provocation, keep your cool. On no account be tempted to do a Sean Penn on some guy's equipment[2]. A cool head and a sense of humor are indispensable in these situations. If, in the heat of the moment, tempers do get frayed and you have just ruined his or her best camera angle with your best body block, be ready with a truly gracious apology. You may have difficulty under some circumstances, making friends with the working press, but do try your level best to avoid making enemies. The former Mossad agent, Victor Ostrovsky recited a curse bandied among his colleagues: "May they read about you in tomorrow's papers." If, in your case they do, at least try to make sure, as far as you are able, that it redounds to your credit.

Then, of course, there are the talk shows. Being on, say, *Larry King Live* is an alluring prospect for someone trying to drum up business. After all, one presidential candidate kicked off a non-existent campaign by availing himself of just such an opportunity, while another sought to bolster a flagging campaign by following smartly in his footsteps. Presidential candidates are in season once every four years. Personal Protection Specialists are a *hot item* at less regular intervals. Sometimes, bodyguarding per se is the featured item. At other times, some particular aspect, such as women protection specialists are the featured story line. Beware the fabled researchers of the major network and cable productions. Their speciality is ferreting out likely subjects for their show's host to interview. They can be very seductive once they have located their prey and they have a well-honed knack for weaseling information out of their victims. Personal Protection Specialists are the repositories of many secrets concerning their principals. That is what makes them appealing subjects for talk shows, rather than their finely-chiselled features or the supposed glamor attached to the job. In these situations, the Personal Protection Specialist must guard his or her principal's secrets as diligently as they would their very lives. A talk show, even for the experienced requires considerable preparation. It is not something to be undertaken lightly. Do not confide to a researcher anything you would not be prepared to say on air. The good talk show guest is one who is knowledgeable and natural. The camera catches—and magnifies—even the slightest whiff of unease. A good television host can draw out his or her guest so as to present that person in the best light[3], but even the most skillful cannot make a silk purse out of a sow's ear. Before agreeing to appear on a talk show, make sure you understand exactly what is required of you. If the setting does not seem right for you, gracefully, even regretfully, decline. Oprah is not for everyone.

Then there is the Personal Protection Specialist as expert. Here, *the event,* rather than personality is the precipitating factor in exciting the interest of the press. Something occurs, say, a noteworthy assassination that sends correspondents scurrying to their laptops the world over. Quickly enough, they gather, more or less, *all the news that's fit to print.* But they want more, that which will make the story intelligible, worthy of a read by an often jaded public.

---

[2] Those who protect celebrities from the world of entertainment have to factor the behavior of the *paparazzi* into their daily schedules.

[3] There are, too, those who, as a matter of style, can do the reverse. David Frost is a master at this, but he limits his use of the talent to the overly pompous. Think twice about accepting an invitation to appear on *Nightline* if you might be so classified. Ted Koppel, too, is a master of the put-down.

In short, they want *background.* They seek out the opinions of those purported to know more about these things than the average man or woman in the street. There is rarely a lack of those ready and willing to express their opinions, especially when this means a chance for seeing them in print. The trick, for the journalist, is finding the person with something interesting and relevant to say and who can say it well. The journalist will generally do the rest. It is not too much to say that the journalist, especially the print journalist, can make or break experts. A brief comment in *Time* or *Newsweek* is worth a ton of worldly wisdom carefully conveyed in classroom and lecture halls. It means *instant name recognition* and a pass to other avenues of mass communication such as television and radio, both local and national and, sometimes, even, international. What an alluring prospect, and how flattering! Dollar signs begin to flash and twinkle and the prospects of book contracts for the more ambitious appear to take on a new dimension of reality. Such possibilities can be quite intoxicating. Before getting carried away by all this, which can begin quite casually enough, it is well to have a look at some of the professional, and personal implications.

It is obviously an advantage to achieve the widest recognition as an authority in your field. There is more than the mere glow of satisfaction attaching to this; there are tangible, material rewards. But in this, as in so many other departments of life, there is no *free lunch.* These things have to be studied from a cost/benefit angle. At first blush, it looks as though control is not much of a problem. The expert knows the subject and can determine what he or she would like to say about it. This is a dangerous illusion. This is very different from being an expert in a legal proceeding. A well prepared expert is difficult, in such a setting, to deflect from his or her chosen path. In print journalism, real control lies with the journalist and his or her editor. Editors are the ultimate arbiters of what gets into print. Even if you <u>own</u> the *New York Daily Post,* it doesn't mean that you will get what you have to say on to its pages; it has, first, to pass through the editorial filter. Starting from the top, if what you have to say, on what you are invited to opine, is contrary to the newspaper or magazine's policy, you will look in vain amid its pages for all the wise and witty things you have said. This is very demoralizing for beginners, especially the naive who have given, generously, some forty-five minutes of their time only to find that not a word of it ever appears in print. Incidentally, unless you are very well known, and very highly appreciated, you will have been very lucky indeed if your forty-five minutes of earnest conversation with a reporter produces more than a single attributed sentence in print. Whether it is worth it or not is up to you. Those with busy schedules may want to think twice about committing their time to such speculative exercises. You will invariably be thanked, handsomely, for your time and trouble, but is that enough? Of course, you may have to cast many times before you actually catch a salmon and there is a certain challenge to this that is absent when you simply go to the fishmonger. And there are, of necessity, penalties for refusal. You may simply not be asked again. Ever.

Many of these same considerations apply to invitations to appear as an expert on radio or television. The taped interview is particularly hazardous in these respects. What you have had to say, though relevant enough at the time, is, on occasion, overtaken by events. The electronic media is especially fast-paced. Anything over two hours old may well be too stale for an airing. While the item may be junked, your cooperation may be kindly remembered by those you have helped. Other, more favorable opportunities may be opened to you thereby. Meanwhile, you have added to your reputation; from such small acorns mighty oaks can grow. If a taped interview does not air, don't blame the reporter, he or she may be as disappointed as you at the waste of effort. Again, even if a taped interview is aired, do be prepared for disappointments in the finished product. Twenty minutes of taping may well be material for no more than a 15 second sound byte. What possibilities there are, here for having your utterances taken out of context! Your few threads are but part of a grander design being woven by the journalist, the editor, and the station or network. To view the whole, you must know the story angle and this is very rarely apparent to any save the most astute of professional observers on the outside. In some ways, the live interview is even more difficult to manage effectively from the perspective of the presenter: time is at a premium. It takes real skill and much training to say something really striking off the cuff in a few seconds. The celebrity may be forgiven for a *faux pas* here or there and the odd bumbling and fumbling for words before the camera. The expert is not usually so fortunate. If you are truly articulate and have something useful to say, and can say it attractively in a few words, this may be for you. If you need time to gather your wits, or are given to lengthy preambles, seek another medium of expression more suited to your style.

Radio is, in many ways the most forgiving medium. One can cultivate a very personal style in a more relaxed atmosphere than is possible through other vehicles of expression. Television often has a nasty habit of focusing upon appearance rather than talent. You may have much that is useful to say, but if they don't like how you look, this may so detract from your performance that you simply don't get on camera.[4] Unfair? Of course. But as JFK is supposed to have said, life is not fair. Television programming is a product, a product, moreover, of a highly competitive business. It has to sell, or it doesn't make it. Radio demands of the listener an act of creative participation. Through the imagination, the listener invests the speaker with all kinds of qualities that may have little or no relationship to real life. What is thus visualized may, indeed, be very far from the truth of the matter. For television you have to present yourself and your expertise in a certain light for a favorable viewing. You have to dress the part. If you have your wits about you, it is possible to give a stellar radio interview on a subject within your specialty, fresh from the shower with no more than a towel for your garb. The listeners are not going to penetrate your predicament, they are going to focus upon what you have to say. Generally, even for a fast-breaking news story, you will be given some time to prepare your remarks. Use this wisely. The great Dr. Samuel Johnson tells us that,[5]

---

[4] The popular image of the bodyguard, male or female, is of someone supremely fit, in the peak of condition. If, in appearance, you don't fit the bill, you might want to consider whether or not they are setting you up.

[5] *Preface to Shakespeare*

"Notes are often necessary, but they are necessary evils." The right kind of notes can be very useful preparation for a radio interview to be conducted over the telephone. Such interviews are usually of two to four minutes in duration, not overly cramping time-wise, but not too generous either. Aim to make no more than five, good succinct points; if you get three of them across, you will have done well. Don't read from your notes. Use them only as a reminder of the points you wish to make. Keep your notes short, simple, and direct. If you find it helpful, use colors for emphasis. You are on radio. No-one except you will know.

Experts are sometimes chosen by the media because they *toe the party line*. What this means, in practice, is that those consulted will voice opinions, which back up what the particular organ of diffusion is trying to get across. This does not, necessarily, mean conformity with the "authorized version." Suppose a network is making a presentation highly critical of the way the government has handled some matter. You may be in private agreement with such a position, but are you prepared, publicly, to express yourself professionally in such a fashion? The media thrives on controversy, but is it good for you? People, understandably, do not often take kindly to criticism, especially where this can reflect adversely on their careers and prospects. The media has a tendency to focus upon what has gone wrong rather than what has gone right. Spontaneous praise, especially for government servants, is a strictly rationed commodity in the media. Experts are all too often selected because of their capacity to criticize rather than simply endorse what others have done. This is hardly an exemplar of *how to win friends and influence people*. Some have a facility for tempering even the harshest of criticism with an essential kindness that takes the edge off the words. Those who do not have this innate facility would do well to ponder the words of Dale Carnegie[6] when he wrote about "How to Criticize— and Not Be Hated for It." It is an art form, and while it can be mastered with sensitivity and practice, it is not proof against the pressures generated by the media. In short, the media is manipulative. It generates controversy to develop interest to drum up business. You must, therefore, expect to be used. The real question, for you, is whether it is in your best interest to allow yourself to be used. This is a very personal choice and one on which you may not, as yet, have formed any strong views. Try to take a long-term approach to the matter. Is a few moments on CNN really worth a professional life-time of more or less sustained aggravation? Ask yourself what sort of a market there is for an opinionated, controversial, know-it-all Personal Protection Specialist? Temper, therefore, your desires to exhibit your professional expertise with a certain prudence. This is another area where taking expert guidance before charging into the media fray is definitely advisable.

Some Personal Protection Specialists will enjoy the distinct advantage of working for an organization that has an efficient, dedicated public relations department. These media professionals will be attuned to the matters we have

---

6 His great book, *How to Win Friends & Influence People,* which has gone into more than 100 printings, should be part of the personal library of every Personal Protection Specialist. It is an excellent, instructive travelling companion.

been considering. Your job is to communicate to them how the latter may affect you with respect to the particular job you do. It is not likely, however experienced they may be, that they will be familiar with your work or how your expertise might be presented to advantage. These media experts are not there just to help out in a crisis. With proper briefing from you they can assist in promoting, wisely, your own expertise and making it available to a wider, receptive audience. Many will themselves have been working journalists and will know what is wanted and how best it might be presented. This is very much a two-way street; as you help them, they will be in a better position to help you. Try to anticipate some of the media calls that might be in the works for you. Knowing how to handle these in advance, and getting a good picture of what to expect, will help you to manage this aspect of your work more efficiently. Politicians and the great captains of industry all employ media consultants to advise them on what to say and how best to say it.[7] There is no abdication of responsibilities, here. Facing the press is, these days, an ever more specialized business. Does it not make a good deal of sense to follow the example of those who have to deal with the media a lot more often than you can anticipate? For those in business on their own account, media relations assume a special importance. This is not an area to learn the niceties of the game by trial and error. Mistakes can be costly, time-consuming, and on occasion fatal. Handling today's media is not just a matter of common sense. If your business as a Personal Protection Specialist involves you in media exposure of any kind, give careful thought as to how you would handle the matter. Consider what help you might need to handle problems which can be anticipated. You may, as a Personal Protection Specialist, as indeed the member of any other trade or profession, spend the whole of your working life avoiding the press. You may even be successful in these endeavors, though if you have achieved any worthwhile standing in your field, it will become a labor of increasing difficulty. If you do succeed, even by association with your principals, in avoiding the attentions of the press, the foregoing will have little application to your case. But you will, given the nature of things, surely be in a small minority of your fellows. The rest of us need help from time to time and the wise seek it from those best equipped to provide it.

I close, here, on a personal note. I worked, for a number of years on the staff of the television program *Canada AM*, the Canadian equivalent of *Good Morning, America* and its likes. I interacted, daily, with the regular procession of famous and interesting, famous and uninteresting, and interesting unknowns, who made their way to our studios. Some were attended by assorted retinues of managers, handlers, and even, on occasion, bodyguards, while others better able to fend for themselves, perhaps, arrived in solitary state. Some were regulars, and others first-time visitors to Canada and the show; all were there by invitation. For all, it was an opportunity to talk to the millions of people all

---

[7] Another book that might be read with profit by Personal Protection Specialists is *Liar's Poker*, Michael Lewis, New York, W.W. Norton (1989). Of Mrs. John Gutfreund, the author notes at page 48: "She employed a consultant to ensure she and her husband received the right sort of coverage."

across Canada, who watch the show every weekday morning. A few needed encouragement in varying degrees, others were blase, while one or two were so inflated with their own sense of self-importance as to be oblivious of their surroundings and those who were there to help them. Our guests fell, broadly, into three categories: the newsworthy; the perennial celebrities; and those whom our producers felt had the special skills, talents, personality, or expertise to contribute to our programming. The show was not only a window on the world; it was a window through which the world entered Canada. The hours were horrendous, and the pay hardly less attractive, and the job carried onerous responsibilities. For me, it was an opportunity to meet and converse with some fascinating people, at interesting stages in their careers, including a young man, who would one day be President of the United States. At the time, I enjoyed it a great deal, though along with the rest, I grumbled and fumbled as we struggled with the problems of trying to satisfy most of the people most of the time. Yet as I look back on the experience so as to pen these few lines, I cannot help but reflect how much more I might have enjoyed, and profited from it, had I only known then what I know now.

NINE

Psychological Factors to Consider When Hiring Personal Protection Specialists

by Bruce L. Danto

TRADITIONALLY, executive protection personnel has been drawn from the ranks of former police officers or military personnel. The basic assumption is that courage as reflected in either type of work plus good physical condition, discipline and familiarity with firearms, are qualities which are of prime importance to the selection of professionals for work assignments in the field of executive protection. The problem that exists when such criteria are so narrowly employed is that such persons are overlooked in terms of what type of judgement they have, what kind of decisions they do make, and what type of skills do they possess for relating to people. Additionally, there is a conversion factor which must be considered for the person who comes from a job where he or she have performed their work under the cloak of a badge and gun or military rank. In executive protection work, such background may be a detriment because civilians cannot be ordered around too easily, or have to be ordered with a different set of skills, as the order given by the executive protection specialist does not carry with it the weight of authority granted by law or some empowering agency. The arrest powers are those of any civilian or citizen. The application of lethal force must conform to the standards of self-defense as seen not only in the criminal law but also in civilian practice because the issues of liability are different. In the selection of applicants for police departments, the Minnesota Multiphasic Personality Inventory test, known as the MMPI, has been used since 1954. Some other tests, like a group Rorschach, a tree drawing test, and a brief psychiatric interview, have been used according to Reiser.[1] Reiser comments that there is no valid psychological profile of what a successful police

---

[1] Reiser, M.: *Police Psychology: Collected Papers*. Los Angeles, CA: Lehi Publishing Company, 1982, pp. 89-104.

applicant should look like. Screening seems to be limited to filtering out those that appear to be emotionally unfit to function as a police officer rather than trying to select those that have the desired personality traits and amplitudes. Thus, the most mentally disturbed applicants will be screened out for not only police work, but for anything, and nothing seems to be specific to police personnel. Furthermore, it should be understood that there has been no screening device that has been successful for the selection of Personal Protection Specialists.

Reiser points out that there is no ready-made measure regarding any test that can be applied ubiquitously in various settings and arrive at valid results. Furthermore, in the private sector there is no civil service guideline to be established so that applicants that ultimately turn out to be unqualified for any number of reasons, not the least of which is the failure to demonstrate a good personality profile for the work itself. The private sector struggles on its own.

There are some interesting things which certainly come to my mind in terms of my experience in the police field. I recall a case of one man who was a former Navy SEAL in Vietnam who received a psychiatric discharge because he was depressed. He applied to a local sheriff's department and was rejected on the basis of his psychological testing. He then applied to a large metropolitan police department in the same county, where he was accepted. When retested by that department, test results caused the psychologist to recommend against his hiring because there were certain depressive features involved in the MMPI. Notwithstanding that, he was hired and did an exemplary job until he was subjected to the stress of training in preparation for a very large international sports assembly. His discharge for the Navy very clearly indicated that he was not a person who could handle stress very well. That turned out to be true and he had a breakdown during the training sessions in preparation for this event which involved 16 hours a day of training. In another case concerning a large metropolitan police department, a man took an MMPI as part of his pre-employment application and on it clearly stated that he had some difficulty in his relationships with people. He was issued a firearm and four years into his service with that department, wound up killing his girlfriend.

Something was obviously missed in both employment circumstances because not enough attention was paid to the interview and to the person's background and history. These little markers, which may at times show up on psychological testing, may take on special significance when viewed from another set of facts, namely background and personal interview.

Vocational testing is another, sometimes misleading, factor in making assessments of who should be qualified for a job just on the basis of areas of interest. Very few tests to date have been able to ferret out those who are good prospects for management capability and for interpersonal skills with the public.

Certainly one way of getting around this problem is to get written letters of reference from previous employers. The problem with that is that previous employers do not always give honest assessments. In point of fact, many are happy to get rid of an employee and part of the tradeoff for getting rid of a problem worker is to write a letter of reference. On the other hand, some employees who are very good become victims of sex and age discrimination, and a supervisor who doesn't like somebody is more likely to write a very poor reference and a poor job performance review. Thus, I see very little value in these kinds of criteria for Personal Protection Specialists.

In my experience as a police officer and psychiatric consultant to many different police departments, I have found that psychiatric interviews for pre-employment are particularly helpful. The interview questions I employ deal with personality and personal background, as well as, experience in relationships. I want to know his/her experience with more weighty questions like decision making, judgement, and crisis intervention sensitivity. In other words, what is his ability to relate to people under conditions that are stressful.

THE ORAL INTERVIEW

According to Terrio, Swanson and Chamelin,[2] at least between 70 and 99% of public and private organizations rely on the interview as a part of the selection process. However, for police departments, the significance of the interview in this process is at the low end of the scale.

All too often the oral interview is nothing more than a highly subjective, last stage, get acquainted session between the applicant and the employer. It gives the employer an opportunity to meet the new employee, advise him of a few last minute rules, regulations and procedures, and wish him luck on the job.

Such a superficial interview is not to be recommended for the employment of a Personal Protection Specialist, or for that matter any employee. Many things have to be involved in a more open-ended type of interview where an effort is made on the part of the interviewer to size up the applicant. At this point the applicant has not received a commitment to be employed by the agency and should not under any circumstance be hired before the interview. It is my recommendation that the interview involve open-ended questions and be free from limited answers because material may be forthcoming from the applicant that has to be explored. If a specific set of questions is provided to the interviewer then he/she is limited from even beginning to look for things which may be of significance to either include or to exclude the applicant. Certainly, a semi-structured interview is preferable because there may be certain standard things the interviewer should keep in mind to ask all applicants, but there should be room left for questions which are relevant to a particular applicant.

STRUCTURED FACTORS WHICH APPLY TO ALL CANDIDATES[2]

1. Police contacts, arrests, convictions, military discipline and discharge status, honesty and integrity.
2. Nature and extent of the military experience.
3. Family and domestic characteristics, marital status and problems.
4. Attitude of the family toward the applicant's interest in personal protection work.

[2] Terrio, L., Swanson, C.R., Chamelin, N.C.: *The Police Personnel Section Process.* Indianapolis, Indiana: Bobbs Merrill Educational Publishing, 1977, pp. 142-182.

5. The applicant's financial status in terms of debts, credit rating and sources of income.

6. Racial and ethnic attitudes.

7. Attitude toward drug and narcotic usage.

8. Work history including technical knowledge and experience relevant to personal protection work.

9. Hobbies.

10. Social and recreational activities.

11. Extent and nature of formal education.

12. Motivation, interests, and goals relevant to personal protection work, and understanding the basic nature of the job and its demands.

13. Reasoning ability, judgement, common sense, and decision making ability, especially in critical or stressful situations.

14. Willingness to confront serious problem situations.

15. Verbal communications, self-expression.

16. Appearance, poise, bearing, self-confidence, ease of talking to a virtual stranger, and presence of a sense of humor.

17. Leadership.

18. Interpersonal sensitivity, sociability, ability to relate to others comfortably and harmoniously, and ease of socializing in a group situation.

19. Attitude and the perspective on importance and social significance of working with community agencies, particularly law enforcement.

20. Knowledge of the community in which the applicant is applying for work in this field, including socioeconomic, geographic and political/governmental characteristics.

21. Dependability, reliability, conscientiousness, sobriety and industriousness.

22. Level of responsibility of this person to take on an assignment and see it through.

23. Emotional health and stability, temperament, reaction to criticism, self-control.

24. Health and physical fitness.

25. Attitudes regarding relationships between and reciprocal responsibilities of personal protection to the community.

26. Why did they leave their previous job(s)? Why did they leave school, if they did not complete high school or college? Such information reflects on the level of maturity, responsibility and determination to achieve on the part of the applicant.

27. Miscellaneous non-verbal behavior, alertness, potential maturity, independence, intelligence, personality, adaptability, sincerity, self-discipline, attitude towards authority, mannerisms, and ability to project a good image.

BEHAVIORAL CLUES

1. Eye contact is essential, not only because it is a measure of truthfulness, but it also reflects interest in, and toward the interviewer. It also reflects signs of discomfort like anxiety or depression.

2. Fidgeting and mannerisms, i.e. jiggling of the foot or picking at the hands or fingers, may very well reflect anxiety.

3. Asking permission to smoke again may be another way of reflecting anxiety and we all know from personal protection work, it's few and far between that one can smoke on the job. We have to be able to live without some personal support by way of tobacco or alcohol while working.

4. Is the applicant able to greet the interviewer appropriately. Whether he extends a hand to be shaken, whether he comments on how nice it is to meet this person or bothers to look around the room to see how it's furnished, all reflect the kind of social ease this person may be able to feel in the interview. This may be what he's going to be doing with high level executives, members of his family or important dignitaries.

5. The interviewer should focus on the way the interviewee's thought process seems to function. He should ask himself whether the thoughts of the applicant seem to hang together or whether he skips around from one subject to another. Significant pauses in his delivery of answers to questions or how he forms questions should be noted. Such facts may have a bearing on communication. People who have serious mental disorders, like schizophrenia, may very well show a looseness or scattering of their ability to hold thoughts together into a logical pattern and to concentrate as well.

6. Questions should be asked by the interviewer about anger, and how anger and irritability are handled by the applicant. In so doing, the interviewer should be observant for signs of "white-knuckling," where a fist is formed into a clenched position. This may indicate anger or antagonism felt but not verbally expressed by the applicant. How anger is dealt with is very important for every Personal Protection Specialist.

DUTY RELATED QUESTIONS

During World War II, The Office of Strategic Services developed a series of task or reality-type questions about realistic situations which could test judgement and perception on the part of an applicant for that particular type of training or duty assignment. It should not be difficult for the interviewer to construct realistic kinds of questions, ones reflecting the broad spectrum of his experience in the field of personal and executive protection. For example, death may occur. Questions about whether or not the applicant has had a death experience, either taking a life of another person or being involved with someone who has, should be asked. They should be questioned about whether they have seen a dead body, one relatively fresh from either a shoot-out or some acute situation like an automobile fatality. Additionally, they should be asked how they think they would feel about having to take the life of another person.

In the same vein, they should be asked also how they think they would feel protecting a principal while under fire. After constructing the situation which illustrates this type of problem, efforts should be made to determine how difficult it is for the applicant to picture making a choice between getting his principal under safe cover versus letting himself become engaged in a gunfight.

Questions of health are always important to consider not only in training, but in the background of persons who seek training or employment at personal protection. It should be easy for the interviewer to construct several questions involving a possible heart attack on the part of the principal, a nosebleed, gastric distress, chest pain, an epileptic seizure and so forth, to see how the applicant would handle such a situation.

In my experience, one of the major problems for police officers and Personal Protection Specialists has been the inability to anticipate problems so that a plan can be developed by which those problems can be managed. The ability to plan ahead, or see ahead, is an extremely important part of the job of a Personal Protection Specialist and should be a priority issue to be raised with the applicant to test his sensitivity and experience in this area.

Judgement, particularly in terms of the employment of lethal force, is a very important issue. If one is training agents to do this type of job, then the level of sophistication should be less than that which would be associated with a person who comes to an agency with such training. Regardless of whichever situation exists, it's important to raise some of these questions in terms of when to shoot situations and what would be done, if for example, a citizen is walking toward them with his hand in his waistband or inside his suit coat. Under what circumstances the applicant would draw a weapon and fire is an important question to ask before you hire somebody. Does he even want to know what the policy is for this particular agency regarding the use of firearms to defend a principal? One of the most basic questions to raise for the applicant is, what does he think is involved in protecting a principal? Does he see this strictly in terms of a bodyguard function or is he sensitive enough to recognize that he may be required to carry groceries or to locate a pumpkin for the family to celebrate Halloween?

I think it's very true that curiosity did not kill the cat. Curiosity as a personality requirement for personal protection work is extremely important. One way to measure curiosity is to observe whether or not the applicant makes any effort to look around the room, or asks questions about the agency: what sort of assignments there are, what sort of dress is involved, and what kinds of protection assignments the agency handles. Without these questions, I would wonder what this persons expects to do by way of work for the agency. How will the person even know whether or not his work assignments will bring him some degree of gratification?

Boredom is a problem which exists for all members of the military, police and personal protection as well. Significant periods may involve doing nothing and waiting for something to happen, particularly if one is stationed in the hallway of a hotel during a period when the principal is asleep or whether one is waiting at an airport for a principal to arrive. How we occupy our time is an important consideration and gives the interviewer an opportunity to evaluate what this person is going to be doing. In the same vein, it would be important to determine how he spends his time for recreational or leisure time activities. If time is spent in the local bar, ogling the girls, or telling war stories, in my judgement, this is not appropriate for the applicant for this type of work.

Some principals, for example, expect the Personal Protection Specialist to hold his end of a conversation. It is important for the Personal Protection Specialist to be literate, to be well read or at least current on news, and to be aware of certain business trends particularly if the executive is connected with a company. Not uncommonly, persons in upper management feel a certain sense of oppression about the lonely lifestyle they're required to lead and it may be that they want to share business questions, exchange information or even at times share personal problems. If this is so, they need someone who can be observant while they also listen attentively.

If the applicant says very little during the interview, speaks in a monotone or gives monosyllabic answers, he's not exactly going to be thrilling to have around.

The interviewer should be sure to inquire about the applicant's experience with firearms, how he feels about carrying a gun, which preferences he has for the kinds of weapons that he knows and has an ability to qualify with. For every Personal Protection Specialist or police officer I have worked with, I will show you a different preference for the type of sidearm that is worn in terms of revolver versus pistol and also the caliber of the weapon.

If at all possible, questions should be raised about the individual's experience in fire fights or combat, particularly if he has been in the military or a police department. Everybody has a different experience with firearms in tight situations. I was a member of a SWAT team as a hostage negotiator and never fired a weapon once. Yet I carried a machine gun and a sidearm. As a homicide detective, I was brought into contact with many killers and never fired a weapon. Currently, I am evaluating a situation where an officer killed an unarmed citizen, and yet in a 12 month period of time, this officer has killed four people in gun fights.

As stated, I believe that questions should be raised about military combat experience. I recall when I was doing psychiatric screening for the SWAT team, there were many Vietnam veterans who denied any kind of post-traumatic stress, nightmares of combat or even dreams of combat, and certainly denied any flashbacks regarding combat. When questioned about military experience involving fire fights, some denied that they had ever been frightened. They gave the impression that they just simply handled it without incidence of any anxiety. Yet, when questioned about how they would handle different combat situations, beads of perspiration would appear on the forehead. It was very apparent they were unable to recognize their own feelings of anxiety. Thus, it's important to understand that it's perfectly realistic for people to become frightened and there has to be an appropriate way of dealing with it. In my experience, if they can't talk about it, they can't deal with it.

Whether or not an applicant has been involved in physical confrontations involving hand-to-hand combat or fistfights, could be important to know about. If a person has had a significant physical fight history or has been involved in physical fights with his spouse or girlfriend, I think it's important to find out why this person seems to have such a history in terms of frequency. This, plus facial scars, may give some clues in terms of how he may handle differences and conflicts with people. Is this the type of person you would want to hire for your agency, who seems to solve everything with his fists? I think not.

Special care should be taken to assess his sexual interest and experience, particularly if the applicant is single. Agencies must guard against the seductive type of agent who may want to exploit, or rather attract, a principal or the daughter of such a person. Minimally, he should be asked whether or not he's sexually active. If single, some questions should be directed about where they find outlet for their urges. In this day and age, the interviewer must be very careful about not only making inquiries as to gender preference in terms of sexual activities, but also should maintain an open policy with respect to gay applicants. This is the way the trend is going in the military, police work and personal protection.

I feel questions about religious practice should be addressed in the interview as well. The interviewer should be satisfied that the applicant is not a religious zealot, one who is more preoccupied with converting members to his faith than he is in doing the work of a personal protection agent.

Earlier a question was raised by me concerning the exposure an applicant might have had to disaster-type or death-type situations. Of equal interest also, is a question concerning how an applicant reacts to death threats, swear words, and threats to do great bodily harm to people. I'm reminded of a recent experience I had in teaching a novice group of students in a professional investigators' class. Material was shown from a collection I have of death threats to different principals that were written, and were displayed on slides. Not only was the language very rough and bizarre, but there were some cartoons drawn by stalkers that showed sexual and sadistic messages, as well as, mutilation of small girls. One of the students got up from class and went out and began vomiting. She tried to explain that she has a ten year old daughter and the pictures of a young girl being tortured, which had been sent to a religious group, were too much for her to handle. Three other students in the class were also offended by the language and content of the cartoon.

I would have to question whether or not these people were suitable for the job because those who threaten the lives of principals, who may indeed be mentally disturbed, use extremely gross language and may send animal body parts, or otherwise gross material, including photographs or cartoons. If the job is to protect against such persons, the Personal Protection Specialist must be emotionally prepared for any type of serious but bizarre language and behavior.

ADMINISTRATIVE-TYPE QUESTIONS

The applicant should be questioned about his/her skills in performing effective communication. As mentioned previously, how the applicant performs in the interview gives some measure of his ability to communicate orally. His choice of language and sentence structure should also give some indication of how well he can handle a report. How he projects his voice with appropriate volume, his choice of vocabulary and his ability to organize and form an answer, all have a bearing on this particular area of interest.

An ability to make independent and critical decisions has already been mentioned, but there are times when checking with a supervisor is very important. There are times when being able to think on your feet is even more important. The person who feels his experience tells him that he is best when he follows his own instincts, is a person who may create a liability problem for the agency.

Situational questions, as mentioned, will help answer the question about his ability to answer whether or not he has appropriate decision making skills and judgement. How he handles various situations in the interview will give important clues to this particular area of concern. What is the applicant's motivation and preparation for personal protection work? Does he see himself as a person who needs to push others around? Is he looking for dangerous excitement to feed his underlying narcissistic needs? Does he have a professional attitude about being of service and protecting people in the most routine kinds of ways? Does he enjoy doing advance work, making sure he knows where hospitals are, and whether he knows how to drive skillfully? These are some important aspects of Professional Protection Service, and these questions must be asked.

The interviewer must determine the type of conduct this person expects himself to follow in context of legal behavior which is part of personal protection work. He should have a sense of what's required for this job so that he can perform job-related functions more appropriately. His work and performance must be within the framework of legal limits and not in terms of some kind of "John Wayne syndrome."

Finally, the interviewer should determine whether or not the applicant is motivated for personal protection work and what he has done to prepare himself for this type of employment. This should involve information about his education, employment, military service history or service as a police officer.

In all of the areas listed above, it is important to determine whether or not the applicant is a team player. If he is a lone-wolf type of applicant, it's highly doubtful he will maintain the kinds of professional qualities that will make him an asset to the agency. He has to be there to backup others, as well as, being able to ask for backup himself.

If the interviewer is not sure of responses to questions in terms outlined in this presentation, then provisions should be made for a second interview to see whether or not questions about the applicant can be resolved by an independent interviewer.

RATINGS

The applicant can be rated in terms of: Adequate, definitely acceptable, below average but acceptable, or unacceptable.

Ideal characteristics should involve the applicant's ability to exercise independence in assuming responsibility and control in situations requiring prompt action.

His ability to analyze a problem objectively in terms of being flexible enough to choose alternative courses of action, and to exercise some judgement and common sense in being able to anticipate the best outcome from alternative courses of action is essential.

He must possess the willingness and aggressiveness to actively assert himself as a Personal Protection Specialist in decision-action situations which may involve considerable pressure and threat.

SUMMARY

The agency interviewer or director of personnel or both, must make every effort to feel that he/she knows the applicant and what the agency is getting in terms of what type is needed. The agency must be satisfied that the applicant's level of training, sophistication, judgement, decision making and interpersonal skills are above the average. Failure to take into account the personal and professional background of the applicant may result in a tremendous backwash of consequences for the agency both in terms of reputation and absolute failure in terms of the reputation to protect its contracts and accounts.

Testing is a tool that's available to offer some information, but what happens in the interview and how the background of this person looks, are infinitely more important variables to consider when making that important final decision to hire an applicant for personal protection work.

TEN

Being Prepared

by Roch Brousseau

*"An expert is someone who knows
more and more, about less and less."*
—*Mark Twain*

AS I SAT HERE THINKING of all the aspects that are required in Executive Protection and having read the first book, *Providing Executive Protection,* I offer you an additional dimension or facet of Providing Executive Protection, or some details of a detail.

If you have spent any time in this profession, by now you know that this business calls for more than a fast draw, a perfect bootleg or the ability to bench press twice your weight. Hopefully, if you have attended the training facilities at the Arcadia Manor (Executive Protection Institute), you were given a taste of what it takes, or a tune-up enabling you to stay sharp and up-to-date. If you have made a commitment to the care of an individual, and if you wish to stay in this profession, a large part of this is your ability to continually grow and modify yourself with this ever changing world outside our door, and more importantly, the needs of your principal.

With many, you are in fact the entire protective detail. With you being the only protective person assigned to your principal, it is your responsibility to insure more than just the protection of your principal. It is often that we are called upon to assist with details that are not covered in a training manual. It is then, when your principal calls on you, or in fact says nothing, but you happen to have an extra shirt or tie in your kit, that you become of value to your principal.

Do you have a kit in your vehicle? If so, what's in it? How often do you do maintenance on it? It should be done on the same schedule as you would your vehicle. What am I talking about? Here is a suggested list, or a minimum, of items you should have readily available for your principal.

- A clean long sleeve white shirt, with button cuffs. Have it cleaned professionally, with light starch, and folded. Ask the cleaner to place collar boards or stays in the collar. Keep wrapped in a plastic bag.
- One solid color tie, dark blue or burgundy.
- A spray type spot remover, such as H2R and a can of spray wrinkle remover.
- Any special medication that your principal may take. Make sure it is in the pharmacy bottle, with your principal's name on it. Aspirin, non-aspirin pain reliever, Band-Aids, baby wipes and a general first-aid kit (Red Cross approved).
- Two legal size writing pads, black ink writing pens, paper clips, etc. (As an added precaution, have the ink pens in a zip lock baggy. The heat in a trunk may cause the pens to leak.)
- A micro cassette tape recorder, and extra tapes and batteries.
- A mini mag light, tape it to the top of the kit, if your trunk light fails, you can have this available to assist you in your search for an item, or if you have to do a minor roadside repair, it will come in handy.
- A survivalist type blanket, foil type is best. They are prefolded in a factory bag, small and inexpensive.
- A quart of water.

As well, you should include any item which your principal uses on a regular basis. This would not only allow you not to have to search for something in a strange town or in the middle of an engagement, but it will allow you to keep your principal calm in a stressful situation, and most of all, keep you near your principal. Remember you are of no value and will not be long in this profession if you were sent looking for something (upon your principal's request) and *it* happens. This is when it will. Remember Murphy's law. All of these things can be easily placed in a briefcase and taken with you as needed.

Additionally, you should have a pocket calendar with you at all times. In this calendar, you should list any medical information needed for your employer. Also include credit card numbers, emergency telephone numbers, as well as the daily agenda for your principal.

Some other suggestions would be:

If there is an auto club in your state, join it. In many states there is AAA. By joining this club for $35.00 a year, you can call 24 hours a day, get emergency roadside service or have your vehicle towed to a gas station or service center, all at no charge. Best yet, they only serve members. They will also take you to the closest hotel if your vehicle is inoperable. You can also call and have a preprinted map sent to you, and/or get detailed directions to any location(s).

It is also wise to establish relationships and contacts with your principal's favorite clothier/tailor, restaurant, etc. Get the telephone number of the people who can do things for you, such as open the store late at night or on a Sunday morning. You never know when you will need it.

For years I handled the protection for a young female executive. As time went on and the notoriety of this individual grew, so did my responsibility. Every aspect, every movement hit my desk, no matter how "insignificant." I had six full-time protective personnel/drivers assigned to her and her family.

I once had a major public event; the logistics and preparation for this event were staggering. All security arrangements were handled by myself and my staff; it was the largest I had ever handled.

Just prior to the beginning of the event, a news photographer, knocked over a champagne bucket. The combination of ice and water in the bucket splashed all over both myself and my principal. My principal was wearing a leather outfit, and the water spotted it badly. Needless to say, my principal was not happy. She was taken to our pre-arranged safe area, to both dry off and cool off.

Having shopped with her at the store where the outfit was purchased, more times than I care to remember, (with many of the employees assuming that I was her husband) I was able to establish a relationship with the store's manager. The store had already closed for the evening, but I had the manager's home telephone number. When I called, the manager was happy to open the store for my principal. A vehicle was sent to pick up the manager, he was given first class treatment. A replacement outfit was picked up and my principal was again happy. Sound easy? It was seven years of work.

You may be thinking to yourself, this is not my job. It may not be, now. But what about your next assignment? Even if it is a temporary assignment, your resources, your contacts become one of your biggest assets. Understanding this part of the profession will help you further your career.

You, as the executive protection specialist, must possess more and more skills; this will only help make you a more valuable asset to your principal. Think about this for a moment: How many times have you accompanied your principal to a business meeting? Have you ever sat and observed the executive secretary for either your principal or another's? Just who runs the show?

A good executive secretary to a CEO or President of any corporation sees all, knows all, remembers everything, repeats nothing and can make things run smoothly for his or her employer. I have, in fact, had to interview with many executive secretaries for EP positions. That goes to show how much they understand their employer's needs, and how much trust is placed in them.

We have two continuous threats in this profession. The first is our ego. The second is thinking everything is under control.

When our ego gets in the way, things stop happening. Part of our job in this profession is to ensure that our employers can move about freely and with a minimum of risk, so they can do their job. Remember this, the men and women we protect affect a great many lives and fortunes. When we can allow them special comforts and reduce their stress, a great deal more than just their lives are made easier. You also should remember, they really would rather go about life freely, that means without us, the protective person. Put your ego away, "thank-yous" are few and far between. Your thanks comes in the form of a paycheck.

The other threat we face is when we think we have everything under control. When we fool ourselves and start to believe in a false sense of security, it is then that your principal will be embarrassed, hurt or killed while under your care. You should pray, that if any of the above happens, you were killed; it is the only excuse that will be accepted.

Your training in this profession is ongoing, until the day you retire or change careers. Do not ever stop your education, training or commitment to this profession. It is the only way that you will keep your client and yourself safe, and more importantly, alive.

"I threw a thousand completions this year, but no one remembers any of them now."

Warren Moon—Houston Oilers, after throwing a game losing interception, knocking them out of the playoffs.

ELEVEN

ETHICS AND TRAITS OF THE
PERSONAL PROTECTION SPECIALIST

by Richard W. Kobetz

IT IS WITH GREAT PRIDE and humility that, as you read this chapter, our first volume, entitled *Providing Executive Protection,* originally published in 1991 is now available in the third printing. Very exciting world events with security implications have come upon the stage, completed their performance and moved on into history. The names involved and the activities engaged in are added to our memory banks and improved protective performances become more obvious. Although the names and events are different and many are variations on the protective services theme, the need for *professional* personal protection increases and that is a growing concern.

We must never loose sight of the main theme, in the perspective of personal protection, that it is a person to person activity. The activity is initiated by someone having a need for a trained person to protect them and the protection is planned and provided for by another "someone." The key point of course is "trained" with the training being built upon a foundation of ethics and traits possessed by the protector. This foundation of ethics and traits are what all instructors at the Executive Protection Institute credit our success to. This is the crucial base to build upon for all men and women who seek to serve as a professional Personal Protection Specialist—the internalization of a canon of ethics and traits for this "Fifth Profession."[1]

We live in interesting times. Honor, which was once the notion of virtue, now means only merit, as in belonging to an Honor Society. The aspects of not lying, cheating or stealing appear no longer to be included as they were in the original definition. Where are our proper role models today? On the opposite

---

[1]   Morrell, David. *The Fifth Profession.* New York: Warner Books, Inc., 1990.

end of the good and evil scale even major organized crime figures who once prided themselves on a "code of honor," now bemoan the fact that there is no longer any honor, only greed and viciousness.

In merely a few decades we as a society have shifted messages to high school and college graduates from, "find your path to success through honor, ethics, virtue, values and discipline; and becoming a worthwhile contributing member of society," to, one of, "go out and get your share of the pie." What pie? The pie of consumerism, high pay for low work standards and no concern whatsoever for others or society. The continuing philosophy of, "It's not my fault if there is a problem, incident or accident. Don't blame me, it has to be someone else's fault. I can't be *accountable* and I refuse to accept any *responsibility*."

This all too often contemporary message coupled with the belief by many that today's students are being educated beyond their intelligence level and ability to comprehend even the purpose of an education, are obstacles in need of solutions. Each of us possesses personal power. The power of choice, to choose what we do with what we are and how we will allow events to affect us. "The power of mind is infinite while brawn is limited." (Koichi Tohei)

For the balance of this chapter I would like to explore the valuable traits and the ethical considerations needed to succeed in the profession of Personal Protection Specialist.

TRAITS

"It's easy to be successful—just do the right thing all the time. . . ."
                                                                    R.W. Kobetz

Traits are marvelous things. Subject to individual interpretation, and of course, all of us believe we possess the necessary traits for success in our chosen endeavors. How could it not be otherwise? On the other hand, what specific traits are needed for success in providing personal protection for a principal. This is one of the first discussion points focused on by many who wish to enter into the work. And work it is, though many fail to understand the full definition of "halls and walls," long lonely nights on an outdoor post and the individual effects upon judgement from sleep deprivation, the reality of fatigue combined with stress.

I commend to your reading the complete magnificent *Message to Garcia*, written by Elbert Hubbard in 1899. When war broke out between Spain and the United States, it was very necessary to communicate quickly with the leader of the insurgents. Garcia was somewhere in the mountain fastnesses of Cuba—no one knew where. No mail or telegraph message could reach him. President McKinley must secure his cooperation and quickly. Someone said to the President, "There is a fellow by the name of Rowan who will find Garcia for you, if anybody can."

Rowan was sent for and given a letter to be delivered to Garcia. How "the fellow by the name of Rowan" took the letter, sealed it up in an oilskin pouch, strapped it over his heart, in four days landed by night off the coast of Cuba from an open boat, disappeared into the jungle and in three weeks came out on the other side of the Island, having traversed a hostile country on foot and delivered his letter to Garcia—are things to be described in detail elsewhere. The point to be made is: President McKinley gave Rowan a letter to be delivered to Garcia; Rowan took the letter and did not ask, "Where is he?" "Where do I get a boat?" "How do I eat?" "When do I sleep?"

It is not book-learning, nor instruction on various topics, but a stiffening of the vertebrae that is needed to cause successful people to be loyal to a trust, to act promptly, concentrate their energies: do the mission—"carry a message to Garcia." The successful person receives his/her assignment and is capable and qualified to do the task. To become capable and qualified is the person's individual responsibility. To anticipate assignments which they have placed themselves in position to receive holds them accountable for their successful conclusions or why are they posing as someone who is qualified to perform the task if they have no idea of what is expected of them or what they are to do with the task? Tasks are specifically detailed more often than not but your job is much broader in context. It is the entirety of your position. The "how" of the profession—that umbrella thought process of everything which must be considered to make things work. In contrast to the specific "what" of an assignment, which can be learned through steps, checklists and guidelines. This is the biggest shortcoming for *wannabees* in the Personal Protection Specialist profession. The failure to grasp the "how" of the world and only seeking out checkpoints of knowledge for the "what" of the world.

It is difficult to grasp non-specific job responsibility over specific task activity. Many people believe for example that ego in itself is detrimental in this field. Not so at all. Ego is like cholesterol, there is good ego and there is bad ego. All people in protective positions must believe they have the capacity to protect others and that when called upon to perform they will do so successfully. You must believe in yourself and be at the same time prepared to do what needs to be done,—block an attack, render first-aid for an accidental injury or avoid an embarrassment for your principal. This is all positive or good ego.

"The less effort, the faster and more powerful you will be."
Bruce Lee

Bad ego comes from those who believe they are prepared to do personal protective work because they have performed in another security or enforcement position and have never taken the time to learn what up-close personal protection really entails. It comes from those who have already made up their mind that they can perform the services of a focused and dedicated Personal Protection Specialist when they suffer from one of the most common inflictions in our society today—being a PWOC (Person Without a Clue). There are still others who believe we can divide the world into persons who suffer from one or a combination of attitudes on protection: stupidity or naïveté.

Fortunately the bad ego is curable through proper and specific training followed by entry level professional positions and an individual acknowledging that they do not know all there is to know nor is there one specific solution to all problems encountered. The lack of a "bottomline" in security positions contributes to the problems in a contemporary sense. In other words the lack of a commonality of achievement and performance where people can approach a position equally with everyone having an equal background of education, training and valid experience. For example, if a group of qualified, medical doctors are discussing a specific medical technique, there is a common acceptance of a "bottomline" regardless of which medical school the doctor attended or where their internship was performed. This "bottomline" having been established, there is now a genuine professional approach to discussion of the medical technique.

We find in providing personal protection as in the provision of the majority of security services, the individual proclaims competency based upon service in another occupation with other trait and skill requirements. Somehow this combined, more often than not, with minimal levels of general training has the individual honestly believing that he/she can perform the services which they advertise. In fact, most of the brochures and letterheads in the security or protective services industry list numerous areas of expertise, many of which individually require lengthy training periods combined with hands-on experience. Remember, it is extremely easy to have a business card, stationery, or brochure printed or do it yourself on a personal computer; calling yourself anything you wish or offering any services. Little wonder that in the eyes of the consumers of these services, the security field must be viewed with some skepticism.

<u>Who</u> People Are. . .	<u>Who</u> They Really Are. . .
<u>What</u> They Say They Are. . .	<u>What</u> Others Say They Are. . .
<u>What</u> They Say They Can Do. . .	<u>What</u> They Really Can Do. . .

These traits, or lack of same, are sincere concerns in the fast growth fields of security and protective services. Traits are individual and difficult to clearly and specifically isolate in their sense of value to this field. Many believe that the A B C traits alone (<u>a</u>gility — <u>b</u>ravery — <u>c</u>ourage) are all that are necessary to succeed in the field of personal protection. All three are important, of course, but no guarantee of total survival as a professional in this field. Many traits are required, but here, for example, are some of the most important ones.

Trait	Definition
1. <u>Adaptable</u>	Able to adjust to changing environments. If you are not comfortable in some environments, learn to be.
2. <u>Courteous</u>	You will accomplish much more for your principal and gain respect for yourself.
3. <u>Dedicated</u>	To your responsibilities
4. <u>Dependable</u>	Not because you are told to do it, but because you see it has to be done and you do it.
5. <u>Ethical</u>	Set a high standard for how you conduct yourself.
6. <u>Flexible</u>	The ability to accept change and respond properly.
7. <u>Honorable</u>	Being truthful, doing right and knowing wrong; performing your duty.
8. <u>Loyal</u>	To your principal

| 9. Self-Discipline | Able to place your needs and wants subservient to your performance obligations. |
| 10. Thoroughness | Be focused. Do what you must do and what you say you will do. |

Many men and women employed in the field or attempting to enter the field will never know why they can not make it. A careful consideration of this list will reveal that there are many dimensions of performance within these traits. They are not "bumper sticker" definitions but require serious thought. If dependability for example is an important trait, and it is, than every action you take will be judged, not merely those that *you* determine to be important. Also, remember that "man," is the only creature on earth, who can talk himself into trouble. *(Control your emotions or they will control you. — Chinese Adage)*

ETHICS AND VALUES

"Knowing others is wisdom, knowing yourself is enlightenment."

Lao Tzu

Definitions

Ethics: the <u>principles</u> of morality, or the field of study of <u>morals</u> or right conduct.

Principle: a general truth; the primary source from which anything proceeds; a basic doctrine or tenet.

Morality: conforming to the principles of good conduct.

Values: the qualities, customs, standards and principles of people regarded as desirable.

Virtue: a praise worthy quality or trait.

"Situational Ethics": a contemporary re-definition which allows you to do anything you wish or "you only lie to defend your integrity."

With respect to ethics and values within the protection profession we face the dilemma of personal conduct, that of definition and interpretation. If we can agree on specific definitions then we can limit the interpretation or judgement of our conduct within narrower parameters.

The very essence of providing personal protection is service, the service of providing safe passage for our employer, the safety and security in all dimensions of the protection function. If we were merely concerned with the mechanical aspects of movement and physical protection, we would not be concerned with conduct. Conduct is governed by behavioral attributes which may be directed by our values, those beliefs that we have internalized into our thought processes which guide our behavior. It is most important for all of us to understand the solid foundation of ethics and values in the influence upon our role behavior as protectors.

How the protector performs his or her role is clearly as important in many instances as what is accomplished. A code of ethical conduct, which is our own internal self-governor, helps us to:

- Refrain from conduct that would be adverse to our client or principal's best interests.
- Conduct ourselves only in the most professional manner at all times.
- Strive for personal excellence.
- Demonstrate high standards of personal integrity.
- Protect and respect the privileged information revealed to us in the course of our duties.
- Avoid activity or interests which are in conflict with the performance of our responsibilities.

In the *Hallcrest Report II's* chapter on Ethics and Values[2], we have a reference to Ethics: discipline dealing with what is right and moral duty and obligation; as a set of moral values; or as the principles of conduct governing an individual or group. Ethics has developed as man has reflected upon the intentions and consequences of his actions.

Obviously our contemporary society has experienced a few incidents which cause serious concern about the "current state of the art."

- Scientists admit in an experiment of skin graft from one kind of mouse to another—that they used a felt pen to fake the results. . .
- C.I.A. employee selling secrets. . .
- Sex scandals abound with ministers and priests. . .
- Political scandals involving all levels up to the Presidency. . .
- Insider stock trading revealed. . .
- Industrial espionage and bribery by major defense contractors. . .
- Pharmaceutical companies lying to Food and Drug Administration. . .
- Medical wastes dumped into oceans. . .
- Sugar water packed for babies as apple juice. . .
- U.S. Savings and Loan financial embezzlement. . .
- Leading business schools now realize the importance of teaching ethics to students. . .
- Approximately 70% of business managers agree ethics of corporations should be as important as profits. . .

In the military model of management style a total body of management philosophy and techniques are used to achieve compliance to direct orders. Soldiers are trained to internalize goals of protecting their territory from invasion by armies and preserve the liberties of fellow citizens. The model makes use of a more focused technique for controlling and directing soldier behavior

---

2 Cunningham, William C., Strauchs, John J. and VanMeter, Clifford W. *Private Security Trends: 1970-2000 aka The Hallcrest Report II.* Stoneham, Massachusetts: Butterworth-Heinemann, 1990.

toward common goals through integration of the goals of management with those of the soldier. In addition to behavioral control induced by simple threat or fear of sanctions, soldier discipline is also obtained. Implied is the idea that there is "one best way" for individuals to behave in pursuit of goals. Discipline has a clear identity and is elaborated in well defined codes and procedures. Results are often associated with high standards and pride in accomplishment.[3]

In the civilian world of professional protective performance we depend upon the values of the individual as developed by training, education, background, family members, friends, peers and adopted social values. These values and developed ethical views are difficult to change or channel into a pre-determined pattern of behavior. We have not set down performance philosophy and techniques or threat or fear of sanctions. The professional performance is judged in other contexts with no model of behavior or standard of performance. Teaching techniques are presently focused on performance example or role model behavior. But gradually by properly performing personal protection we will achieve higher standards reinforced by pride in accomplishments and recognized professional performance. Our goal is to obtain a body of knowledge, doctrine and principles which will emphasize "What is right—not who is right."[4]

CONCLUSION

"To win one hundred victories in one hundred battles is not the highest skill. To subdue the enemy (attacker) <u>without</u> fighting is the highest skill."

Sun-Tzu

It is clear that many will be called into the profession of Personal Protection Specialist for a wide variety of reasons. Most of these reasons may be attributable to fantasy, finances or fame, and the excitement of what is believed to be the lifestyle of someone who protects another. Not much thought will be given to the performance requirements; the need to first clearly understand what the discipline is about—and what it is not about. The reality that the first program attended is the first step in a new career direction and the realization that continuing conditioning and education or training will be required for the entire duration of career performance. As in all career attempts there is an arbitrary 10% top and 10% bottom division of ranking within a group of achievers. The majority of candidates fall into the mid-80% scale with a tremendous potential for growth through accomplishments to rise upward within this range.

Those who achieve the top 1% positions in this field have several characteristics in common. They are totally committed to what they do. Their attitude is positive, expressed clearly and recognized by others through their performance. They understand and practice good communication skills by: not reading into another's words their own personal responses but realize they must

---

3   I.A.C.P. *Managing For Effective Police Discipline*. Gaithersburg, Maryland: International Association of Chiefs of Police, 1976.
4   Barefoot, Kirk J. and Maxwell, David A. *Corporate Security Administration and Management*. Boston, Massachusetts: Butterworths, 1987.

consider what the other person means; they listen more than they talk; they ask the proper questions; they never assume that everyone knows what they are talking about. Achievers recognize that without clear understanding there is no effective communication. In personal protection the ability to communicate is extremely important and failure to recognize and practice the rules will cause problems.

Ultimately, it is you who will "make it" and become a success in this very old but now reborn emerging profession. No one qualifies you for success—you qualify yourself. You are in charge and in control of yourself, constantly aware of what could happen and what you are prepared to do about it. The principles of the protection profession were set many centuries ago, but, like old wine in new bottles on the shelves we are constantly re-examining and improving protective measures. Some of the bottles will break, some will spoil but most will be quite acceptable and consumable. What the profession of Personal Protection Specialist seeks is the true top 1% performer who will become vintage, the rare, but achievable level for consumption.

> *In order to achieve victory you must place yourself in your opponent's skin.*
>
> *If you don't understand yourself, you will lose one hundred percent of the time.*
>
> *If you understand yourself, you will win fifty percent of the time.*
>
> *If you understand yourself and your opponent, you will win one hundred percent of the time.*
>
> *Tsutomu Oshima*

TWELVE

Intelligence Gathering—
Operative and Operations

by Michael C. Miller and F. C. Miller

PREFACE

When we first began addressing the subject of Intelligence Gathering years ago, and because we monitor activity throughout the world, we usually answered the question about terrorists by saying that your chances of coming into contact with a terrorist operation were pretty slim. You and your principal stood a better chance of being "collateral damage" resulting from workplace violence, a better chance of being a victim of violent criminal activity (kidnap and murder included), a better chance of attracting the attention of some nutcase stalker, even a better chance of being wiped out on the freeway—than you did mixing it up with terrorists and terrorism. Now however, we must advise that things have been strategically and methodically changing since that time, and *will* change even more radically in the months and years to come.

The frustration that accompanies seeing and understanding repugnant, violent, "seemingly" illogical patterns emerging and taking shape on world screens is intensified when that knowledge falls on deaf ears in a complacent or neatly maneuvered society. Those of us who track and monitor criminal and terrorist activity on a global scale have an obligation however, to place ourselves and our methods at the disposal of our professional colleagues who are entrusted with being more alert, more responsive, more responsible, and more precise in their comprehensions.

The ignorance, arrogance and violence of mankind intruding into the lives of others is the stuff of which history is made—complete with its ups, downs, cycles and repetitions. On the horizon, we see that the seeds of old adversaries have sprouted new branches, reaching out into new territories, new global geographies—complete with advanced technologies, ever increasing numbers and a zeal perhaps unparalleled in modern history. At the same time, fundamentalist extremists of all denominations and "separatists" are spreading like wildfire, polarizing conflict after conflict, and they too are lighting up the map with new alerts every day. *The forthcoming dangers in these expansions and networking should not be underestimated.*

Personal observations from an "Intel" point of view shows the world at war with no indication that it's going to let up anytime soon. Being aware on a daily basis of all the factions who are emerging and growing, fighting and killing, stealing and kidnapping, assaulting and bombing one another in every corner of the globe, makes Intelligence Gathering more than a full time job.

We cannot in good conscience simply imply "business as usual" even though for the past several years the "terrorism" picture has appeared to remain static. This seemingly quiet time has been strategic time for malefactors to fall back, regroup, recruit, retrain, refinance and ultimately to more efficiently return. No we cannot say "business as usual." To say such a thing would invite the justifiable anger from any one of the tens of thousands of people directly affected by the attack on the World Trade Center. It would not be unreasonable for any of the additional tens of thousands of people who were targeted for death, injury and terror July 1993 in New York buildings and tunnels to also take exception to such a statement, nor the innocent people killed or injured in Europe, Asia, Africa or the Middle East. Personally, we see it as "the handwriting on the wall" and will continue planning accordingly. You do as you think best. If you think it best to try to get ahead of the "curve" pay attention to this worthy book. Learn things that may save a few lives—not the least of which is your own.

However strongly we may wish to more fully address the global emergence of a number of formidable, fanatically motivated and increasingly more technically sophisticated oppositions, we will turn our attentions to matters closer to the subject at hand.

In this chapter we will address the subject of Intel from many perspectives—including philosophical, positional and operational perspectives—and will *focus our attention* in this chapter on Intelligence Operations <u>within the Corporate Entity itself.</u> We select this specific area because it relates to the Corporate Principal *where he or she is most closely associated and identified.* How to structure Intel both from within and outside the Corporate Entity will also be covered. The growing activity against Executives and public figures both locally and worldwide shows us an emerging war. These "mini wars" may have only a half dozen (or less) combatants on each side, but the results are no less lethal—and no less predictable. We will use the analogies of warfare routinely for one simple reason; they fit. *Be advised that what we will teach is the ideal, the highest standards of this profession. Being the best is sometimes not possible to accomplish, but you have a responsibility to reach for those high standards, not only for your sake, but for your principals' and your colleagues'.*

I suppose we should proceed by describing what this specialized area of "Intel" is, and what it isn't, before we discuss how it works. We'll begin first by describing what it isn't—(because we all need a good laugh on occasion).

WHAT CORPORATE/CELEBRITY INTEL IS NOT

The image conjured up by most executives and celebrities when you begin talking about "Intelligence Operations" and "Intelligence Gathering" must be one of intrigue, midnight rendezvous under dim street lights, trench coats, slouch hats, microphones hidden between silk sheets (or under the azaleas), assassinations and guys named Ivan, Wolfgang or "Code name - Bogart." (The pale expressions on their faces always give them away!) Many of the principal's misconceptions, his hesitation and his fears, legitimately come from images of sinister types cultivated in the movies and novels having to do with cold wars, hot wars, secret agents and international spy agencies—and until this stage in his life and career may not have had any reason to distinguish between world war cloak and dagger intrigue and Intelligence Operations as they more closely relate to the world of Corporate Executive or Celebrity Protection.

WHAT IS A CORPORATE/CELEBRITY INTELLIGENCE OPERATION?

An Intelligence Operation in the Executive or Celebrity Protection world is tasked with locating information on potential or real circumstances or conditions of any harmful or embarrassing nature which already exist or may be emerging. Then we are charged with assessing the risk and threat factors—and presenting such information in a format beneficial for the Operational Protectors (and/or the principal) to know—whereby measures may be put into place for avoiding or dealing with them.

An efficient Intelligence Operation builds those same "concentric circles" of protection around the Principal and the Protective Team, only it is done *with layers of knowledge and information.* Intelligence is gathered on the destination, on immediate area problems and topography, on assets available at the location, on avenues of travel in and around the area, on problems facing the area or region in question and on national issues which may effect the principal(s). Information is developed on problems which may directly affect the executive related to his or her identify, position, affiliations, beliefs or industry. Intelligence is also gathered which might indicate the potential for the Principal becoming "collateral damage" as the result of actions *not directed against the Principal,* but simply by having the misfortune of being in the wrong place at the wrong time![1]

Intel is The "Skilled" Art of Searching Outward, ahead of, in front of, and all around the Principal (outer concentric circle) to search out, find, and

---

[1]   Recent Examples:
•Cardinal Juan Posadas Ocampo assassinated 5/25/93 in Mexico was reportedly not the intended victim, "a case of mistaken identify" when about 15 men opened up "on what they thought was a drug baron." • None of the 8 people killed and 6 wounded in the mass killing of San Francisco 7/1/93 were on the shooter's list of intended targets. • None of the 6 people killed or 1000+ injured at the World Trade Center 2/26/93 were known to be personally "targeted" by the perpetrators.

identify every potential or real risk, danger, threat or embarrassment to that Principal—whether he or she is stationary, moving forward a short distance, or traveling halfway round the world. The searched for Intelligence Information is found and then given to the Executive Protection Professional who then uses that Intelligence Information to put his own plans and skills into operation to protect that Principal from those real and/or potential dangers which Intel searched for and found.

Intel Is The "Skilled" Art of Searching Inward, the inner concentric circle, to find those areas of weaknesses in the principal's facility (or wherever else the Principal is associated) and the habits, patterns, or system which leave the principal, (and perhaps his associates, his family, his property, his product and/or his employees) vulnerable and/or wide open to hostile activities—including assault, kidnapping, armed confrontations, stalking, hostage, corporate espionage, even murder.

An Intelligence Operation is also an "internal audit" used to detect flaws in the overall protective profile of the entity in question. It is an operation which develops the "yardstick" by which *risks* and *threats* are measured (the *analysis* part of Intel), allowing for the appropriate entities to remedy the situation; and is an operation which views everything with an immediate, local, and a "global" eye when approaching a potential problem.

The Intelligence Operation is the *reconnaissance* eyes and ears which goes out on its mission in advance and gathers information on the assets and opposition before anybody else, thus allowing for *avoidance* preplanning decisions to be made given all the options. It is the unit which checks "all the way out" (to the "outer concentric circle") for hidden agendas and traps which will impact the Principal (by virtue of seeing everything as it relates to other events). It is the unit which then comes in *behind* the Protection Detail and supplies updated information which has suddenly developed and will impact the assignment. The Intel Operation will then support the information needs of the "assignment-focused" Protective Detail, and assist or direct them by assessments and observations on the information obtained.

An Intelligence Specialist who does on-going, professional "Recon" has a wealth of information at his command. Directing his area of expertise to the needs of the Personal Protection Specialist, the individual client, or the corporation—Intelligence Specialists help the PPS leader to determine whether or not he will need additional personnel assets (and what kind), where additional back doors may be located, what the bad guys down the street or across the border are up to (and how fast they're approaching), what new M.O.'s or weapons types his mission may run into, and what other activities he and his Principal may come face to face with either in their own city or across the ocean.

As an Example: The PPS must get his Principal safely in and out of a Middle East country. The PPS knows his job and he does it well. He's already taken care of his on-site, his security team, his drivers— and he's ready to proceed—but **not** without advance Intelligence/Recon assistance. With the help of Intel, he discovers that the luxury hotel where his principal is registered ("where everyone who is anyone stays") complied with construction safety regulations only on the bottom three floors of this and other hotels before the local building inspectors began to take bribes and look the other way. Every floor above the third level are disasters waiting to happen. What's more, earthquakes and landslides have *already* cost many lives in some of those glamorous, unsafe buildings thanks to natural disasters (a fact which was carefully kept from the principal's travel arranger!).

Another Example: You're accompanying your principal to a locale far from home. Your job is to access all the particulars including risk and threat levels. Putting the Intel person on the job in advance, you discover that the authorities are co-opted (induced by whatever means to cooperate with the bad guys), language will be a nightmare, radicals are moving rapidly in the general direction of your principal's destination, and trying to find your way out in an emergency doesn't look promising. Letting the Intel Specialist know that your principal is not going to be deterred (he believes what he reads in the paper and in the travel brochures) and you're not comfortable about the risk level, you tell him you need another back door out. Because the Intelligence Specialist has been tracking that area of the world, because he's been tracking it in connection with other Intelligence Operations, because his job is to categorize a wealth of information—he can tell you that, "The most efficient way out is to use the same method and route as the local cross border smugglers! It should take you 15 minutes to escape, you'll need plenty of cash, and you'll need someone with sea navigation experience on stand-by."

The Intelligence Operation is also the tool for finding out *why* something happened. This may allow for planning so that it doesn't happen to someone under your protection. You have to ask yourself "why" something happened when it did and "how" it happened when it did—and until you understand those points, the "what" will not be of much use to you.

That's what an Intelligence Operation is.

WHAT IS THE COMPOSITE OF A SUCCESSFUL INTELLIGENCE SPECIALIST?

An efficient, skilled Intelligence Specialist is part investigator, historian, observer, listener, reader, researcher, navigator, map-maker, scientist, warrior, bodyguard and puzzle-maker. He must be experienced in many disciplines and in many skills. He must be politically astute, grounded historically and not prone to propaganda. He must be a tactician, experienced, disciplined, attentive to details, savvy and scrupulous. He must be able to find flaws in the system, dangers in the destination, risks, elevating or declining threat levels, smoke screens, strengths, weaknesses and even hidden agendas. He must examine people, places, buildings and patterns—and absolutely cannot afford distractions, smoke screens or sleight of hand.

You must find yourself the most "knowledgeable" person connected to the assignment, knowing all the pieces, all the players, all the options and all the plans. Yet you may not be in charge of the detail or the events. You probably will not be next to the Principal; you may not be going on the trip or the detail;

and most likely you won't be getting any Hero badges for it all going correctly. You put all the tools in everyone's hands so they can plan, and you had better be dead bang on target every single time you report.

Your gender makes no difference, since it is your disciplines, experience, character, and skills which are the considerations. (For the sake of brevity, we will use the "editorial" he throughout this chapter, indicating that we are referring to both men and women.)

You need the ability to work alone, since you are most likely to be visiting (if only electronically) the destination ahead of the Advance Team—if there is one (you may be the Advance Team). It may be the Team Leader of the Protection Detail who is the Intel Specialist as well, in which case it will be a real test of organizational and time management skills—and being resourceful enough to draw on the skills of others to accomplish the task.

You need a lot of the investigator in you and a great deal of historical appreciation. Things have a habit of "cycling" and being repeated by those who weren't paying attention the first time. "Investigating" the past can often give you clues to current activity. As it has been said, "there is nothing new under the sun, only variations of how it is done." This applies to governments, to corporations, to radicals and extremists, to the general population, to terrorists, to armies, to nations and to individuals. You must study, investigate, pay attention and learn from the successes and mistakes of others.

You need to recognize propaganda when you see it and you need to be a bit of a "scrounger". You'll find that there are as many sides (and slanted versions) to a story as there are people involved. "Scrounging" through all the rubbish is something not everyone is willing to do; pulling out all the propaganda is something not everyone is capable of doing.

You have to understand the application and importance of the information obtained. An asset in this field is experience such as having worked your way up to Protective details or operating as Team Leader. Another asset is "life experiences" since much of what you see and hear may not have a direct bearing on the assignment as it was given, but as secondary information could prove to be invaluable. Experienced, wiser, older heads are far more qualified to pick up on obscure, seemingly unimportant information. You have to "know" people, something not acquired by the advantages of youth. An Intelligence Operator is the logical promotion upwards of a successful field operative Protector. With the experiences gained, the information needed is far more easily identified and becomes of value much quicker. (Many times, you will find the successful field operative automatically doubling as Intel because his skill and experience may superbly qualify him.)

> "Great part of the information obtained in War is contradictory, a still greater part is false, and by far the greatest part is of doubtful character. What is required of an officer is a certain power of discrimination, which only knowledge of men and things and good judgment can give. The law of probability must be his guide. . . . It is then fortunate if these reports in contradicting each other show a certain balance of probability,

and thus themselves call forth a scrutiny. It is much worse for the inexperienced when accident does not render him this service, but one report supports another, confirms it, magnifies it, finishes off the picture with fresh touches of colour, until necessity in urgent haste forces from us a resolution which will soon be discovered to be folly, all those reports having been lies, exaggerations, errors, etc., etc. In a few words, most reports are false, and the timidity of men acts as a multiplier of lies and untruths. As a general rule, every one is more inclined to lend credence to the bad than the good."[2]

—Carl von Clausewitz

You must have an aptitude for putting together giant puzzles, covering both time and distances. Taking the beginnings of Islam and Judaism and understanding them, helps to put current day conflicts in better focus. Understanding "the troubles" of Northern Ireland is made easier by going back a few hundred years to see what the problems were then. Connecting what happens in the deserts of the Sudan to events formed in New Jersey no longer seems to be such a stretch of the imagination. Developing information on an explosive device used in London, England and doing the same for one used in Sunnyvale, California can make pieces of a puzzle fit like a glove. Sometimes, it is like playing a Global "connect the dots" game in order to make sense of events. You begin to look at everything as if it was a "what's wrong with this picture?" exercise, and when you do see what's wrong with the picture—you win!

You must be a keen observer allowing very little to escape your notice. You must understand and respect basic principles and natural laws, enabling you to see "what's coming—before the facts."

You have to have a "relaxed mental attitude" about the world at large. If you don't, you cannot be completely objective in your findings and reporting for one thing, and for another you will probably end up "washing out" because the sickness of the human mind and "man's inhumanity to man" is where you will spend most of your time while looking for the relevant information you will need.

Being "thickskinned" doesn't hurt either, because you are going to work yourself half to death getting an assignment completed and then the Principal will go ahead and do what he or she wanted to do in the first place at the risk of compromising "your" mission.

You should have a better than average understanding of languages and cultures. Winding your way through international languages, beliefs, religions, loyalties, etc., is a formidable task. If you're working Intel on a global scale, such skills are imperative. If your concentration is on a local or national scale, the demands may not be as great at the moment, but you're still not off the hook. What appears to be on the horizon and in place involves many cultures and languages; be prepared. With regard to global Information coming in from

---

[2] Clausewitz *On War* Chapter VI "Information in War"—page 162 (first published in 1832).

other countries—be advised that other languages may look entirely different by the time they forage their way through translations (and propaganda) and wind up with you. Be prepared to track back and get it right.

We must point out that this profession is one where you routinely end up with information in your possession which could be damaging if it ended up in the wrong hands. We encourage people putting together an Intelligence Operation to *immediately and thoroughly weed out* those who are snoops, gossips, kiss and tell types or busybodies. (There *is* a difference between those descriptions and Intelligence Gathering!) Such types are not only dishonorable, they are unstable, dangerous liabilities.

Intel is not the place for neophytes, laziness, mediocrity, political players or part-timers. A good Intel Specialist must be experienced, seasoned and have historical, global and attention-to-detail perspectives.

WHAT IS THE DIFFERENCE BETWEEN INFORMATION AND INTELLIGENCE?

For our purposes, Intelligence is Information "of value" in a usable format. There is such an enormous volume of information coming at us all at once, that it is a little more than data at best—until something of value or relevance to us is noted.

Example: The fall of east Germany is information. Stasi agents going into private enterprise as Intelligence Officers and marketing their "skills" throughout the world is Intelligence (information of value) which might have an effect on your business.

Example: The fact that the Irish Republican Army exists is information. That three separate escapees from Maze Prison have been found in California, living and working in the same geographic area, is Intelligence (information of value).

Example: That the "Soviet Union" and the "KGB" no longer exist is information. That the same people who were "KGB" under the Soviet Union still occupy the same building, hold the same jobs, have the same basic assignments and still operate (inside and outside of Russia) under the same principles, but under a different name, is Intelligence (information of value).

Example: That there are several books published which detail the making of explosive devices is information. To learn that an employee of your Principal's company has been arrested for making pipe bombs at home is Intelligence (information of value).

THE PURPOSE OF AN INTELLIGENCE OPERATION

The purpose of an Intelligence Operation, (regardless of whether it's conducted by Corporate in-house, an independent agency, part of contracted security or a Protective Program) is that *it supports the Protective Team* in their endeavors by identifying every known *threat*, every possible *risk* and identifying every possible *asset*. The Protective Team is then given information which may well mean the difference between success and catastrophe.

Once a person becomes (or is perceived to have become) "celebrity" by way of his or her importance, wealth or fame—that person is a prime candidate for being targeted for trouble. "Celebrity" not only has its perks, it has its nightmares. The same principle holds true when John or Jane Q. Citizen is targeted—just because they're "Americans" and/or because they can be used as a handy "bargaining tool."

Within the corporation, that person who is "high profile" is also a "corporate asset" and not only has the right, but the **obligation** to be protected from danger. Should anything happen to this person, the *entire* Corporation is affected. Every employee, manager, executive and vendor will have reactions to the event, and attentions will be diverted to this topic for a period of time. The company makes the headlines in a negative way, stocks go down, insurance rates go up, employee morale goes down, attention is diverted from productivity, legal and P.R. departments go into a panic and journalists begin digging for sensational corporate and personal "dirt"—and will broadcast everything they know, or think they know, to the rest of the world. What's more, all the holes in the Corporation's protective system are exposed to the world; "experts" make public commentary on the "obvious mistakes made;" and heads begin to roll within the company. All this before the funeral is over.

Another purpose for Intelligence Gathering is to "know your enemy." If you think the Bad Guys are just walking into situations unprepared and charged full of emotion, you are sadly mistaken. We learned this during the early 1970's while providing protection during the Leftist "anti-war" demonstrations. It was great fun in those days to take them "head on" and fight the rock throwing crowds, but youth gives way to maturity and we learned that by looking to the sides and rear of the crowds, we could locate the "orchestrators" of these "spontaneous demonstrations of social concern." We identified them and began keying off their movements in order to intercept and frustrate the demonstrators. This proved to be just as much fun!

In his book, *The Minimanual of the Urban Guerrilla*, Carlos Marighella set the stage in 1969 for years to come. His strategy is much to be admired by the professional. Condensing from the book, you'll discover that many of the points he makes require one thing in common—Information.

- Do not incorrectly estimate the enemy
- Know the state of mind or emotions of the enemy
- Use the element of surprise
- Have better knowledge of the terrain than your opponent and use that advantage
- Have greater mobility and speed than the enemy
- Take total command of the situation
- Do not fail to plan, thus forcing yourselves to improvise

Your opposition may be narco-terrorists, eco-terrorists, extremists, kidnappers, stalkers, assassins or social/political activists. They may be using FAX machines, portable computers, or electronic "bulletin boards" to communicate nationally or even internationally. They may be using such tactics as "bugs," theft, planting personnel or surveillance against you and your Principal. They may be tapped in on your cellular telephone calls and your radio frequencies.

They will rely heavily on Intelligence Gathering activity!
The Bad Guys use Intelligence Gathering to their own advantage.
They know the Who, What, Where, When, Why (and How) their targets have been chosen. The more difficult it is to penetrate the target's protection *unnoticed or unchallenged*, the less likely any disastrous situations will occur. If an employee's armed and deranged husband can't get through the tough security operations at work, lives may be spared (including the Principal's). If the kidnappers can't identify and locate the children of the Exec./Celeb., you may be attending their graduations (not their funerals) next spring. If the bad guys can't identify any of the residence locations of the C.E.O., there may not be any shocking headlines tomorrow. Otherwise rational people have to stop thinking it's "the other guy" or their family members who will be victimized. Your Principal is the other guy! Counter-Intelligence is a must!

There isn't a single year of recorded history which isn't to our advantage in learning the benefits of Intelligence Gathering. History teaches us to be thorough, to be factual, to keep our perspective while doing whatever we do and to apply the information we learn. Intelligence Information from a historical perspective will give us the advantage—once we are placed in an adversarial role with another person or entity.

On terrorist Abu Nidal and his Intelligence Directorate (Intel Ops). "To an outside observer, there seemed to be periods when the directorate was intensely active and others when it was dormant. But an inside source told me that even when no operations were being mounted or planned, the directorate was always vigilant. Security arrangements at airports and seaports had to be constantly reviewed, alterations to visa and immigration stamps monitored, and a host of other subjects kept up to date; the training of staff was a daily preoccupation. 'It was work at the time,' the source said. There were no periods of rest at all. The directorate could not afford to pause for a single moment."[3]

Sun Tzu, about 2,400 years ago in ancient China, was respected then and now as a philosopher of war and strategy. Throughout the ages there have been many variations on "Good Intelligence is the Prelude to Victory." In his "Use of Spies" chapter, he talks of the "foreknowledge" of generals which allows them to be victorious. "This 'foreknowledge' cannot be elicited form spirits, nor from gods, nor by analogy with past events, nor by astrological calculations. It must be obtained from men who know the enemies situation." He went further to write, and this is aimed at you personally, "Generally in the case of armies you wish to strike, cities you wish to attack, and people you wish to assassinate, it is necessary to find out the names of the garrison commander, the aides-de-camp, the ushers, the gatekeepers, and bodyguards." It was Sun Tzu who said, "Know your enemy and know yourself and you can fight a hundred battles without defeat."[4]

In his book on Mao Tse-tung, USMC Brigadier General (ret.) Samuel B. Griffith interprets the writings of Mao from Mao's 1937 Yu Chi Chan (Mao Tse-

---

3 *Abu Nidal: A Gun For Hire* by Patrick Seale 1992—page 187.
4 *Sun Tzu's Art of War— The Modern Interpretation* by General Tao Hanzhang—1990. (Sun Tzu lived approximately 500 B.C.)

tung on Guerrilla Warfare). "Intelligence is the decisive factor in planning guerrilla operations. Where is the enemy? In what strength? What does he propose to do? What is the state of his equipment, his supply, his morale? Are his leaders intelligent, bold, and imaginative or stupid and impetuous? Are his troops tough, efficient, and well disciplined, or poorly trained and soft? Guerrillas expect the members of their intelligence service to provide the answers to these and dozens more detailed questions.[5]

From Carl von Clausewitz, Prussian war philosopher and Director of the Military Academy in Berlin (1818 to 1830), "By the word 'information' we denote all the knowledge which we have of the enemy and his country; therefore, in fact, the foundation of all of our ideas and actions."[6]

Germany's General Irwin Rommel stated "Know your enemy" as a principle in his book on tank warfare, so American General George Patton read Rommel's book before engaging Rommel in battle during WWII.[7] (Germany lost that war if you haven't been following history. Don't laugh, I was asked not too long ago which war the Germans were in and which side they were on.)

"World War II taught Americans that, in the words of William J. Donovan, 'good intelligence was no more mysterious than *McGuffey's Second Reader* and just about as sinister.' During the war, agents of the Office of Strategic Services learned that a few minutes spent with the brakeman of a freight train destined for occupied France produced more useful data than Mata Hari could learn in an entire evening."[8]

During the early 1970's, we had opportunity to work undercover on a college campus. The FBI was looking for an anarchist past-president of the SDS (Students for a Democratic Society) who had been drafted and was now wanted on army desertion charges. We knew he was currently back on the campus hiding out and agitating the local Leftists. Unable to locate him, we decided he must not look anything like the available photos we had of him taken during his previous activist period, so we ran an intelligence research operation on him. We finally came up with a few high school yearbook photos which allowed us to see him as he really looked. The arrest came two days later. The "twist" or punch line in this story is that this imaginative fellow knew he was going to be watched during his former days as SDS president, and made certain he was always identified and photographed *in disguise* during that period when demonstration surveillances were conducted by local law enforcement. When things got too hot for him (as in this effort to identify him) his "disguise" was to look like himself!

Should the student choose to ignore the lessons provided from thousands of years history (I can only guess it is there for us to learn from); should he choose to ignore the really great tacticians who have come before us and made pronouncements as to the important of Intelligence; and should the student forget the sheer logic which dictates that you don't approach any situation without as much information as possible, we submit an example from recent publicized

5   Mao Tse-tung on Guerrilla Warfare by Samuel B. Griffith, USMC (Ret.)—page 22—1961.
6   Clausewitz On War—Chapter VI "Information In War"—page 162.
7   "The Patton Papers."
8   Central Intelligence and National Security by Harry H. Ransom 1958—page 16.

history where Intelligence Gathering was indeed of prime importance to the perpetrators but deficient in behalf of the Corporate victim—and where the consequences of those deficiencies proved to be fatal.

Mr. Sidney Reso of Exxon was a man of value and importance both to his family and to Exxon. According to reports, some training had been supplied to Exxon personnel in matters of Protective service, professionals were called in to give the benefit of their experience and wisdom, and someone in a decision making capacity (non-protection more than likely) decided what would be best for all concerned and the security program went forward according to those decisions. Trained drivers met Mr. Reso at work and transported him around during his work day safely. Protective and Security personnel conducted their business according to the dictates of Administrators and other decision makers, and all the while some yutz husband and wife team ran a successful surveillance on Mr. Reso for several months. The result is known to us all. Mr. Sidney Reso is no more. An ex-employee of Exxon Security used the obvious, known weaknesses in the system to his advantage and the rest of the executive world trembled at the thought of this successful kidnapping. So what is to be learned?

1) The bad guys use intelligence gathering to their advantage, and they take time to prepare it.

2) The bad guys use intelligence gathering to find weaknesses and openings in the system or program.

3) Intelligence information doesn't usually come to you—*Go look for it.*

4) No one at Exxon knew that anything was afoot. "IT" came to them.

5) Intelligence gathering in Exxon's own "backyard" in the form of an operation to see that all was well with their executives—might have been a useful thing (a.k.a. counter-surveillance).

5) Exxon was the actual target; Mr. Reso was only the tool for getting to them. It was nothing personal.

7) A half-hearted or compromised plan—is not "better than nothing." It only serves to point out to people like Seale exactly where the holes in the system are and how they can be exploited.

We give this example because we want to break down some preconceived ideas about an Intelligence Operation, not for the sake of criticizing anyone at Exxon. Looking "inward" is seldom done, because the majority of people think of Intelligence as the art of only going *out* and to gather information about the other fellow. While that is true in part, why not apply the same "disciplines" to other areas—such as looking "inward" to see what critical information can be readily obtained about your operation, your client, your CEO, your celebrity or you personally? Keep in mind that all records of our "having passed this way" adds to the Intelligence files of someone!

Never forget—all purpose, technique and finesse becomes unimportant *if you as the Intel Specialist are waiting for information to come to you when dealing with critical issues.* When "IT" gets to you, there are seldom any opportunities for anything other than reacting to a bad situation, <u>reacting</u> from a negative position, reacting in someone else's game, and with their rules. Bad business!

HOW TO DEVELOP AN INTELLIGENCE PROGRAM

You "Plan, Plan, Plan!" Begin with asking yourself some realistic questions. "What is it that I really want and/or need to do?" Do I contract out all or part of the research? Am I going to be the researcher as well as the analyst? Am I part of the PPS Detail and taking the Intelligence Gathering over as a "coordinator?" Ask yourself what your expectations are. If you can't answer these questions yourself, get someone in the business to help you.

Determine if what you have decided to do, or have been tasked with doing, is "do-able." Remember that there are a lot of misconceptions and false expectations from those who do not understand Intelligence Gathering. Don't get yourself in too deep!

Next, ask "who will use this information?" Are you supporting an Executive Protection Detail? Are you providing information for a Corporate Intel operation? Are you dealing directly with Executives and Celebrities? Determine what criteria the User will accept to validate your findings.

PLAN for the growth of your information storage. If your information is stored in a "database" in a computer, plan for the growth requirements of the hard disk storage size as well as the increasing amount of memory needed to run the program. If your information storage is a "hardcopy" system, plan for the physical growth of the area needed for storage. You also need to build an indexing system which can be expanded or altered at any given time. (I can't imagine why anyone would still choose to use hardcopy, with technology such as it is, but I present it for your consideration anyway.) You should build your files in separate "layers" or sections, to prevent any one file from becoming enormous. By breaking it down and devoting separate sections or files to National data, Individuals and Groups, Special Reports on events or locations for example, you can more efficiently handle problems associated with growth.

Determine where all this information is going to come from. Identify in advance as much as possible—your resources as well as your sources. PLAN how you are going to get the information, what format it will be stored in, and how it will be accessed as the demands for information are made. Depending on the format, develop the appropriate ability to "cross-reference" the information so that one effort or command brings up all relevant data for that subject. Cross-referencing also will help you prevent duplication of efforts.

Unless you are starting an Intelligence Firm, (an agency with both national and international perspective) PLAN to be specific in the information you are going to pursue. If the problems of Winnie Mandella in South Africa have no bearing whatsoever on your client(s), don't waste the money, time and energy following those developments. If the situation changes, and it becomes an issue to know what the Mandella family is up to, buy the information somewhere and get caught up that way.

Determine to the best of your ability what the "negatives" of your assignment will be and PLAN how to overcome them. If you recognize for example, that you are designated or regarded a "non-profit generating, administrative expense" within a corporation, determine how else you might serve the corporation in your capacity as an Intelligence Specialist. And you absolutely must attempt to develop *support* from the executives, because their lack of professional understanding may be more focused on their concerns over the costs of the staffing.

We'll share with you some of the "logic" of P&L (profit and loss) types covering this subject: The cost of an in-house employee is estimated at anywhere between two and six times the actual salary paid. This includes work space, equipment, benefit packages, taxes, insurances, telephones, utilities and a host of other considerations. Therefore, "they" (the decision makers) conclude that "the cost for Intel, outweighs the need for it." When this kind of logic is offered, you'll begin to understand how and why so many other mindless decisions fall into place. **Not** generally computed in: the costs in lives, injuries, product, real property, stocks, lawsuits and the ever popular (other) innocent victim—the insurance industry.

Corporations may choose (if they address the problem at all) to contract an Independent Intel Professional on an "as needed basis" to avoid the estimated expenses listed above. The plus side of this will come *only* from hiring top level professionals or bona fide "Specialists" who can provide the absolute highest level of service quickly and efficiently. The minus side is twofold in that if the true "Specialist" isn't engaged, mediocrity in service will result (which may also kill the project). One usually finds (if the problems are addressed at all) that in-house personnel are seriously and dangerously limited to reliance on very costly, periodic "Dial a Disaster" or "Dial a Travel Advisory" service. Such services may have their place as an *adjunct,* but in the hands of non-Intel, non-educated personnel, a Protective mission can *easily* be compromised, endangering both the protectors and the C.E.O., or even worse, end in disaster. Fortunately there are other things that an Intelligence staff can address within the Corporate structure which will "justify" the staff's existence. We will review some of the options and problems in the following section.

If you recognize that incoming information should not be handled by a non-professional, *do not assign this function to clerical personnel.* If, in your planning, you see that keeping current will possibly have a negative impact on the operation due to the volume of information to be handled, determine what your options will be so that you can defeat the criticism before it starts.

Identify and track your sources. You may wish to code this information into the reports and keep the actual information separate from the database. This will depend on your sources and to what extent, if any, you need to protect them.

PLAN how the information will be provided to the Users. Do you FAX it? Do you put it on an electronic "file server"? Do you provide it "hardcopy"? Do you mail it? Do you hand carry it?

PLAN to routinely recheck all facets of the program including the satisfaction of the User, to ensure that you are still providing the service everyone expected at the beginning.

PLAN that your sources are not going to be adequate for your needs at some specific moment in time. Know what your options are before that need arises and draw from them. Intelligence Specialists not only "know", they "know *who* knows!"

You can PLAN to generate or obtain a considerable amount of relevant Intelligence Information from openly accessible sources. Analysis findings by government sponsored research labs (Los Alamos), private companies and major corporations (such as Motorola) state that information from the "open sources" of publicly available information can give them from 85% to 95% of the information they need to run an effective, efficient Intelligence Operation capable of supporting the Intelligence Gathering needs of their entire corporation—including the Protective Services.[9]

Example: Using information from openly accessible sources, you research Italy prior to a trip by your Principal. During your research, you learn the usual "informative" things you require. *If you continue to dig however,* you may pick up on the fact that the Italian government won't allow for the exchange of money at their banks to pay for ransom demands. In fact, they will *freeze* bank funds if they suspect a kidnapping. You determine there are kidnap gangs working certain areas and make a couple of telephone calls to confirm this all to be true. Is that information useful to you in planning the boss's travel protection in Italy? Does that make you, and your Intelligence Operation, useful to the boss? Were you able to identify a working threat against a carrier or destination and assist the Protective Detail in being able to *avoid* it? All the Intel information was actually available from open sources. It takes skill and technique to find it. *(Bear in mind* that finding relevant information versus recognizing and understanding it are still two distinctly different topics.)

Information from confidential sources is generally not "confirmable" due to the secretive nature of both the information and the relationship to the source. Using them can blow up in your face. Don't try to cultivate them unless absolutely necessary. How are you going to justify revealing your cultivated "secret source" if something goes dramatically wrong as a result of the information obtained? There are very few people in whom we place unqualified trust. If you do use an unqualifiable source say so in the report. That way the information is available, and all parties know its value.

The bad guys are going to start their Intelligence Operations someplace, so why not start with the public information that is most readily available to them? Major executives and celebrities living in secluded areas of the countryside take out building permits in their own names. They license their personal vehicles in their own names. They fill out change of address cards in their own names. (These are a matter of public records, since the post office makes this information available to the public and businesses routinely.) All this information is either a matter of public record or can be obtained with very little difficulty. Publicists or P.R. Departments see to it that the Execs' pictures are in the press as often as possible, that their incomes and promotions are publicly noted, that their itineraries are published, that their benevolent gestures are duly noted and so on. (Executives and Celebrities can be their own worst enemies and bring problems on themselves if they aren't careful about their P.R. campaigns!)

---

[9] "Tactical Technology" newsletter—1/6/93—Phillips Business Information Inc. quoting Robert Steele at the Symposium on National Security and National Competitiveness: Open Source Solutions.

Example: Mr. Charles M. Geschke, President of Adobe Software in Mt. View, California, reportedly came to the attention of two young males after a high visibility article regarding his philanthropic work appeared in a local newspaper. A short time later, *(their surveillance and planning accomplished)*, Mr. Geschke was approached in the parking lot of his office building by the two and subsequently became their unwilling guest—for a period of five days. The ransom was paid. Mr. Geschke was rescued and the two males were (barely) captured.

Conclusion—*Go looking for information* (Risks and Threats) if the program is to be of any service to the ones who need it. If you wait for it to come to you, the game is already half over. This isn't stepping out of the role of Intelligence Gathering, this is using it on a more productive level. Look up, look down, look left, look right, look inward and then look outside. Turn your Intelligence Operation loose on the company or your boss (with permission of course) once in a while and see what develops through publicly accessible records and information sources. It's smart business! We did this on one client and came up with no less than 136 pieces of information *from only one single source* for a one year period. We were able to identify the family members, ages, work history and income of the client, marital history, educational background, the family residence address, the real estate purchasing history, hobbies, location of his second home, work associates, type(s) of vehicles driven, driving habits, travel patterns and so on. This person makes himself a nice target! By the way, this person insists on his privacy from any protective details and security period. He doesn't like them around. They make him "uncomfortable."

COMPUTERIZING

One of the biggest advantages of this information age is the ability to merge it with high technology—a.k.a. "computers." "The computer" allows us to expand *far* beyond what we thought possible even a few years ago. Computerized operations so far *surpass* the traditional information retrieval systems, it is almost not to be believed (and we have been party to both types of operations, so we know whereof we speak). We designed our own Intelligence Operation for the largest possible expansion of information, including the discovery of new patterns emerging, easier discovery of "networking" or serial operations, new groups and activities just beginning to evolve, even how to find additional information we already had (and didn't know we had) and so on. If one knows how, the merger of Intel and high tech as a finely honed technological weapon, can send an Intelligence Operation to new heights you wouldn't have thought possible.

We will address portions of this topic so that you may see what we mean. Please refer to the attached diagram to aid your understanding. The descriptions are short due to covering a wide range of topics, and are not meant to over simplify, but to give you a small glimpse of what is possible.

The storage and retrieval of information using a computer system far exceeds that of the hard copy system. ("Hardcopy," a.k.a., paper reports, paper files.) As an example, on a corner of our desk is the equivalent of *at least* 500,000 pages of written material—and it is all sitting under a coffee cup. (Why the cup is there I don't know.) That does not include what we have in the computers themselves or what we can access through dozens (if not hundreds) of computer accessible "archives" which would give us *incalculable* amounts of information. How many filing cabinets would that take for you to duplicate? And how would you "back up" your information files—or where?

How many times have we all heard something and thought it sounded familiar but we just couldn't put it together? How many times have we worked on a case and recalled a bit of information which opened up a dead-end investigation? Being conscientious professionals, it drives us up the wall. Suppose you have a database with 1000 separate cases. Learning how to turn that high tech machinery into a first class technological weapon, you can establish a system so streamlined, so formidable—your jaw will drop. One day you read a report that says the weapon used was a pipe bomb which exploded on impact, the vehicle used was a small motorcycle, the M.O. was to throw the device from the moving motorcycle, the victim was a manufacturer of widgets and the perpetrators were identified as "one each—unknown male and female." This all sounds familiar to you, but you don't know why. Using a streamlined high tech system to go with that high tech machinery, you could actually come up with the same identification information in several parts of the country over the past four years and everything matches! The computer found the other information out of those 1000 reports. And you could accomplish this feat—in a matter of minutes. You have a pattern. Your "perps" are back in business!

"Data basing" information in a computer has provided the opportunity not to miss an important point in a report once it has been identified as being important. We can pull up a report by name, number or topic, pull up a database by topic and then we can research what we need. With this type system, *you* can search an entire database for a specific name or even a single phrase which was entered one time. No more depending on memory or volumes of Indexing notes.

The transfer of hard copy information from one point to another which has been relegated to phone conversations, the mail services or even "overnight" priority mail is now accomplished by FAX (Facsimile) or by E-Mail (Electronic Mail) to or from any point in the world with the right set up—and now FAX and computer E-Mail can even be handled all at the same location. FAX machines can be purchased in the $300 range and will also double as phone answering machines and printers; modems for computers come complete with the software and can cost as little as $100. Automatic scheduling programs can be set up on the computer for sending (or receiving for that matter) E-Mail during the off hours thus reducing the cost of transmission and freeing up the phone lines during business hours.

"Scanning" information from a source outside the computer is a simple task no more complicated than using a photocopier these days. There are black and white or color "scanners" from the hand-held variety that you run over a document (like you were painting it with a brush) to small units which fit desk top where you simply put the document on it and follow the software directions to duplicate the document into the computer. This allows you to include published maps, hand drawn sketches, original handwritten documents, pictures, receipts *or any other document* not created within the computer. The item then can be printed out from the computer just like any other document. The applications of this technology are only as limited as your needs, or your imagination.

Computers "talking" to each other only requires compatible software programs, modems, phone lines (or cellular/satellite connections) and very little else. Diagrams, maps, reports or pictures can be sent to or from the field by anyone having the appropriate equipment and software. "Encoding" for privacy can be as simple as using a "picture language" font which is then converted at the receiving end, or the computers can be "scrambled" by various types of phone add-on devices you can purchase anywhere.

"Art and graphics programs" for the computer have allowed us to manufacture overhead transparency presentations (in color) as well as the attachments to our reports and writings including the simple ones we have produced for this book. The graphics and printed words on the page can be done in a fraction of the time it takes with hardcopy "cut and paste" the traditional way. Items are aligned, spaced, and sized to our specifications, and one is only limited by the ability to find the right graphic, or to use the art program to its fullest potential.

C.D. ROM technology is so advanced (Computer Disk Read Only Memory means that you cannot alter the contents of the disk itself) that you can purchase entire books of information for a fraction of the cost of buying the book itself. (We have one book that we purchased on C.D. ROM for $10.00, which cost us $30 for the actual book.) When we aren't using the C.D. ROM drive for information research, we put in a C.D. and listen to music through the computer! We can draw from the C.D. and send information to any other location by the means described above.

"Still" Photo technology is so far advanced that one simple "C.D. ROM" drive can hold dozens of photos and allow you to display them on the computer screen, edit them for quality, enhance them for clarity, or crop them for focusing on a specific item in the photo. (Letting the computer effect the clearing of haze, focus, sharpen, or change the hue and brightness.) They can be reduced or enlarged, layered over one another or run in comparison with other photographs. You can process photographs taken by other people and conduct "forensic" research on the photos to determine content and/or whether it is an altered photograph. (By the way, there are examples of this type of analysis done with photos of Lee Harvey Oswald which concludes that certain photographs were indeed doctored.[10] This analysis is based on the technology of the computer only in 1992, and is almost outdated as of this writing. They do not even address C.D. ROM technology.) The applications again are only limited by your needs or your imagination.

"Video" technology and the computer is as simple as learning how to

---

10 *Photo Computer Image Processing And The Crime Of The Century* by Ralph D. Thomas—1992.

manipulate the software. As an example, with the appropriate software and devices you can take from regular VHS tape and put it into the computer where you can analyze it, edit it, add sound tracks (if you want) or conduct "forensic" research on the video—and then put it back on VHS.

"Voice print" technology was once the exclusive domain of the forensic scientist. Not to minimize their scientific "know how" in analyzing the information, computer technology exists today which will allow you to look at voice prints for yourself (and even print out a hardcopy).

"Artificial Intelligence" has advanced to the point where there are now in existence computers and programs which allow you to talk to the computer (giving it verbal commands) and the computer has the "ability" to "talk back." Consider being able to ask your computer to research a 500,000 word database for a specific name! "Hands free" computer operation is not that far away.

"IF YOU DON'T KNOW WHERE YOU ARE GOING, HOW WILL YOU KNOW WHEN YOU GET THERE?"

There are so many terrific quotes regarding planning (or the lack thereof) that it probably would be deserving of a book all its own—and you could probably fill a book! One of our favorites is *"People don't plan to fail, they fail to plan."* We still see entities attempting to develop Intelligence Operations without benefit of sitting down to determine *who* the users are, *what* the needs really are, *where* to find the information needed, *why* certain areas need to be addressed, *when* they need to have everything in place—or even *how* everything should come together, *how* to correctly format it, and *how* to plan for delivery of the information once it is obtained. (This doesn't even address putting in place some mechanism which would allow for the plan to be *changed* at any time, *redirected* to a specific need—or a *complete directional change* if required.) These people don't have a plan; what they do have is an expensive way of gathering a lot of information or data. They are justifying a paycheck (for a short period of time) and hoping that if they're asked "just the right question" they may be able to scramble through all that mess for a correct answer. In a time when personnel resources are not easily obtained, devoting people to "gathering information" without a definite plan is a sure fire way to have the entire project fail in short order.

As a basic principle, you should understand that Intel is never a sporadic, do it whenever-you-get-around-to-it, or when somebody yells for it—venture. Events move too quickly for a person to "plug in" once in a while to some news source and develop the critical information needed for a Protective detail. Intel is never part time; it is an on-going process.

Contracting out the "basics" can be a planned option which allows for the *Operations people* to focus more of their valuable time on the specifics within an assignment. As an example, you could let someone else do your report on Germany (using their resources, time, money and equipment) then buy it when you need it. You can also reverse the order and let the contracted agency do the site specific work (acting as a "shield" for you) so that your corporation or client is not "broadcasting" his or her intent to be somewhere at a particular time.

When the question is asked of you, "What if (this) happens?" the Intelligence Operation should already have (or at least have access to) the answers and probabilities. The answer to, "So what do we do about (this)" should be something mapped out by the Intelligence personnel as well. Your job is to do your homework—and have it ready for the questions you'll be asked by the Protective team leader. The practical application of information is a Protective Detail's forte. You only need go as far as the preface of the book *Providing Executive Protection (Vol. I)* to find a key statement by Dr. Richard Kobetz. He is describing Executive Protection practitioners when he says, "They *avoid* problems and they can deal with any emergency—they are Personal Protection Specialists."[11] The italics are mine for emphasis. Having the information needed to recognize potential or emerging challenges—is the **prelude** to *avoiding* and/or preparing for those challenges, and that vital information must come from someplace.

An Intelligence Specialist has to be able to find the details that may only show up as "secondary" or tertiary information (or buried even lower), has to be able to understand the big picture from a global scale, and has to understand how it all fits together. Then there has to be the ability to communicate the findings so they can be understood. None of it will do you or anyone else one ounce of good if you cannot present it in some useful format to the "end user," and that my friend has everything to do with you personally.

Conclusion—*Plan* before you involve yourself in something that will drain your time and resources. If your efforts over a period of months cannot answer the first few questions asked of you, consider that the planning was inadequate. Plan, ask questions, plan some more and then decide if it is "do-able." Then start gathering information. The rest will follow. Be flexible!

> **"A Plan which has never had to change,**
> **wasn't much of a Plan to begin with."**

MISCONCEPTIONS ABOUT INTELLIGENCE GATHERING

The most succinct description I have heard to date is "Belshazzar actually saw the hand writing on the wall, as did many others, but it took Daniel to tell him what it meant."[12] (Isn't that beautiful?!)

The first misconception we will address is that "anyone can work an Intelligence Gathering Operation"—it just ain't so! You can collect magazines, newspapers and periodicals from all the trade journals you want, for as long as you want—or until your house is a fire disaster from floor to ceiling. You can download data from bulletin board services day and night, sort them into your own software package (of your very own award winning design) and have information going back to the stone age. You can buy every Security newsletter subscription on the market and you can have video tape of CNN back to their first

---

11 *Providing Executive Protection* (Vol. I) by Dr. Richard Kobetz—1991—page 7 of the "Preface."
12 Dr. H.H.A. Cooper at the Academy of Security Educators and Trainers 2nd Symposium on Business Intelligence—Winchester, Virginia 1993.

day of business. You can cut and paste to your heart's desire, edit until you are blue in the face and quote all the sources you want in reverse alphabetical order if it pleases you. *"Now what are you going to do?!"*

Another misconception is that you will be talking to a reasonable, intelligent and concerned professional clientele 100% of the time when it comes to Intelligence Operations and it's beneficial value to the protection of life and property. Again, it just ain't so.

- Client: "What's the risk? We don't see any risk."
- Intel: "'Risks' Sir, do not *volunteer* themselves until it's too late. You have to go looking for them."
- Client: "We don't use Intelligence. That isn't the way we do business."
- Intel: "You are only *half* right, Sir, that isn't the way you do business."
- Client: "Our plan is that our people will tell us if they hear or see anything out of the ordinary or suspicious, then we put our people on it right away. It's more cost effective that way."
- Intel: "No it isn't. First 'they' have to notice it, then 'they' have to understand it, then you had better hope 'they' remember to tell you about it." *(Some plan!)*

(We do want to qualify this; there are people who legitimately ask and want to know *what the risks are,* as opposed to those people who state their viewpoints as some sort of stupid challenge in an attempt to cover up their ignorance.)

OBSERVATIONS ON WHAT TO LOOK FOR

There are certain things we look for in gathering information. A lot of skill, technique, and sixth sense develop over a period of years, but in the end one must rely on *basic principles,* doing your homework, understanding human nature, history, and common sense. Hype, propaganda, smoke screens, ("diplomacy"), naïveté, wishful thinking, ignorance or arrogance have no place along the road toward becoming a skilled Intelligence Person. Here are a few things *to look for.*

- "Different Name, Same Game." Everybody and everything has a name and there are mental pictures (as well as recorded histories) which go with each name. Governments, confederations of governments, groups, individuals and other entities are known to change their names and represent themselves as whole new ball games. The naïve often take the name changes at face value (which was the preliminary desired result). A widely questioned example of this is the USSR (which is now called the CIF) and their KGB (which has apparently gone through about five name changes recently according to their own people). So tell us, where did all of those life long dedicated to their beliefs, high-stepping, scowling, hard line, world conquering, American-hating, communists go? Madison Avenue (the American heart of advertising genius) knows that when a product is generating a negative reaction — keep the product, but change its name! If the "Dregs of Society" criminal or terrorist group needs to change its strategy and tactics, their first move logically should be to rename themselves the "Darlings of Society." Different name, same game.

- "Symbols." Terrorists, anarchists, gangs and other such types of the world think, talk and act in symbolic terms. This is both a *unifying* and identifying technique historically fostered by those who cultivate naïve or hostile recruits. They adopt symbols of identification which stick with them—regardless of what they're calling themselves at the moment. (i.e., red stars, anniversary dates, raised clenched fists, names of dead "heros," military jargon, etc.) They see targets in *symbolic* perspectives (also part of the psychology of desensitizing any feeling or emotion for later targets.) They see reasonably defenseless specific (soft) targets as "symbols" of something they may be afraid to attack directly at the moment. ("Shining Path" in Peru seems to absolutely hate busses!) They make symbolic gestures and they talk in symbolic phraseology. A good example is an "Operational Field Unit" of the I.R.A. "taking its war to the oppressors" (by exploding a device in a trash container outside a retail establishment in London on such-and-such day to "commemorate" something or other).

- "Key Phrases and Buzzwords." Ideology (or lack thereof) can be tracked by watching key phrases used in "releases" given in interviews and in painted graffiti. (Much like the "Symbols" described above.) Oppressors, Liberation, Brothers and Sisters of, the Brave Patriots of, Comrades, Freedom Fighters of, the (XYZ) Army, and a host of other such terms give you clues as to what to expect. This type of specific phraseology if used consistently points you to a series of things: Are you still dealing with the same people? What is their basis for their grievance? What is their *stated* philosophy? What does that philosophy say they must do next? Are they hiding behind a "revolutionary" philosophy is order to carry out criminal activity? (This will tell you what types of people may be associated with the group.) Are they going to be high level risk takers or not? Has the group changed their tactics and actions but retained the same "philosophy?" Have there been changes in leadership behind the scenes? Are their actions consistent with the stated philosophy? The list goes on and on.

- "Backgrounds." Each photograph we see is analyzed for the content of the background. We look for deliberate poses, props, and items or events in the background which were staged to give a specific impression to the viewer, perhaps even on a subconscious level. Finding these things isn't always easy since their job is to give the impression that it's a candid photo taken of the subject. By photo analysis you can not only obtain additional information, but can also tell how sophisticated the propaganda effort is or is not. (Something like playing "what's wrong with this picture?")

- "Brag Books or Autobiographies." We constantly look for books on the bad guys and even on the good guys from time to time. Just as you might buy a good book on elite fighting forces or on the counterterrorist units around the world as a tool to help you learn something useful, so can a book written on or by an activist group or a CEO. Fortunately for those of us in this profession, many interesting people have put their "thinking" or history between the covers of their books. Like the investigative technique of sitting quietly, let the person being interviewed fill in all that quiet with talk.

• "Coincidences, Patterns and Inconsistencies." On the Global scale, we obviously look for patterns emerging which show us some sort of connection between seemingly unrelated groups. In our profession, there is basically no such thing as a coincidence. When the same type of explosive device shows up on three continents, is delivered in the same fashion, is made of the same type of materials and is triggered in the same fashion—you should discern what's taking place. By the same token, if there are "inconsistencies" in the patterns, you may need to dig deeper to see if there aren't a number of people acting independently under the same name. Coincidences, patterns and inconsistencies should also tell you if the group in question is not well financed yet, not sophisticated enough to follow the same patterns, has to depend on the resources they can get their hands on at any given time, etc. Variations in weaponry, or consistencies in the types of weapons found might also tell you the status and sophistication of the individual or group in question **or** you're looking at a deliberate smoke screen *designed to cause you to underestimate.*

SOMETHING YOU NEVER WANT TO FORGET

This seems like a good spot to play "hardball" on the subject of just how important good Intel is to the people with whom you professionally associate, your "colleagues." The Intelligence Specialist is usually that skilled, experienced professional who has worked his way up through *many* ranks and knows how vital it is to get the right information—clearly, concisely, and completely—into the hands of those men and women who are operational in the field. That Intelligence Specialist *knows* he or she may be holding the safety, the future, and the lives of those field operatives and/or their principals in his hands, and he dare not, he will not—permit himself any *careless* errors or oversights that may jeopardize his colleagues, their reputations, or their Principals. Therefore (we'll share with you a "Profiles Principle") the Intelligence Specialist will view everything he does from a *"four way navigational fix"* before he presents it! Qualifying the veracity of the source (first navigational fix), double checking the accuracy of the information (second navigational fix), researching historical, geographical, natural and human factors (third navigational fix), assessing time, risk and threat levels (fourth navigational fix) is the most professional and *honorable* way an Intelligence Specialist carries out his role.

WHAT TO DO WITH THE INFORMATION ONCE YOU HAVE IT

• Do nothing. (This may sound odd, but consider it.) One option you *always* have is to do nothing. This does not contradict anything you will read here. We always include the option of "do nothing, or do nothing different . . ." in our assessments to the client. It is realistic; it is a probability.
• Cross-check the information with that you already have. Determine if it is useful, corroborative, accurate and presentable. Log it so that it is "cross-referenced." This way, when developing the "big picture" you can access each relevant piece of information at the same time.
• Put the information in its most valuable and useful format. If the infor-

mation calls for charts and graphs, make them.

- See that the information is protected. Copies are stored in secure areas, encrypting software is used on the computer, locks are on doors and cabinets, and storage sites are away from the primary work area. These are all ways of protecting information.

- Eliminate "the paper trail." We don't care if they are "just newspaper articles, magazines and old reports." If they can be found all in one location (such as the trash basket), they can give your opposition an indication of what interests you, and how much you know about that subject. Consider options such as shredding everything and then dispersing it into the trash in separate lots. Erase computer disks. Do not "delete" records, reports or files. "Delete" only lets you rewrite over the previously used portion of the disk you no longer need. It does not get rid of the information and it can be recovered in its entirety with very little effort.

INTELLIGENCE OPERATIONS TRADITIONALLY

Intelligence operations traditionally have been as diverse and as creative as the men and women involved in them (a subject far too lengthy to cover here). However, one of the most basic has been the circle of influence or "who do you know?" method of operation drawing from colleagues, friends, business associates, intra-professionals, snitches, operatives, law enforcement contacts, "strategically positioned' individuals and so on. Information was given, shared, purchased, traded, or part of a reciprocity relationship. Those involved invested a great deal of blood, sweat, tears and time in their efforts—and many, many contacts had to be generated and maintained.

INTELLIGENCE OPERATIONS TODAY

One still maintains his own circle of influence (always a critical part of your Intelligence Gathering efforts). With the addition of growing technologies, coupled with the resultant "international access," it has become less difficult in some areas to run an Intelligence Operation. Beginning with the principles covered in this chapter, add access to publications from all over the globe, international researchers just waiting to be asked questions, government sponsored publications (by many governments) on almost any topic, maps, broadcasts and archives from all over the world full of information on every subject discussed for decades. You personally can buy spy satellite photos and listen to the news broadcasts from around the world. You can watch the missiles hit Baghdad, the Berlin Wall come down and the tanks roll into Red Square—and videotape for analysis in your own living room. Today, a good deal more information can be obtained not based just on the blood and sweat of relationships or the politics of the moment, but rather because there are now *endless avenues* of information. One just needs to know where and how to locate all those additional avenues.

THE INFORMATION AGE AND INTELLIGENCE GATHERING

As we referenced previously, the image conjured up by most executives when you begin talking about Intelligence Gathering must be one of deep cover operatives and "illegals." Very often these people are afraid of what we might learn about them (what we may already know) and are afraid of what covert mischief we might do while working in their behalf—and get caught later. (Shades of Watergate!) It does take some measure of educating the client if it is a first time venture for him into Executive Protection and Intelligence Gathering Operations.

This is an "information age." There are books available filled with lists of people to contact around the world. There are C.D. ROM disks for sale which include *millions* of names, addresses, telephone numbers and "information bits." There are satellite photos for sale, (including photos from Russia) which cover the globe many times each day. There are bulletin boards with information services on them which instantly connect you with people, agencies and companies around the world. There are newspapers, wire services and magazines archived into the billions of articles. There are cross reference indexes, reverse directories, SEC filings, business licenses, foreign corporation filings, credit checks, court records—all providing information. The airwaves are full of news stations from radio and television. There are short wave and long wave radio bands as well. Cordless telephones, cellular phones and speaker phones are broadcasting secrets at us as we go by block after block. There are Police scanners, C.D. radios and Ham radios adding to the information exchange—plus military, government and other such secretive traffic we normally don't have access to. We routinely amble right through the middle of it all (this age of information) as it is broadcast, transmitted, trucked and hand carried from one point to another. For any person to say that they have to rely on covert operations to gather information that would support an Intelligence Operation is to have completely forgotten to turn the calendar pages for quite a few years!

"Finding" information is only part of an Intelligence Operation, and probably the easiest part. In this age of Information we are literally drowning in the stuff. How to find it, where to find it, how to screen it, filter it, analyze it, understand it, see through it, see where each piece fits one with the other, cross-match it, project it to its natural conclusions and how to develop reasonable countermeasures based on your findings—*that's* what an Intelligence Specialist does! "Dial-a-warning" services may get your attention, *but now what do you do?*

A knowledgeable Intel Specialist can take information, (piles of it), and drag the valuable items out of it piece by piece until all the garbage is gone and nothing remains but the useful. The Intel person doesn't gather information for the sake of gathering it, but to find that information which is useful. To make it useful, it has to be relevant, it has to be accurate, it has to be delivered in a timely fashion and it has to have meaning to the recipient. If you generate great information, but present it buried in such a way that the reader has to make a part-time job out of deciphering it, then the information is not useful. "Where the rubber meets the road" is where the value is to be found.

Conclusion—*It is more than possible to run a highly proficient Intelligence Gathering Operation* drawing from resources available openly and from other professional contacts. In fact, you most likely cannot keep up with the deluge of available information on any given subject. (How and where to locate it, how to sift through it, how to analyze it, and how to put the whole thing together and what to do with the finished product—*that* is part of the art of being a professional Intelligence Specialist!)

What you do and how you do it will reflect on "the boss." Labor Relations violations, invasion of privacy, "spying" and industrial espionage charges can sometimes be no more than a half step away. Keep it clean! (As a point of clarification, we do not discount the use of Undercover Operations, Covert Operations, Pretext Investigations, Counterintelligence, Countersurveillance or any other legal means of gaining enough information to neutralize the efforts of the opposition. It simply has to be justified according to the *threat level against the Principal.)*

SOME DEFINITIONS OF INFORMATION TYPES

• *True.* (Documented, corroborated). This may include photographs or video of the event in question, independent verification aside from the initial source, or some other measure of qualifying the source supplying the information.

• *False.* (Disinformation or Misinformation) Disinformation includes such things as releases of information "intentionally" giving the wrong impression or information; information contrary to the facts of the matter. Misinformation incudes such things as releases of information "unintentionally" incorrect.

• *Available or known thru publicly available sources.* (Open Source Information) This includes releases via Newspapers, wire services, magazines, trade journals, TV interviews, radio reports, etc., which require little or no "insider" contacts.

• *Given.* Information freely given or unsolicited, with no expectations or promises of compensation. Also—Information supplied willingly for compensation or for some other motivation.

• *Taken.* Information obtained by interrogation or coercion.

• *Uncheckable.* This would include Governmental "Releases" from a closed society, single source reports of an event not yet having taken place, confidential sources which would be compromised by any checking process, etc.

• *Raw.* Information such as maps, facts without conclusion, data or statistical information only, etc.

• *Tainted.* Information given, obtained or presented in such a way as to compromise or discredit the entire report if used.

SOME DEFINITIONS OF SOURCE TYPES

• *Self-serving.* This would be from someone planning to gain by their actions. This would include motives such as revenge, profit, seeking protection, eliminating competition, etc.

- *Reliable.* A source known to be accurate by virtue of past history of information given, access to information of the type given, able to support statement with alternate sources.
- *Unreliable.* Deemed such by lack of history for supplying information, not known to have access to the type of information presented, not known what motives are for presenting information, person with known motives which might "taint" information and so on.
- *Public Access Information.* This is the Open Source type information that can be obtained through normal public channels with little or no "insider" ability.
- *"Official".*

   1) Statements released by an entity for one purpose or another. Any information given this way is suspect, for it is designed to give one specific impression. If the statement is supported by documentation that can be confirmed independently, the statement is less suspect.

   2) Credible information released personally by a known official source within an agency or company, the information not being part of an official release of information to the public.
- *"Unofficial"* connections. Persons within an agency or organization not connected to the information release procedure who advise on a subject or event.
- *Other.* Includes Under Cover Operatives, "snitches", etc.

WHEN IS A FACT NOT NECESSARILY THE TRUTH? WHEN IT IS A STATISTIC.

Part of the "art" of Intelligence Gathering is having the ability to look at something with a "different set of eyes." Not accepting information at face value, but instead turning it upside down and inside out until the reality is exposed—*that* is doing a righteous job!

We are going to attempt to teach the novice what the "old pros" have known for years, namely that: *"Statistics generally do not answer questions for us, they only give us more questions."*

Part of our firm's Risk Analysis is finding the truth in the facts and statistics which are provided to us at the beginning of any Risk and Threat Analysis project. For example, a major Corporation recently hired us to determine their overall Risk Level. Part of what disturbed the department that hired us was the fact that security manpower had not only been reduced by about 90%, but the security department was attempting to tell the rest of the Corporation that there was a "dramatic decrease" in the number of thefts reported throughout the company (of about 90%—corroborated by charts, graphs and statistics no less)! The reported "decline" in the number of thefts was being offered as "proof" that the security department really didn't need the previous personnel. This really bothered our client because it just didn't "logic out," but yet it had come from "professionals" complete with all the charts and graphs. There really were only three answers to be arrived at by our analysis of the Security Department reporting:

1) That the security people were the thieves—and the problems were reduced by reducing the department,
2) that the program overall was working "miraculously" or
3) that the reporting procedure and conclusions were invalid.

Our Analysis brought to the attention of the Corporation that:

1) They could not possibly get an accurate accounting of how much they were losing, because they did not keep close track of Capital Assets released into the company.
2) Internal auditing consistently could *not account* for the whereabouts of at least 50% of the assets in question at any given time.
3) Both employees and managers were so tired of trying to find someone to report thefts to—they no longer even bothered, and with such a staggering reduction in security, there was no one to do anything about it anyway.
4) The measures for documenting property movement within the company (designed to reduce the number of personnel involved with massive amounts of paperwork)—actually *defeated* any chance for an accurate property movement control system.
5) The *reported* number of thefts or missing property was not an appropriate corporate "yardstick" due to the fact that (obviously) *not all thefts were being reported.*

We were able to give this Corporation a much clearer picture of their losses and needs for accountability in statistical reporting. The company was confirmed definitely "at Risk" from internal thefts, and the methods in place for controlling this activity were deemed wholly inadequate. So much for *statistics!*

Regarding Executive Protection and statistics, we see that Workplace Violence listed as the #1 cause of death for women, and the #2 cause of death for men relevant to fatal occupational incidents—overall the second leading cause of death. Applying this to Executives however, we need to go further and determine what an "executive" is by definition, how many are listed as having been killed "on the job" and were they the intended victim or "collateral damage?" Taking it further, the overall leading cause of death related to occupation appears to be Transportation. How many executives are killed and injured each year as a result of driving themselves as opposed to having the right kind of vehicle and a professionally trained driver?

Suppose we give you the statistic that "approximately 85% of all kidnappings are not reported" and nothing more. Telling executives or public figures then, that there is a need for them to be more prepared for this potential, requires additional efforts to generate the agreement that this statistic is either correct or not. If the statistic is true (which is impossible to determine if they are unreported) it is still useless. What is useful is a breakdown of categories indicating *who* is most likely to be targeted, *why* they may be targeted, *by whom* they are likely to be targeted, and for what *purpose* they are likely to be targeted.

Suppose then, we only give you the statistic that "approximately 50% of all assassination attempts are successful." This, if correct, (and there is no way to prove how many "undetected" attempts occurred) does not provide the "break down" of additional, important information. We would like to also know (just to begin with):

1) the number of assassinations where the victim was completely without protection
2) if the victim had protection that was defeated
3) if the victim had protection and the assassination actually came from one of the protectors

To rightfully use the "assassinations" statistics, one would have to divide out the executives, political figures, "celebrities," military and police entities, gang figures and so on. Then one would have to determine which were actually "murdered" and which were "assassinated." The statistic as it stands by itself is not sufficient.

We could continue with this type of analysis, but you get the point. We aren't arguing about the statistics, or making comment on those people who have provided them—we *need* the numbers. If you are being given statistics, if you are using statistics or if you are generating statistics, please bear in mind that the title for this section says it all. The Intelligence Operation can be tasked with looking into the statistical process, the statistical information given, the statistical information not given, and be a valuable asset in determining the legitimacy of the statistical reporting—which has direct bearing on the Risks and Threat Levels of the Executive Protection program.

TRAPS!

Getting caught up in "new speak" is a trap. Accepting the labels people put on themselves or events is a trap and is intended to slant the truth away from what the deeds actually tell you. The "Shining Path" organization in Peru, for example, is not a rosy cheeked, idealistically wholesome group of boys and girls. This is a Maoist philosophy based organization, not even a political force trying to obtain anything legitimate for a segment of the population other than themselves. The words say one thing, but the deeds tell another story. To believe them to be revolutionaries, separatists or anything other than anarchist-criminals is to do them justice undeserved. "New speak" softens the impact of the deed in many cases, while amplifying the impact in other events. Read the newspaper with this in mind. You'll begin to see what we mean.

"Political Correctness" is a sensitive issue for yuppies and politicians having public experiences, not for intelligence work. Strip away all the vocabulary of the day, because in a short while this "talk" will be out of vogue and your report won't be worth a damn. In fact, it will look stupid if anyone ever goes back to it. "Vertically Impaired" will never permanently replace "short". Trust us on this one.

"Legalese" is another trap which can dilute an intelligence report to the point where it contains nothing useful (or at least give that impression). Yes, it is correct to not refer to someone as a murderer, child molester or terrorist until such time as it has been proven. At the same time, if your report is couched in so many "alleged" and "alleged to have" that they look like beads on a string, you had better take another look at what you are doing. If your reporting reads like, "It is reported that the alleged suspects may have possibly done it, but it is unproven—and I might point out that they haven't been convicted, and all of the evidence is circumstantial"—you haven't written much of a report and you aren't helping anyone. You are just doing a job—and not a very good one at that. Dig deeper. The event either happened or it didn't. Say it! (Or at least don't say all that other stuff!)

"Withholding" information is also a dangerous practice. If someone or some group you admire and think the world of has their hands dirty in some way, you put it in the report if it is relevant! Period. It isn't your right to determine which truths the Principal or the Protective Detail should know, they should know them all. Be fair and unbiased to a fault. That's your job.

"Cop Talk" is right for the person who finds himself or herself in public service. An officer who arrives at an incident is no one's friend and no one's enemy. He reports the facts (oftentimes in the third person to further remove himself) and when solicited for an opinion the officer replies, "It isn't up to me, it's up to the courts to decide." In "the business" you discover the truth based on facts and findings, you make your findings as clear as you possibly can, and you report them that way. "Mutual Combat between two parties" is not the appropriate description for the Irish Republican Army sniper ambush of a Royal Ulster Constabulary patrol who returned fire.

"Damage Control" is a language and methodology used to minimize the impact that an investigation or findings might have regarding an event or in response to an investigation into a situation or circumstances. Listening to it, and taking the information at face value, is to invite trouble. It is "cousin" to propaganda.

"Spin Talk" is the dubious art of (usually political but not limited to) *explaining to you* what your own eyes and ears just saw and heard. The "spinner" is the intermediary between the possible fumbling or ineptitude of the speaker which may have prevented you from "understanding" (or catching on to) what was so carefully and eloquently choreographed. The spinner "interprets" for you and attempts to tell you what you "should" have heard—regardless of how inane the speaker was, and attempts to redirect the foolishness away from the speaker—to you. The artful spinner also attempts to redirect whatever emotions or conclusions you draw, to make you feel the desired emotions, and conclude the desired conclusions. If you conclude that the speaker is an idiot and two and two *are* four, the artful spinners groan at your stupidity, nudge you into embarrassment, and explains the correct responses—whatever "they" decide the correct responses should be. This "explaining" is tedious, but can be quite effective. This isn't propaganda per se, it is propagandizing the rhetoric or insanity just given.

SOME "PITFALLS" OF INTELLIGENCE GATHERING

• The misconception that all Intelligence is some sort of "spook" operation that deals in the nighttime environments can sometimes be a challenge. The West considers itself an "open society" and sees itself playing by a more gamesmanship set of rules and generally believes that it isn't "American" to spy on other people (or at least to admit it). This silliness is capitalized on by the *real* game players.

• Corporate Legal Departments are filled with people who went to college to learn how to "just say No" in a multitude of different ways. They will see this as a problem operation, although they too could benefit from a well run operation. They are a potential stumbling block.

• Lest the "shoemaker's children go barefoot," internal Intelligence is called for if for no other reason than to determine your "friendly" adversaries. Those adversaries may be bureaucracies or individuals within the organization you are serving, and may be motivated by jealousy, corporate politics, empire building, or credit taking. They just might be amateurs who think they can do a better job and want your position because it sounds like more "fun" than they are having. Each of these can trip you up at any time, so be careful.

• Misuse or leaks of information are of concern to everyone. If information isn't well protected, there can be serious complications should that information be compromised. In the early 1970's, Portland Oregon experienced a loss of some information from the Police Department Intelligence Unit. Added to this, the Leftists ran surveillance on the Police, determined which cars were "unmarked" Detective cars, and published all the information. In Scotland during 1992, some bad guys broke into the Police station and stole all the records detailing terrorist and counterterrorist activity. Adding to their embarrassment, the Police had to hire Security Guards to protect the Police building against further unlawful entry when the EC (European Community) met in Scotland in early 1993.

• Questionable gathering practices such as Break and Enter, Taps, "Dumpster Diving" or Coercion can lead to the compromise not only of the operation, but of the company or the Principal. Sometimes "going all out" on behalf of the Principal is needed; most of the time it is not.

• "Tainted" information in one document diminishes all the work done previously and all the work for some time to follow. If the work has been altered to give a different impression without qualifying or noting the change(s), no benefit will come of it.

• Databases may be used in the discovery phase of litigation if it becomes known to exist and sources can be compromised. The "plus" side to this is if you are using "open source" information, you will have little difficulty or problems.

• The Users don't always know what they want in terms they can express. You have to figure it out and be on target. Remember that the Principal probably isn't speaking the same technical "language" as you are. (Example: To the Principal, a "shooter" is something you find in a bar—in our business it is one who fires weapons.)

BIASED PERSPECTIVES

Talk about a balancing act! On one hand an Intelligence Operative has to evaluate information and come up with conclusions and prognostications, and on the other hand keep personal likes and dislikes out of the picture.

If you are personally for or against anything, it had better not show up in your Intelligence Reports. Objectivity is the name of game, and no report can afford to be "tainted." You *may* sort out the propaganda as it is being disseminated by the media or the bad guys, you *may* make note of the outright fabrications in any information coming in, and you most certainly *may* qualify the "veracity" of any contributing information or parties of the report. Your job is to peel back layers of all kinds of information until you ultimately get to the truth, but always remember that you are tasked with providing factual information, not personal beliefs. (A favorite example of biased observations is attributed to an American Indian Chief, who supposedly asked a reporter, "Why is it when your people win it is a great military victory, but when we win it's a bloody massacre?")

Don't sensationalize your own reports. If "it sells newspapers" is your justification for sensationalizing an incident to the point where it may invoke fear or reactions in others, your "novelistic" talents are being wasted, real lives are being put in jeopardy, resources are being wasted, and business decisions will be made on *bad information.*

Moses and Company is a great example of good Intelligence, good stats—and wrong analysis based on biased reporting. By all accounts, after a lengthy time in the wilderness nearly 1,000,000 Jews arrived at the outskirts of Canaan—what was to be their "promised land." Twelve men, each a Prince, were sent into the land by Moses for recon and intelligence gathering under orders from God. When they came back, all twelve had the same Intelligence Information because they all had observed exactly the same things. But from there, they split into two separate analysis, conclusions and recommendations—(a.k.a. "Risk and Threat Analysis"). The majority report was presented by ten men who were so terrified for their own safety, they "tainted" or biased their report. From their personal perspectives of fear and terror, they reported it would be disastrous to go in because there were "giants" in the land (who got bigger and bigger as the report was passed on) and they wouldn't stand a chance. The minority Intel Report (two) said the place could be taken. Yes, there were giants in the land, but they (the Jews) had all the assets on hand to do the job, including instructions and "fire cover" from God Himself. The land was worth taking and therefore they should get on with it. The biased Risk and Threat minority Intel report spread panic like wildfire and they made a hasty retreat back into the desert. Point? If the principal listens to those who don't understand they must give a *complete, unbiased, truthful* Intelligence Analysis—he loses. The rest, as they say, is history and one million Jews wasted the next forty years wandering in circles before they regrouped at the *same* spot, adopted the minority Intel report, and finally took the land.[13]

Conclusion—"*The whole truth and nothin' but the truth,*" no matter what you think of your personal opinion. If your opinion is worth something, and it isn't appropriate that you share it with others in the Intelligence Reports, please write your own book and say whatever it is you feel the world should know. You may very well be right! In any case, keep it out of the Reports!

---

[13] *Holy Bible,* New Scofield Revised Edition—*Numbers 13:1&2.*

ADDRESSING THE CORPORATE
INTELLIGENCE GATHERING OPERATION

My first "take" on this subject is that *an Intelligence Operation within a corporation is NOT a security department function.* Yes, Intel does involve factors of security, investigations, the Executive Protection Detail (I wouldn't put that in the Security department either by the way!) and other contacts with Corporate Security. Nevertheless, an Intelligence staff should fall under the auspices of the Risk Management group, the Office of the President, the Executive support staff or similar Administrative department. What's more, Intel should be as far removed from the political arena of the corporation as possible, so that Intel is not hampered by inter-departmental in-fighting.

At the risk of offending some of you, Security Managers and Directors all too often want to be "involved" with things like Intel because it looks important and "fun." They get a real hankering to know what is going on from the inside track. Nevertheless, they should never be involved or making decisions which they are not qualified to make (by virtue of their lack of knowledge), but may be permitted to do (by virtue of the positions they hold). Intel and Security are related, not one and the same.

A person or group who only "plugs in" to an electronic bulletin board on demand and passes on "travel advisories" is not an Intelligence Staff. A person or group subscribing to monthly security periodicals or trade journals is not an Intelligence Staff. At best, someone is performing a clerical function—and the clerk doesn't even know how to recognize a travel advisory unless the bulletin board calls it that. *Not following and understanding the information* which causes there to be an "Advisory" in the first place, is dangerous business. Unless you can provide the full picture to the person requesting the information, he or she is probably going to get into serious trouble. (This is like Noah saying "It's going to rain." Not understanding rain, and even getting his information from an "unimpeachable source," *Noah had absolutely no idea* how hard it was going to rain when it finally did!)

You may not be able to justify a Corporate Intelligence staff based on the Protection of executives alone. (Of course, lose just one executive and see just how valuable an Intelligence staff suddenly becomes—and what price all the "decision makers" would <u>now</u> have gladly paid "<u>then!</u>") Corporate groups such as travel or event facilitators, risk managers, legal, insurance departments, corporate security, environmental health and safety, crisis management and business recovery planning—as well as the Executive Protection personnel—are but a few of the corporate people who could benefit from a well thought out Intelligence Gathering Operation. Providing the corporation with a unit whose task is coordinating information gathering efforts reduces the possibility for someone in the corporation "not knowing" information of importance when it was available all along. They just need to know who to ask. This is one entity which can assist in breaking down the traditional "walls" between various corporate departments without inhibiting their ability to function effectively as separate departments. Projects such as **Risk Analysis** and **Threat Assessment** can benefit by having someone look at the Global Picture through the eyes of an

Intelligence Operation, rather than the person who views it from their own particular focused point of view (how it effects their own individual department).

Benefits? Suppose you are running an Intelligence operation. Your routine efforts may have alerted you to the increases in such matters as Industrial Espionage by foreign nationals who are working in conjunction with their national Intelligence agencies. This information affects your client. (By the way, an estimated 20 "friendly" nations are currently targeting American business technology and business secrets by covert or any other means available.) Discovering this, measures could then be put in place to identify and minimize risks, and countermeasures can be instituted. ("'For every American company's success, there are many more failures. American companies, more or less across the board, are three to five years behind their counterparts in Europe and Asia when it comes to business or competitor intelligence' says Herb Meyer, formerly of the National Intelligence Council. According to Michael C. Sekora, who once headed the Defense Intelligence Agency's Project Socrates, the real problem is attitude: American companies don't realize the United States is in an 'economic war' with foreign competitors. Meyer more or less agrees. 'American companies can be alarmingly naive about what foreign competitors may be willing to resort to,' he says.'"[14]) And this is only one of the possible benefits, one of the possible discoveries! Not losing is winning! *You now have an Intelligence Operation which just paid for itself.*

When a firm like ours goes into a company to provide an Intelligence Analysis, we look at all facets of the company and find where the Risks are by reviewing areas such as executive protection, information gathering efforts (protective, security and competitor intelligence), manufacturing, facility protection, property movement, insurance coverages, transportation, personnel safety and security in the workplace, physical security, information security, public documents about the corporation, communications, employee termination procedures, joint venture projects with foreign companies, crisis management, business recovery planning, emergency services available in the immediate area (including hostage negotiators, SWAT teams, explosives technicians, rescue personnel), access by "hostile" information gathering entities and so on. In other words, we develop a "baseline" of Risk Levels as they measure up with the rest of that industry *and* against events or trends locally and world wide. We then make a determination as to what the protective measures in place should be at any given time and develop the plans for escalation to higher levels of alert as circumstances change. We assist in identifying Threats, as opposed to Risks, plan for how the company will escalate along with the Threat and put the appropriate countermeasures in place. What was once a Risk Analysis project can also then be turned into a Tactical Assessment (planning as if to attack the entity as an aggressor would) once the information has been obtained. This is of enormous value to the client if they understand the concept. If you can gather all this information on the corporation, so can someone else—whose intentions are less likely to be "benevolent" to the client.

The above analysis could and should be performed from within the com-

---

14 *Friendly Spies* by Peter Schweizer—1993—page 260.

pany, but seldom is. What generally happens when an analysis begins from "in house" goes something like this: for openers, Company politics have a way of making people "uncooperative." Personnel within the corporation don't like other departments looking over their shoulders, and individual departmental efforts generally only focus on what is relevant to that particular department. When done internally, "personalities" get in the way and there seems to be great difficulty in simply addressing the issues. No one wants to "look bad" (even at the expense of not fixing what is so obviously wrong). This would ideally be where an internal Intelligence Operation, supported at the highest levels of the corporation, can step out of the executive protection role and be of considerable value to the whole corporation—especially if it is an objective, neutral operation with no political axe to grind. It is also a good way of determining what is going on "in your own backyard" which may turn out to be problems for the executive(s) under protection.

Another point relevant to the subject of Corporations (and a sad situation) is the exceptional crisis going on in the United States today regarding the ineptitude of "middle management." This ineptitude compromises executive levels by the endless pouring out of bad advice and counsel. If there is a corporate "choke point," that is it. I doubt that at any other point in recorded history there has been the percentage of incompetent managers as exits today. If at all possible, deal from either above or below management as often as you possible can. If you are fortunate enough to find a really competent manager to deal with, give him or her all the support you can; these people are probably fighting for their corporate lives! You can better accomplish your important tasks if advice falls on the ears of those more willing and waiting to be counseled, rather than someone who will become a stumbling block to others because he doesn't want to look bad.

An Internal Intelligence Operation gives some measure of independence and self-sufficiency, since the reliance on others for information is greatly reduced. One is given the ability to then cross-check and network with others of the same type to determine the authenticity of information obtained on an activity, person, group or event. By developing knowledge on what information the opposition has the ability to obtain, the Intelligence Operation can also engage in preemptive actions as needed or even guide "disinformation" projects of their own to protect the Principal.

Why have an Intelligence staff? Intelligence isn't something suited for everyone (pun intended). More times than you would like, you will find yourself in front of some "decision maker" in the security profession who can't even understand the questions, much less the answers! (How they got there I have no idea.) To convince these people that such an operation is worthy of consideration is enough to prove that the pay just isn't good enough for what you do. But back to why even consider having an Intelligence Operations staff.

Any Protection Team with no knowledge of what to expect, no knowledge of what's going on at the next destination, no knowledge of which risks have escalated into threats, no information on the opposition's players and how they operate. . . . will be turned into a bodyguard detail who's chances of survival in an armed confrontation are little better than 10%. The first desire of any Executive Protection Team is the *AVOIDANCE* of an encounter with hostile persons, not dealing with a confrontation. Avoidance happens based on Intelligence information, not *clairvoyance.*

A Corporate Crisis Management Team is helpless without the Intelligence information (regardless of the source) letting them know what damages have been done, what resources are available to them or what they might expect next from the opposition if it was a man-made crisis such as the World Trade Center. (Most Intelligence and Protection Operations aware of Islamic extremists worldwide weren't surprised by the World Trade Center incident per se, only that it wasn't done sooner.)

A Risk Management group *without anyone developing information on topics that will affect the management of risks,* can only hope for the best, and exercise the dubious option of over-insuring. Hardly a "plan." This is not cost effective, reduces profits and leaves the insured (people or assets) still very much "at risk" from all the known and unknown dangers. This type of "insurance protection" only plans for a course of action at the time of "worst case scenario"—*paying off for the loss* of people and/or assets. Regardless of the premium amounts involved, I doubt that the insurance companies consider "paying off" as one of their favorite activities when it would have been so easy to minimize the risks in the first place by just knowing they existed. *Intelligence Specialists and Intelligence Operations are the foundation for Risk and Threat Analysis—and without these activities, no effective protective, preventive or proactive program can evolve or be implemented.*

Corporate Security departments, without benefit of Intelligence activity to tell them that a particular crime trend or threat is taking shape, can only react to events as they happen. Simply *Reacting* demonstrates that whatever protection measures were in place (if any)—were inadequate. It also shows that they had no viable plan to begin with.

The point then, is that all Corporate entities must depend on information if they are going to plan. It never ceases to amaze me that corporations (or public figures) will devote resources to market research (intelligence), competitor research (intelligence—call it what you like) and then somehow think that Intelligence Gathering should not be part of the Security or Protective Services network—or that this type of information just somehow shows up at the right time. Talk about stopping short of the finish line! We, as Intelligence Specialists, develop that critical information from a multitude of sources and then present it as it is called for. Information is Strength and it is Protection. Information allows you to identify risks and minimize the potential of their ever being realized. Information allows for recognizing threats and then placing a "value" on the threat so that the proper safeguards might be put in place.

Too many times we see really good Security Practitioners from the various disciplines stymied in their attempts to do an honest, professional job. Corporate Administrators (including Security Managers or Directors) attempt to make decisions regarding Intelligence Operations and Executive Protection

Programs—based in total ignorance, deficiencies and/or what appears to be deliberate attempts to scuttle the program even at the expense of executives who should be receiving the protection. When you see resistance to these type programs, and it is abnormal resistance, look for hidden agendas. At the very least try to find out the real meaning of the message being sent.

AMERICAN BUSINESSES NEED TO FACE SOME HARD FACTS

"Keeping up with the competition" is nothing new in the corporate world and no one gives competition a second thought. It's what you do. There is an element, however, who's purpose it is to out-do, steal, injure, embarrass and outright destroy people, property, ideas, reputations, facilities, images and symbols—and episodes of this nature are on the rise daily. We're no longer in an age of unruly neighborhood kids with pea shooters aimed at first floor windows. It's the angry revenge types, the local political axe to grind group, the local "we want ours" types or the international politically or "heavenly inspired" terrorists who are catching the unwary "what's the risk?" types off-guard. American businesses have been too busy cutting deals to realize who else has everything lined up to cut their throats. Intelligence Specialists and Intelligence Operations go out looking for information to find those things out . . . . that's their profession.

The principal, the celebrity, or the corporation who doesn't know where his own vulnerabilities lie, where he's wide open to potential or real danger, or who may be "out there" planning to kidnap, injure or kill him or those close to him—is potential trouble looking for a place to happen. Without good Intelligence Operations, the principal won't know if someone else with whom he associates is under a very real, very dangerous threat—(which may well remove him from that association—*permanently*). Furthermore, without good Intel, the principal may simply be "in the wrong place at the wrong time" and pay dearly for this oversight because he didn't turn his Intelligence people loose to get the lay of the land. (I wonder how many people are in the general social or business areas of others who know at this moment they are being "stalked" or "targeted?" Do these targeted individuals *warn* everyone with whom they associate that they too could be in the line of fire?)

WHEN THE CORPORATE EXECS
BECOME THEIR OWN WORST ENEMY

A most important point to remember here is that *the most useful weapon at the disposal of the terrorist/criminal is the naïveté of their targets.* These people can hardly believe what happens to them *even while* it's happening! This is due in part to the "Who would want to hurt me?" attitude which assumes that everything must happen on a basis personal to them. This syndrome is beautifully capitalized on by those who *do* want to hurt them. It also happens to compliment the carefully orchestrated defense tactics of "the bad guys" (and/or their associates) as observed on the T.V. news so often, seen chuckling and denying that such "imaginary" enemies could exist—or looking pitiful and unimposing—or adamantly denying such a thing and swearing oaths to God in their denials. People have the tendency to believe it is "the other guy" to whom disastrous things happen, and this disarming Public Relations tactic the bad guys so often use in the media helps to cultivate disbelief in the existence of such malefactors. This tactic has been in use for years by organized crime, gang members, terrorists, political enemies, corporate schemers, national predators and other similarly disposed individuals and groups.

Another point. Mr. C.E.O. (the one who doesn't want Intel Specialists or Executive Protection Specialists or even Security looking over his shoulder knowing his private business)—advertises his travel plans, endorses his favorite restaurants and haunts, shows off his blue ribbons at the shows where he enters the competition each year, smiles for the camera on the front page of business magazines, makes his address and other personal information a matter of open, public record, takes the same route and parks in the same place at work and at home every day—and blushes modestly for photos in every brag book he's "fortunate" enough to be featured in. (This guy ought to blush!) And in some cases, this fellow feels duty bound to fill some of those books from cover to cover with all sorts of confessed misdeeds, reasons for doing them, associates involved, strategies, and more! (Just the sort of things needed for learning about personal weaknesses!) Mr. C.E.O. has provided every conceivable ounce of information needed to set himself up as a target, a victim, a hostage, a ransom payer and a bargaining tool. And in the process, he's endangered his family, his associates, his Corporation and all kinds of other innocent people around him. But he got his way; he kept his privacy . . . . right??

The scenario above, multiplied by the number of C.E.O.'s within an industry can permeate and endanger corporate life like a bad rash. Weaknesses, peccadilloes, naïveté—coupled with lack of understanding about skilled, professional, honor bound, discrete council—spell disaster on the horizon.

THE WRONG BACK DOOR OUT—THE INSURANCE COMPANIES

The Insurance Industry is bearing the brunt of Corporate failure in the area of any professional or realistic "Executive Protection Plan" and hopefully they'll catch on soon. We did an Intelligence Analysis recently for a major corporation and in our report advised them of serious, gaping holes in their Executive Protection Program. Their Execs were prime targets, and nothing was in place to effectively protect them. That same Intelligence Profile showed their entire corporation in the same inadequate, unprepared position for handling criminal, political or natural disasters. "Do you want our recommendations about what to do about this?" we asked. "No, we're okay," the Security director answered, "we have a plan." And with that, he leaned over his desk, opened a drawer, and pulled out an envelope which he handed to us. In his hand was *an Insurance Policy!* An Insurance Policy was *not* the way to guard against disaster, crazies or criminals! An Insurance Policy was *not* going to shore up the holes in the Corporation's vulnerabilities! An Insurance Policy was *not* going to educate his C.E.O.'s about the facts of life! An Insurance Policy was *not* going to protect the lives and safety of his C.E.O.'s, their facilities, their property or their employees! This man was lining up like so many others in Corporate America who aren't taking care of business—to let the ***insur-***

ance companies pay for their mistakes! (We thought we were the only ones who had ever experienced such outrageous conduct and irresponsible attitude, until it came up in conversation between several consultants at a seminar, and we all marveled at such foolishness.)

The situation described above tells us many things, none of them good. In any case, it is a pitiful situation which leaves the insurance company to pick up the pieces when "IT" happens and all goes very wrong.

Corporation Conclusion—*When Things Go Bump In The Night.* The whole system of Corporate Intelligence and Corporate Protection is generally so full of holes that little by little—media, historians and biographers are going to have an absolute field day writing about it.

Personal Observations: "Threats" continue to change and more now than ever, both Executives and Celebrities are prime targets worldwide—regardless of where they're from, where they're staying, or where their next destination may be. The Executive or Celebrity either adjusts to the changes, or runs the risk of becoming a statistic of the times. Too many "decision makers" are ill-equipped for the job of determining the protection levels for the Principal, yet they do it anyway and base their findings on their own lack of understanding of risks, threats, trends, game plans, politics, history, cultural differences, circumstances and situations. They are either naïve, arrogant, ignorant or incompetent—and worse yet, many try to cover up with "need-to-know" secrecy. The only other options left are for the Principal to remain a potential tragedy in the making or step up to the responsibility personally. The executive or celebrity who makes Intelligence and Protection decisions for themselves is one thing—*if* the impact of wrong decisions only effects them. But they must take into consideration the repercussions their decisions will have on innocent family members, bystanders, insurers, stockholders and employees—all who will be victimized indirectly, or will have a direct part in paying the price for failure. There is a definite, provable need for finding skilled professionals capable of "reading the handwriting on the wall" and advising the decision makers of what it all means. In this "information age," there is no excuse for ignorance.

**Information is the key to knowledge, and
knowledge is the key to success.**

GLOSSARY

- OSCINT = Open Source Intelligence. Information which is publicly and legally accessible with little or no restrictions and which is obtained openly.
- HUMINT = Human Source Intelligence. Information obtained from an individual either openly or covertly.
- Competitor Intelligence = Using legitimate, available resources to determine what the competition is planning, doing or capable of enacting.
- Counterintelligence = Becoming aware of opposition intelligence efforts and taking measures to counteract those efforts.
- Countersurveillance = Running a surveillance operation to determine if surveillance is being conducted against your principal, your corpora-

tion, your operation—or conducting a surveillance against a known surveillance. (a.k.a. Looking over your shoulder)

- Disinformation = The intentional release of false or misleading information designed to give a specific impression or bring the recipient to false conclusions.
- Misinformation = The unintentional release of false or misleading information.
- Principal = The person or entity being protected.
- Concentric Circles = "Rings" or circles, drawn one outside the other. It is used here to note the "layers" (perimeter to inner circle) of protection afforded the client.
- End User = The person ultimately receiving or using the product. In this case, information.
- Economic Espionage = An activity against a corporation or national entity, generally conducted from the inside, in an attempt to gain access to business secrets and strategies—the purpose of which is
  (1) to influence key personnel in such a way as to promote failure of the entity or
  (2) to gain the necessary information to alter the competitive advantage in favor of the perpetrator(s).
- Industrial Espionage = An activity against a corporation, generally conducted from the inside, in an attempt to gain access to company secrets and confidential documents for the purpose of the theft of company knowledge, materials or assets. It can also be for the purpose of influencing key personnel in such a way as to promote failure within that corporation.
- Format = How a computer document or file is physically structured.
- Database = Information contained in a computerized document or file.
- Mole = A person placed or cultivated "deep" within an organization or agency, designed to conduct a normal daily routine life style until such a time as activated and "surfaces" to perform a specific task.
- Covert = A secret, hidden or disguised operation.
- Risk Analysis = A methodology which looks at both known and anticipated situations, conditions or circumstances to determine:
  (1) that all relevant conditions and circumstances are researched to determine potentials for risks;
  (2) that the risks are categorized and appropriate protective countermeasures are recommended; and
  (3) to put in place a system of periodic checks that will ensure that nothing has changed that would upset the balance between the circumstances as they have been identified and the protective measures in place to control the risks.
- Threat Assessment = A methodology whereby situations, circumstances or conditions are researched and evaluated, generally with a known cause for concern.
  (1) A threat is identified and the potential for escalation is measured.
  (2) The ability of the Threat to be carried out to its conclusion is determined.
  (3) The appropriate protective measures (or countermeasures) are put in place based on the findings.
- Assets = Something of value, such as:
  (1) People in positions to effect the positive outcome of a mission, i.e., "assets in-country" denotes people in a country available for the assignment and able to contribute to the mission's success.
  (2) Material items of a positive value.

Example:
Basic Travel Assignment
Flow Chart - Intel Ops

The Intelligence Operation takes the lead in developing all data relevant to the assignment, conducts a Risk Analysis and Threat Assessment, makes Recommendations and reports findings.

The Team Leader/Operations Leader is given the information with all support documents and determines which assets must be devoted to what portions of the assignment.

The proper personnel are brought into the assignment and each need is addressed—additional protection, transportation, insurances, personal staff, logistical support, P.R., legal and so on.

Intel Ops turns to a support role, watching for changes in data or circumstances previously reported.

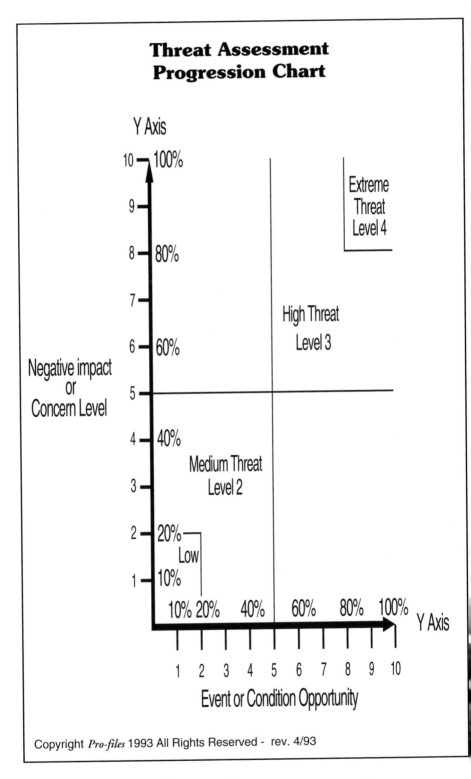

Threat Assessment Progression Chart

Y Axis

10 — 100%

9 —

8 — 80%

7 —

6 — 60%

5 —

4 — 40%

3 —

2 — 20%
Low
1 — 10%

Negative impact or Concern Level

Extreme Threat Level 4

High Threat Level 3

Medium Threat Level 2

10% 20%   40%   60%   80%   100%   Y Axis

1   2   3   4   5   6   7   8   9   10

Event or Condition Opportunity

Threat Assessment Progression Chart
NOTES

Negative Impact or Concern Level

1 = Report or Intelligence Received
2 = Confirmation Received
3 = Target Identified
4 = Impact Is Quantifiable
5 = Preplan/Contingency In Place
6 = Safeguards Deemed Inadequate
7 = Target Is Vulnerable
8 = Target Loss Beyond Acceptable Levels
9 = Measures Available Will Not Stop Action
10 = Technology, Revenue, Corp. Secret, Personnel Most Likely Will Be Lost

Event or Condition Opportunity

1 = Report or Intelligence Received
2 = Confirmation Received
3 = Is It Possible To Do?
4 = Is Activity Historically Successful?
5 = Perpetrators(s) Identified?
6 = Perpetrators Have The Ability For Job?
7 = Counter Efforts Confirm Activity?
8 = Is Law Enforcement Able To Intercede?
9 = Counter Efforts Have Failed to Halt Effort?
10 = Is Is Probable That This Event Will Happen?

Simply put, this chart allows for the progression of information to be evaluated as a Threat is recognized or reported. As you progress up the chart scale, each question answered in such a fashion as to not stop the continuance escalates the threat. When an answer is reached which stops progression, back off 1/2 step (to the point in between markings) and that is your "score" for this event. Both numbers are then added, divided by 2 and you have a final Threat Level indicator number.

This chart is given in "generic" form, and the conditions may be changed to suit your personal environment as you see fit. The principle here is that each step is an escalation—with the 50% level being the "turning point" when the odds are tipped in the favor of the perpetrators. The final entry (#10) is to be the ultimate circumstance indicating no more steps need to be taken by the perpetrators to accomplish their goal—the event will happen next given all the exiting circumstances and conditions.

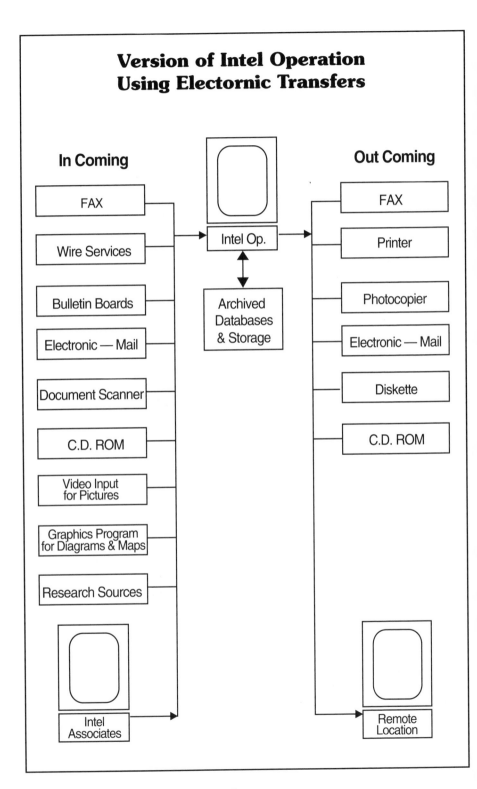

Version of Intel Operation Using Electornic Transfers

In Coming

FAX
Wire Services
Bulletin Boards
Electronic — Mail
Document Scanner
C.D. ROM
Video Input for Pictures
Graphics Program for Diagrams & Maps
Research Sources

Intel Associates

Intel Op.

Archived Databases & Storage

Out Coming

FAX
Printer
Photocopier
Electronic — Mail
Diskette
C.D. ROM

Remote Location

Example:
Intelligence Operation Coverage Of A Principal As It Relates To Executive Protection "Concentric Circle" Concept

Principal

Inner Circle
Immediate Information regarding the Principal, Risk and Threat Analysis on situations directly affecting him and his family, working with known factors. "Informational Counter-surveillance."

Middle Circle
Risk and Threat Analysis of the workplace, his home environment, analysis of the local area(s) he frequents and information analysis regarding known business and personal associates.

Outer Circle
Risk and Threat Analysis of travel destinations, events he plans to attend, world events relevant to him and/or the business environment he is associated with in particular. Working with Intel Ops. from "host" locations, field support for traveling E.P. Detail. Advance Team support.

As Concentric Circles are normally shown

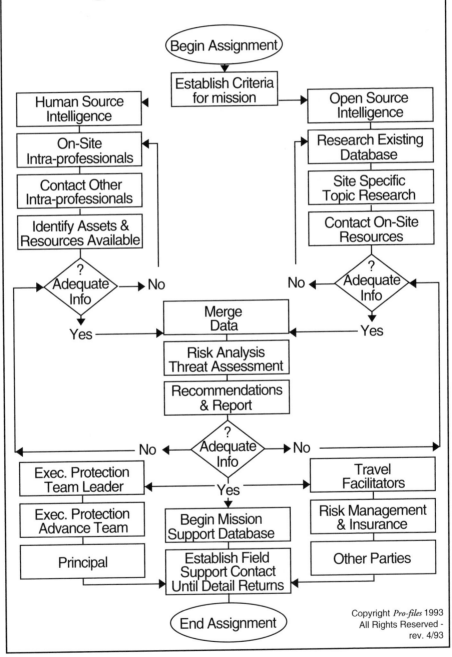

Example:
Advanced Corporate Or Travel Protection Assignment Flow Chart —Intel Ops.

Begin Assignment

Establish Criteria for mission

Human Source Intelligence

Open Source Intelligence

On-Site Intra-professionals

Research Existing Database

Contact Other Intra-professionals

Site Specific Topic Research

Identify Assets & Resources Available

Contact On-Site Resources

? Adequate Info — No

No — ? Adequate Info

Yes

Merge Data

Yes

Risk Analysis Threat Assessment

Recommendations & Report

? Adequate Info

No — ? Adequate Info — No

Exec. Protection Team Leader

Travel Facilitators

Yes

Exec. Protection Advance Team

Begin Mission Support Database

Risk Management & Insurance

Principal

Establish Field Support Contact Until Detail Returns

Other Parties

End Assignment

PART III

Protective Operations

THIRTEEN

Mission Moscow

by Bill Besse

AS RECENTLY AS TWO YEARS AGO the number of private security companies in Russia could be counted on one hand. The recent rapid expansion of this industry can be attributed in Moscow, St. Petersburg, and the heart of mother Russia, in cities formerly closed to visits by westerners and, indeed, many Russians, to two main factors. First, many officers from the overgrown former KGB, GRU, and Ministry of the Interior find themselves searching for opportunities to utilize what they know so well. Secondly, more than 3,000 organized criminal gangs, and countless street thugs, criminals, and con artists have established a strangle hold on many privatized commercial concerns and much of the budding entrepreneurship seen on the streets of Moscow. Contributing factors include a complete absence of property laws. There have been only attempts at banking or lending laws. In Russia, there is no law which covers kidnapping or extortion. The Russian Mafia has infiltrated the private security industry before the industry could organize itself. Corruption of governmental officials and the police runs unchecked and widespread. The problems identifying, communicating with, training, and maintaining reliable security services in the CIS are indeed a challenge. On the other hand, the opportunity is unprecedented and unlimited.

The basics of any service business, i.e., finding a need and providing a service that fills that need, are present and without question, are great. The Russian people, Russian business, and western business attempting to establish a foothold in these locales all need to feel safe. The Russian government, whatever that may be, has not proved itself capable of providing this necessity.

Thoughts of how successful my two weeks in the Russian Federation would be studying these issues, quickly vanished as my Luthansa flight out of

Frankfurt settled into its final approach to Sheremetyevo.

Registration and check-in at the Ukraine Hotel at 2/1 Kutuzovsky Prospekt became an experience in patience. The Ukraine sits on the Moskva River, not far from the Russian White House. It is one of the taller structures in Moscow topped with a "ruby star." Moscow covers an area of over 870 square kilometers with a population greater than New York, 2 1/2 times as big as London, and eight times the size of Paris. Late October brings a damp, gray cold to Red Square. As we watched the Red Square Guard march in precision goose steps, I lost myself in thoughts of fallen friends, far away places, and times influenced so heavily by the men behind the brown, brick Kremlin wall. A light snow falls and is highlighted by the lights from St. Basil's Cathedral, at the end of the square. How could this be so? How could I be standing here in the cold Russian night? The world is rapidly changing.

There is a tremendous effort in the Russian Federation to convert services once provided by the government to the private sector.

In 1992, there were nearly 120,000 crimes against business concerns, according to best estimates. There were 4500 cases of government corruption reported. The Russians seemed to have been paralyzed into non-action.

I listened as Yuri Vidochkin, President of the Baltic Bank stated, "The government should do everything possible to stimulate a free market economy." He also stated that there was a complete absence of free market ethics/morals; that a profit at all costs mentality had taken over. Due to 75 years of Communist ideology, the country has a very low moral standard rendering it ripe for crime and corruption. In addition, overbearing administrative practices had a great influence and interfered with market relations. Municipal services are poor. Telephone service is based on old technology and has broken down. The private sector must drive this turnaround. It was clear the government was hopelessly mired in a survival mode.

General Victor Budanov is straight out of Central Casting. The former KGB General, tall, well muscled, nearly bald, with a chiseled, serious face and dressed in a below-the-knee black leather coat, knows how to get things done in Moscow. Budanov is now President of the International Association Security of Business and Priority. He heads a country wide partnership of Russia entrepreneurs, who have entered into the private security business. Some of them include:

Commercial Security Agency
Novo
Centurion (Koskon)
Security (Joint-Stock)

Several training centers have been established. I visited one, 40 minutes outside of central Moscow. It was once a training center for the Soviet Foreign Intelligence Service. Located in Odintzova and run by Andrey Zimin. This Private Security Training Center Villa is staffed by former KGB personnel. Entry level, as well as supervisory, technical, and special issues training is provided to personnel sponsored by various security companies. Professional exchange with western private security experts is highly desired and needed. Western technical information regarding security devices/technology is desired and sorely needed. In meetings with members of a group calling itself Former Members of the Russian Foreign Intelligence Service, I learned that highly skilled investigators, interpreters, technicians, intelligence analysts and personal protection specialists from the former KGB 9th Directorate are available if one knows where to look. Vetting is possible and absolutely necessary. A number of Russian companies are attempting to establish data bases needed to conduct due diligence, and risk assessment. Taking on a Russian business partner requires a careful vetting process. You must know who it is you are dealing with. You could end up taking on one of the 3,000 Russian gangs mentioned earlier.

No one has to convince Russians about the wisdom of layering security into concentric rings. Moscow avenues radiate outwards like spokes of a wheel and are linked by a series of concentric rings.

The first ring is formed by the walls of the ancient Kremlin. The main Moscow squares and the remains of the Kitai-Gorod fortification are arranged around them. The next ring, in a bend of the Moskva River, is formed by the boulevards. The fortress wall fringing Bely Gorod followed this ring in the Middle Ages. The names of the squares Yauzskiye Gates, Pokrovskiye Gates, Petrovskiye Gates and Nikitskiye Gates, testify to ancient times when there really were gates flanked by watch towers in the city walls. The suburbs and fringe settlements of Bely Gorod were ringed with moat and an earth rampart where the wide Garden Ring (Sadovoye Koltso) now runs.

Ancient times are recalled by the names, Crimean Rampart (Krymsky Val), Earth Rampart (Zemlyanoi Val), Rampart Street (Valovaya Ulitsa). Roads branched out in all directions from the Kremlin to Tber, Novgorod, Smolensk, Kaluga, Serpukhov. Next comes the steel ring of the Circle Railway, the city's outer boundary in 1917, linking up many railway lines running from the capital.

The giant ring-radial pattern is completed by the ring of the Moscow Motorway.

Providing a protecting envelope around corporate assets with physical, information, and personnel security techniques widely utilized in the west can be achieved in the Federation. However, quality service issues, employee relations issues, and public relations issues must be addressed in depth and in detail if a Russian security company is utilized. These terms are non-existent in the Federation. Technical expertise is present; they know security. Blending the security into the corporate environment or life-style of a protectee is a problem.

The General Manager of our Russian subsidiary is a bright, independent, highly active American female, a challenge indeed for any protective detail. She jogs, she loves to travel, enjoys nightlife and believes she should drive her new red Volvo, anytime, anywhere. Our Russian contract protective detail could not or would not relate to her pace. They could not solve these issues. Their response to her active, long work week and active weekends was to suggest she change to accommodate their inflexible, narrow methods. She requested that they loosen the coverage; she bumped into them every time she moved. She went out to dinner with friends, they insisted on sitting at the same table. When she objected, they informed her that she should stay out of their business, they knew what was best. No amount of counseling on my part could convince these guys that they should learn to blend the security to fit the situation. This is an area that is in need of improvement. We now have our own employees training to perform these critical functions.

The contractor's agents are probably busy bumping into someone else's frustrated GM—not good for their continued growth.

The Armory of the Moscow Kremlin is one of the largest depositories of national wealth in the world. The collection of 12th - 19th century armory art is rich and varied. It includes the coat of mail that belonged to the military leader, Prince P. Shuisky. The coat was later taken to the tsar's treasury and presented by Ivan the Terrible to Cossack Chief Yermak Timofeyevich, the conqueror of Siberia.

St. Petersburg was the capital of the Russian Empire for more than 200 years. During that time, the city began to embody the spirit of Russia in its palaces, its architecture, its flourishing trade and in the organization of its day-to-day life. It was built to a comprehensive plan conceived by Peter The Great. It is one of the world's most beautiful cities. Its 300 bridges earns it the deserving name "Venice of the North."

Security in the former Soviet Union requires a rebirth and redefining. The long, rich, proud history of the Russian Republic has been completely suppressed by the Communist regime. Initiative of the human spirit has been repressed. Russian security professionals need our assistance in defining customer service, quality, and pride in ownership. These are all features critical to providing protective services.

Professionally designed, and managed security services can contribute to social, economic, and political security in the CIS. Now, more than ever before, the Russian people have an increased awareness of the potential for personal freedom, personal security, safe streets, and work places. The private sector can play a key role in this transformation. Highly professional security companies sensitive to the rich Russian history and culture, and who are capable of importing expertise in service, quality, training, and marketing can establish themselves as leaders in this endeavor.

Where does the protective detail fit? Who supervises the protective detail? Who does that individual report to? How does the protective detail get things done within the corporate structure? Does it work better outside of the corporate structure? How does it collect and analyze intelligence? Regardless of the location; Boston, Dallas, or Moscow, these are questions which must be resolved if the people who make up the detail are going to survive as employees of the corporation employing them. Miscues in organizational design can also be fatal to the Corporate Security Director coordinating this flurry of activity, perhaps a continent away.

Anyone who provides any kind of service to a corporation of any size at all, must educate themselves quickly and expertly about the culture of that corporation. What are the core values? Who drives the corporation toward these values? Is there powerful influence within the corporation whose values are different?

It is going to be difficult to educate a Russian for example, who has no concept of entrepreneurial spirit, creativity, open rapid communications or brainstorming/problem solving. The people designing, and implementing a corporate executive protection program must understand, in detail, the core business. They must be sensitive to the public image their CEO, Chairman, or other protectee wishes to project to colleagues, family, stockholders, friends, and enemies alike. At the same time, they must apply the techniques necessary to ensure the protection is of high quality, at all times. In the case of an executive who jogs, the protective detail must have a jogger who can accompany the protectee without suffering a cardiac arrest, or worse, slowing down, or generally interfering with the protectee's workout. Diversity, and cultural differences can detract from, or contribute to, the success or failure of a protective program.

It is my opinion, that in order to provide personal protection to a female executive or celebrity, the protection must include a capable female protection specialist. Situations involving powder rooms, dressing rooms, hospital stays, etc., must be planned for, or anticipated. From a management and quality service standpoint, building diversity and a range of interests/expertise into the protective detail, offers great flexibility and the ability to respond to the global demands of most corporate executives, entertainers, and entrepreneurs, male or female.

Diversity played a great role in Russian history. The Hermitage, one of the world's truly spectacular museums, was created by Catherine The Great with the aid of her distinguished Russian and foreign advisors. It is a product of the Russian Age of Enlightenment. In 1764, Catherine bought, in Berlin, a magnificent collection of paintings for her new royal residence, the Winter Palace. It consisted of 225 canvases by Dutch and Flemish masters which provided the nucleus of the Hermitage collection, as we know it today. Later still, in the reign of Catherine II, three more palatial buildings were erected on the banks of the Neva to house the ever growing Imperial collection. It came to be known as the Hermitage, in keeping with the fashion at royal courts, throughout Europe, for monarchs to seek refuge from the strict demands of court etiquette by relaxing in the company of their own intimate circle in private apartments filled with all manner of rare objects and works of art. Today, Hermitage Museum has a collection of three million exhibits representing cultures and civilizations of many nations and peoples ranging from the Stone Age to present.

Ideally, the security function should have the support of upper management. Organizationally, the function should be placed and empowered with adequate resources and access to strategic corporate wide plans and issues. Those responsible for executive protection must have a clear, complete picture of potential risks and exposures if proactive countermeasures are to be effective. It will be far more cost effective to implement security into the plans, than to react to incidents after the fact, due to the lack of intelligence. Corporate wide physical, information and personnel security systems must all blend into the corporate culture and support the core business goals. If these programs or systems detract from overall goals they will be perceived as a liability.

Those responsible for the security of the chairman, CEO, President or other protectee must develop close lines of communication with a wide range of support personnel. Healthy relationships with the protectee's staff, family, flight crew, public relations staff, mail room, legal counsel, financial advisor, personal trainer, medical personnel or anyone else who influences his/her day to day activities, are imperative. Useful protective intelligence regarding the comings and goings of the protectee's business and personal relationships will flow much easier if everyone has a clear understanding that security plays an important role in corporate planning and has access to decision makers. Those charged with protective services must have the final say on transportation, hotel arrangements, emergency medical procedures and the management of public appearances involving large crowds. These responsibilities must be explained to other staff members with tact and finesse.

The persona that makes up many corporate founders, chairmen, and CEO's calls for a customized protective posture, which allows this unique, creative, perhaps somewhat eccentric individual, personal freedom to do the things which brought him or her success in the first place.

A design isolating the celebrity or popular, inspirational company president from adoring, well-intentioned fans or followers is doomed to failure. The protectee in these circumstances can be insulated with the use of carefully planned entrances and departures using rear hallways, stage doors, nondescript vehicles, curtaining, and crowd diversion.

This must be carefully planned with detailed advance work and must compliment the protectee's image, aid in his or her movements, and generally make their life easier. No matter how many times we work on an appearance in the Georgia World Congress Center or the Chicago Hilton Hotel & Towers, we walk that facility over and over and over until we know it as well as its own employees. The importance of this cannot be overemphasized. Advance and intimate familiarity with a facility is the foundation of every protective assignment. When the schedule changes begin, and they will, knowing where meeting rooms, restrooms, street level exits, rear hallways, and phones are located will turn you into a star in the eyes of your charge. Success breeds future success; the initial success is crucial to building credibility within the corporate competitive hierarchy.

"The speed of the leader, is the speed of the crew." The 24-hour a day, 7 day a week, protective detail demands an extraordinary energy level, and commitment within the protective detail. The leader must demonstrate that he/she is willing to do whatever is asked of individual members. Training, communications, problem solving, and all the personnel issues associated with "normal employees" must be addressed professionally and promptly in order to maintain operational internal security.

All of the above mentioned issues translate into English, Spanish, or even Russian. Global competitiveness and the new world order, cultural diversity, and a growing, not diminishing need for highly professional private security expertise, demand continuing development of the art called, "Providing Protective Services." The 1990's will call for closer and closer relations between security professionals around our shrinking globe.

FOURTEEN

Reducing Liability Exposure Through Minimizing Opportunity for Violent Acts

by Oliver O. Wainwright

THE UPWARD SPIRAL OF VIOLENT ACTS in the workplace has become a national issue in the United States. This is a highly complex area which challenges the professional astuteness of corporate security directors, attorneys, human resource managers, medical specialists, public relations managers, top corporate executives, and law enforcement executives.

While the first concern is to prevent the loss of life, the second focus is on the prevention of incidents and reduction of exposure to serious litigation. Both of these issues are serious matters which are thoroughly documented through credible research.

The National Institute of Occupation, Safety and Health (NIOSH) has produced a study which shows the following facts:

- There are 25,000 homicides per year nationwide, 7000 are workplace fatalities per year.
- January 1, 1980 through December 31, 1988, there were 6,956 work related homicides.
- Homicide is the #1 cause of work related deaths among females — 42%.
- Homicide is the #2 cause of work related deaths among males — 12%.
- The largest number of victims are in three categories: sales, service, and management.

Frequency of events by geographical areas is as follows:

49%	South
8%	Northeast
19%	North Central
24%	West

The types of incidents occurring include:

Homicides	Arson
Attempts	Product Contamination
Assaults	Bombings
Sexual Assaults	Extortion
Sabotage	

Categories of individuals involved are:

Employees	Ex-Employees
Temp/Part Time Employees	Vendors
Contractors	Customers
Family Members	Unknowns

On the litigation side, Liability Consultants, Inc., a Framingham, Massachusetts security and legal consulting firm, has produced a report on major developments in premises security liability. This report shows the following facts:

- From 1983 to 1992 the average settlement in premises security cases was $545,000.
- The average jury verdict during the same time frame (1983 to 1985) was $3.5 million dollars.
- States with the most cases were: New York, Texas, Florida, and California.
- State appellate courts are changing the rules on negligence, making it easier for plaintiffs to sue.
- Employees are finding ways to sue employers and avoiding the worker's compensation bar to recovery.
- Some property owners have been held liable for crimes that occur off their property on some one else's land.
- In premises security cases, the law requires a plaintiff to produce evidence of the foreseeability of criminal conduct occurring on a premises in order to establish the defendant property owner's legal duty or responsibility to prevent the injury producing incident. Absent this evidence, a defendant could argue that the incident was an independent, unforeseeable act which could not have been anticipated or prevented.
- Foreseeability does not require that the property owner know who will commit the crime, when it will occur, or what type of crime specifically will occur. It is a legal concept that requires property owners to take the risk of crime into consideration while managing the day to day affairs of their business.
- The traditional rule on foreseeability in use in many jurisdictions requires proof of a prior similar act before the property owner would be aware of, or on notice, that an event similar to the one committed against the plaintiff could happen. Referred to as the "prior similar crime" rule, this traditional rule precludes recovery by the plaintiff in the absence of such evidence. This rule has its basis on the theory that a property owner must be aware of the risk (foreseeability) generally, before a legal duty to prevent it would apply.
- A significant legal trend has been developing during the past ten years.

Several state supreme courts have held the "prior similar acts" rule to be unfair to plaintiffs. These courts have stated that the rule has the effect of victimizing plaintiffs twice; first, when they are victims of the attack, and second, when they are unable to recover in a law suit if they happen to be the first victim of a crime at that location. The traditional rule resulted in giving defendant property owners "one free bite" by not holding them responsible for security until the second attack.

- The trend is to replace the old rule with a broader rule, or test. One of the new rules is known as the totality of circumstances" test. This newer test allows plaintiffs to present evidence other than prior crime to establish the foreseeability of the criminal act.
- The following cases illustrate how different courts came to employ the newer "totality of circumstances" test. The sample cases are:

  Early v. NLV Casino, 678 P.2d 683 (Nev. 1984)

  Isaacs v. Huntington Memorial Hospital, 695 P. 2d 653 (Cal. 1985)

  Galloway v. Bankers Trust, 420 N.W.2d 437 (Iowa 1988)

  Mullins v. Pine Manor College, 449 N.E.2d 331 (Mass. 1983)

  Small v. McKennan Hospital, 403 N.W.2d 410 (S.D. 1987)

This phenomenal thrust of foreseeability and the "totality of circumstances" test creates major management issues as socio-economic conditions continue to spark workplace crime and serious acts by disgruntled employees. Organizations and managers can no longer use the "not foreseeable logic" as the rationale for not implementing effective pro-active security measures.

OBJECTIVES AND STRATEGIES

There is a "clear and present danger" in not being prepared to prevent or manage events created by violent or disgruntled employees. The consequences for such a significant shortfall may include: the loss of life, serious damage to corporate reputation, serious liability suits, and business interruptions. Each of those conditions could adversely affect the existence of any corporation as it is presently known.

Real concerns over the threat and the actual occurrence of violence in the workplace and passive actions by disgruntled employees continue to grow as various economic, social and cultural pressures impact individuals, organizations and communities.

This presentation focuses on the role of Corporate Security in developing strategies for a response to the threats, violent episodes and passive actions which have significant impact on the corporation. First, it must be assumed that the Corporate Security Director has membership on a multi-disciplined response team with representatives from human resources, safety, medical, legal, corporate communications and public relations. Outside experts should be earmarked for membership on the corporate team; those experts should be identified to respond on a quick contingency basis. Review of several cases and corporate programs shows that the typical outside experts could be psychiatrists, psychologists, private hostage negotiators, law enforcement hostage negotiators, specific Employee Assistance Program (EAP) resources, and attorneys specializing in labor relations.

The Team's objective is to assess the likelihood that an individual might act in a manner that is either intrusive, alarming, or violent.

The response team resources are used proactively in pre-event planning. Those same resources are used during the actual events. Post event or post mortem analysis become very important because it could be an effective framework for retrospective assessment.

In the review of previous cases, it has been noted that provisions must be made to provide service for members of the workplace who were not targets of violent or disgruntled actions but did experience some traumatic feelings and reactions. If those individuals are permitted to go without attention, the possibility of adverse actions against the company could grow with respect to poor image, low productivity, and conceivably monetarily if civil actions were to emerge. Resources to aid planning in this area may come under the broad heading of Humanitarian Assistance. Some of the organizations well positioned to provide such service, particularly counselling services are: The American Psychological Association and The American Red Cross.

The American Psychological Association maintains a Disaster Response Network. All psychologists participating in that network must complete a "Mental Health Provider Training Course" offered by the Red Cross. This organization can be reached in Washington, D.C. at (202) 336-5898. The Red Cross also runs a Disaster Services Human Resources System which is designed to provide various types of humanitarian assistance.

IDENTIFYING EARLY WARNING SIGNS

With the proper resource and response team structure in place and under the leadership of a member of management, the Corporate Security Director should be thoroughly prepared to focus on the early warnings or "Red Flags" that are brought to his or her attention by management. In many situations, the early warning may come from other sources, both internal and external.

Various researchers have identified the typical early warnings or "Red Flags;" some of them are:

- Inappropriate Written Communications
- Cards
- Flowers
- Pictures
- Unwanted Letters
- Trespassing
- Stalking
- Surreptitious Entry
- Etc.

S. Anthony Baron, Ph.D., author of *Violence In The Workplace: A Prevention And Management Guide For Business,* shows the early warning signs at three levels culminating in a final act of violence:

Level One
- Refuses to cooperate with immediate supervisor

- Spreads rumors and gossip to harm others
- Consistently argues with co-workers
- Belligerent toward customers
- Makes unwanted sexual comments

Level Two
- Argues increasingly with customers, vendors, co-workers, and management
- Refuses to obey company policies and procedures
- Sabotages equipment and steals property for revenge
- Verbalizes wishes to hurt co-workers and/or management
- Writes sexual or violent notes to co-workers and/or management
- Sees self as victimized by management (me against them)

Level Three
Frequent displays of intense anger resulting in:
- Recurrent suicidal threats
- Destruction of property
- Use of weapons to harm others
- Commits murder, rape, and/or arson

TAKING ACTION

Proper security planning and countermeasures can provide a strong position against serious liability suits which can easily arise from those pressure situations caused by violence in the workplace.

Generally, the first step to be taken by the Corporate Security Director is to investigate an early warning signal. Most investigations are done against a backdrop of serious concern for the privacy rights of the individual. To be on the safe side but yet move swiftly, the Security Director should have at his or her call, those appropriate expert resources that provide proper forensic examination that will stand up under cross-examination and withstand any attempts at being discredited by expert witnesses. This is a critical capability in evaluating the seriousness of a threat, particularly if there is a requirement for assessment of one's potential for violence.

The prevailing quest to protect employees' privacy rights will always make this a high professional risk for the Security Director and management team members. However, it should be made known to all members of management that credible analysis provided by the proper experts can reduce the risks. Those with certification and long-term experience in the following areas have been found to be excellent resources when conducting threat assessments:
- Forensic Document Examination
  (handwriting, typewriters, computers, etc.)
- Psycholinguistics
- Voice Print Analysis
- DNA Specialists
- Controlled Substance Specialists
- Quantitative and Qualitative Chemical Analysis
- Forensic Accounting

- Psychologists
- Photograph Interpretation
- Fingerprint Analysis
- Threat Assessment Organizations

From the onset the Corporate Security Department's work with these experts should be approved and monitored by legal counsel.

Additional investigative actions might include thorough research of internal records in: human resources, finance, benefits, security, internal audit, and the legal department. Employee Assistance Program records and medical files may be researched only upon approval of counsel, the medical professionals and social workers.

Because of the variety in state legislation, counsel's advice and even direction are critical during the investigative phase of corporate actions relating to the assessment of violent threats or the evaluation of actions of a disgruntled employee. Special focus areas that need the aid of the legal department include the following:

- Verification of background information on in-service (current) employees
- Acquiring medical information
- Researching credit and financial information
- Soliciting references
- Surveillance activities (human and electronic)
- Psychological tests
- Personality tests
- Drug tests and drug use
- Polygraph
- Arrest records
- Convictions
- Past work relationships
- Family and personal relationships
- Past conflicts with managers and co-workers
- Psychiatric history
- Prior discipline
- Health
- Alcohol tests and use

Advice from counsel is critical as the security department must avoid "unreasonable intrusion" into the rights and privacy of those who are subjects in incidents involving violence or reflecting disgruntlement.

Concurrent with the initial investigative steps, the Security Director should conduct an in-depth security survey. It should begin with the best efforts to compile professional and personal specifics about the target of the threat or actions reflecting disgruntlement. That early background information in the survey may reveal some facts or indicators bearing on motivation and rationalization of the originator.

The employment of security technology and procedures is influenced by findings in the investigation conducted in concert with the law. Just as the investigative procedures were utilized to achieve the best results and avoid serious liability, the physical security process must conform to the standards of protection and avoidance of serious legal suits.

The prevailing thought in the selection and use of security technology is the coordination of systems, components, procedures, and training of the human elements.

The major technologies to be coordinated include: closed circuit television (CCTV), alarms against intrusion, fire alarms, access control, security lighting, and special purpose alarm signals. Reliable components tested by reputable laboratories such as Underwriters Laboratories, National Bureau of Standards, or one of several private testing laboratories are acceptable. A complete maintenance schedule must be established and followed. Critical analysis must be done to create redundancy and backups to proprietary systems.

Training is a critical component in avoiding liability. Some of the major subjects for members of the security force and those with direct responsibility in handling this issue are:

- The proper use of force
- A proper focus on privacy
- Stress management
- Interview skills
- Report writing
- Testimony in courts and hearings
- An overview of support services internal and external
- Team building
- Dealing with difficult people
- Managing change
- Termination training

Robert Bonnevie, PsyD., Vice President of Manchester, Incorporated, specializing in psychological assessment provides a clear focus on the topic of workplace violence relative to training. He emphasizes creating policies and procedures regarding verbal and physical threats. Bonnevie also stresses the need for staff training and liaison with law enforcement and security counterparts in other corporations as significant activities in managing this complex issue. We should maintain an up-to-date list of security professionals in our industry as well as in other industries. Local law enforcement authorities (the chief or his representatives) should be familiar with the employer and the employer's premises. The law enforcement organization may also be a source of critical information for this problem in various facilities.

REPORTS AND FINAL ACTION

Protocol for processing information is another key element in effective organization to manage incidents and to avoid serious liability. A typical diagram for the protocol in handling incident information is shown in the chart on the following page.

An Incident may be generated by an employee internally or by an outside intruder. The incident could be a carryover from an external happening. In either case, an incident report containing the main descriptions of who, what, where, and how should be reported to a representative of the threat assessment team. The team may initiate simultaneous actions:

- An Investigation
- A Security Survey

The findings from the investigation may cause some modifications in the survey. The information or findings are converged and presented as recommendations to management. Finally, management directs some action. Law enforcement liaison and communications should be upon direction of counsel.

This protocol may appear to be cumbersome and bureaucratic. However, the organization that conducts training and exercises will find internal methods of expediting actions and even refining its flexibility.

The final action that can sharpen a company's efforts in reducing liability is to conduct an effective post mortem on an actual event or specific exercise. This will provide a retrospective assessment that could become the benchmark for corrections and future actions.

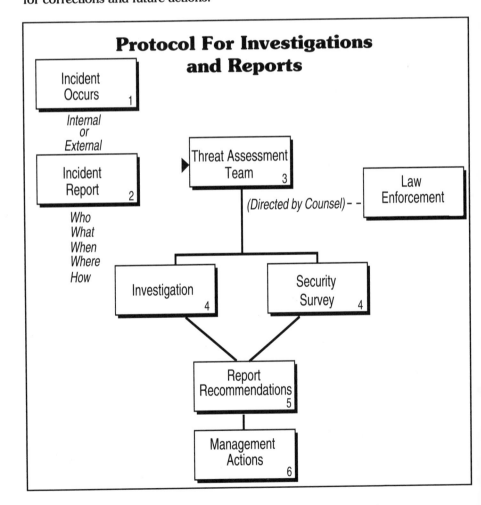

Protocol For Investigations and Reports

Incident Occurs 1

Internal or External

Incident Report 2

Who What When Where How

Threat Assessment Team 3

(Directed by Counsel) - -

Law Enforcement

Investigation 4

Security Survey 4

Report Recommendations 5

Management Actions 6

FIFTEEN

Dealing With Confrontations

by Dennis Van Deventer

ONE OF THE FUNCTIONS of an effective Personal Protection Specialist (P.P.S.) is to protect the principal from confrontations. Generally speaking, a confrontation can be defined as *an encounter of a negative nature.* Webster defines a confrontation as "a face-to-face meeting involving a conflict or challenge—the clashing of forces or ideas." Defined in this manner, it is readily apparent that a confrontation is a threatening situation. It may threaten the life, the safety, the security or the peace of mind of your principal. A confrontation can also threaten the image and interests of your principal and your principal's organization.

Just as with a criminal act, three elements must co-exist for a threat element to perpetrate a confrontation: motive, opportunity and capability. When protecting a principal it is helpful to consider each of these elements in the light of your principal's activity and profile.

For example, who would benefit from a confrontation with your principal? This benefit is much more a matter of perception in the mind and view of the perpetrator than a matter of reality. Most perceived benefits from a confrontation are actually intangible. Yet in the mind of the perpetrator these benefits are very significant achievements. Let's examine some possible motives for a confrontation.

REVENGE

Revenge is the motive when the perpetrator feels victimized by your principal or organization. Often a confrontation with your principal appears to be the only way or the best way to "get even." Settling the score, addressing a grievance or a perceived inequity are all contained in the motive of revenge.

Generally, the perpetrator has suffered a perceived loss and is hurting. Often the perpetrator has taken all he or she can take and is "not going to take it anymore." Now it's payback time. Now it's time for your principal to find out what it feels like to suffer as the perpetrator has suffered. That's the general scenario. Keep in mind, we're not talking about an assassination attempt (though there is always a potential for violence due to the emotional content of the situation), we're talking about a confrontation—a very negative and vengeful encounter. This is an experience to which your principal, should not have to be subjected.

As a protective professional you must ask yourself, "Who might have revenge as a motive against my principal?" Consider disgruntled and former employees, members, clients or associates. However, don't limit your thinking to your principal's professional or business life and activities. Also think about your principal's social life and activities. Recently terminated relationships of a social or romantic nature can easily produce perpetrators with the motive of revenge. As you go through life with your principal, maintain a confidential list of those who might have some sort of score to settle. Be aware of those who might perpetrate a confrontation motivated by revenge. This is a necessary part of your threat assessment and advance work for every movement.

POWER

Power is the motive when the perpetrator simply wants to prove a point. The message here might be: "See? You're not so safe and untouchable after all. See what I can do?" Or, "I can get you anytime I want and I just proved it." Often the perpetrator simple wants to scare your principal and make your principal feel insecure and vulnerable. This motive is similar to, but distinct from, the motive of revenge. The power motive is similar to the revenge motive in that as with the revenge perpetrator, the power perpetrator who feels insecure, inadequate and powerless, wants your principal to feel just as insecure and powerless as a result of this confrontation.

However, the power motive is distinct from the revenge motive in that the perpetrator often has no specific injustice to redress. Sometimes it is simply a case of the perpetrator proving something to himself or herself. In evaluating potential confrontation perpetrators motivated by a desire for power, also consider those whose weakness or inadequacy has been "spotlighted," as they would see it. Take note when the success or achievement of your principal is contrasted against the weakness, failure or inadequacies of someone else.

Put another way, when your principal wins, who loses? Such contrasting scenarios, however, are not always present or necessary to signal the likelihood of a confrontation with a power motive behind it. Some perpetrators find the "rush" or "power trip" of a confrontation with someone whom they regard as powerful an end unto itself. Such individuals and groups often become repeat offenders as they become addicted to the euphoric exhilaration of the confrontational experience.

Those who perpetrate the power motivated confrontation are often content with anonymity. Sometimes anonymity is a big part of their objective in creating the confrontation. In such cases the perpetrator is satisfying a strong personal desire for power and/or enjoying the rush of the achievement. It is also important to note that in power-based confrontations the perpetrator(s) will not easily give up on the idea of achieving the intended goal.

ATTENTION

Attention is the motive when the perpetrator wants the recognition associated with a confrontation with your principal. This recognition may or may not be limited to your principal's awareness and acknowledgement. Sometimes such perpetrators pre-arrange media presence and coverage. Through the confrontation the perpetrator is telling the world "*I'm* the one who did that—that was *me!*" This subject craves attention and recognition and desperately wants to be noticed and identified.

The reasons for this desire for recognition are many and varied. These perpetrators can be very creative and unconventional in the pursuit of their goal. "They"ll know who I am after *this!*" has led to many a confrontation. The threat of arrest may have little or no effect on these perpetrators. They may actually desire it for the additional attention it will bring.

SPONTANEOUS OR ESCALATED CONFRONTATION

This type of confrontation is not premeditated or planned in advance. However, as the protective professional assigned to your principal, you must be prepared in advance for this situation. This confrontation is incident-specific and emotion-driven. It can begin with anything from a spilled cup of coffee to an accidental bump in a crowded subway. The unpleasantness that follows results from your principal's response and the input of the other party. Rude comments, shouting, even physical assaults are not uncommon if the situation is allowed to go unchecked. Human pride and vanity are all that is needed to fuel this confrontation. And every human alive has these commodities in great abundance. Know your principal well. Consider your principal's personality and character, for you must be able to discern quickly and accurately the potential for this type of confrontation.

Although there are any number of potential motives for an unpleasant encounter, and numerous possible ways of evaluating them, you will find that almost every confrontation that you will ever deal with, is motivated by one of the aforementioned factors of *revenge, power* and *attention*. Even the spontaneous escalated confrontations are partially or entirely driven by elements contained in these motives.

CAPABILITY

Now a word about the capability of the confrontation perpetrator: **never underestimate it.** As a protective professional you prepare for and live with the element of surprise. There is no good excuse that will cover you for: "How was I supposed to know they could do that?" The answer is obvious. It's your *job* to know. That's what you're being *paid* for. That's why you're *there*. Enough said.

OPPORTUNITY

Of the three essential elements necessary for a confrontation to take place, this is the one over which you have the most control. By your professional, intelligent and resourceful actions you can greatly minimize or even eliminate the *opportunity* for the confrontation perpetrator to achieve his goal. So, just as you must never underestimate the potential capabilities of the perpetrator, don't underestimate your *own*. Think ahead, plan ahead, use your creativity and resourcefulness. Make positive suggestions to your principal. (You don't always have to give your reasons why.)

In protecting the principal you must always remember three things: control, control and *control*. Do your utmost to control every situation to achieve the important goal of protecting your principal. It's that simple *and* that challenging, but *always* worth the required effort.

In reading this material you are probably looking for some specifics regarding your response to various confrontations. (Actually, some very specific detailed procedures are provided for you a bit later in this chapter.) Confrontations are as varied as life itself. However, part of the reason you became a protective professional is because you like the challenge, the intensity, the spontaneity and the variety of the job. That's what makes it interesting and almost addictive to the right person. So in dealing with and responding to confrontations, remember that there is an element of "playing it by ear." If you have your act together and you're always thinking ahead you'll *know* what to do and you'll *do* it.

In general terms when dealing with confrontations, you want to practice avoidance. Stay away from confrontations—*far* away. Establish properly acceptable levels of control. Can you totally prevent all confrontations? No. You will never be able to do that. However, you *are* able to prevent *most* confrontations. Don't underestimate the importance of this fact.

When the inevitable unavoidable confrontation occurs, remember the solid protective principles contained in this book and taught at the Executive Protection Institute. Most important among these are:

1) To quickly assess the threat level (and theat potential) of the situation.

2) Place yourself (or another member of your protective team) between the threat element and the principal.

3) Cover and evacuate.

You will notice these are listed in ascending order. That is, as the situation or threat element increases, the next successive step is implemented. and yet in general terms, in principle they apply simultaneously at all times to all situations.

Under *no* circumstances should you consider retaliation as one of your options. To do so would cause you to become a participant instead of a protector and would pose a serious compromise to the security of your principal. It could also seriously compromise your principal's opportunity to legally respond to the situation at the appropriate time and in the appropriate manner. Your mission isn't retaliation. **Your** mission is **protection.**

In many (if not most) cases, your principal's life centers around a corporate environment. Often the person you must protect conducts daily business in some form of corporate headquarters. In such a situation it is essential for you as the Personal Protection Specialist to have good communications and a good working relationship with the director of security at the corporate headquarters. One of the essential subjects for the two of you to cover is the subject of confrontations and how to deal with them.

Your corporate headquarters is probably the highest profile location that your principal ever visits. It is also the most obvious location for the perpetrators of confrontations to target for their premeditated activity.

In some cases you are not only the protective professional, but also the director of security for the corporate headquarters. If that is the case you must not allow corporate security matters to distract you from your primary mission of protecting the principal. In reality, that should be the focus of your corporate security decisions. Every good corporate security decision—every enhancement to your corporate security systems—should make a positive contribution to the protection of your principal.

PROTECTING THE PRINCIPAL

Having said that, let me say that *ideally,* although you may be the director of corporate security and although you have the decision making authority in security matters, you should assign a full-time P.P.S. to the principal. This would be someone who can be with, and focus on, the principal's security exclusively. You may assign yourself to the task or you may establish a rotating schedule depending on the needs of your situation. Such decisions need to be carefully discussed with your principal at the right time and in the right manner.

What follows is specific information and procedures regarding confrontations in the corporate environment. It is written from the perspective of the director of corporate security, but can be used by anyone having the responsibility of executive protection.

CONFRONTATION PROCEDURES

PRIMARY CONCERN — PROTECTING THE PRINCIPAL

In the event of a potentially embarrassing, threatening or hostile confrontation, your primary concern remains the same: protecting the principal. To ensure the maximum security for your principal, the following procedures should be followed:

1. When it is determined that a potentially hostile or threatening confrontation is likely or imminent, contact the P.P.S. assigned to the principal. Give him or her the exact or likely location(s) of the confrontation, number of subjects involved (with descriptions), vehicle descriptions with plate numbers and registered owners from police files, any known statements, demands, or questions issued by the subjects and any other pertinent information. It will be his or her responsi-

bility to keep the principal out of the confrontation area(s), and to inform you of any movements of the principal in advance if possible.

NOTE: Even through the confrontation may occur in an area of corporate property away from the principal's location, exercise caution, realizing that threat elements often use a confrontation as a diversionary tactic to camouflage their primary mission.

2. Known or potential target areas and buildings (especially those frequented by the principal) must be secured immediately when the confrontation appears imminent. This can be achieved by placing radio equipped officers in the buildings or areas to be secured. Depending on the circumstances this coverage can either be conspicuous and high profile for maximum deterrence (i.e. uniformed officers) or covert.

3. The subjects involved in the confrontation should not be able to determine whether or not the principal is on the premises. Do not confirm his or her presence or absence to any outsider.

4. Should the confrontation escalate and the threat level become elevated, the P.P.S. assigned to the principal may need to move him or her to a safer location. You must be informed in advance to ensure a secure movement for the principal.

5. Should it become necessary to move the principal off the corporate property the movement should be covert. By being informed in advance you will be able to ensure the security and success of the movement.

NOTE: If you have reason to believe the threat element has knowledge of the principal's location, you may wish to use one or two decoy vehicles, complete with conspicuous protective personnel going to different locations. Under such circumstances, disguising the principal and changing the personnel who normally accompany him or her is appropriate procedure.

A. **General Guidelines for Making Contact With Individuals or Groups**

1. Appearance is very important. You represent the principal and the organization. A sharp appearance will elicit a more positive response from those whom you contact. Dress according to corporate guidelines or standards. Dress appropriately for the occasion and the location of your deployment. You should appear credible, professional and authoritative. However, your appearance should not be so unique as to make you conspicuous or call attention to yourself.

2. A smile can help to disarm subjects who are defensive. Use yours.

3. Maintain positive eye contact with the subject(s). This shows that you are sincere, interested and service oriented. It also shows the subject(s) that you are watching and can describe appearance, etc., and that you are courteous but not intimidated.

4. Use a pleasant tone of voice whenever possible.
5. Be service oriented. Initiate a contact by asking, "May I help you?"
6. Remember the "positive alternative" principle. Example: "I can't let you inside the building to use the phone, but please let me direct you to a public telephone nearby." Whenever possible help them achieve their goal or solve their problem.
7. Always use tact, diplomacy and professionalism in your choice of words and conduct. Keep in mind the rights of the visitor as well as the rules of the corporation. Some visitors may be looking for the opportunity to bring a lawsuit against the corporation. Decide in advance that every contact will be a positive contact from your vantage point. If the contact is not going to be positive, let that be up to the subject(s) being contacted.

   Remember there is no need and *no excuse* for rudeness, abuse or discourtesy on your part. Be a professional and maintain professional control of yourself and of the situation. Be professionally courteous and professionally aware. Use discretion. Measure your words and realize that some people are listening for "quotable quotes" to use against you, your principal or your organization. Don't play into their hands.
8. If you must observe suspicious persons, try not to be offensive or invasive. Try to be inconspicuous while observing them.
9. Often a friendly, diplomatic contact is more effective in determining a person's reason for being on corporate property than surveillance by stealth.

B. Determine Whether or Not a Contact is Necessary

A contact is necessary when you observe:

1. Violation of corporate rules or policy. Demonstrating, unauthorized entrance into buildings, soliciting, distribution of flyers or any other unapproved material, unauthorized photography, and unauthorized use of corporate property or facilities are typical examples of violations. In these cases immediate contact is appropriate.
2. Suspicious behavior. After briefly observing a visitor whose behavior is suspicious, contact him and try to determine his reason for being on the grounds.
3. Undesirable persons. Disgruntled former employees, intoxicated, mentally or emotionally disturbed individuals and vagrants are examples of undesirable persons. Contact with these individuals is essential.
4. Indecent or inappropriate dress. This is extremely sensitive and subjective and requires a great deal of tact. You should have no doubts regarding the inappropriateness or indecency of the dress of the visitor before making contact. Determine corporate policy in accordance with the wishes of your principal or other designated authority.
5. Unlawful activity. Any violation of local, state or federal law on your corporate property requires an immediate contact.

6. Injured or ill person. Any person in need of immediate aid must be contacted.

C. Determine Whether or Not a Visitor Should Leave

1. Attitude. Is the person cooperative or uncooperative? Is the person displaying destructive or inappropriate behavior?
2. Time of day. Normally, no visitors should be allowed on corporate property after a specifically designated time.
3. Person's reason for being on the premises. Is it for an appointment, or just to walk around, or is it to cause a problem? Either a short period of observation or a brief conversation will usually reveal the reason for the person's presence. Sometimes observation, experience and discernment will be required to determine the real reason.
4. Appearance. Will the person's presence greatly detract from the corporation's image? For example, a filthy, foul smelling vagrant should not be permitted to sit in the doorway of the main entrance where he would be seen and come in contact with employees and invited guests.

A Note About Exceptions: You are responsible for making wise decisions regarding legitimate exceptions to the above guidelines. You could be held responsible if you allow someone to visit who then harms someone, damages property or steals valuables. On the other hand, you could tarnish the public image of the corporation by being overly restrictive or prohibitive in your approach to visitors. Such decisions require training, experience and discernment.

D. Guidelines For Asking Visitors to Leave

As a security officer you have the right, and the responsibility, to ask any visitor to leave that you conscientiously deem necessary. However, the following points should be carefully considered.

1. Often you can tell undesirable visitors that the facility is private property, but that the public is welcome to take tours (if your facility has such a program). Then if there is interest, give the details regarding tours or direct them to the proper area or person.
2. If the visitor has legitimate business or reason to be visiting, you might expedite that business before asking him or her to leave. Your courteous manner will enable the visitor to leave with a sense of positive achievement. Or you may decide that the circumstances require that the person leave immediately.

    In any event it is always better for people to leave in a manner that enables them to maintain their dignity and self respect. This minimizes the potential for problems both at the time of the contact and in the future. Don't set anyone up for the need to "get even" with you, your principal or your organization.
3. Sometimes it is necessary to be extremely firm and insistent to get your point across. In such cases there is still no need to be rude or

abusive. Consideration of the person's rights must be taken into account. Lawsuits may result from your wrong choice of words, tone of voice, or from any physical contact.

You must strive to maintain professionalism and emotional control. Remember that some people are looking for "quotable quotes." Some even provoke a confrontation in order to record it with concealed electronic equipment. Don't play into their hands. Smile and thank them for their cooperation and understanding.

4. <u>Anytime</u> you ask a person to leave the grounds a report should be written documenting the contact and giving information on the subject's description, conversation, disposition, etc. This report is kept on file for legal protection and for future reference should the same individual return.

NOTE: Decide that you want every contact to be a positive contact. Let it be up to the *other* individual to determine whether or not it will *remain* a positive contact.

5. If the person refuses to leave, notify your supervisor. The supervisor may decide to call the police at this point. This must be decided carefully because calling the police may involve media coverage which could do more harm to your principal and organization than merely allowing the person to stay on the property for a period of time under close observation.

Also, calling the police may make it necessary for you to testify in court, which could engender negative publicity. These considerations should not deter you from contacting the police when it is warranted and in accordance with your corporate policy. In any event, the arrival of your supervisor, your assistant or uniformed security personnel is a clear indication to the subject(s) being contacted that the situation has just escalated to a higher level and is more serious in nature. This of itself may cause the subject(s) to voluntarily withdraw.

Remember: if you want them to leave you must provide them with an avenue of retreat. Never block their egress. Whenever possible, allow an honorable withdrawal. Let the subject(s) leave with their dignity intact if possible. Smile and thank them for their cooperation and understanding.

6. Let such people know that if they don't leave you may have to call the police to have them removed from the property. Sometimes people will leave as soon as they know you are considering calling the police.

7. Sometimes the police require the security officer to make a citizen's arrest for trespassing before they will remove the person from a facility. This can easily be done by following your standard operating procedures. If you have no corporate S.O.P. for this, contact your local law enforcement agency for information and consult with your corporate legal counsel regarding the establishment of such procedures. All cor-

porate security and P.P.S. personnel should be trained in these procedures.

E. Guidelines for the Potentially Violent Confrontation

If you anticipate contacting a potentially <u>violent</u> person, always alert another officer so that he or she can be nearby and respond quickly to assist you if needed.

1. Before making the contact, take the opportunity to observe the subject for a moment. Pay particular attention to the subject's hands. This may enable you to notice any danger signs (such as a concealed weapon) and formulate a plan for approaching and safely handling the situation.

2. If you decide to make contact with a potentially violent subject you should have another officer with you for reasons of safety (for backup) and legal liability (to be a witness to what happens).

3. If more than one officer is involved, only the lead officer should do the talking to avoid confusion. If both officers have the same rank, the first one on the scene should assume the responsibility of the lead officer.

4. <u>Your</u> attitude and behavior is very important. Treating a subject with contempt, hostility, or excessive force increases the likelihood of resistance, violence and litigation. Do nothing to escalate the situation or to provoke a violent response from the subject being contacted. Do not corner the subject. Project calmness, friendliness and confidence.

5. Position yourself at an angle to the subject, giving yourself optimum defensive capabilities.

6. Allow at least five feet between yourself and the subject at all times to minimize his grab zone and maximize your reactionary gap. Always maintain the tactical advantage.

7. Be aware of the <u>subject's hands</u> at all times.

8. If his hands are concealed in any way, ask him to please keep them out in the open.

9. Do not let the subject corner you in any manner. Don't let him force your back to the wall. Don't let him close in on you. <u>Maintain control.</u>

F. Guidelines for the Violent Confrontation

1. Should the individual show himself to be violent or threatening violence, take note of exactly what the individual is saying and doing as this information must be included in the required report. Keep other people away from the subject and be aware of possible accomplices in the area.

2. In such cases the police should be contacted immediately. Depending upon the situation, the subject may be told that the police are on the way. This may cause him to cease and desist. If not, it will let him know the seriousness of his actions, and the firmness of your resolve.

3. Do nothing to block the individual's avenue of retreat. If the individual wants to leave—*let* him leave. Police can be given a full description of

the individual, his actions, his vehicle description and license number and direction of travel. Remember your goal is to reduce or <u>eliminate</u> the threat on your property, not to *preserve* it. Your mission is *protection,* not apprehension.

4. If the individual poses a legitimate and reasonable threat to himself or others and refuses to leave before the police arrive, it may become necessary to restrain him.

5. If the individual must be restained, use the minimum amount of force necessary to do the job, make sure to have sufficient backup involved to reduce the likelihood of injury, and to provide competent witness(es) to your actions and those of the subject.

6. Once the individual is restrained, check him for weapons and detain him in a secure area until the police arrive.

G. Emotionally Disturbed Persons

1. When in doubt, you may anticipate that <u>any</u> suspicious person may also be emotionally disturbed and mentally unstable.

2. Such persons may become violent at any time with or without provocation. It is important to maintain proper distance in dealing with them. You should have a silent partner with you for backup.

3. In a friendly, courteous manner, greet the individual. I recommend: "Good day, may I help you?" Use a warm friendly smile.

4. The ball is now in the other person's court. Some response is called for. <u>Listen</u> carefully to his response. <u>Watch</u> for changes in mannerism and body language. <u>Show interest</u> in the person and his remarks. Let him *talk.*

5. Don't over-react to anything the subject says. <u>Accept what you hear</u> (no matter how far-fetched or "off the wall"). This helps to keep the subject at ease and encourages further communication which could prove very helpful and informative.

6. Avoid making any judgment calls on what the subject says. Don't ridicule or belittle the subject or his ideas. Project yourself as someone who is concerned and wants to help.

7. If you <u>must</u> make a <u>negative</u> statement or <u>deny</u> a request, quickly follow up with a <u>positive</u> option. If possible show how the positive option is superior to the original request or intention. Always show this from the subject's point of view in terms consistent with his desire or objective.

<u>Example:</u> The subject wants to see your C.E.O. to give him some "important information." You explain that the C.E.O. isn't available right now and you invite the subject to write down all the important information. You may say: "I'll see to it that this is properly delivered in person."

NOTE: it may be properly and personally delivered to the trash can after a thorough review, or it may be delivered to an "E.D.P." (Emotionally Disturbed Person) file or "Threat" file

depending on its content. You can explain further that even if the subject were to see the C.E.O. in person he'd "only have a few minutes and a thorough presentation of this important material would not be possible, but with a letter the material can be thoroughly reviewed and given the consideration it deserves."

Offer to supply the subject with writing materials and a place to write. This is often preferable to having the subject leave and bring back a written statement. This approach has several advantages:

a. If enables you to put the subject in a place of your choosing away from public view and under control while it buys additional time to check out the subject if necessary while you have him in "voluntary custody."

b. It gets the subject's information and purpose more quickly.

c. It provides a signed document which may become important as evidence in the future.

d. It eliminates the imminent need for the subject to return.

When the subject gives you the written information, treat it with respect. Project <u>closure</u> to the subject as if this action <u>resolves</u> the matter and is a significant <u>achievement</u>. Let him know he's done a good job and has <u>accomplished his mission</u>.

If the subject believes the document should be confidential, respect his wishes <u>conspicuously</u> in his presence. Allow him to seal it up in a "secure envelope." Give this document the respect <u>he</u> thinks it deserves.

8. Reassure the subject that his concerns will be addressed and that he has done the right thing by coming to you.

9. Ask the subject how you or the C.E.O. could contact him about these matters in the future. Obtain name, address and telephone number in a non-threatening manner. Ask to see identification so you can be sure no one is misrepresenting the subject. Make note of relevant numbers or information in a natural and unthreatening manner.

Ask the subject if he has any professional references who know him in the area such as doctors, etc. Make note of doctors, counselors, etc., and contact them later. They can provide helpful information on the subject and may be able to notify family members of his whereabouts, etc. Often, when a subject mentions a doctor, you can ask, "Are you taking your medication?" This information will be helpful when you contact the doctor later, and his response may provide additional helpful information.

10. Escort the subject off the grounds while maintaining friendly conversation. Often a subject handled in this manner will never realize that he's being ejected.

NOTE: In dealing with E.D.P.s always maintain control of the situation in a non-threatening manner. Should an escalation

of force be necessary you can then act from a position of advantage.

11. It may be necessary to contact the police to remove the subject.

H. Procedures for Group Confrontations

When an unauthorized group shows up on corporate property the following procedures should be followed.

1. Contact your supervisor informing him or her of the situation and request backup.

   NOTE: The supervisor will then contact:

   a. The P.P.S. assigned to the principal (see section "Protecting The Principal").

   b. Your corporate legal department and your corporate public relations department and inform them of the situation (group size, location, activity, etc.).

   c. The local law enforcement agency. This preliminary call to the police will inform them of the situation at present and lay the foundation for subsequent calls as the situation develops. This prepares them for the possibility of police intervention and adds credibility and liability protection to the situation at hand.

   The time of call, the name(s) of persons spoken to and the specifics of the conversation should be documented.

2. Observe the group, taking note of the number of people, any conspicuous weapons or objects that could be used as weapons (e.g. signs, flags on poles, nearby rocks, bottles, etc.), and any apparent purpose in their presence and actions.

3. If possible, photograph the group from various angles.

4. When backup personnel arrive make contact with the group, maintaining a secure position at least seven feet from the nearest subject.

5. Use the standard "Good day, may I help you?" It may be necessary to inquire if there is a leader or spokesperson for the group.

6. Listen carefully to what is said as it must be included in the required report. This information will also be essential in your evaluation of the group.

I. Group Evaluation Guidelines

1. <u>Determine the Size of the Group</u>. The size of the group has a direct bearing on their capability and the potential for problems. This information also has a direct bearing on your response and the options you will employ. You must know the size of the group you are dealing with. Often the presence of a group will itself draw a crowd. Sometimes a group will have a second or third "wave" ready to move in on cue or at a pre-determined time. Sometimes those who appear to be onlookers are part of the group also. It may be necessary to ask nearby onlookers "Are you with them?" Try to isolate the group from unrelated bystanders.

2. <u>Determine if the group is cooperative or uncooperative</u>. To control a cooperative group you may have to do little more than direct traffic. An uncooperative group can be extremely difficult to control, depending on a number of elements.

3. <u>Determine if the group is organized or disorganized</u>. A cooperative group which is well organized can be more easily controlled by working through its leader and chain of command. A disorganized, uncooperative group is the most difficult to control. Since they have no organized plan or leadership, you may be faced with random spontaneous incidents of disorder and violence. Be mentally prepared for this possibility.

NOTE: Uncooperative groups do not have to be violent to evade control. They can passively resist attempts to control them. They can form human barricades, occupy buildings, and block access to essential areas and thoroughfares. They can chain themselves to each other and/or to buildings and objects to force arrest and bodily removal. Generally these actions are the premeditated operation of an organized, uncooperative group.

4. <u>Determine Whether or Not Women, Children, Elderly, Infirmed or Handicapped People Are Included in the Group</u>. The presence of these individuals will affect your decision regarding which of your options will be employed, and the manner in which any option will be employed. Some groups will deliberately place such individuals in their ranks, hoping that the physical actions you employ will appear to be excessive, abusive, and insensitive. If that is their intention you must not play into their hands.

5. <u>Determine Whether the Group is Violent or Non-violent in Their Intent</u>. Group mood and intent will have a direct bearing on what you do and what you can expect in response.

6. <u>Determine Whether or Not the Group is Violating the Law</u>. If the group is in fact violating the law this will enable you to elicit a stronger response from local law enforcement, and will afford you enhanced liability protection. Possible violations include: unlawful assembly, trespassing, disorderly conduct, disturbing the peace, public intoxication, obstruction of vehicular or pedestrian passageways, blocking or denying access to public or private buildings, damage to property, vandalism, lewd, obscene or indecent communication or conduct, assault, battery, etc.

J.   Guidelines For Considering Your Options

Generally speaking, when dealing with an unauthorized group you have four possible options. The option you employ will be determined by your evaluation of the group as previously discussed. A brief discussion of each option follows.

1. <u>Monitor the Group</u>. Security personnel may take up carefully chosen

vantage points from which to observe the group. Members of the monitoring team should be in constant communication with the security team leader regarding size, activity, location and mood of the group being monitored. This monitoring enables the security leadership to gage the group's activity and intent, and anticipate further control measures.

a. Monitoring is appropriate when a group is determined to be nonviolent or is posing no immediate threat.

b. Monitoring is appropriate when further control measures are deemed unwarranted or possibly provocative.

c. Ideally, monitoring is accompanied by communication between the security team leader and the group leader if the group is organized. This enables security to express official interest and intent. The message being "We just want to make sure everyone is safe and secure," and "We have an interest in protecting our personnel and property."

d. Monitoring can be an effective way of gaining the confidence and cooperation of the group's leadership and its members.

e. Monitoring can enable security to gain control of the group without employing more severe measures.

f. If communication with the group's leadership is working effectively, the group may be diverted from their original purpose and intent and may even abandon their stated goal. Positive pressure can be placed on the group's leadership to channel the group into an area that is less disruptive and "safer for all concerned."

g. During the monitoring process security can have the group photographed and/or videotaped. This not only provides documentation of the incident and its participants but it can also provide an effective deterrent to violent or criminal activity.

People are less likely to commit unlawful acts if they know you have photographed their faces. And, if needed, photographs and videotapes can be used as evidence for prosecutions or litigation.

To be most effective the group members must <u>know</u> that you are photographing them and documenting their presence. Photographers should be in uniform or otherwise identified as part of your organization so they will not be mistaken for members of the press and so the group members will know they are being photographed by the official control force.

Photographers should be close enough to be easily seen but not close enough to be provocative to the group or endangered by the group.

2. <u>Contain the Group</u>. Containment limits the group to the area they are presently occupying.

a. Containment is appropriate when you determine that the group intends to move into an undesirable area from a security standpoint.

b. Containment prevents outsiders from joining with the group.

c. Containment is useful to protect personnel and property in adjacent areas.

d. Groups can be contained by barricades, stationary vehicles, effective perimeter patrols and barriers such as walls, trees, hedges, and water-filled barrels. Lawn sprinklers can be activated to deter the group from moving into certain areas.

e. Depending upon the size of the group, public address systems may be used to inform the group regarding the designated boundaries.

f. Containment procedures can send a definite signal to the group that there are limits to their actions and that there is a committed determination to establish and enforce those limits.

3. <u>Block the Group</u>. Blocking the group denies access to specific areas and physically prevents the advance of the group.

a. Blocking is appropriate when the group begins to move.

b. Blocking may be used to protect a facility or area that is a potential or actual target.

c. Security personnel in close formation, vehicles, and barricades can be employed in a blocking operation.

d. Do not block their avenue of retreat.

4. <u>Disperse the Group</u>. The intent of dispersal is to fragment the group.

a. Dispersal is appropriate when it is determined that all other control measures have been ineffective.

b. Dispersal is appropriate when the stability of the situation is rapidly deteriorating.

c. Dispersal is most useful with a smaller group in an urban site.

d. If dispersal is warranted the local law enforcement authorities must be informed and involved.

e. Target areas must be well protected prior to the dispersal operation.

NOTE: Target areas are areas likely to be targeted for action by the group, but also include any areas of concern from a security standpoint.

f. Dispersal routes must be pre-determined prior to dispersal to prevent increased disorder and violence from spreading over a wider area. Do nothing to block the group's avenue(s) of retreat. It may be necessary to tell the group which route(s) to take to safely leave the area.

g. Methods of dispersal include proclamations, assertive security formations and movements, and the use of chemical agents. Depending upon the group's size and location, activating lawn sprinklers may be an effective method of dispersal.

K. Other Considerations in Dealing With Group Confrontations

1. If the group has some specific questions or demands, contact the appropriate public relations and legal personnel in your organization immediately while you continue to monitor the group. Tell the group you hear their questions or demands and are contacting the appropriate personnel to get them an answer.

2. If the group wants to engage in some "ceremony" which does not threaten personnel or property, under certain conditions you may determine to permit it as it may only last a short time and preventing it could provoke an undesirable escalation. However, discretion is advised.

3. At no time during a group confrontation should any security officer become rude or abusive in dealing with the group. All security personnel must maintain emotional control and proper professional bearing.

4. As mentioned in the first section of these procedures, keep in mind that group confrontations are sometimes used as diversionary tactics to distract and occupy security forces while the threat element initiates its primary mission elsewhere. Regardless of what the group does or fails to do, keep your focus on protecting your principal.

A FINAL WORD

Though you can never totally eliminate the possibility of a confrontation occurring, you can approach the situation with confidence and dramatically increase the odds for a successful resolution of the matter. That can be done through the implementation of your well thought out plan of action consistent with sound protective principles. Remember, you can't give what you don't have, so spend the necessary amount of time in preparation so you can give the first class professional protective service that your principal deserves. I hope this chapter makes a positive contribution to that goal.

SUGGESTED READING

Broder, James F. *Risk Analysis and the Security Survey.* Stoneham, Maine: Butterworth Publishers, 1984.

Buckwalter, Art. *Surveillance and Undercover Investigation.* Woburn, Maine: Butterworth Publishers, 1983.

Headquarters, Department of the Army, *FM 19-15 Civil Disturbances.* Baltimore, Maryland: U.S. Government Printing Office, 1985.

Shackley, Theordore G., and Oatman, Robert L. *You're the Target.* McLean, Virginia: New World Publishing Ltd., 1989.

Yeager, Robert. *The Failure to Provide Security Handbook.* Columbia, Maryland: Hanrow Press, Inc., 1986.

SIXTEEN

Corporate & Private Security Advance Work

by Charles H. Blennerhassett and Jerome H. Glazebrook

A COMPREHENSIVE EXECUTIVE PROTECTION PROGRAM will encompass a multitude of disciplines, e.g., vehicle security, residence security, etc. Advance work is a critical component of a total program. It is during this planning stage that we attempt to avoid putting our principals in embarrassing and/or dangerous situations. Remember the 5 P's: *Prior Planning Prevents Poor Presentation.* It is a discipline that is difficult to master as it requires not only the proper training but years of travel, both domestic and foreign.

This chapter will explore the inner workings of advance work in the private sector. Dealing in reality, as opposed to fiction.

An advance can be defined as "Activities and arrangements made prior to and in connection with the visit of a principal."

Following are the four basic reasons for conducting an advance:

1. Minimizes the risk to a principal.

2. Establishes a secure area for a principal.

3. Provides valuable information.

4. Allows the principal to expend the majority of his/her time on business related activities and minimize time exhausted on un-related activities, e.g., hotel check-in, car services, etc.

Some corporate security departments conduct advances as a part of their daily security activities. Others, do so only under specific circumstances, such as overseas trips, when their principal's threat level accelerates. A fair statement would be that generally foreign advances present the greatest degree of difficulty. That is not to understate the importance or significance of stateside advances.

The current economic conditions have had a tremendous impact on corporate America, resulting in re-organizations, down sizing of departments, lay-offs, reduction in budgets, etc. Security departments, like other departments, find themselves with reduced budgets, and now more than ever they must justify expenditures.

Conducting advances is an expensive undertaking. Following are approximate cost factors relating to a two day advance of London:

- Home base: New York / Destination: London
- Airfare: round trip business class $ 3,892.00
- Taxi: round trip airport to city (2) $ 155.00
- Car service: (8 hrs to run routes) $ 320.00
- Hotel room: ($300.00 per night) $ 600.00
- Meals: $ 130.00
- Salary of advance man, (based on 30k) $ 250.00
- Approximate total cost: $ 5,347.00

The aforementioned list is not intended to be an all inclusive list of expenses that will be incurred, as there are numerous intangibles that will have a direct impact on the cost, such as the complexity of the itinerary and the threat level, etc. Cost factors can be reduced by such methods as flying coach as opposed to business, (those of you who have had the unpleasant experience of flying coach for eight hours in an aircraft filled to capacity will not relish this method of cost reduction), and staying at a less expensive hotel until the arrival of your principal. Others may choose not to run the routes prior to the arrival of your principal; bear in mind your principal will have serious misgivings of the advantages of an advance if you get them lost after spending two days completing an advance. Then there is the other side of the coin, cost increase. Some security professionals require that they fly first class, and/or the car service may be needed for more than the one day, etc.

Time required to successfully perform an advance will depend on numerous factors. Following are several factors that will contribute to determining this time frame:

- Will the advance take place in the United States or abroad?
- Complexity of the itinerary?
- Length of trip?
- Is trip intended to be pleasure or business, or a combination?
- Will your advance days encompass holidays and/or weekends?
- Number of principals involved?
- Current threat assessment?

The body of an advance can generally be broken down into five areas:

1. Pre-Advance:

The pre-advance is a critical component of the total advance, as it will lay the foundation for the entire process. A thorough, in-depth pre-advance will help ensure that the advance is accomplished in an efficient and successful manner.

Following is a list of activities that will generally take place during a pre-advance:

- Review the proposed itinerary
  - Dates of trip
  - Check for typos
  - Lodging
  - Business or pleasure
  - Special events
  - Special needs
  - Principals participating
  - Transportation
  - Contacts
  - Scheduling conflicts
  - Specific clothing needs
  - Reconfirm itinerary with the appropriate person(s)

- Secure post advance report and review. As most principals repeatedly frequent the same locations, it is to your advantage to maintain detailed post reports. You will find these reports a valuable asset when conducting your pre-advance. Post reports should include the following information.
  - Dates of trip
  - Security personnel involved
  - Purpose of trip
  - Transportation, ground & air, with contacts
  - Problems encountered
  - Pertinent contacts
  - Trip synopsis
  - Copies of letters of appreciation
  - Location of trip
  - Principals involved
  - Lodging, with contacts
  - Emergency phone numbers
  - Maps, surveys
  - Trip itinerary
  - Weather incurred

- Research: The following research should be completed during the pre-advance:
  - Location, climate, terrain of area to visit
  - Type of government; primary religion
  - Are passports necessary?
  - Are visas necessary?
  - Are shots required?
  - United States Embassy/consulates phone numbers
  - Currency and conversion rate
  - Customs restrictions
  - Terrorist organizations that operate in the area

- Official holidays
- Review State Department background notes or equivalent
- Obtain phone numbers for lodging, airline and car service contacts.

Following are several sources where the aforementioned information may be located:

- Newspapers
- US Government Printing Offices
- Bookstores
- Tourist Centers
- Foreign Consulates
- Travel Agencies
- US Embassies

- Phone calls: The individuals you need to meet with on your advance are often times very important and extremely busy individuals. It is always prudent to call in advance and reach a mutually agreed upon time to meet. Following are several contacts that should be made prior to departure:

- Airline
- US Embassies
- Hotel
- Police
- Car Service

- Car service: Generally a car service will be selected during the pre-advance phase. Selecting a car service that will provide you with the quality, dependability and professionalism that is a pre-requisite in the business of executive security, can be a time consuming task. One method of narrowing the field is to solicit recommendations from your fellow colleagues. We have all listened to the horror stories of dead batteries, ran out of gas, no spare tire, air conditioning or heat inoperative, revoked drivers license, etc. This is not to say there are not excellent services available, there are, it just takes some research to locate them. Following is a list of areas to explore when evaluating a car service:

- Company name, address, phone and manager or owner's name
- Procedures for screening prospective drivers
- Number of vehicles in fleet
- Maintenance of fleet
- Minimum charge
- Billing cycle
- How long to obtain backup car
- Possible to have current DMV report on drivers used
- What type of equipment is in cars
- Years in business
- References
- Dress code for drivers
- Type of vehicles used—year, color
- Charges per hour
- Gratuity added to bill
- Time required to book service
- Request two sets of keys

- Items to go with advance person: Following is a list of items an advance person should consider taking with on a trip:

- Proposed itinerary
- Copy of hotel confirmation
- Copy of principals passport
- Emergency Bio on principal
- Cash
- Credit cards
- First aid kit
- Travel umbrella
- Camera
- Travel flashlight
- All pertinent contacts and phone numbers
- Passport information on accompanying security persons
- Business cards
- Spare doc kit for principal
- Tape recorder
- Small tool kit

A quick word about traveling aboard an aircraft on your advance. Most of us would certainly rather travel in casual clothes as opposed to a suit. If you choose to travel in this manner it is a wise person who carries top side a suit along with other incidentals. I have been told by persons, "I have been traveling for ten years and have never had my luggage lost." My response is always the same, "Better safe than sorry." In my opinion the negative results of attending a business meeting in casual clothes far outweigh the inconvenience of a carry on.

HITTING THE ROAD:

Here is when all those long hours exhausted on your pre-advance begin to pay off. If you have conducted a thorough, detailed pre-advance your mood while traveling to the advance site should be relaxed and confident relating to the upcoming events. On the other hand, if you have shirked your responsibilities and cut corners you will probably find yourself feeling apprehensive and unsure. Confident and relaxed beats apprehensive and unsure every time. This is not to say that the person who has covered all the bases will not encounter issues they had not planned for. Advance personnel must always expect the unexpected and remain flexible at all times. Let the on site work begin.

2. **Transportation:**

There are numerous modes of transportation that an advance person will encounter, e.g., commercial and private fixed wing aircraft, helicopters, cars, trains, buses, and ships. The mode of transportation most commonly encountered are vehicles and aircraft.

- Vehicles: This is an area that if not properly advanced can turn an otherwise well executed trip into a complete disaster. You have already taken the first step towards success by conducting the car service evaluation, thereby selecting your service wisely. The next step is to ensure the vehicle and driver that you are going to use meet your standards in every respect. As previously mentioned, ideally you would require a copy of the drivers DMV; at the very least you should inspect their drivers license to ensure that they have a valid license. Drivers should be thoroughly briefed on what their responsibilities will be and guidelines they should follow while driving your principal. An inspection should be performed on the proposed vehicle.

Following are several areas that you should be concerned with during the inspection:

- Physical appearance, dents, etc.
- Headlights, high & low beam
- Brake lights
- Spare tire
- Windshield wipers
- Interior lights
- Reading lights
- Tires
- Tail lights
- Turn Signals
- Windows
- A/C, heat
- Horn
- Telephone

- Routes: Selecting the safest most expeditious route will generally require driving the routes at least once prior to the arrival of the principal. Some persons will think this is not necessary as the driver that has been hired assures them that he knows the area inside and out. A principal's time is often at a premium and I seriously doubt that they will appreciate being delayed because of road construction or any other delay that could, and should, have been avoided. Keep in mind road conditions are oftentimes in constant change. Detailed primary and alternate routes should be reduced to writing and accompanied with maps. Following are several areas that you should be concerned with when selecting a route:

- What is the date and time the route will be used.
- Remember holidays and weekends will have a different traffic flow than the average week day.
- If you will be passing business or industrial areas keep in mind shift changes.
- Bridges that open to allow ships to pass.
- Train tracks and tunnels.
- School zones.
- Overpasses and underpasses.
- Road construction.
- Special events, —parades, demonstrations, sporting events.
- Traffic lights and stop signs that you will encounter.
- Hospitals, police stations, fire houses and medical facilities.

Above all else, remember that the condition of the routes you have planned to use may vary by the hour, so always plan ahead and remain flexible.

- Commercial Airports: The advance person should be thoroughly familiar with the airports to be used. Your current threat assessment will dictate the degree of assistance you will request from the airport authorities and police, for plane-side pick-up, police escort, etc. As a courtesy to the airport police, you should inform them of your principal's arrival and/or departure information, regardless of whether or not you request their assistance. Following are areas you should be familiar with at the airport:

- Daily passenger ranking
- Airline administrative offices
- Baggage area
- Airline clubs
- Police office
- First aid stations
- Lost & found office
- Customs office
- Private telephone
- Gift Shops, news stands
- Ground transportation area
- Restaurant
- Ongoing construction
- Estimated time to allow for retrieval of luggage
- Obtain airport map
- Inner airport transportation
- Location of religious stands or other groups that hand out material

- Time Zone
- Ticket counters
- Lost baggage area
- Gates
- Paging phone number
- FAA phone number
- Information office
- Currency exchange
- Restrooms
- Hair salon
- Business facilities
- Closest hotel
- Estimated time to allow for check-in
- Estimated time to clear immigration & customs

By completing a proper advance you can avoid putting your principal in embarrassing and sometimes dangerous situations, like areas where groups hand out material and/or solicit contributions, or construction areas, etc. In addition, when the luggage is lost, and it will eventually happen, you will know where to go and who to contact.

- Commercial Airlines: Remember, you set this appointment up during your pre-advance. Contact with the airline of your choice will generally be initiated during the advance of the airport. Meeting the Passenger Service Managers and/or Station Managers and obtaining direct phone numbers will prove to be invaluable. Airlines are generally very helpful when it comes to assisting VIP's.

During this meeting you will discuss any special needs you may have — specific seating, board first or last, luggage first off, or special menus. Following is information that will generally be discussed during a meeting with airline personnel:

- Obtain airline contact and direct phone number.
- Confirm flight information and seat assignments.
- Proposed arrival and/or departure gate.

- Check on backup flights.
- Model of aircraft (DC10,747, etc.)
- Aircraft originates out of what city?
- Contact for airline club and phone number.
- Is there a telephone aboard the proposed aircraft?
- Any expected delays?
- Special arrangements for luggage.
- Special boarding arrangements, first or last.
- Special medical request, e.g. oxygen.
- Request airline representative meet the aircraft and assist your principal.
- Request private holding room.

When confirming seat assignments remember that even on the same type of aircraft, seating configurations will vary from airline to airline. Never assume that a particular seat number will always offer the same comfort and convenience. When flying coach, generally, the greatest amount of leg room can be obtained in seats immediately behind a cabin bulkhead or in an emergency aisle. A word of caution to those advance persons meeting an arriving principal on flights from coast to coast, or overseas, these flights have the potential for arriving ahead of schedule. There are many factors that will influence arrival time, e.g., air traffic, head or tail winds, etc.

- Private Aviation Facilities: Many principals that require protection travel by private aircraft. Private aviation facilities can be found at large airports, such as LaGuardia in New York, or small airfields located throughout the world. Below is a list of areas that you should check during your advance of the facility:

- Name, address, phone no., of service that will handle your aircraft
- Are there any noise restrictions
- Length of runway
- Maintenance & fuel capabilities
- Meeting facilities
- Security for airfield
- De-icing capabilities
- Police jurisdiction
- Clearance for plane-side pick-up
- Closest major airport
- Hours of facility
- Are night landings permitted
- Restrictions on aircraft allowed
- Customs clearance availability
- Catering services
- Restrooms & phones
- Hangar space for rent
- Emergency response crew at airfield
- Nearest hospital with trauma unit

3. **Hotels:**

Principals oftentimes reside in public lodging of some fashion, hotels, inns, resorts, etc. This is another critical part of the advance. It is the place where your principal will most likely spend a good deal of his/her time. It is also an area where there are many uncontrollable intangibles that can rock the boat: room service is late, food is cold, noisy room, heat not operating properly, etc.. How happy do you think your principal will be if you arrive at the hotel and the service staff is on strike, or a foreign government delegation is staying at the hotel, holding elevators, blocking traffic at the front of the hotel, etc. On the other hand if you have covered all the bases, your principal will enjoy a pleasant stay while at the hotel. Make no mistake you will have your work cut out for you. When you consider that you will be dealing with a multitude of people and personalities, including front office management, concierges, room service, and bellmen; all with different personalities, all of whom are important if you hope to have the ideal visit. It will be necessary to cultivate each and every one of these persons to accomplish your goals. Following is a list of activities that will generally be conducted during an advance:

● Meet with hotel management to discuss the following:

- Confirm reservations
- Specific amenities to be provided in room
- How to handle phone calls
- Special events in hotel
- Possible to re-key doors to room
- Name of concierges for all three shifts
- Pass on any special needs
- Go over all services offered by hotel — limo service, safes, fax, etc.

- Arrange payment of bill
- Names of managers for all three shifts
- Other VIP's in hotel
- Request same maid clean rooms during stay at hotel
- Request extra keys
- Possible to hold elevators
- Newspapers are available at what time

● Meet with the Director of Security to discuss the following:

- Schedule and itinerary
- Specific security needs
- Type of fire detection system
- Closest hospital with a trauma unit

- Request tour of hotel
- Current and past security problems
- Number of hotel security on duty per shift
- Is security staff armed

- Are emergency exit doors accessible from stairwells
- Elevator certificates
- Crime rate for area of hotel

• Conduct a thorough inspection of principal's room. Confirm that all appliances, lights, locks, plumbing, etc. are in proper operating condition. In addition inspect the room for unsafe conditions — sharp corners, excess wiring, etc.

• Generally principals appreciate having a room or suite that is located in a quiet area. When selecting such a room it is imperative to stay away from: stairwells, ice machines, vending areas, elevators, rooms above or below meeting rooms or lounges, etc.

• Place by the principal's phone(s) information on how to reach their security personnel.

4. **Sites to be visited:**

During a trip you are likely to visit numerous locations, office buildings, theatres, restaurants, etc. In this section we will look at two locations that are frequented often by a principal — restaurants and office buildings.

• Restaurants: Following are several areas to consider and discuss when conducting an advance of a restaurant:

- Manager's name
- Hours of restaurant
- Smoking or non-smoking
- Interior lighting
- Arrange for specific seating
- Special requirements
- Private rooms available
- Any special events on the proposed date
- Arrange for payment of bill
- Maître d's name
- Obtain menu
- Dress code
- Seating capacity
- Time to be allowed for dinner
- Location of restrooms and telephones
- Entrances and exits

• Office Buildings: Many principals will undoubtedly visit an office building at some time during their trip. Many businesses have tightened the security in their buildings, e.g. requiring all visitors to sign in and be issued identification badges, all visitors to be escorted, access control, etc. This added security is most welcome by executive security personnel. However, it can also delay the movement of a principal if the proper clearance has not been approved ahead of time. Below are areas that we should discuss and consider during the advance:

- Contact person & phone number
- Entry requirements
- Tour of building
- Area crime index
- Security at building
- Is security armed

- Backup power supply
- Sole tenants or multiple tenants
- Hours of building
- Fire detection system
- Closest hospital with trauma unit

- Smoking, non-smoking
- Evacuation procedures
- Restrooms, phones
- Where to park car
- Secure area where car is going to be parked
- Elevator inspections

ARRIVAL OF THE PRINCIPAL:

The moment of truth has arrived. Soon all of those long days will start to pay off. You have covered everything from a to z; you have considered countless alternatives to your operational plan; you have contingency plans for contingency plans. Yet you still find your mind running through all the possible changes your principal will make when he/she arrives. The sign of a true advance man. (Between these two writers is over thirty years of conducting advances and neither one of us can remember a trip going exactly as planned.) So your principal arrives, you meet his/her plane-side with the help of the airline representative, the car is waiting, door open, interior at a comfortable temperature, the principal is whisked off to the hotel. No delays on the way to the hotel, how could there be, remember you ran the routes. Of course because you did a proper advance you have already checked-in your principal and you hand him/her the room key in the car. You arrive at the hotel, bellman waiting to assist, enter their room where they find their Don Perigon, 1976 of course, chilled to just the right temperature. Now the questions begin, how much time to get to . . . . . ?, are you sure . . . . . . ?, etc., you confidently answer all the questions. At the end of a long day you sit down to have your dinner, usually around 11:00 p.m., exhausted but feeling proud of a job well done. Congratulations!

5. **Post Advance:**

You return from another successful trip, hopefully! The post advance is an integral part of the total advance. The success of a trip is a collaborated effort, with many people having been instrumental in achieving the final objective. Just as a football team can not win with only one player, neither can an advance be successful without the assistance of many persons — hotel staff, driver, airline personnel, etc. Generally many of these contacts will be able to assist you in the future. It will behoove the advance person to ensure these valuable contacts by showing proper appreciation. Those responsible for advancing for a notable personality may opt to forward an autographed photo to those who assisted you. At a minimum a thank you letter from your principal should be forwarded to those who assisted on the trip. I can assure you that this practice will pay enormous dividends in the future.

Now is the time for the aforementioned post report to be completed and filed for future use.

As you can see from this chapter, advance work is as demanding and complex as it is important. To be completely successfully the advance person must be meticulous in his work, covering every possible angle. The advance person must possess enormous self-discipline as he/she is generally working alone and the opportunity (and temptation) to take short cuts is always present.

Advance work is also extremely rewarding as you have the gratification of knowing you were an important part of providing a safe environment for your principal.

SUGGESTED READING

H. H. A. Cooper, *On Assassination*
Burt Kapp, *Bodyguarding: A Complete Manual*
Dr. Wess Roberts, *Leadership Secrets of Attila the Hun*
Tony Geraghty, *The Bullet Catchers*
Duffy Ricci, *Target Hitler*
Peter Hoffman, *Hitler's Personal Security*
Pierre DeMaret & Christian Plume, *Target de Gaulle*
Reber and Shaw, *Executive Protection Manual*
Reed Travel Group, *International Air & Travel Handbook*
Tony Scotti, *Executive Safety and International Terrorism: A Guide for Travelers*
Roger E. Axtell, *Gestures: The Do's and Taboos of Body Language Around the World*
William W. Forgey, M.D.: *Travelers' Medical Resource*

SEVENTEEN

Protective Operations in the Corporate Environment

by Robert L. Oatman

A GREAT DEAL HAS BEEN WRITTEN about the most visible and, some say, the most glamorous aspect of executive protection—operations. Enough to fill a small library. But precious little material has been published about the administration of an executive protection program, and the complex maneuvering necessary in the highly charged and intensely competitive corporate environment. This chapter is intended to expose the reader to the kind of real administrative experience that drives the executive protection operation of one of the country's largest Fortune 500 corporations, and to the lessons of that experience.

This viewpoint is predicated on the experience of having established a protection program "from scratch," a scenario involving the introduction of a consultant's recommendations to build an operation from the ground up, with a fresh, professional perspective. This kind of grand opportunity rarely presents itself. But when it does, the experience of years of protective operations management can be brought to bear on the development of a custom tailored, dynamic and vital organization.

There are a hundred lessons to be learned and rules to be followed in this kind of environment, and I don't pretend to know them all. Nor do I intend to present all of them here. Instead, my purpose is to discuss broad topics that can shed some light on running a vibrant protection operation within a corporation. And while this may all sound like a lesson in corporate survival, it is more importantly a lesson in the security management of a corporation's most important asset—the chief executive officer. If you and your program are successful, well managed, vital, team spirited, imaginative and smart, then the opportunity to minimize risk to your CEO is significant.

PROGRAM DEVELOPMENT

The first building block in the development or restructuring of a protection program is the examination of the threat environment and developing a realistic risk assessment. You can't determine, or justify, the nature of the program unless you determine the nature of the threat. Consider the total protective environment (corporate and private) of the principal and, if necessary, his family. Conduct incisive, informed and realistic examinations of risk particular to the principal, as well as general risk factors that all the citizens of the world confront.

Be thorough but be reasonable. Don't, for example, emphasize the threat of terrorism unless reality makes such a confrontation probable. That is usually not the case. If your examination of risk exposure is well researched, balanced, and credible, then your proposed program will hold more weight for those who make the decisions.

Don't let a risk assessment that is a year old drive the direction of your program. A threat analysis responds to a fluid environment that can gradually evolve, or alter radically, in response to a wide variety of stimuli. Have periodic reassessments conducted to be certain that your program is responsive to the risk.

The traditional idea of relegating the "security guys" to a basement closet, only to be brought out in an emergency, can be aggressively countered by demonstrating the importance of your immediate presence through a *credible* risk analysis.

Begin program development with a well-thought mission statement, describing goals and objectives. It is critically important to establish a dialogue with the decision makers in the organization—the chief of staff, corporate counsel, the budget director or controller—in short, anyone in your chain of command who will review and approve the various aspects of your program.

Recognize from the beginning that your enthusiasm for a concept (or for a capital budget item) may not necessarily translate into reality. Compromise is usually the foundation of success. The motivation that drives corporate America is profit, and your demonstrated enthusiasm to develop and use resources wisely will serve you well. Get to know and understand the budget process and recognize its limitations. If an emergency or unforeseen circumstance requires that you ask for a budget variance, be prepared to thoroughly justify it, and have alternatives in your mind. Avoid placing yourself in the embarrassing position of seeking approval for an acquisition, only to be told that the resource already exists within the corporation, or can be acquired better and more effectively through another route. Failing to do this only demonstrates that you haven't done your homework, or, more importantly, don't understand corporate dynamics.

The evaluation of travel and expense reports from your staff needs close attention. Be certain that you are intimately familiar with corporate expense policies and procedures and that you follow them to the letter. This is particularly relevant if your program is a new one, since it will be the subject of intense scrutiny, as any new players are.

Be exceedingly careful in the selection of your protection personnel. Conduct thorough background investigations, including discussions with current and former associates and employers. If you know your CEO, you know what kind of people he or she likes and doesn't like. Use that knowledge, in combination with criteria such as talent and experience, to make personnel selections. If your corporation has a large security staff, consider hiring from within for the protection program. This shows company loyalty, smart resource management, and creates an interesting career path opportunity that may help to minimize turnover expectancy among the security staff.

Personnel costs can amount to 85% of your budget. Attempt to minimize that encumbrance as much as you can by using off-site contract protection specialists wherever possible. The use of established, approved protection teams, who meet your criteria, can be very useful, especially in distant domestic sites and overseas locations. They know the language, the customs, the local players and you only pay for them when you are in town. If your operation requires advance work, an overseas operative can spend a few hours at the visit site before arrival, as opposed to sending one of your own people out two days ahead.

If you are the director of your protection program, don't lose touch with reality. Work the street yourself on occasion, both to demonstrate and tune your proficiency and to keep a good operational handle on the protection environment. It also shows your principal that you aren't afraid to get your hands dirty, and that you can provide both operational and administrative leadership.

Don't skimp on advance work. Any protection professional worth his salt knows the value of site preparation, both in terms of safety and that magic word, "facilitation." Facilitation is worth its weight in gold because, while it provides a level of comfort and convenience to the principal, it adds immeasurably to the security mission by minimizing unnecessary exposure to risk.

Emphasize training. I can't say enough about the need to train, prepare, drill, evaluate and reevaluate the effectiveness of your program. Training keeps your people interested, alert and proficient. If they drive the principal, have them take driver training. If they carry firearms, have them qualify frequently. If they carry "step-down" weapons, be sure they know how to use them (the ASP is a very effective tool that has found prominence among protection teams lately). To the extent possible, develop in-house training programs that are cost-effective and realistic. You are better off, for example, ensuring proficiency in emergency medical protocols than training for counter-terrorism defenses.

In my opinion, the emphasis on the use of firearms is sometimes overdone. I can't recall a single assassination attempt that was stopped by return gunfire from protection officers. Events simply happen too quickly to respond. I'm not for a minute suggesting that firearms not be carried. They should. But the reality is that you, and your principal, are better off preparing for situations favored by the odds. Firearms training and proficiency is important, particularly from a liability standpoint, but your training should be broad-based enough to establish proficiency in many other areas as well.

Reevaluate the direction of your program, and the procedural implications of your established operations, to see if you can do things better. Be imaginative and proactive. For example, the conduct of counter-surveillance activities can reveal the presence of individuals who are watching your principal. Watch for the watchers—you are being paid to be smarter than they are, and you can be, if you learn to anticipate. Don't rely on comfortable assumptions. The perpetrators of the Reso and Weinstein abductions came from within, from their own "trusted" associates. This is a good lesson for us all.

If you feel that you need a fresh perspective, don't let your professional pride interfere with the thought of seeking advice from someone outside of the organization. It's not an admission of weakness to seek help, it's a statement of strength and maturity that can reveal vulnerabilities you can't see.

You don't need to become an expert in the rapidly advancing world of security hardware technology, but you do need a good working knowledge. Keep up on this area by reading trade journals and by talking with your counterparts in other organizations who confront the same problems. I would also highly recommend the use of a security consulting firm that has engineering expertise to serve as your representative in any dealings with security hardware vendors and installers. They will save you heartache and money. Some hardware vendors will try to sell you whatever they think you need, and not necessarily what your circumstances say you need. A consultant with engineering expertise can design the best system for you, leave the procurement and installation of systems up to others, and serve as a watchdog over the entire process. You can avoid becoming a victim of budget overages and ensure the installation of a high quality system, relevant to your needs.

Establish a well-informed protective intelligence network. It's hard to defend yourself if you don't know what to expect. One of the most useful aspects of protective intelligence is liaison with local, state and federal law enforcement agencies. Seek them out. Talk with their chiefs. Cultivate social and business contacts with them. It's an easy approach if you have a law enforcement background yourself, and the returns on this particular investment can be very profitable.

THE LINCHPIN—PERCEPTION

The survival of an executive protection program in the corporate environment (and your continued employment) can be a very tenuous position indeed. To begin with, the very nature of your presence is negative: You don't contribute to the bottom line; you aren't a profit center; if you run a 24-hour program, the corporation may not fully support your budget, requiring your protectee to contribute personal resources; you serve as a constant and unpleasant reminder of the dangers inherent in today's world; your principal may feel that your presence is, at best, a burdensome intrusion; fellow CEO's may look at your chief executive as an oddity when they themselves go about their day unprotected; you embody the nagging feeling in the back of your protectee's mind that he isn't "man enough" to take care of himself; and finally, your presence is usually welcome only for as long as the memory of the latest kidnapping headline lingers in the mind of your charge.

These are difficult negatives to counteract, but they can be minimized or even eliminated with smart, aggressive adherence to the canons of corporate culture. If you can first recognize those rules, and follow them, you can survive, and even thrive. One of the most difficult tasks of maintaining the confidence of corporate leadership is supporting a positive perception of your program.

The first commandment to remember: "Negative Perception Will Kill You." Regardless of your program's effectiveness, the perception that is held by others—often uninformed, inaccurate and contrary to reality, can scuttle a protection detail just as surely as if it were sunk by gross incompetence.

How does one build and maintain a positive perception? This question is easier to answer than it is to accomplish, but there are some suggestions. First, it is necessary to get the right players on your side and make them believers in you, your program, your subordinates and your abilities as a *corporate officer,* not just as a narrowly limited protection specialist. Skill in executive security and protection is an obvious central requirement. But it is just as important that you be perceived as a respected, effective, well-informed and articulate executive who can represent the CEO and the corporation in its best light. The development of a comfortable dialogue with the major players, keeping them informed, seeking their advice, being accessible, reaps huge dividends.

When I speak of conformance with corporate culture, I mean that you must be savvy enough to recognize current trends within the company, and flow with them. Look for the *big picture* and follow its direction. Understand the corporate philosophy and mission, as well as the chemistry of key personnel. Build your operation with corporate ideals as the underpinnings and you can't go wrong. You, and your organization, will be perceived as being team players, in step with everyone else. Rid yourself of the mind-set that because you are "security," and have access to the principal, that you are privileged and don't need to conform to the rules. The resentment that this approach builds can turn around and bite you.

Demonstrated performance is one way to help assure positive perception. But it takes time to establish a good track record. And many aspects of executive protection are latent, misunderstood and rarely, if ever, seen in detail by anyone but the chief executive. It is therefore important that the benefits of the program be sold to the senior leadership and, if necessary, to the Board of Directors.

The central tenet of an executive protection program, the one that can truly counteract the argument that it's an expensive, intrusive extravagance, is this: **It permits the chief executive to live safely in, and move efficiently through, an increasingly dangerous world. The immediate lack of concern over personal safety allows him or her to concentrate fully on the business at hand.** That's your primary selling point. It involves a well managed combination of protection and facilitation. But it cannot be achieved unless the CEO first has confidence enough in the protection program to allow him or her to forget about security issues and leave the worrying to you.

The kidnapping and killing of Exxon executive Stanley Reso, and the claustrophobic abduction of Harvey Weinstein in New York demonstrate the real, close-to-home hazards of being a prominent chief executive. If your CEO has even moderate curiosity, he or she will want to know about these things. Be prepared to keep him or her, and other superiors to whom you are accountable, informed of such protective intelligence and trends. It is important that you be able to brief them, incisively and accurately, about recent events involving security and protection incidents. The development of a presentation format, no matter how informally structured, allows you to provide accurate, consistently focused information about events as they unfold.

You, and your protection specialists, should be able to describe an event in detail, the progress that authorities are making toward resolution (as in a kidnapping), a critique about how it could have been avoided, and any suggestions or reminders to your principal to avoid similar incidents. To do this, you need intelligence. Read as many articles from mainstream publications as you can get, subscribe to an information service, watch broadcast news services early in the morning. In short, stay informed and on top of events. The last thing you want is for your CEO to say, "Did you hear about that kidnapping last night?" only to return a blank stare.

AVOID A NARROW FOCUS

The mission of an executive protection team is inherent in its name: The protection of key executives. And, as those of us who are experienced practitioners know, the management of an "EP" program involves a bewildering variety of minutia: we live and breathe details, details, details. Don't let anything fall through the cracks. That's a good, healthy perspective to have on the management of your operation. But it shouldn't blind you to the need and opportunity to establish a leadership role within the corporation by championing other causes.

If possible, expand the narrow corridor of executive protection. For example, the development of a crisis management program, or a corporate communications center will help to support the primary mission, while making the executive protection office a more central part of the corporate community. The development of your mission statement should include consideration of related roles and activities, without losing your primary focus.

Finally, THINK about everything that you do. How will your managerial decision affect the chief executive; your immediate superior; your subordinates; the stock holders; or the corporate environment and its associates? How will it be perceived? Is there a better way, a more cost effective way, a smarter use of existing resources? How will your decision impact the *big picture?*

Think through the dominoes that will be triggered by your decision and attempt to predict the consequences of your actions and decisions. Hindsight is always a clear perspective, but you get paid for seeing through the clouds of foresight. Many of the decisions we make in this business can't be given a lot of time for thought. It's often more reaction and gut instinct than anything else. But management decisions can frequently be made with time enough for good judgement to predominate.

EIGHTEEN

Corporate Aircraft Security

by W. Greg Light

IT IS ESTIMATED THAT Fortune 500 companies in the United States operate some 1500 aircraft. Although commercial air carriers are required to comply with a rather stringent aviation security program administered by the Federal Aviation Administration there is no such program or requirement of the general aviation population.

Commercial air carriers are required to comply with the Air Carrier Standard Security Program (A.C.S.S.P.). This program was developed by the Air Transport Association in 1975, submitted to the Federal Aviation Administration and after receiving the approval of the F.A.A., was implemented by almost all U.S. air carriers. It is now mandatory that all U.S. air carriers operate under this program. The A.C.S.S.P. simply assures that all airlines will operate under a single, standard security program.

Some areas administered under this program include the training programs for Checkpoint Security Screeners, Inflight Security Coordinators and Ground Security Coordinators. It establishes requirements for baggage and cargo security, checkpoint security screening operations, physical security and general guidelines.

Although this program has no effect on the general aviation community it is important to note that strict requirements are met by the commercial counterpart at one side of the airport. A security program in your area of operation may be all but nonexistent.

The F.A.A. does require airports throughout the country to have some type of security program in effect. Some airports have a very effective security program in place but, most airports still operate with the open door policy. The actual airport security system may only be a fence with open gates and some of those fences are only 3 feet high.

Recently I was conducting a vulnerability survey for a corporate flight department. I arrived at the airport and my first observation was a lone security guard walking the ramp area. He was a real professional. His dark blue uniform, red tennis shoes and three foot nightstick portrayed an imposing figure. I immediately walked over to one of the corporate aircraft parked on the ramp and I was challenged by our security professional smoking a cigarette next to our future 30 million dollar fireball. I told him I was an airline writer and I wanted to see the inside of this aircraft. He not only obliged me by opening the unlocked aircraft but, invited me inside for a closer look. He left me alone inside the aircraft. I left the pilot a box with my business card in it. It was found by a flight attendant a week later after flying overseas with the company CEO. All of the parties concerned were very relieved to find only the business card in the box. As for my friend in the red tennis shoes, I haven't had the pleasure of seeing him again.

This chapter will discuss the concerns of the Personal Protection Specialists and their relationship with, and in, the corporate flight community.

FLIGHT CREW COORDINATION

This section has been placed first and with due regard. Your ability to deal with people and keep your ego in check will never be more important. I know I will make few friends with this next statement but, two of the biggest egos are about to come in contact with each other. Being a pilot and Personal Protection Specialist, I can attest that both professions have strong egos and on occasions, do clash.

A note to the Personal Protection Specialist. If push comes to shove, the pilot will win. Ultimately, the pilot of an aircraft is charged with the sole responsibility for the safety and security of his or her aircraft. Your job is to develop a strong working relationship with your corporate flight department.

I have watched corporate security departments and executive protection teams all but forget that a corporate flight department exists. There are a number of factors that contribute to this. Corporate flight departments usually enjoy some autonomy. First, the location is removed from the actual day to day operations of the corporate office. Flight department personnel have little contact with the corporate community and almost no contact with the security department. If your company utilizes a charter service for air transportation the contact will only come when you arrive at the airport for your flight. The fault does not always lie with the security department. The responsibility for implementing an effective security program involves the flight department as well. The following are a few suggestions for implementing your program.

1) Schedule monthly security meetings with your flight department. Discuss security concerns, travel security planning and air crew concerns.

2) Conduct joint training sessions involving executive protection movements, aircraft fire fighting, aircraft evacuation procedures, inflight

security procedures, hostage negotiations and crisis response. Involve corporate management whenever possible.

3) Develop a Crisis Response Plan and <u>TEST THE PLAN TOGETHER.</u>

4) Assign a Security Liaison and Flight Crew Liaison to keep channels of communication open.

5) Have your flight crew personnel provide you with an aircraft familiarization inspection. Learn the aircraft! Your security search will be made easier if you know the aircraft and your flight crew will be more receptive to you searching the aircraft.

6) If your security department subscribes to Lexus/Nexus, ASNET or any of the other security computer networks provide your flight departments with regular security briefings prior to flights.

7) Learn aircraft & aircrew terminology. Know what each person's job entails and learn the chain of command.

8) Develop, design and write a Standard Operating Procedure for security procedures and crisis response. Have the final draft approved and signed by your company CEO.

9) Never attempt to search or board an aircraft without the Captain's permission. Remember, it is their airplane.

You will find that flight crews are always willing to work with security and flight crews should always find security willing to work with them. Make the attempt to work together. It will be the beginning of a beautiful relationship.

RAMP SECURITY

Whenever possible keep your aircraft in the hanger. Although keeping your aircraft in the hanger does not assure 100% security, you can reduce your risk. If a hangar is not available or if the aircraft is away from home base and *Remain-over-night* (RON), keep these procedures in mind.

1) **ALWAYS** use the aircraft's alarm system. Even if the aircraft is only going to be parked for a short time.

2) Do not allow anyone on the aircraft unless they are closely supervised by flight crew members or security personnel. This includes fuelers, cleaners, ramp personnel or any non-company employee. This is particularly true at foreign airports.

3) Flight crews should be provided with all emergency numbers including: police, fire, bomb squad, FAA, FBI and corporate security 24-hour numbers.

4) Aircraft should be parked in a well lit area, away from perimeter fencing. If the threat level warrants, consideration should be given to having your corporate security agents placed on 24-hour guard of the aircraft.

5) Flight crew personnel should visit the aircraft at least once a day to check security and check for tampering. If alarm systems are not used, then security seals should be used and checked for tampering.

6) Aircraft keys should never be left with FBO (Fixed Base Operator) staff.

7) **ALWAYS** conduct a security inspection of the aircraft prior to your departure.
8) Flight crews and security personnel should leave contact numbers with FBO staff in the event of emergencies or suspected aircraft tampering.
9) Company logo's and/or organizational identification should be removed from the aircraft's exterior.
10) No cargo, luggage or inflight items should be placed on the aircraft unless inspected by flight crew or security personnel.

HANGAR SECURITY

1) Hangar the aircraft whenever possible.
2) Use the aircraft alarm system, even when the aircraft is in the hangar.
3) Use a picture I.D. system and enforce it 100%.
4) Equip hangar facility with efficient physical security measures, i.e., card access systems, motion detectors, fire suppression & alarms, surveillance cameras, etc.
5) Hangar should be well within the secured airport perimeter and well lighted inside and outside.
6) Access to the hangar area, flight control, dispatch and all operations areas should be denied to anyone without escort and security clearance.
7) Employee parking should be separated from visitor parking.
8) If hangar doors are left open for ventilation, expansion barriers should be used to deny or slow access.
9) Excellent housekeeping throughout your facility will reduce your fire risk, as well as personal accidents.
10) All flight operations personnel should be trained in security procedures and reporting of violators.
11) Regular security and safety inspections should be conducted.
12) Consider an outside consultant to perform annual risk assessments and vulnerability studies. A qualified consultant may be able to see problems you cannot.
13) Vehicle parking and storage of items on the ground should be at least 25 feet from fence line.
14) Posting of all emergency numbers including law enforcement, fire and security at all telephones.
15) Maintain a current copy of your security procedures and crisis management plan at your hangar/flight operations area. This should be kept out of public view and provided to only those with a need to know.
16) All flight plans and itinerary should be secured and information provided to only those individuals with a security clearance.
17) Maintain positive key control of flight operations area, hangar,

perimeter gates and aircraft. Conduct a periodic audit of keys, access cards and I.D. badges.

18) Consideration should be given to passenger screening and parcel/cargo screening areas, as well as equipment.

AIRCRAFT and AVIONICS THEFT

One of the largest threats to aviation security is the theft of aircraft and avionics equipment. Although aircraft theft usually occurs more at airports near border areas, it can still occur anywhere in the world. The use of alarm systems and high security locks on your aircraft will not prevent a theft but, it will serve as a strong deterrent. A greater risk is presented for the theft of avionics equipment. In 1993 there was approximately $1.2 million in reported losses from aircraft burglaries. The following procedures may be considered as preventative measures for aircraft and avionics thefts.

1) Aircraft alarm system should be employed at all times, even when the aircraft is in the hangar.

2) High security locks should be installed in the aircraft.

3) All avionics equipment and removable items in the aircraft should be marked for positive identification.

4) A color marking (entire coverage of color stripe marking). In addition to engraving the aircraft registration numbers or any other unique identification marks or symbols. The addition of this combined effort will act as a visual deterrent.

5) Non-installed items of value or of unusual interest should be removed from the aircraft whenever possible.

6) Inventory of the aircraft contents should be taken and results kept on file at your flight operations area. Photographs of the aircraft's exterior and interior should be taken and included in the file.

AIRCRAFT ALARM SYSTEMS

Since I have mentioned aircraft alarm systems previously I would like to include some general information regarding the systems that are available today. As with most alarm systems, you have the option of using on-board, or portable systems. The preference is given to on-board systems since these provide better protection using the aircraft's power supply and remain with the aircraft regardless of its location. These systems are also harder to defeat. Remember, aircraft alarm systems are similar in nature to automobile systems only in the fact that they move with the item you are attempting to protect. This is where the systems similarities end. Aircraft alarm systems take time to install. They must be installed by trained avionics technicians and approved by the Federal Aviation Administration. The systems are expensive and the cost can range from $100,000 to $250,000. This is really not expensive when you consider you are protecting an aircraft that ranges in price from $3 million to $50 million dollars upward. Shepherd Systems, Inc. manufactures an alarm system that alerts of tampering by using a pocket pager. The range of this system varies but it can operate up to 10 miles. A system that I am quite impressed with is manufactured by Securaplane USA. This system can provide you with alert times, zones and an actual play by play of the persons intentions attempting to tamper with your aircraft. This is done using a radio system which supplies you with immediate notification and/or a complete report of any security violations when you return to the airport. You can even dial up the aircraft for a status check from your hotel. The range of this system is around 10 miles, greater range can be provided using a portable repeater system.

A portable system I have come to rely on is "The Agent" manufactured by Intellitech Industries, Inc. This system is completely portable. The benefit of this system is its portability. You can use this system for aircraft, hangars or hotel rooms. It comes complete with wireless PIR sensors. You can add door sensors, magnetic switches and panic buttons. This system also works with a portable radio system. It provides immediate notification, as well as maintaining a record of violations including time and dates. It is self-contained in a briefcase and weighs approximately 18 lbs. I have used this system as well, and I can highly recommend it. The drawback to using a portable system is simply the fact that sensors or other parts can be misplaced or forgotten and people can forget to charge the system. Remember, you cannot install any of the sensors permanently in the aircraft.

HIJACKING

Although hijackings of corporate aircraft are rare, they do occur. Each year one or two private aircraft are hijacked. The hijackers' reasons are not always clear and the reasons are not always important to us. What is important is that we have the ability to prevent hijackings. By using some or all of the methods discussed in this chapter we can reduce our risk. Consider the following suggestions to reduce your risk of hijackings.

1) Baggage inspection of all carry-on baggage. This can be accomplished rather quickly and should be employed when transporting any unknown passengers.

2) Screening of all passengers. Using portable or hand held metal detectors can not only locate weapons or items used as weapons but, it can also act as a strong deterrent to attempted threats.

3) Positive identification of all passengers prior to boarding.

4) No hitchhikers! It is not uncommon for people to seek free transportation. Unless the individual is cleared by your flight operations and security department do not transport them. A written procedure should be adopted and adhered to regarding transportation of company and non-company personnel.

5) Hijackings are most likely to occur during the hour of operation. Any suspicious activity should be reported and checked immediately. If you are in doubt, take a delay on the flight rather than risk an unwanted passenger.

6) Remember, a good, consistent physical security program can be a deterrent in itself but, nothing can replace the human element.

INFLIGHT SECURITY PROCEDURES

1) Flight crews should frequently review security plans and procedures with the security department. Whenever possible the flight crews and security should conduct briefings on security matters prior to any trip, particularly during an increased threat level.

2) If the cockpit is separated from the cabin by a door, unauthorized personnel should not be permitted into the cockpit.

3) Pilots of the aircraft should be familiar with the transponder codes and code words used by the tower personnel to declare or notify them of an emergency.

FOR SECURITY CONCERNS THESE CODES AND CODE WORDS ARE NOT BEING PRINTED IN THIS BOOK. THAT INFORMATION CAN BE OBTAINED BY YOUR FLIGHT CREW THROUGH THE FEDERAL AVIATION ADMINISTRATION. FLIGHT CREWS SHOULD BE THOROUGHLY FAMILIAR WITH THIS INFORMATION. THE MISTAKEN USE OF THESE CODE WORDS OR TRANSPONDER CODES CAN RESULT IN A GREAT DEAL OF INCONVENIENCE TO THE AIR TRAFFIC CONTROLLERS AND THE FLIGHT CREWS INVOLVED.

4) Cooperate with the hijacker at all times.

5) Make every effort to notify the air traffic controllers of your position and destination, as well as any other vital information.

6) In the event of a hijacking or unauthorized person on board your aircraft you should make every effort to land at the nearest available airport. Get the plane safely on the ground using any pretext.

7) Once on the ground, get the passengers off the aircraft and then the flight crew members.

8) Allow the law enforcement authorities to deal with the hijackers or other disturbances.

AIRCRAFT BOMB THREATS

The regular search of aircraft for sabotage devices or illegal substances prior to commencing your flight should be common practice. As the threat level increases, so should your degree and intensity of the search increase. Particular attention should be paid to areas that are most easily accessible to the saboteur. This area is most likely the exterior of the aircraft. Areas such as wheel wells, jet engines, inspection ports and service ports. This inspection can usually be done in conjunction with the pilot or by the pilot during their preflight walk around inspection of the aircraft. Remember to secure any doors or inspection ports you have opened for your inspection. If, during your inspection, you find a suspicious or unfamiliar device, it should not be touched or disturbed in any way. The appropriate security organization should be contacted immediately.

After searching the exterior move to the interior. Begin your search in the forward section of the aircraft. Start your search in the flight deck or cockpit area. Check all areas including the logbook/flight manual storage area, oxygen mask storage, ceiling and sidewalls and inside the first aid kit. Move slowly toward the rear of the aircraft. Be sure to check the galley area extremely well, including ovens, cold storage and trash areas. As you continue your move to the rear check all storage areas including under seat stowage, oxygen mask compartments and seat back pockets. Check the lavatory area including trash bins, towel storage, water access ports and light fixtures. In general conduct a very thorough, complete search. Your search should be conducted the same way, in the same manner, without interruption each time you perform your search.

If manpower and time permit, I would suggest developing a cross-check system. This is the type of search bomb technicians perform. It simply involves two security agents conducting the same search. One starts at the front of the aircraft, the other at the rear. The agents pass each other in the search and continue searching until the one stops where the other began. A second set of eyes may sometimes see what one set misses. Familiarization of the aircraft you are searching is mandatory. Without a complete and thorough knowledge of the aircraft and the equipment on board, you will not be able to perform a complete search. In addition, I would suggest taking a class in explosives identification and recognition. You do not need to be a bomb technician but, you do need to know what explosives look like and the damage that can be incurred. Remember, anything can be a bomb!

DRUG SMUGGLING

General aviation aircraft are involved to a great extent in the drug smuggling business. Passengers, flight crew members, ground crew staff, as well as professional smugglers can reap the profits of using your airplane to transport their goods. Your aircraft searches should also include searching for drugs and related contraband. Not only can you stem the tide of illegal drugs coming into, or being transported around your company, but you may be saving your company a great deal of money and a great deal more embarrassment when your aircraft is seized by law enforcement or customs officials for transporting drugs.

CONCLUSION

This chapter will only provide you with general guidelines in establishing your corporate aircraft security program. It cannot substitute for experience and continued training. Aviation security is a relatively new field. It is a growing concern for security professionals and flight professionals alike. Developing mutual respect and a professional relationship with your counterparts will pave the way toward building your program.

The following is a list of alarm manufactures, equipment, and professional organizations mentioned in this chapter: • Shepherd Systems, Inc., 358 Baker Avenue, Concord, MA 01742 (508)371-3000; • Securaplane USA, 3830 E. 44th Street, Suite 534, Tucson, AZ 85713 (602)745-6655; • Intellitech Industries, Inc., 1300 Shiloh Road, Kennesaw, GA 30144 (404)514-7999.

NINETEEN

Long Guns and the
Personal Protection Specialist

by Craig Fox Huber

LONG GUNS, for the sake of this writing, include all shoulder fired or hand held weapons, excluding handguns, which are capable of delivering effective small arms fire onto a protectee or security personnel from ranges beyond those considered practical for the primary weapons carried by the security personnel. These same long guns can be employed by security personnel to extend their own effective range of defensive fire. Included in this category of weapons would be rifles, particularly sniper rifles, assault rifles and shotguns. Although sub-machine guns, which are often nothing more than machine pistols with some type of stock attached, aren't technically long guns, we will address their use here and include them in this category.

Long Guns, when compared to handguns, are generally considered to give two advantages to their users. The first is range, and the second is firepower. Firepower can be defined in terms of quantity, quality, or both. The question of range is a little more involved. "Longer range" can be anything beyond the range at which most people are effective with a handgun. This can be the limited range of the riot shotgun, or the more extended range of the assault rifle. Longer range can also refer to that which is beyond the area normally observed or controlled by security personnel, or that which is, in fact, beyond the physical capability of the human eye. This is the realm of the Long Range Weapons System or Sniper Rifle.

Though private sector Personal Protection Specialists (P.P.S.) aren't often forced to defend against a long gun attack, they do have to be aware of the possible threat posed by subjects armed with such weapons, and the limited viable response security personnel can realistically employ as individuals.

Security personnel also need to be aware of the usefulness of long guns in the defense role.

If we look at effective security as LAYERS OF PROTECTION, and we are trained to do so, it is easy to see that in order to provide protection from long gun attack we need more layers of security. The layers have to be deeper (involve more security personnel) than what we, in the private sector, are used to dealing with, and the layers would have to be "tempered," or flexible, instead of just "hardened."

NEGATIVE

One of the biggest problems security teams have to face when considering long gun attacks is the same problem they face when dealing with any attack. In most cases security has to "react" rather than act. This is particularly true in the private sector. We can't neutralize a suspected threat by action. We must wait for the threat to materialize before we can take action against it.

It is, practically speaking, impossible for any individual bodyguard to defend a protectee from a long range assault by a dedicated sniper. The same can be said of an attack, against a principal, mounted by several people armed with assault rifles or sub-guns.

It is, however, possible to reduce the risk of such an assault by being aware of your surroundings (aware of an area much greater than you customarily try to control), by gathering all the information possible on those who might pose a threat and by limiting the movement of your client in areas susceptible to such attacks.

One aspect of long gun attacks that security personnel must take particular note of is this: Such attacks are often directed towards the security personnel themselves. An assault, with abduction of the principal as its goal, is helped along immensely by the removal of the security personnel, just prior to or in conjunction with the arrival of the grab and run team.

It is standard procedure to attempt to neutralize the protection and the driver before any move is made on the principal. This is especially true when security consists of a single bodyguard and a driver, who may or may not be a member of the security team. If this can be accomplished while both are dismounted it avoids damage to the vehicle and gives the attackers another option in escape. Using the principal's own vehicle to move him away from the point of attack simplifies the logistics of the maneuver, lowers the risk of alerting anyone of what has happened and serves to quiet the abductee and make him easier to manage, since he is still in "his" element. If the limo is full of bullet holes and the windshield is blown out, it kind of screws things up.

From a threat to compliance stand point, the removal of one's bodyguard by a long range marksman, tends to weaken the resolve of the principal to resist politically or financially motivated demands. It directs the principal to a certain type of activity or inactivity, for the benefit of the opposition. The message is, "It could have been you, or a member of your family."

POSITIVE

In the private sector, the "Long Gun" which security teams are most likely to encounter in use against them is the sub-machine gun (SMG). As unpleasant as the possibility is to consider, there are some positive aspects to the SMG being the weapon of choice for most bad guys. The first of these is, most bad guys are just as susceptible to the hype we are fed in the movies and on TV as are the uninformed good guys.

Hardly a movie is belched out of "Hollyjungle" today which doesn't have some totally untrained individual picking up an UZI or MP-5, casually working the mechanism, as if it had arrived on the delivery table at the same time he did, and going into righteous battle with his enemies. Despite overwhelming odds and great loss of blood, usually the result of tortuous injuries inflicted by the same bad guys who were stupid enough to let him get his hands on one of their weapons in the first place, he defeats numerically superior forces armed with everything from assault rifles to rocket launchers. And he never runs out of ammo!

The facts are: The sub-machine gun is not so easy to master, it does not guarantee a sure win to its user, or the sure death of its intended target. Usually these weapons are loaded with standard handgun ammunition, which is not particularly effective in stopping vehicles in their tracks or in penetrating standard body armor. These weapons just aren't as available as the anti-gun press would have you believe. And sub-guns are more difficult to conceal than handguns and much less effective than other long guns.

Many assaults with this type of weapon prove ineffective because most people overestimate the capability of the weapon and start shooting long before the threshold of their own or the weapon's capability, has been reached. The high cyclic rate of fire which attends most sub-machine guns, and their relatively small magazine capacity, can prove a greater disadvantage than the perceived advantage. In the heat of the moment many people "shoot dry" before any real damage can be done to the target.

The use of vests by the principal and the team, the first step taken to "harden" the target when an elevated level of risk is detected, greatly enhances their chance of surviving a sub-gun attack.

Lest you go off half cocked and optimistic, don't forget the possibility of a trained assault team, with fire discipline, armed with sub-guns, loaded with armor piercing rounds, and a plan. The only effective defense in this case is advanced intelligence gathering and avoidance.

THE OTHER SIDE OF THE COIN

The long gun, in many forms, can be a great asset to the Personal Protection Specialist, especially when employed in the *team* scenario. Long guns properly deployed in conjunction with tactical communications can greatly improve the effective level of security you are able to provide.

"Long gun personnel" deployment allows the security team to control a much greater area of response, can give advanced warning of potential threats and can neutralize a high level attack on the principal more effectively than almost any other response possible.

SNIPER RIFLE/LONG RANGE WEAPONS SYSTEM

In the hands of a trained and experienced long range marksman, a sniper rifle can extend the circle of effective protection from arms length, or practical handgun range, to 500, 1000 or even 1500 meters, engaging a threat long before it can harm the protectee. A team backed up by such a "system" has a tremendous edge, in confidence alone, over one not so equipped. The only effective way to neutralize a sniper threat to your principal is with intelligence gathering and a counter sniper.

REAL FIRE POWER

A well placed team member, armed with any of today's better assault rifles, can dissuade a large and dedicated force of attackers bent on injuring or abducting the principal. With proper ammunition (and what is proper for one scenario may be totally inappropriate in another), the assault rifle can disable attacking vehicles, give cover fire to a retreating team and principal or be used offensively to neutralize a threat or clear a path for the team to advance through to safety with the principal.

Where concealment and light weight or mobility are perceived to be more important than raw fire power, such as in a vehicle or on board a private aircraft, the SMG, in the hands of properly trained and experienced personnel, can be used to provide many of the functions the assault rifle can. Again choice of the proper type of ammunition for a particular job is critical. Some teams employ quickly interchangeable, color coded magazines to provide the load flexibility needed for both assault rifles and sub-machine guns to be used most effectively as defense tools. I generally use blued magazines for standard loads in sub-guns and assault rifles, nickled or stainless mags for one type of special purpose loads and some other form of marking for yet a third type of load. For instance I will load military "Full jacketed" loads in blue steel mags, "Armor Piercing" loads in nickeled magazines, and if I carry tracer ammo I will wrap red plastic electrical tape around the base of those magazines.

A riot shotgun such as the Remington 870, which an extended magazine, loaded with the proper ammunition, can arguably be called the finest close quarters defensive weapon in the world. A dedicated PPS, armed with such a weapon and firing from cover, can almost always turn away an assault mounted against his principal or any fixed installation under his control, even by a numerically far superior force.

A security team having all four of these weapons systems available and in place can present a perimeter which would be difficult or impossible to breach except by an all out military style assault. (See the four drawings—With and Without Long Gun Support—Airport and Estate on the following two pages.)

THE PROBLEM

As pointed out above, an attack by long guns is almost indefensible for the individual PPS. The Secret Service deploys two full teams to deal with this type of threat. The Counter Assault Team made up of Special Agents, and the Counter Sniper Team made up of Uniformed Officers, both of which have responsibility for dealing with long range threat. In addition the Secret Service has practically unlimited resources of man power and equipment at its disposal and it still can not guarantee the safety of its principal from long gun attack, pri-

WITH LONG GUN DEPLOYMENT — AIRPORT

(1) Sniper deployed on terminal roof controls entire perimeter fence and gate area. Area immediately behind plane not covered. **(2)** Assault Rifle deployed by personnel using vehicle for cover control area behind plane and fence line from point "A" to point "B". **(3) & (4)** Security personnel armed with shotguns and or assault rifles control gate and fence line from point (B) to point (A). All positions are supported by at least one other long gun position.

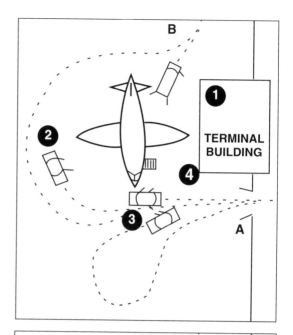

WITHOUT LONG GUN DEPLOYMENT — AIRPORT

Assault can come from any point on perimeter. Attacking personnel can take control of high ground and control movement in and around plane and terminal building.

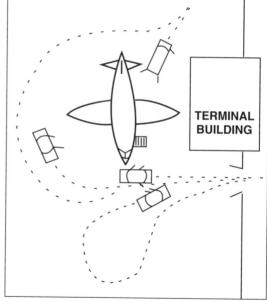

marily because of the exposure to the public demanded by the principal's job.

Avoidance of high risk areas is the most effective defense available to the individual. The list of such areas is so long that to be fully effective the defense plan would restrict the movement of the principal to a level unacceptable to most people who employ security. Stadiums, Country Estates, City Streets, Public Parks, Construction Sites, Jogging Trails, Shopping Malls, Any Window, Regularly Traveled Route to or from the work place, recreational site, or home,

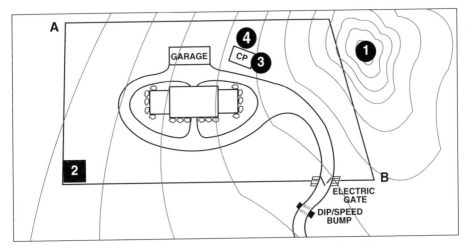

WITH LONG GUN DEPLOYMENT — ESTATE

(1) Sniper deployed on high ground controls entire perimeter fence and gate area. Area behind house and buildings not covered. **(2)** Assault Rifle deployed in tower controls access by vehicle, area behind buildings not covered by sniper and fence line from point "A" to point "B". **(3)** & **(4)** Security personnel armed with shotguns and or assault rifles control gate and fence line from point (B) to point (A). All positions are supported by at least one other long gun position. Combination of "Nite Sites" and area flood lights give 24 hour long gun support capability.

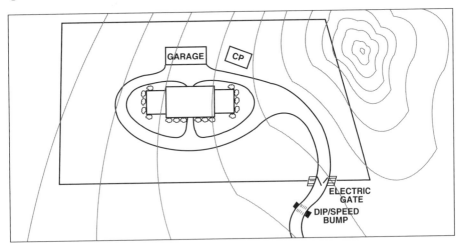

WITHOUT LONG GUN DEPLOYMENT — ESTATE

Assault can come from any point on perimeter. Attacking personnel can take control of high ground and control movement in compound.

all provide a potential sniper with access to your principal. Unless your client is willing to be turned into a mole, and to travel in an armored vehicle from secure place to secure place, it is all but impossible to protect him or her from a sniper.

If the protectee is a low profile, high-dollar client, an extremely successful but unpublicized financier for example, the risk of a long gun attack aimed directly at the principal is low. Much lower than it would be if the client were a politician, show business personality or high profile money man like Donald Trump or a woman like Ivana. The risk level of a long gun supported assault with abduction as its goal is also quite low in comparison.

INCIDENTAL THREAT

However there is another area of great concern to the PPS with regard to a long gun attack. This is the possibility of his or her client becoming the victim of an assault aimed at someone else.

If your client is going to be sharing a stage, dais, opera box, viewing stand or arena seating with a high profile, high level-of-threat individual, or if he or she is going to be sharing common transport with such a person, then you must consider your principal to be under the same level of threat as the higher risk individual.

RANDOM VIOLENCE

Another area of threat which exists is that of random violence. Your client is always susceptible to injury from an assault aimed at no one in particular. Freeway shooters, gang hit men, and other "wackos" present a threat to everyone, including your client. More and more of these assaults involve long guns in some form or another.

THE SOLUTION

Limit the exposure of your client to such high level threat by avoiding repetition in route selection, limiting the time your client is in the open during routine movements, and severely limiting the knowledge of your client's movements and whereabouts to a strict "need to know" basis.

Only those members of the family and staff, and those business associates who are directly involved with the specific event, should be briefed regarding the movement of the principal to and from the event. Even the drivers involved should always have three routes planned and be told by the Detail Leader which of the routes is to be taken at the last possible minute. Switch vehicles as often as possible and if two vehicles are used, move the principal's position in the vehicles on an "irregular" basis. As always, the most effective way to deal with threat is avoidance of the threat. Avoidance is far more effective than having to deal with an assault underway.

Use "low profile" transportation when possible. Stretch limousines draw unwanted attention to the security conscious. Standard luxury cars are much less conspicuous and are harder to track through traffic. The standard Cadillac, Town Car or New Yorker is also considerably easier to maneuver, in the event of an assault or other problem one would wish to avoid or escape from, than are the longer limos.

Where possible it is advisable to have the principal's vehicle armored. The passenger area can receive extra protection by having drop curtains of Kevlar® installed above rear and side windows (which prevents the attackers from establishing the protectee's exact position in the vehicle), and extra plate installed on the back of front and rear seats. The headliner and floor boards of the entire vehicle should also receive extra layers of protection as should the fuel tank, oil pan and radiator. "Run on Flat" tires are an excellent addition to the vehicle as are *kill switches* which can be activated by the principal or security personnel seated in the passenger area. The kill switch prevents the assault team from making use of the protectee's vehicle, as discussed earlier. Another useful addition would be the closed circuit ventilation system supported by an oxygen bottle in case of a gas attack. In the event of attack which cuts off all chance of escape or retreat, or if the driver is taken out, the principal just "buttons up" and waits for help. This is sometimes referred to as the "turtle shell" defense.

In the event your principal is going to be in close proximity to a higher risk level individual you should co-ordinate your security efforts with those of the HRL individual. Do not allow yourself to be separated from your protectee. In many cases the security for the HRL person will try to close you out of the security loop. They will tell you your client comes under their protection when he is in contact with their client. This is particularly true when dealing with government agencies. Don't believe this for one second. If the fecal matter gets involved with the ventilation system your client will be abandoned by the other security team, as should be the case.

In fact, in extreme cases the security for the HRL person might feel your client increases the threat to their protectee and decide to terminate him themselves.

Good advance work and threat assessment are two of the most effective defense tools available to the Personal Protection Specialist. Learning who your client's enemies are (primary threat) is the first step in threat assessment. Gathering all possible intelligence about those people is the second step. Knowing their modes of operation, level of dedication, their employees who might be used to carry out an assault against your client (secondary threat), the weak points of the "threat's" own security, all may give you the needed edge to avert a possible assault.

This gathering of intelligence is particularly important if there is the remotest possibility that a long gun attack might be employed against your client.

An important part of the advance work, which needs to be done for every location where your client will spend exposed time, is to establish a working knowledge of the "high ground." This might be a hilltop controlling a view of his estate, a roof top near his business or the roof of a neighboring home. In a team situation one of the primary responsibilities for your protectee's safety lies with the team member who controls this high ground.

Sometimes it is possible to secure the cooperation of local law enforcement units, when you can prove a short term elevated risk exists to one of their prominent citizens. One of the best ways to make use of this assistance is in control of high ground near your principal.

Remember the dictum of the Personal Protection Specialist, "Expect the Unexpected, Do the Unexpected." The advantage in a long gun assault lies almost entirely with those doing the assaulting. They get to pick the place, the time, the weapon and the personnel who will carry off the assault.

Each of these advantages must be dealt with separately and neutralized if possible.

Example: Alter the time of departure from home and work place each day, and alter the routes traveled as much as possible. The home and work place are both known so you must be extremely cautious as you leave or approach them. Have five or more possible routes planned. The detail leader should decide at the last moment which route will be taken. Don't be afraid to ad lib and change the route as you go. Sometimes this action will be dictated by traffic or other activity. Make unscheduled stops to throw off anyone who has timed the route. Long gun attacks depend on perfect timing. Have the driver slow down or speed up periodically. Use decoy vehicles.

Example: Several years ago, the security team leader for an extremely

Left to right: Rifle with scope, military weapon with regular magazine, and assault weapon with banana magazine.

wealthy lady learned of a planned assault on his principal. He had planted one of his own men in the employ of his protectee's estranged husband. He learned the "hit" was to be carried out by a sniper and the shooter was a former marine. The team leader had an investigator put on the shooter for two weeks, during which time the protectee was kept under wraps. At the end of the two weeks the team leader sent a copy of the accumulated file to the shooter. Included was information on the shooter and his family as well as details of the planned hit. Being a former marine himself, the bodyguard had written "Semper Fi" across the cover of the file in magic marker. The shooter quit, left town in fact. It might have been the contents of the file, but it was probably the simple greeting that turned the trick. The divorce became final before a replacement shooter could be recruited, eliminating the monetary motive for a killing. Good intelligence gathering was the effective counter assault in this case.

Never allow the principal or the team to become predictable. Don't frequent the same restaurants on a regular basis. "We always go to 'the Club' for dinner on Saturday night." This is a good way to get in harm's way. "I like to take River Road to work every morning." That's another. Team members or individual protective personnel must guard against becoming predictable themselves. Don't always go to the gym or the range at the same time each day or on the same days each week.

THE ARSENAL

There are a variety of Sniper Rifles that will work for the security team, the best of these are based on modern turn bolt actions such as Remington's Model 700. The most practical caliber for a Team rifle is probably the .308 Winchester (7.62x51 NATO). There are literally dozens of options available but the .308 is proven to be extremely accurate and effective to beyond 1000 yards. Excellent match ammunition is available in this caliber from all three major domestic manufacturers. Special purpose loads are available from a variety of sources. Recoil is light, particularly in a weapon that weights close to ten pounds. A synthetic stock and top quality fixed power scope in the 6x to 10x range, attached with solid mounts, almost complete the basic system. A one inch wide, adjustable, nylon sling is a must. A good eight or ten power binocular is almost as important to the long range marksman as is his rifle.

Some people like a stock mounted bi-pod, I'm not one of those and neither is Carlos Hathcock. There is a tendency to become dependent on the bi-pod and there are too many instances where it can not be effectively employed. These gadgets have a tendency toward folding up, or in some other way failing, at the most inopportune time.

When considering assault rifles, the variety is once again staggering. For private sector personnel I recommend one of the better semi-automatic models. In trained hands these units will accomplish what is needed without the hassles involved with full auto weapons ownership and transport. The various AR-15 models and their clones, the Ruger Mini-14 and any of AK clones chambered for the .223 cartridge will work. A better choice might be the newer versions of the AR-15 chambered for the 7.62x39, the Mini-30 (Ruger) or one of the standard semi-auto versions of the original Kalashnikov also chambered for the 7.62x39 round.

The best of the sub-guns for security work are the UZI, the MP-15 and the MAC-10. There are still those who feel Sub-Machine Gun development peaked with the old Thompson M-1928 and the Schmeisser MP-40, however these old warriors are very heavy and nearly impossible to conceal. All of the newer items are available in semi-auto versions which make a lot of sense for private sector use.

If full automatic weapons are employed by the security team, three round burst mechanisms must be employed.

The Grendel SRT Rifle in .308 cal. is a light defensive weapon which folds into a compact 30". Clip-on 3x12 Tasco Range Finding Trajectory Compensation Scope.

Most of the major domestic firearms manufacturers produce a serviceable fighting shotgun. Remington's Model 870 is probably the best known and most widely used model for this purpose. Winchester makes the Model 1300, Mossberg the Model 500 and Ithaca the Model 37. All are available in battle dress of various degrees. The old Winchester Model 12 and the older Model 97 were offered in police and military models and are still fine choices if they can be found in good shape at reasonable prices. There are several imported shotguns that will also work quite well for security purposes. I personally prefer pump action weapons over semi-automatic weapons for serious social functions. There are a growing number of "pros" who have opted to use Remington 1100's or Franchi's semi-auto for their fighting shotgun. These weapons **almost never** malfunction, if maintained properly and fed proper loads. The 870 that I have had for over twenty years has **never** malfunctioned, ever.

In Europe the weapon of choice, for many bodyguards doing estate duty, is a short barreled double gun loaded with buck shot. These are carried slung barrel down, over the left shoulder with the left hand on the barrels, and can be gotten into action "most rickee tick." In small towns where the protectee is the "patron" these same weapons are often carried at all times and in plain view by the guards. The mere presence of such a weapon is a great deterrent.

A shotgun does not require great skill on the part of the shooter to be effective, and everyone knows how damaging a round of buck shot can be. The draw back to this weapon is that it can not be used with good conscience where there are innocents in proximity to the bad guys. The shotgun is an indiscriminate neutralizer.

UNDER ATTACK

The principles of action differ very little for the security specialist whether an attack on his client is by handgun or long gun. The basics, slightly modified, apply. Arms Length, Cover, Pray, Remove! As soon as the attack starts you will want to get yourself and your principal under some sort of substantial cover or out of the line of fire, whichever can be accomplished most quickly.

The idea of merely throwing myself over the protectee just doesn't appeal to me. Besides which, this is not a very effective way of protecting the client, unless you happen to be wearing a Class III vest at the time the attack starts.

A ballistic blanket, stored rolled and anchored in the rear window well, can be quickly deployed over the principal in case of assault. This tactic works equally well for long guns or handgun attack and is particularly effective against sub-gun assault with the added benefit of giving protection from broken glass and other shrapnel. Another advantage of the ballistic blanket is that it removes the client from sight. Snipers are trained to shoot at what they can see, not at where they think a target might be.

Ballistic vests stored in the vehicle can be used as a makeshift ballistic blanket. Unless they are stored in the trunk, which they should not be. (Of course the vests are better employed being worn. I have had some difficulty convincing clients to wear a vest unless there has been a specific, verified and recent threat. After an unsuccessful attack, clients will sometimes wear a vest without argument, for several days!) Keep the principal low in the vehicle and make sure his or her head and upper torso are fully protected.

The best tactic to employ in the event of a long gun attack is to remove your client from the killing ground as quickly as possible. If you are in a vehicle at the time the attack is initiated, the best way to accomplish this is to remove the vehicle at high speed from the area. The only time you would want to remove your client from a vehicle under attack is if the vehicle is disabled and is being penetrated by projectiles or is on fire. If you decide to leave the vehicle it is a good idea to take the ballistic blanket and/or vests with you.

If your client is attacked at his home or place of business, your tactics change very little. Your first responsibility is to protect the client and remove him or her from harm's way, not engage the threat. Once the principal is safely out of the line of fire the job of security (Individual or Team) is to keep him safe until authorities arrive. This may mean engaging the attackers with return fire, however in most cases the attack will be broken off very quickly if it is not instantly successful.

In very rare instances you may have a team member in place and a set of circumstances existing which would allow security to neutralize the attacker(s) before, or as soon as, the attack is initiated. It is not likely to occur in the United States. If you are employed by a head of state or are working for a powerful and wealthy client overseas, a member of a Royal Family or on a government contract, there is a chance you would have the manpower and the sanction to take this type of action. Books and movies have done a great deal to glamorize this aspect of security work. If Security does its job properly there will be nothing to write about.

The guns to choose from are extensive when it comes to long guns or assault weapons.

PREVENTATIVE MEASURES

Long guns can be used very effectively to prevent attacks from being successful. Notice, I have said "prevent attacks from being successful," not "prevent attacks." In this country you are unlikely to be able to initiate an action against a suspected threat. However, you can respond to an attack effectively, especially where the protectee is in his home or at his place of business. The "home" here would include permanent dwelling, vacation home or yacht. Place of business would include office or private aircraft while parked at a private terminal.

The most probable application the PPS will encounter for unrestricted use of long guns is aboard a private craft on the high seas. Here the threat to one's client is more likely to be directed at the vessel and its contents rather than a specific individual, although that possibility can not be ruled out.

On the high seas there are fewer constraints on the actions one can take to protect a client and his property. Actions at sea are governed by the international law and court which recognizes the right of individuals to protect themselves and their property in the absence of any law enforcement entity.

There is very little application for a sniper rifle at sea. Shooting from one moving platform at a target on another moving platform is not what the sniper rifle is intended for. On the other hand, shotguns, assault rifles and even submachine guns definitely have a place in the seagoing arsenal. The riot type shotgun loaded with buckshot is very handy for repelling boarders and, loaded with slugs, will do an admirable job of disabling an attacking small craft. Slugs make the shotgun a fairly effective weapon out to 100 yards. The sub-gun really comes into its own aboard ship. In the confined spaces, and while negotiating slippery ladders and decks, the sub-machine gun allows a free hand to help stabilize the shooter while providing adequate fire power to deal with boarders. At the same time, the sub-gun's rounds are not as likely to penetrate into the heart of your own vessel as are those of the heavier assault weapons. Still, a good assault rifle properly deployed can dissuade even the saltiest pirate.

There are times when it is possible and feasible to deploy long gun personnel along established travel routes. This is particularly true in situations where the client travels long distances on private roads such as on larger estates or ranches or where there is intelligence that indicates a specific spot as a potential ambush location. Again, there won't be much of this in the U.S., but overseas, particularly in Central and South America, you may find an application for this type of deployment.

The key to the long gun is control. With the sniper rifle the control sought is that of the high ground. This may be the hilltop behind a residence, the roof of an adjacent office building, the tower at a private air terminal or a "hide" overlooking a travel route. The control sought with other long guns is that of the access route to the protectee. Shotguns, assault rifles and sub-guns can all be used effectively to turn back an attack. The most effective deployment involves a cross fire using shotguns and/or sub-guns to create a barrier between the protectee(s) and the threat and to use assault rifle fire and sniper fire to neutralize the attacking party.

In a team situation, where you have the luxury of deploying long gun personnel in a prevent defense, priority one is control of a high ground vantage point. Priority two is control of access to your principal. This may be a complete perimeter or a central hallway. Whatever the access route or routes are determined to be, there should be two posts per route. The first post is manned and the second post, somewhere between the first post and the client's sanctuary, allows the security personnel to engage a threat, fall back and re-engage. This gives the client time to secure himself in the sanctuary, gives the detail leader time to cover the client, and allows the security team to "fold over" the client, protecting itself and slowing the assault. Priority three is a react team to engage and neutralize the threat.

Remember, as much as you might want to do battle with the threat, your responsibility is the welfare of the client, not the decimation of the bad guys. The team leader, especially, must remember to stay with the principal. If, after a shooting attack has concluded, you haven't fired a round but your client is safe and sound, you have done your job. If after a shooting incident you have killed all the bad guys but your boss is history, you blew it!

TWENTY

Learning to Recognize and Manage The Abnormal Personality

by Bruce L. Danto

GUIDELINES FOR THE EXECUTIVE PROTECTION PERSON:

When training is available for persons who are responsible for protecting principals, the major amount of emphasis is placed on appearance, manners, firearm safety and management, and various strategies to bring about a successful exit from danger to the principal.

Very little is known about the kinds of behavioral clues that executive protection specialists might be able to employ when dealing with persons who pose danger to a principal. It is the intention of this outline to provide an introduction to that particular area of training.

INTRODUCTION:

The Personal Protection Specialist becomes familiar with certain signals, such as facial and eye movements, expressions, movement and postures of the body, as well as the driving styles and reactions of a person who sees a car containing a principal. He soon learns to watch for out-of-the-way things, such as bulges in clothing; side glances (as if one were looking to see that the coast is clear); a look-out outside a place where a principal is scheduled to visit so that they may tip off a plan to injure, kidnap, or kill the principal. These kinds of meaningful signs, plus many others, may indicate that criminal behavior is in the making. They may represent psychological clues which support or lead to suspicions about criminals on the part of the executive protection specialist.

It would not be surprising for a protection specialist to pull himself up short if he saw someone walking up to gain entry into a facility holding a principal. If that person has a multi-colored mohawk hair style, bikini shorts, sandals, and a long package, it would be suspicious. Almost anybody could spot this person as somebody to check out, particularly if he is carrying a long package which might hide a rifle or some weapon—even a sword.

By way of contrast, if a person dressed nattily, carrying a zippered brief-case, a business hat, and looked spic and span in a nice suit approaches, the average executive protection specialist might drop his guard and feel less worry about that person. One might not even consider questioning what is in the zippered briefcase.

However, if an appointment has not been made in advance, assuming that this is a business deal and he would need to have an appointment, it would be suspicious. If this person has brownish stains on his fingers from cigarette smoking, he then becomes more suspicious as heavy smoking may reflect excessive anxiety.

If we add to the scene that the "visitor" establishes no eye contact, is sitting on the agent's desk and nervously moving his foot back and forth, we know that this is an individual who has a great deal of anxiety. Any sign of anxiety to this degree should alert the security specialist that this person needs to be watched and checked out before having access to the principal.

If the visitor happens to be a woman who is dressed in a mini-skirt (hardly the right attire for a business meeting with your principal), is very seductive and flirty, sitting on your desk with her legs crossed, or in a chair across from you where you can see the middle of her belly-button, one would have to ask why she has to get this much attention from you. Is this a diversion on her part so that you will not think about looking into her purse, or you will not check out the credentials because your sexual fantasies have been called into play? These fantasies have been squirting black ink over your glasses so you will not see the rest of what she is really there to do—namely, possibly kill the principal or his security agent.

There is body language associated with abnormal behavior. When a person learns the clues, it makes it easy to recognize a mental disturbance. For the executive protection specialist, it is important to recognize these clues to determine whether or not simple or psychological management can be employed to deal with them and get them out of the circumstance which might otherwise bring them into contact with the principal. Whether the police will have to be called, as this person might require court-ordered emergency 72-hour holding order, can be determined by careful assessment.

The workings of a human mind can be assessed by observing the function and basic operation of a person. We all have a "green-light" system involving all of the biological and inborn forces called drives. We have needs for sexual pleasure, food, water (and thirst fulfillment), aggression, as well as needs for general creature comforts such as warmth, the security feeling of a bed with the weight of warm blankets on us, and so forth. These instinctive and basic biological drives make up the "green light" system. They always want the pleasure of being fulfilled. This system, which never seems to be fully satisfied, really enjoys being satisfied.

Mother Nature is funny about biological givens. Everything in nature is made up of equals and opposites. Balance, or homeostasis, can never really be achieved in that system. Thus, as you might expect, there is also a "red light"system, which is contrary to pleasure. It promotes control and inhibition of the drives. The "red light" system is commonly called the Conscience or Superego. It consists of all the social values which keep us in line in terms of rules and expectations required of civilized persons.

Imagine the constant war within the mind if these two systems were in open opposition to one another. There would be a tug-of-war between the feelings of "I went to," and "but you can't." Were such a conflict to persist, the average person would be reduced to total frustration much like biting his or her nails down to the bone.

Once again, Mother Nature came to the rescue and figured out a pretty good way of achieving a balance between these opposites—by creating a structure for the mind called Ego. Thus, the Ego has a tough job to do in maintaining peace between these opposites. In order to acquire and maintain such effectiveness, the Ego has certain basic functions. Knowing about these functions can help anyone trying to assess a possible psychological abnormality.

Once this interaction is understood, the executive protection specialist can begin to feel greater security and awareness of the citizen he meets while on duty. In addition to achieving an understanding of that person, he will also know how to handle him and head for the safe areas that will favor the citizen's ability to achieve or maintain control. The specialist will be better able to emotionally support the disturbed person so that everyone's safety will be enhanced. Comfort can be achieved by everyone involved.

REALITY TESTING:

The first function is called reality testing. This is defined as any person's ability to sense what is happening and what is real and not real. Certainly, if a citizen has been shot at, has received threatening letters, and there are possible witnesses to either threats or attempts at violence upon him, it would be fair to conclude that this person has a realistic picture of his personal danger. If he appears nervous, frightened, agitated, uncertain about what to do, or is asking for help, then the officer has another measure of the person's reality testing—namely, that he shows his feelings appropriately. He talks of a danger which is real and appears to be responding realistically.

For example, a principal has received death threats. Suppose the principal is involved in a highly controversial political situation or business situation, such as a conflict between management and a union. Suppose a brick has been thrown through the window of his summer home. In spite of all this the principal, as chief executive of the company, decides that this is all unimportant and highly unnecessary. Then he attempts to go out for walks without security staff with him and decides that he wants none of his security personnel to be armed. Suppose he then decides to drive separately, having his security force follow him, and then engages in a game of cat and mouse, leaving his security forces trying to find him.

The above circumstance does not necessarily represent a psychotic condition but it certainly does indicate that the principal is contributing to his own high risk of danger. Thus, it will be important to direct particular attention to the protection of the principal as well as the threat which seems to come from outside the principal's residence. It might even be necessary to seek psychotherapeutic intervention by a psychiatrist to help the principal recognize how self-destructive his acts really are and how he is endangering not only himself and his family but also his security staff.

On the other hand, if an elderly person approaches a security specialist in the state of minor anger or upset and relates a story about people in the company spying on him or implanting a television set in his toilet to broadcast his bowel movements on the air all over the company to embarrass him, the security officer should view this complaint in light of poor reality testing. There is little likelihood that such a story could either be true or possible.

Suppose, according to family members or coworkers, that a woman has buried money in the snow or torn up a check amounting to thousands of dollars, and she happens to be the aunt of the principal or an employee of the company. When questioned, she says that she did this to prevent the bank from stealing her money. Her actions obviously do not make sense. She is employing a typical paranoid logic—that is, justifying a distorted or false idea about the bank being against her and then doing the very thing she accuses someone else of trying to do, namely, destroying her money.

The average security specialist must exercise great care so that he does not assume that a person with a problem is a "nut." No matter how strange the story or the person telling it, this may be a potential witness to a planned effort to kidnap or damage the principal or his family or some other officer of the company. Most psychotic persons, such as the man who complained about his television-bugged toilet, will reveal their broken reality in terms of something terrible or personally menacing. However, his disturbance does not mean that he is stupid or totally at a loss to comprehend all reality. Wouldn't it be embarrassing to the protection specialist and his department if such a disturbed person actually saw an assassin enter the building and had written down the license number of the car? Being paranoid, he wanted to offer help to the security department. If the protection specialist thinks about a television in a toilet, he stops listening to a description of the assassin or the license number that could be checked out and he will miss not only protecting his principal but also the opportunity to apprehend the wrong-doer before someone gets hurt.

The chronic mentally ill, non-violent person who presents a break from reality can be handled by the average protection specialist. Certainly if some older person beckons his help to protect him or her from coworkers or even a principal plotting against him, they can be told by the agent, "I am glad you came in with your complaint. I can understand what you are upset about. We certainly do not want anything to happen to you. We will keep an eye on your place. Let us know if anything else serious is happening. Here is my name and number (or my card). Feel free to call."

The above approach might be called "humoring" a person. It is effective in working with chronically suspicious and paranoid-type persons who feel that others are plotting against them. This type of person must be approached as if his concerns were serious and important. To laugh at him or argue with him about the unreality of the claims would be to invite him to become more defensive and entrenched in his distorted views of the world, the security agent, or his company. Do not turn dealing with such a person into a debate.

If this same person is violent, quiet assurance and plans for custody might be necessary if he has not been in psychiatric treatment with a physician who can prescribe tranquilizers. Very often, if the situation permits, inviting the angry and disturbed person to sit down and have a cup of coffee or have a glass of milk will help to defuse his anger, and certainly listening to him without challenging him will go a long way toward calming him down.

If he has lost contact with reality only and has relatively good impulse control, there is very little need to employ more than simple reassurance and concern. Such support coming from a security agent makes this principal or employee feel less isolated and more secure in the knowledge that somebody recognizes his humanness.

IMPULSE CONTROL:

Impulse control is the second Ego function. Every security agent knows about this function because working in any police or protective assignment forces him to survive confrontations with people who have lost control of aggressive impulses or who have gone off the deep end in terms of drinking or drug use so that control is badly compromised by an intoxicant.

Obviously, it is one thing if that aggressive person threatens to get a gun and start shooting; it is another if he has a gun and has not yet fired it. Furthermore, if he is sniping or blowing up television sets and windows or lamps at home, he has lost control. Intent or threat alone versus action on the threat or action without the threat gives the situation a different tone.

If the security agent is present at a scene where a shooting has occurred, or there has been fighting or destruction of property, impulse control as a function must be evaluated regardless. If possible, the agent should learn if the person has had a history of being impulsive or provocative. By the latter I mean acting like big bad Leroy Brown, the meanest man in town, meaner than a junkyard hound, with a razor in his shoe and a .32 caliber gun in his pocket. This latter person is a fighter who is provocative, has a short fuse, and everybody knows that he is a walking time bomb.

Important for the security agent to observe would be scars on the face of that person which might have resulted from fighting. Certainly scars that are jagged are frequently seen with persons who have been involved in bar fights. If the scars are very thin, calm, and regular, with suture marks on either side, then those can be assumed to be surgical and non-traumatic type scars. On the other hand, if there are punctate scars, like someone has punched a pencil into the face, and there is a little crater, the scar might indicate that the person has epilepsy. He has had seizures and fallen, bringing about injury to his tongue, jaw, or cheekbones, and sometimes the forehead.

As a security agent is talking to the person, does his fist tighten with white-knuckling occurring? Is he chain-smoking? Again, are there yellow nicotine stains on his hand? Does he avoid eye contact? Is he rubbing something on his waist that might appear to be the butt-end of a revolver? Does he cock his head on occasion as if he is looking for some source of voices coming from up in the ceiling or somewhere else around the room which might indicate that he is hallucinating? Does his whole body movement appear that he is in an offensive posture, ready to pounce on the agent?

If he is hearing voices and turns his head to try to find out where the voices are coming from, there might be a command hallucination ordering him to attack somebody because of some crazed, psychotic idea.

If there is a lifeless quality to his whole body movement or his eyes so that it makes the security agent feel that he is talking either to a zombie or a store mannequin, this certainly might mean that he is psychotic and suffering from a severe mental illness where he has been drained of emotional tone and is most likely schizophrenic.

In my experience as a police officer, security agent, as well as a psychiatrist of 31 years experience, I can tell you that when the subject you are looking at looks at you and makes you feel as if he is looking right through you like you do not exist, and he is yelling or is angry, that means that he is dehumanizing you; he is behaving as if you are not really there and just staring through you. Once that occurs, the officer must be alert. It is possible that he is in very real danger of being seriously injured or killed.

The way I have dealt with dehumanizing coming from a psychotic, dangerous or homicidal patient is to keep talking whether he talks or not. I let him know how badly he needs me, that I can see he is upset and disturbed, and that he is lucky and fortunate to be there with someone who is trying to understand and help him. What this says to the subject is that you, the security agent, are necessary to his life and he will be less likely to want to destroy you on that ground alone.

Once the subject begins to look at you, he or she can see you (realize you are there). Even if there is a smile that looks like it is an inappropriate smile, then you are about 50% of the way home. Keep talking and letting him know that you are glad to see that he finally sees you, that he can focus on you, and that it is important for you to know what you can do to help him. You need him to talk to you. Once this happens, he will quiet down and become more serious about recognizing the value that the security agent has for him.

In the event that the security agent finds he is facing a gun pointed at him by somebody who is rather crazed, disoriented or irrational, it becomes important for him or her to talk more softly to indicate that with a gun pointed at him it makes it that much more difficult for him to know what he can do to help. The security agent should ask the person with the gun whether a deal could be made so that the gun would either be pointed at the floor or put on the table away from the agent, who will make no effort to grab the gun. This piece of advice might very well cause my readers to have serious questions about my experience as it runs in total opposition to all the things that their karate instructors have taught them about self defense. All I can say is that this does represent some of my experience; I have faced guns and have been shot at more times than I can count.

It never fails for me to feel that I do everything possible to make the person with the gun, or the anger, feel he is in control. By doing that, I am inviting him to assume control in an appropriate way—namely, impulse control. Each time he does what I want, underneath it all, between us, I am in control because he is doing what I am asking him to do. As he continues to perform what I am asking him to do, I know that I am ahead; that I am winning; that I am managing him very well. Furthermore, I am reasonably certain that I am going to get out of this situation alive.

I reward and compliment him on his willingness to be cooperative so that we can both be safe. I tell him that I am convinced that he really does not want to harm anybody; that he really does want to be heard and has a legitimate complaint. I am more than happy to give him the opportunity to be heard. As we progress toward that point, I then tell him I will do what I can to get the appropriate people to help him; that I think it is time to seal the deal by letting me take possession of his firearm. I tell him that it is necessary for us to have the gun because we can guarantee we will get help for him.

To those still doubting the wisdom of this approach, I can tell them that I am still alive, that it has worked, and that I have had many people pull guns on me. I end up feeling very grateful for the way I handled them.

For many people, a firearm becomes necessary so that they can feel powerful and competitive. When they are treated as I suggested, so that they know they have power and have a voice, the gun then becomes less necessary. If you are dealing with an extremely paranoid person or a professional hit man or terrorist, none of this talk is going to work and it then becomes every man for himself.

Fortunately, the subject of this work concerns the mentally disturbed person and the rules which I am describing fundamentally apply only to that kind of high risk, face-to-face contact.

Behavioral signs can be important in assessing danger from the standpoint of impulse control. If the subject suddenly averts his eyes from those of the security agent, hesitates a little longer in answering questions, or displays a slight smile at the corner of his mouth before answering a question, he may be lying. This is important to determine as it should alert the officer to question and press on. Someone complained about this citizen for a reason, and the security agent should feel that it is important enough for his own safety to be sure that he can trust the subject as an informant or somebody to have contact with a principal or any other member of a company within the administrative or supervisory section.

Most people may feel very insecure when they are approached by a security agent. Some of the signs of insecurity are seen in the increased body movements in terms of restlessness, i.e., tapping the foot toward the floor, cracking knuckles, or sweating. Sometimes the voice rises in pitch and intensity as the individual becomes more upset and possibly hysterical.

All of these signs point to impaired ego function and serve as a warning of impending danger or violence. Although many psychiatrists disagree about being able to predict danger, the average security agent is familiar with many of these signs if they have had any previous experience in law enforcement or have had good training. When a citizen is upset, the security agent can say, "I can see that you are pretty upset. Take it easy! It is important to keep the lid on so that we can see what needs to be done to help you." This statement supports the basic notion of maintaining emotional control.

The agent can look for an opportunity to comment further, "I am glad to see that you are handling yourself better. There is no need to shout. I can see that it is important for me to listen. I am pleased that you are keeping your cool," or "keeping control of yourself." If impulse control appears to be shaky, it is always helpful to invite the subject to be seated some distance from the agent. This has control value, prevents the subject from being able to leap forward so easily and puts some distance between himself and the agent. He can also suggest the subject have a drink of water (never alcohol) in view of the agent. He can follow him to the drinking fountain and should never take his eyes off the subject during that evaluation.

When standing face to face with a person who looks as if he is agitated, it is always best to take one step backward. The reason for this is clear to those of us who have had contact in prison with disturbed persons. There is a concept called "Body Buffer Zone" which means, "You cannot come any closer to me or I will have to get violent with you to maintain distance between us." Thus, if you take one step backward you are not retreating; rather, you are giving him a little more space so that he doesn't feel that you are crawling up his back. This sometimes is called homosexual panic, seen very commonly in men who are terrified about having contact with another man—even in a security situation.

In managing the person with poor impulse control, the agent must ensure that he or she does not act in a provocative manner. Such behavior may signal the citizen that he should either feel defensive about the agent or prepare for physical combat. The agent, usually in plainclothes, should unbutton his coat before talking to the subject. If done before the subject, such an act during the interview might be an alert type of behavior, making him believe the officer feels threatened or wants his gun or slapper handy. If the agent is toying with a night stick or gun, if in uniform, he is possibly signalizing to the subject that he is ready for a fight and is ready to lose control of himself. The agent may not be aware of his behavior. A senior agent should view his partner in such a light to possibly save him from injury in the long run.

The underlined point for the agent is that he serves as a model of behavior that he should want the average citizen to identify with. He must exercise reasonable caution so that his model is not based on either insensitive or naïve notions but should be as polite and mannerly as possible.

OBJECT RELATIONS:

The term "object relations" describes the third Ego function which an agent should view in a citizen. This relates to the basic style in which the citizen or subject gets along with others. Is he genuinely friendly or surly? Emotionally remote, or a loner? Is he a family person, friendly toward his children? Does he pet his dog affectionately; does he have friends that he jokes around with on his job? All of these observable qualities reveal whether the subject is trusting of others, is able to appreciate the rights of others, feels a sense of human warmth, values life, and is a reasonable person in general.

If it is known through personnel records or reports that this individual has been a wife or child abuser, and has gotten into fights with people on the job, then I think it is important to know that this is a person who does not get along with others very well.

Rationalization is an ego defense which frequently gets people into trouble. They seem to break the law, feeling that they are justified. This type of rationalization has been seen from smuggling or buying industrial secrets, to taking secrets from the national defense—all under the guise that some patriotic statement is being made toward human rights. We have had government equipment broken by people who protested the Viet Nam War, and we have had fishing boats damaged in order to protect various species of fish, such as whales. The security agent has to be careful and know when rationalization is being used to promote justification of an act of violence in the mind of the criminal.

The Ego has an integrated function as well. This means that we should profit, or at least learn, from experience. Once we are burned, we learn not make careless contact with stoves, hot vessels, or loose wires. Many people, however, especially habitual offenders, repeat the same type of behavior, e.g., sometimes criminal and other times self-defeating behavior despite many divorces, previous arrests, business losses, and the like. When this behavior is considered to be wrong on the part of the company that hires you to prevent it, and this person continues to pursue anti-social corporate behavior, it would appear as though he has not profited from his own experience since he has been caught several times. Some would argue that he wants to be caught and discharged from his job or sent to prison if he is threatening the life of an important person because he feels guilty. Perhaps being institutionalized meets unconscious passive dependency needs for control to come from the outside. Others might argue that there is a defect in his personality or ego-function and that he becomes locked into a pattern of behavior regardless of the underlying reason. Protective agent investigators may exploit this defective Ego function to help solve problems within the corporation or government agency because it helps establish a method of operation by the suspect.

This type of behavior is commonly seen in psychopaths or sociopaths. It is also seen in persons suffering from a particular learning disability or attention deficit disorder. Both types cannot profit from experience. Psychopaths can be recognized when they exhibit some of the following types of behavior: lying; the use of force and threats to intimidate others; melodramatic acting; resorting to power-oriented ploys of behavior; and demonstrating through his behavior or attitude that the rights and lives of others are unimportant. Persons with this type of disorder are never able to show accountability for their own behavior and often rationalize and deny it, lie about it, or blame others. Scruples and moral values are completely missing from their personality.

A learning disabled person, as an adult, may very well become a part of the anti-social or sociopathic population. He may progress from the simple types of anti-social and silly behavior to criminal behavior, then to petty criminal behavior, and then become felonious. He may, along with his psychopathic counterparts, develop problems with substance abuse in terms of alcohol and drug abuse, which further inflames his aggression and makes it difficult for him to maintain control of himself.

INTELLECTUAL FUNCTION:

The intellectual function, another important Ego function, involves the ability of a person to operate with intact memory, ability to absorb information, and understand written and verbal material as well as to apply it.

Certainly, one of the most apparent examples of impairment is the mentally retarded citizen, of which there are three types. Essentially, the security agent will have contact with the first two. The first type is educable and has an I.Q. somewhere between 70 and 90. He can achieve a third grade reading and arithmetic level and can work in a job which requires some reading and spelling, such as being a checker in a stock room. He can pass a driver's test, can drive, work, and be self-sufficient. The trainable retarded person has an I.Q. between 50 and 70. This person can be taught to perform simple, common, routine tasks like cleaning offices, domestic service work, and dishwashing. He will not be able to understand written instructions or signs and will not be any better able to understand a confession that he is asked to read than the educable one. The last one, the institutional or untrainable type, is usually confined to a chair or bed, has no bowel or bladder control, and must receive constant supervision.

It is important to understand this type of citizen because he frequently becomes employed and becomes a member of the work staff. This individual may get into difficulty and may be induced by other people to commit crimes against the company or persons as he is so suggestible.

People from another country cannot always understand English or read signs. The security agent should be alert for prominent accents and ask persons who appear to be foreign if they have a reading problem. It may be important, particularly if signs have been infracted, to give them a sign to read to make sure they do, in fact, know how to read. This may make the difference between someone trying to get away with something and someone who had innocently wandered into an area because he did not know he was in the wrong place.

In regard to a police matter, I should state that some years ago I was asked by a newspaper reporter to assist a woman who had served four years for the murder of her baby. It was alleged that she had starved her daughter, who died at one month of age. The mother had reared two other children. The third child had a harelip and cleft palate. The baby died in her crib on the very day the pediatrician weighed her and told the mother the infant appeared to be in good health. No doctor examined the baby and she was in a pathology cool drawer without medical pronouncement of her death. At autopsy, no effort was made to check the liver for congenital malformations; and material in the stomach, which might have been food, was never analyzed by a pathologist. The town almost lynched the mother and she was convicted.

Four years later, an appeal for a new trial was granted because the judge had given incorrect instructions to the jury. After my investigation as a forensic psychiatrist, there were more than reasonable grounds to doubt her guilt. In addition, she had signed a confession which was, in fact, by a mentally retarded woman with an I.Q. of 67. The confession had been obtained after driving her in a police car approaching speeds of 100 miles per hour.

The final verdict on a new trial was acquittal. In all probability, the infant had died from congenital liver disease. The mother was freed from jail and is leading a new life. Because of her low I.Q., she did not fully appreciate the injustice she had endured.

AUTONOMOUS FUNCTION:

The final major Ego function, the autonomous function, serves to protect the Ego from the personality so that it will not be destroyed. For example, what happens when we feel overwhelmed at times? Some of us faint; in that manner, we withdraw. Fainting is like pulling the covers up over our eyes and turning out the lights. It prevents us from being overwhelmed by anxiety. Getting stoned on street drugs or alcohol and removing ourselves from pressures of the time may keep the Ego intact and offer a kind of holiday, i.e., "getting away from it all." It helps to preserve autonomy. With substance abuse, the problem persists no matter how stoned we get and in time, if we intensify our chemical approach to problems, we start taking ourselves away from family, work achievement, and normal competition. We weaken our chances for happiness and basic survival, and then the way in which we strive for autonomy via some chemical agents leads to further pressures and problems.

The average person rarely realizes that for many who feel overwhelmed, a psychotic break or so-called nervous breakdown in actually a protection. Hospitalization or seeing a psychiatrist or mental health professional helps to harness or control anxiety. Hospitalization removes the person from the combat stress of his or her personal problems. Medication will help relieve anxiety or depression. Talking with a caring person, such as a psychiatrist, social worker, or psychologist provides a trained and sensitive therapist to share a burden and learn from in terms of developing effective coping mechanisms. In many cases, a breakdown rallies friends and relatives around a patient's flag and more effective communication is open. In the short term, a person achieves a better state of psychological balance or autonomy. That initial falling apart is soon replaced by a more significant building up of resources, and controls possible new directions for a better life.

In addition to Ego functions, there are other signs which may predict abnormal behavior. For example, tattoos tell a great deal about a person and have long interested psychiatrists. Some tattoos are ominous and frightening-looking, such as angry animals or vicious-looking snakes; those with blood dripping from a knife; or a knife through a heart or eye socket of a skull. Tattoos with faint ink and the name of a man on the arm or shoulder of a male citizen may not only mean he is a homosexual but that he has also done time in prison, particularly if tattoos extend over the chest and back. There is a great likelihood that this person has been tattooed in prison. The words "love" and "hate" tattooed on fingers or knuckles reflects a deep struggle between feelings of love and hate for people. This may suggest that this hate may break through like a tidal wave. When I examine someone, I always ask about tattoos, if a person has them, and what they mean to that particular person.

The agent should look at the hands and fingers of persons they are talking to for signs of nail-biting, which is a sign of anxiety. The woman who sits with her skirt pulled up in a revealing manner is testing the agent and being subtly seductive. This behavior seems to please a number of younger agents and pulls their attention from investigative duties. Constant observation is necessary as those persons might pose a threat or danger to the parties being protected.

The security agent must always ask himself, "Why is this person throwing herself at me? Am I really that irresistible, or is she out to control me through sex?"

ANXIETY AND RESISTANCE:

Many people may show signs of anxiety, though not necessarily because of guilt or fear of security agents. They simply may feel uneasy because the officer is standing too close or has physically touched them in terms of what I said about the "Body Buffer Zone."

If the agent senses that a person is tensing up as he is approaching him, the agent should back away slightly, as I suggested, by stepping back at least one step. If it becomes necessary to handcuff the subject, be very careful about this as some people are set off by being touched. This does not mean they are resisting arrest; it means they are trying to defend against their own unconscious homosexual anxiety. It is always important to ask a subject if physical contact makes him/her feel uneasy.

DRUGS AND BEHAVIOR:

With any abnormal behavior, the agent should watch for the odor of alcohol or signs of drug use, i.e., staggering gait, slurred speech, dilated pupils, reddening around the outside portion of the eyelids (away from the nose), or the odor of inhalant drugs. A body search frequently reveals the presence of an intoxicant and acknowledged history also helps. Certainly the subject can be taken to a hospital emergency room for a medical opinion about the intoxicated state as well as for detoxification.

The agent should be careful not to judge the intoxicated subject as being just another drunk or junkie. They may be having a diabetic crisis; a hypoglycemic attack; prelude to epilepsy; having just had a seizure, in a state of postictal confusion; having an impending stroke; an attack of high blood pressure; a blood clot in the brain due to a fall resulting from the use of drugs or having been bludgeoned in a hold-up.

The agent should be sensitive to what he or she observes about the total behavior, not just what his own nose reveals. He or she must ask meaningful questions and note the general appearance and condition of the whole person, satisfying his or her curiosity by what appears to be unusual or abnormal behavior.

During the interview itself, he must notice what the subject says and does not say. What did his body say? Does his behavior reveal feelings appropriate to what is being said, i.e., "I feel angry; I feel sad; I was upset when I saw the man hit the woman?" The agent must learn to check with others for further or corroborating information about the subject to have a more complete picture of this person.

At the same time, the agent must make his own Ego sources and functions available to the subject. He must ensure that he is not behaving provocatively. He must reward control shown by the subject and cooperation extended to the officer during the contact. He must avoid arguments, if at all possible. Professional restraint, judgment, and action on his part might make his contact with the disturbed person meaningful and supportive. The disturbed or abnormal person will well remember how he has been treated by the agent. If he has been put down, it will make it difficult the next time he has contact with this person. He can be assisted in feeling that the agent is not judging him, hounding him, picking on him, or threatening him. There will be times when physical restraint is necessary and helpful—perhaps the subject is too disturbed to cooperate or he must be saved from self-destructive behavior. At some future time, he will be able to acknowledge the need for such restraint. The agent can explain why it is necessary to secure the citizen in handcuffs. I have had to make observations of patients on the ward who required being placed in leather restraints, and citizens who have required cuffing as a means of calming them down for security purposes in my role as a police officer.

It should be understood that not all areas of abnormal behavior can be covered in this document. Hopefully, the agent can develop a feel for the need to observe, manage, and work toward the development of a sense of trust in the person who presents himself in some kind of abnormal manner. The security agent is not expected to be a psychiatrist. What he is expected to be is someone who is sensitive and sensible; someone who can observe and, at the same time, respond with management that is appropriate. He should know that once any eminent threat is under control resources in the community can be used in terms of contacting the appropriate police agency or PET chain (Psychiatric Emergency Team), which will come to the site in most communities and make an evaluation as to whether or not an involuntary 72-hour holding order is necessary to administer to this particular person.

In my experience, most agents get injured because they have provoked the wrong response from the citizen or suspect.

Like most security agents who are armed, I have been armed since 1965 and have pulled a gun only once, even though I was also on a SWAT team for four years as a hostage negotiator. It is nice to know that my friend is at my belt, but it is better to know and rely upon the lips that make up my mouth and the brain which makes it possible for me to get a more accurate picture of danger and a more fruitful way of dealing with the abnormal person.

PART IV

Practical Matters

TWENTY-ONE

The Notebook Computer:
A Portable Powerhouse for the
Executive Protection Specialist

by Peter J. Brown

THE 21ˢᵗ CENTURY IS JUST AROUND THE CORNER

With the aid of a modem, a laptop or notebook computer, a CD-ROM drive, and a GPS satellite system linkup, you can instantly transform any hotel room, automobile or yacht into a state-of-the-art command post. Add your usual array of communications and telecommunications gear—everything from pagers to fax machines—and you can perform a wide variety of tasks. In the 1990's, we routinely employ electronic hardware in the field of executive protection that was a mere dream just a decade ago.

Portable protection systems have been around for years, whereas the portable computer is a relatively recent innovation. Now, it surfaces everywhere, and costs very little. Its capabilities are boundless. A notebook computer with full-color displays and graphics software can easily fit into a briefcase. It allows you to carry the equivalent of a full library in a package weighing much less than ten pounds.

And this technology is not emerging in a vacuum. The next generation of telecommunications technology—a broad selection of personal communications systems—is already on sale. An endless list of possibilities is now within reach. What will be the next development, for example, in remote video surveillance technology?

Look at what a detail leader can accomplish today while in transit, and doing so in an affordable manner. The affordability factor is a significant area of concern for security professionals, except in those rare instances where money is no object.

Today's tiny computers will become even more capable in the near future as flat panel displays and a dazzling array of wireless systems combine to permit instantaneous and simultaneous two-way—or multipoint—voice, video and data transmissions.

Remember, the 21st century is just around the corner.

In this chapter, we will refer to the notebook computer as an "NC" in order to differentiate it easily from the conventional desktop or PC computer.

NO EASY ANSWERS

This laptop revolution raises many questions. Does the NC meet the needs of the protective services specialist? How can this hardware be used in the most efficient manner to enable the protective services specialist to better serve his or her principal? What future pathways are emerging in terms of new applications of software and hardware, and how will these developments affect the way you conduct your operations?

Where does the executive protection professional find an appropriate balance between his or her needs and what is available today in terms of sophisticated equipment? Do these systems help security personnel in terms of providing useful and accurate information in the fastest way possible, or do they actually undermine the effectiveness of the user by diverting him or her from more essential tasks?

These are just a few of the questions which must be considered, along with critical procurement and support costs. Can these costs be justified, or do they handicap an otherwise smoothly functioning organization by bleeding away funds that might be better applied to other equipment or training?

Finally, there is one central practical question. Will this device make your life easier, by being easy to operate and by reinforcing your primary mission? We think the answer is yes.

There are no simple answers to all these questions. Each individual and each organization must determine how to best apply often limited resources. In terms of the framework that we are seeking to establish here, the answers are secondary to the overall effort of introducing what may be, for many readers, a totally new way of managing and processing information that is vital to the protective services mission.

KEEPING UP WITH THOSE WIRELESS WONDERS

On the hardware side, this chapter is not intended as an exercise in product review, nor are we concerned with any comparison of the different software packages and their advantages or disadvantages. We are simply sorting out the beneficial ingredients, and attempting to identify ways in which you can begin to, first, see some of the benefits of the NC approach, and second—if you decide to go ahead and acquire one of these devices—effectively begin the transfer process from the paper-only to a shared paper/electronic mode of managing information.

This notion of transferring or otherwise transforming one's way of conducting routine operations is especially important. Some readers are going to

Essential state-of-the-art portable command post tools for the Executive Protection Specialist, including an RCA satellite dish, Street Atlas USA, and a laptop computer.

be far ahead of the curve, already using the systems outlined here. You might be described as wireless wonders awash in all sorts of exotic hardware, while other readers who have shunned computers for whatever reason in the past, will be tempted to hold firm regardless of the persuasiveness of this chapter. In particular, these pockets of resistance are our chief target.

At the same time, we want to avoid broad generalizations. It is no secret that while some people enjoy encounters with new ideas and new technologies, others are not so enthusiastic. There is a term for the most powerful form of resistance which often surfaces in these circumstances, it is called "machine fear." As a former computer instructor with field training experience, this writer can attest to the power of this phenomenon. We will not be able to solve the mystery of this hidden force, but we can help to overcome some of the anxiety and discomfort that accompanies it.

We are not trying to cast aside or otherwise undermine traditional forms of information management with respect to executive protection. We want to make the transition from the old manual style to a more flexible NC format as easy as possible.

Our primary concern is that you at least consider this approach, and that as part of this process, you take what is spelled out here as a blueprint. We want you to either devise your own customized system to best suit your needs, or consider a more rapid and perhaps more efficient option.

Affordable all-in-one emergency management software packages which are easily updated by the user and configured to meet a number of different requirements for executive protection specialists as well as other emergency response personnel are beginning to appear. We previewed one of these software systems which is called SoftRisk. It was created by SoftRisk, Inc. in St. Simon Island, Georgia.

SoftRisk includes many attractive components. Numerous response and communications-related functions are drawn together in a very coherent format, so that a systems operator can perform several tasks simultaneously. This is a sophisticated and comprehensive software package; however, it is very user-friendly. Like anything else, however, it does require a good deal of practice and hands-on experience to master.

SoftRisk is not the only package of this type of the market, and while it costs nearly $9000—that's the price as of mid-1994—it can save the user a lot of time. Because we are not involved in reviewing and evaluating specific products here, we do not have an interest in comparing SoftRisk to other competing software packages.

At the same time, this does not prevent us from pointing out the obvious. Creating a computerized database with all sorts of lists, maps and other important ingredients is time-consuming. What might appear to be a very expensive software package is perhaps not as expensive as it looks when you take into account all the hours required to create and blend together the underlying software structures that enable the programming elements to fit together into one nice neat package. This is not only time-consuming, but it lends itself to what can become a very troubling scenario.

If one individual emerges as your team's designated systems guru, and if this same person oversees all the development and design tasks associated with your system, you better be sure that you have selected someone with better than average communications skills. Otherwise, little details and minor adjustments to the software may spring out at a time when they are least expected or desired, freezing the entire system or causing unwanted delays.

Purchasing a package means that while you still have to load all the data and mapping information, you can avoid the burdensome structural stages, and the above-mentioned pitfall, to name just one. Do not misunderstand what is being said here. Products like SoftRisk are not rigid and inflexible. You can adapt them to meet your own set of requirements. SoftRisk includes many elements or formats such as WordPerfect, PCX or Paradox which represent the universal building blocks for all sorts of software packages. This is an important consideration, especially for a system that has to be constantly expanded or updated.

While performing vital file transfers or communications functions—sending out faxes or whatever—SoftRisk does not go into a state of suspended animation. It allows the operator to continue along, simultaneously accessing or activating other parts of the system and thus moving through any pre-patterned emergency response plan in the most efficient manner.

SoftRisk also allows for data and maps to be interwoven into a single coherent mass. This keeps lots of information at an operator's fingertips. You want geographical information to be tightly configured to any relevant information about that specific area, and you also want to be able to move quickly from a descriptive text or burst of data to an accurate map or graphic depiction of the information at hand. Jumping back and forth between graphics and text can be difficult, but SoftRisk does this easily and automatically.

Again, the SoftRisk approach is offered here as one of many possible solutions. Budgets are budgets, and although your budget may not allow for this product, you should at least be aware of the trend in terms of emergency response software packages. More of these packages will no doubt appear in the future, and those currently on the market will be refined as more features are added. Rest assured that prices for these packages will drop eventually.

Many readers will no doubt view the keyboard and activities associated with using an NC as an administrative function rather than part of a coordinated, highly organized and mobile protective services operation. This is a very risky attitude in a fast-moving world where much of your decision-making hinges on accessing vast reams of intelligence data. We can only urge you to adapt now to the most sophisticated techniques available.

Besides, the keyboard itself is being displaced by a mix of new character recognition system and electronic clipboards. These are bypassing the conventional keyboard, and calling out to anyone who wants to cling to pens and the old reliable handwritten approach. Widespread applications of even more amazing voice recognition technology cannot be far off.

We mention this only to emphasize the unpredictable nature of the electronic world. It is constantly evolving, so any attempt to proclaim one way of doing things as the superior way is a bit questionable. We are not attempting to do so here. We are just sharing ideas.

SECURITY IS A TECHNOLOGY-INTENSIVE BUSINESS

Providing executive protection is a complex task that involves, among other things, the routine handling of vast amounts of information. This preoccupation with information management can be ranked as one of the more detailed and time-consuming elements on the executive protection menu. In years past, data gathered in the field and deemed relevant to the performance of executive protection assignments could only be handled and stored in hand-written form. Notebooks and numerous scraps of paper became the standard way of keeping track of lots of details and observations.

This practice is by no means obsolete today. Paper continues to serve as a reliable and proven tool for the protective services specialist; however, with the rest of the corporate world adapting to the presence of a whole new generation of NC's, electronic notepads and portable word processing devices, the top providers of executive protection are slowly embracing this new yet highly capable line of hardware as well.

The security industry as a whole is a technology-intensive business. It has been this way for years. Surveillance, identification, intrusion detection and other specialized forms of electronic security systems are commonplace. The acceptance of both the reliability and integrity of all this equipment has allowed the security industry to restructure itself. Look at CCTV technology as a good example. CCTV systems now enable a single guard to monitor large scattered areas while—if required—simultaneously performing other functions such as screening visitors.

Working in the field of security today requires a thorough understanding of a wide range of electronic devices. Knowing their capabilities and their limitations is critical to the task at hand. By being too dependent on hardware or by failing to provide adequate redundancy in the design of an integrated network of systems, one invites trouble. And yet, networks and systems that were considered sophisticated and state-of-the-art just a decade ago, are now seen as obsolete. These have been overhauled and replaced with even more capable later-generation hardware.

A LOT OF POWER AT YOUR FINGERTIPS

A rapid access memory with enormous storage capacity all combined into one rugged, reliable and easy to operate package. That's it in a nutshell. Today's NC can put a lot of computing power at your fingertips, anytime and anyplace. Portability has been made more attractive in this instance by the presence of longer-lasting batteries, which not only provide hours of power, but can be quickly recharged.

But computer power is only remotely important to the flawless performance in the realm of executive protection. Right? Well, it depends on how you view such things as the importance and proper role of a mobile command post when you are on the road. Mobility adds much to the appeal of an NC; however, in this network-intensive world, mobility is only part of the story.

This profession is perhaps no different from many others in that precise information management is critical to success. What does set protective services apart from other jobs is that the sorting and prioritizing of certain bits of vital information can have a direct bearing on the survival of a given individual as well as on the survival of an entire protective detail. This is not an exaggeration.

Counter-surveillance, for example, is just one ongoing information-intensive activity that is part of a required set of procedures for ensuring adequate security. Any pattern of questionable or suspicious activity which could indicate some degree of preliminary planning by a potentially hostile individual or group needs to be identified, tracked and treated with an appropriate response.

For our purposes, let us label the first sign of an unusual activity focused on your principal as "Episode A." Within the context of your routine security operations, you can create an appropriate imaginary event, and plug it in accordingly to this hypothetical scenario. Besides, we are not concerned with the episode or encounter itself, but rather with what happens to the data as it moves downstream, that is, through your organization after the initial point of contact.

While many unwanted intrusions can develop quickly and with explosive repercussions, many first encounters of the kind we are concerned with here are very subtle in nature where a protective services specialist has to rely upon his or her instincts as the sorting process begins. Is this a mere distraction or is this the first phase of what could ultimately become a very nasty and damaging incident?

What registers and what does not is quite relevant to this chapter, but we are more concerned with the flow, the handling and filing of all information relevant to this type of event after the immediate reaction phase is over.

Logs containing the time, place, and specific details of the incident need to be updated along with an entry in a specific incident file, new or updated. In your command post, such data can be instantly added to computerized files or it can be filed in written form with a scheduled entry into your intelligence database at a later specified time.

If necessary, all appropriate personnel on duty must be alerted to the presence of a specific threat. In sequence, the next shift needs to be alerted so as that shift takes over, this incident is given priority status as far as a possible flashpoint is concerned. Two or more successive shifts encountering episodes triggering high levels of alert do not constitute what might be defined as a routine situation.

If such a sequence takes place, your database should be absorbing all the details of these incidents as quickly as possible, reassigning the random file opened for Episode A with existing files on groups or patterns of behavior. Thus, the first step involves the delicate process of either merging Episode A into the larger fabric at hand, or highlighting the uniqueness of the event like an isolated strand or thread.

Episode A cannot float in a vacuum. You must determine the relationship between Episode A and any other incidents to preserve your edge. If the other side gains the edge, you are in big trouble.

And all data relevant to Episode A should be cross-indexed or cross-referenced as quickly as possible in order to help identify and establish the magnitude of the threat. Quickly accessing the best possible picture of the overall threat to a particular principal and his activities allows for immediate corrections in levels of response, as well as rapid adjustments to what is often an ever-changing schedule.

The key to avoiding the creation of parallel files—files where common elements are not merged together and therefore a more complete picture of an incident or subject is never assembled—is to establish a set of easily understood ground rules for the use of keywords and file headings. If you are uncertain about the proper way to file a piece of information which you feel is vital, don't rule out the quick creation of two files where one is a "tickler" which serves as a temporary holding cell for such data until the data can be relocated at a later time to an appropriate file.

VERY FILE-FRIENDLY

You are not going to become a computer whiz overnight. Nor are you going to be flooded with data. This means you can take your time to acquaint yourself with an NC. Do not underestimate the value of simple exercises involving simulated incidents. This emphasis on imagination can yield immediate results in terms of helping you and your detail to become more proficient and comfortable in the routine handling of a computer and its contents.

The concept of a file needs to be explored as well. Files can be batched together for a variety of purposes. A moment ago, we mentioned the possibility that parallel or isolated files which share common elements might take shape. These problems associated with file management in general can be solved with a little input from an experienced computer operator. Look for help from inside your company, or tap an outside consultant. Try not to delay the process of identifying and obtaining competent assistance in this regard. Like anything else, a few pointers early on can help to avoid major mistakes and improper operating procedures.

Quick access is where the NC approach can run circles around the old paper-stuffed notebook. Sure, readers will say that the human brain is the best computer, and while that won't be disputed, there are numerous examples of incidents where a whole roomful of brains failed to find the right answer because somehow someone failed to share the right information at the right time.

Again, gathering information and sharing information are two different matters entirely. For information to be shared, it has to be processed and then stored. At the same time, instantaneous inputs of critical data are not to be expected. Nobody is suggesting, for example, that somehow a protective services specialist is going to leap to his or her NC and enter all the details of a particular incident just moments after it occurs.

At some point, the data entry process will take place in a quick and efficient manner involving as little time as possible. How much time is necessary? It is hard to accurately project the time requirement, and yet record-keeping and file-related activities are already part of the job at hand.

An NC enables the user to access lots of stored information rapidly. In addition, this data can be stored both in chronological form—date and time—as well as in various files. What makes this approach so attractive is the way in which any computer—portable or not—is so dependent on files and how that dependence on the part of the machine parallels your needs and operational requirements both on a long term and day-to-day basis.

All computers portable or otherwise can be loaded with software packages which contain different desktop applications such as notepads and calendars in addition to a standard word processing capability. Files in the word processing mode—where you can create your own database dedicated to various incidents, settings, threat scenarios or whatever—are stored and indexed automatically in alphabetical order.

This concept of creating a customize database for an NC may sound like an enormous undertaking—awkward and somewhat intimidating to the novice computer user—but it is a remarkably simple concept. Just think of the machine as being very file-friendly. Keep in mind that any database starts with nothing and can grow to infinite proportions. As you familiarize yourself with your selected hardware and software, you can begin to tailor-fit the manner in which information is stored and categorized to best suit your needs as well. But remember, *garbage in, garbage out.*

One of the exciting new twists to the portable computer field is the creation of a line of desktop PC's which are equipped with "ports" where you simply insert the smaller NC to allow a larger PC to instantly access and store what has been entered into the NC. This is a very attractive feature, and yet we must omit a detailed discussion of the PC/NC connection here.

Incident-related files along with schedules and advance sheets will no doubt constitute the bulk of your constantly changing files. Other files containing important medical and biographical data or fixed diagrams and maps can be created and stored indefinitely. Medical information stored on a $3^1/2$-inch diskette—these small floppy diskettes are inserted into the front of an NC like popping a videotape into a VCR—may seem a bit obsolete when tiny microchips are capable of performing the same function.

However, the small diskette offers plenty of flexibility, and a standard ten-pack of diskettes represents an enormous amount of storage capacity. Each diskette can be labeled appropriately.

Here are some of the fixed or unchanging files that you can easily store on a diskette for use at your convenience:

— Medical Data
— Maps and Routes (Note—we will explore the GPS dimension in a moment)
— Buildings, Layouts, Floor Plans
— Staff and Contact rosters
— Registration data for vehicles, weapons, etc.
— Checklists

YOUR NC IS A BACKUP UNIT

Keep in mind that your use of computer technology has a strong underlying motive which can appeal to your principal in no uncertain terms. The concept of the NC being constantly carried by a protective services detail may seem somewhat out of place, that is until the day when your NC is suddenly transformed into a spare or emergency backup system because your principal's NC malfunctions or becomes otherwise unavailable.

While this is a rare occasion, it only takes one instance of this type for you to instantly win over anyone who is skeptical of the NC approach to protective services operations.

Besides, if your principal is using NC technology, and if all his or her aides and associates are immersed in this electronic environment, don't you think that your incorporation of the same technology and organizational methods enhances your credibility? Yes, you can continue to cram all sorts of notes into your pockets and carry an address book, if that's the only option available to you for budgetary reasons in particular.

But the corporate world is going to continue to embrace standards of performance which are evolutionary. When it comes to mobile telecommunications and computer-related activity, the longer you wait to ease into this new dimension, the greater the gap you have to fill. This is a skill like any other. Besides, it can be lots of fun. Your kids can always act as troubleshooters if everything else fails.

THE FEAR OF INTERCEPTION

When it comes to any form of cellular or wireless communication, one should never assume that the signal in question cannot be intercepted. To assume otherwise is foolish, and risky. Besides, it flies in the face of overwhelming evidence that the sophistication of techniques routinely employed by unseen interceptors, whether they are harmless hackers or more dangerous parties, continue to evolve.

In this chapter, the NC is presented as a tool for information management and for enhancing command post capabilities while on the move. As a result, the encryption or encoding dimension of NC operations is part of a larger picture involving your overall adherence to secure communications procedures and practices. The NC simply plugs into that grid via conventional modem or fax/modem.

Because the NC is a powerful tool, and not just a passive device or some sort of electronic bottomless pit into which you dump vast amounts of raw data, you should be very careful when you link this device—or any computer—to a network, either wired or wireless. You are no doubt aware of how quickly a skilled operator can penetrate a network, and then prowl the innermost depths of the electronic cavern in question without being detected. Once inside, the penetrator can lie dormant for months if he or she so chooses.

A solution to your concerns about secrecy might lie in a box of 3½-inch diskettes. As you will quickly discover, your NC has two disk drives, one permanently fixed in the guts of the machine and one that requires the presence of a diskette. Remove that diskette, and unless you have transferred a file onto the hard drive inside the NC in question, the contents of the files on that specific diskette are instantly sealed off.

While this may seem too primitive and burdensome an approach, it is a safe way to proceed until you become more familiar with the operating characteristics of your machine. But bear in mind that as long as you do not use your NC as a point of transmission or as a reception device, it's just as secure as your old paper-filled notebook. The procedures that kept that notebook and its contents secure—if they worked successfully—should be applied to the NC.

Remote penetration via electronic means of your NC while it is operating cannot be ruled out entirely; however, such an undertaking, especially in urban areas where layers of electronic transmissions at all frequencies are so concentrated, is very difficult if not impossible indeed. Chances are that if your protective detail is so closely monitored, someone has already planted a pinhole camera or series of cameras in order to watch your every move.

A reader might be inclined to think that we have solved a problem here. We have not. An NC user in a protective services role will be drawn to the down loading process by virtue of his or her job responsibilities. It's almost too good to be true. Vast amounts of intelligence data—the quality of which is never to be taken for granted—await you. As multicasting and other network enhancement measures become more common, along with what is known a the "browse and burst" capability, users of various commercial databanks will multiply quickly.

"Browse and burst" is a technique which allows a systems operator to acquire large blocks of data in a single burst. This data is stored and then screened at a later time when the systems operator can "browse" or break down the large block of data into its smaller components. It's like telling a library to send you every book on every stack, and then being able to select the one book that you want to read at your leisure.

Again, once you have acquired all this data, the verification process is another matter entirely. Hopefully, everything you receive is accurate and up-to-date. Sound too fantastic? In the real world, no such flawless flow of facts exists. Like everything else, it's up to you to figure out what is real and what is not.

SCHEDULES AND CALENDARS

With schedules and calendars constantly in a state of flux for travel-intensive protective services details in particular, NC's offer enormous advantages. With built-in calendars and notepads—the electronic equivalent of all those little scraps of paper—the NC funnels time and date-related data far more efficiently than any handwritten system.

Readers, who have functioned flawlessly in the past without the benefit of any electronic device, may find the above-mentioned claim a bit exaggerated. And yet, anyone with highly-organized, detail-oriented scheduling skills is going to immediately appreciate the advantage, rather than any disadvantage, that the NC offers.

The ability to instantly generate an updated, and revised written schedule with the push of a button is another feature of the NC that requires additional hardware, in this case a portable printer. But what a difference in terms of rapid turnaround time and neatness. Again, we seek to identify possibilities here, not to condemn past practices.

THE MAP GAME

A CD-ROM drive added to your NC can open a whole new world as far as travel plans are concerned. This writer used "Street Atlas USA" which is made by DeLORME Mapping to produce detailed, street-level maps of the entire U.S. Other similar CD-ROM-based maps are available on the market. "Street Atlas" allowed us to jump from a street map of Shelby, North Carolina to a dirt road in Jackson, New Hampshire (population approximately 450) in under 60 seconds.

This type of map enables the user to search for locations via zip code, phone exchange or place name—even street name. It allows for different scales using a variable magnitude setting. It also allows the user to set off in any direction from a given point. This is a great feature for anyone looking to plot alternative routes.

The convenience and flexibility of this system is quite amazing. This writer could operate the system with relative ease in only a matter of minutes.

For pinpoint accuracy in transit, DeLORME offers a Global Positioning System (GPS) software link called "CPS Mapkit SV" as well as full hardware packages including the CD-ROM drive and GPS receiver under the designations, "HV" and "HVG."

As a vehicle moves along, the MapKit operator in the vehicle can see exactly where the vehicle is located. A "bread crumb" function details the route taken, and another feature allows for mileage projection between points.

This CD-ROM mapping capability is ideally suited for protective services details who engage in multi-site stops or visitations in unfamiliar areas. Of course, a local contact serving as a coordinator is recommended, and yet the availability of a GPS link is very advantageous in the event that a detail, for example, elects to do a rapid advance and site survey with little lead time.

Leaving aside this particular CD-ROM accessory, the little Toshiba T1900C NC which was used by this writer to explore the powers and capabilities of NC's in general came with a fantastic color graphics feature. This enables the user to quickly draw detailed maps—ideal for distinct site survey purposes. Such maps can be stored and updated with attached files of descriptive text.

In this instance, for example, this writer used a so-called "Paintbrush" accessory tool, part of the overall Windows software package which was built into the Toshiba T1900C unit. It took less than five minutes to generate a full-color map of the outside of a hypothetical hotel complex where a helicopter landing was taking place. All the assigned vehicles and personnel were located on the map, along with routing information. Printouts were available in less time than it took to produce the map in question.

This capability may exceed your requirement, but it demonstrates nonetheless how flexible and adaptable an NC can be. Because we are exploring the future applications of this technology as well, do not be surprised if photo scanning and live video feeds are soon included as part of the NC operating environment. This will not happen overnight, and it will not be an inexpensive feature at first, but the day is coming when a vehicle or mobile command post will include all of these options linked to one portable terminal.

SO MANY TOOLS

Readers are aware of a long list of other electronic tools of the trade. In fact, there are so many tools out there, that we obviously are not able to devote space to all of them. Again, many readers—our wireless wonders—are already tapping into the more automated realm of portable computer technology, and they are doing so without giving it a second thought.

In the law enforcement community, the process of integrating portable computers into routine operations is proceeding at a brisk pace. The National Institute of Justice, for example, in conjunction with law enforcement personnel in St. Petersburg, Florida, and Los Angeles, has helped to redefine the concept of an Automated Reporting System (ARS). Work in this area in St. Petersburg, for example, dates back over a decade, beginning with what is called "PISTOL," or "Paperless Information System Totally On-Line."

In this respect, many police officers from police departments that use this hardware are well-versed in the routine operation—and glitches—of portable computers. While a new series of guidelines and input requirements will no doubt be encountered as the switch is made from law enforcement to executive protection, any previous exposure to this technology and to its advantages and constraints makes the orientation period that much easier and shorter.

Drawing any parallels between public and private sector initiatives in this regard is not easy. The resources available to public sector agencies may not be infinite, but in the field of electronics or telecommunications, there is a broader base of support and expertise. The public sector must also cope with extremely large volumes of data with instantaneous linkups or access to even larger national databanks, whereas the private sector faces a different set of priorities.

Privacy in the information age is another concern as electronic pathways expand and overlap. What might seem convenient and easy—all sorts of facts at your fingertips—may prove to be a legal quagmire and downright inaccurate as well. Keep in mind that if you expand your computerized approach into the dimension of intelligence gathering and if that process leads to the creation of what are, in effect, personnel files which delve into the private lives of others who might pose a threat to your principal, you could be walking through what could easily become a minefield. This writer is not a lawyer, and nothing here constitutes a set of recommendations in terms of what is legal and permissible. A word of caution in nevertheless necessary.

We have tried to initiate a process that involves an open mind and a willingness to explore new methods and new technologies. At the same time, the emphasis here is on the adoption of different and perhaps innovative information management techniques. We are not trying to increase the time spent on paperwork; we are looking at ways to improve your operational proficiency.

Intelligence gathering is one thing, billing and financial record keeping are something else entirely. For those security consultants who serve multiple clients, the ability to file financial and accounting data via electronic means equates to fewer headaches, especially if you are on the road for prolonged periods of time. We have omitted the formalized business applications of NC's, including the use of spreadsheets and standard computerized accounting practices for obvious reasons.

Blending all the details, in the world of protective services, into one coherent mass is quite difficult. Whether you are currently computerized or not, you probably did some creative problem-solving as you read this chapter, imagining how one or more aspects of your job could be squeezed into an NC. Now, it's up to you to translate the hypothetical application in your mind into reality.

The introductory phase of such an undertaking is bound to seem time-consuming, but your patience will be rewarded. Don't try to master the whole machine at once. Bite off a small piece and chew on it for a while. Look at the amount of time you have available and set your own pace. Play with the NC, get comfortable with it and be realistic. Sooner than you realize, you will slip into the electronic era. And you won't ever look back.

Acknowledgements: The author wishes to thank the Computer Services Division of Toshiba America Information Systems, Inc. in Irvine, California for the use of a Toshiba T1900C, and Ms. Traci Hayes of Maples & Associates in Irvine, California for her rapid and efficient handling of my request for such equipment. DeLORME Mapping of Freeport, Maine quickly provided the "Street Atlas USA" on CD-ROM. Thomson Consumer Electronics, Inc., in Indianapolis, Indiana provided a model of its new Ku-Band satellite dish, part of Thomson's RCA-brand Digital Satellite System (DSS). Thanks to "SoftRisk, Inc. in St. Simons Island, Georgia" and a special thanks to Eli Badger for sharing his computer insights.

TWENTY-TWO

Professional Dress for the Female P.P.S.

by Tobie L. Naumann

TEAM LEADERS TAKE NOTE:

Although this chapter is directed to women, it should not be over-looked by anyone in the field. The guidelines it offers are basic and make for good advice to female teammates. It enhances the effectiveness of a team leader to see that all members of the team, men and women alike, are properly attired for the mission and situation at hand.

Men, for years now have dominated the field of Executive Protection Specialist. However, times are changing, and women are now being requested frequently for specific assignments. With this, women have encountered special concerns relating to their attire. For men it's like breathing, they know how many suits they need, the number of shirts, shoes and personal items required.

For women it's not that simple. Much thought must be given to organizing and preparing their wardrobe for travel. The old adage has always been that the Personal Protection Specialist is to blend in, not to stand out, to be there, but not be there. For women that is a tough order to follow. Because of today's fashions, it's almost impossible to blend in. If a women chooses to wear a trendy outfit she is then drawing attention to herself. If she chooses too conservative a dress, she sticks out like a sore thumb. One of the first things a woman needs to do is to research the fashion trend of the city or country to which she will be traveling.

This can be accomplished by calling a good hotel in the area where you will be working and asking the name of a reputable women's clothing store. A conversation with a fashion consultant at that store may give you hints as to the acceptable business dress of the area. The only way you will blend in is to know what the professional women are wearing in that locale. Keep in mind, principals come in all shapes and sizes, and women are women wherever you go. You must always remember: never out-dress your principal, and your appearance is a very important part of your job.

Here are some hints that remain consistent no matter where you go:

1. **Suits**
   a. Selection of a double-breasted verses single-breasted suit may depend on your need too carry a firearm.
   b. Always purchase a fine quality suit that will be wrinkle resistant, such as wool, or a wool crepe blend. Wool gabardine is also a good choice as it transcends seasons and travels well.
   c. Have the suit properly tailored to accommodate firearms or radios.
   d. You may want to have a pocket put in the suit for small personal items such as lipstick or comb, when carrying a handbag is impractical.
   e. Purchase jackets, skirts and dress slacks that are interchangeable for versatility. Dress slacks should only be worn when the assignment dictates.
   f. Skirts should not be too straight, too long, or too short. Keep it practical. You must be able to run or walk with comfort and at a fast pace in your skirt.
   g. Fortunately pants suits are again in fashion in the business world. This is good news for the PPS as they offer a comfort and flexibility that skirted suits do not. One caveat however, make sure the suit is a traditional classic cut and is well-tailored. A good choice would be a wool gabardine suit in navy, black or taupe.
   h. By investing in good quality suits you will not only always look and feel good, you will actually cut down on maintenance time and expense. Good wools are wrinkle resistant and, as a natural fiber, should not be over-cleaned. You can keep them fresh and neat by hanging them to air after wearing, and spritzing inside the collar and underarms with alcohol when you take them off.

2. **Blouses**
   a. No plunging necklines or sheer fabrics.
   b. Rounded necklines are easier to accessorize.

3. **Stockings**
   a. It is imperative to know the acceptable colors for the area where you are working. Stay with colors of a conservative nature. For example: tans, taupes, blacks, creams.
   b. A support type stocking may be preferred for long hours on your feet.

4. Shoes

a. Be Conservative. A pump works the best. Choose the color and inch size of heel carefully.

b. Your shoes should be functional and flattering on your feet. Proper fit and comfort are imperative.

c. No sporty flats unless the outfit or assignment dictates. However, low healed pumps are now acceptable and in vogue for professional dress.

d. Shoes must be clean and polished at all times. Repair heels and lifts as needed.

5. Accessories

a. Should be kept to a minimum.

b. They should enhance your outfit, not overpower it.

6. Jewelry

a. Wear costume jewelry as opposed to fine quality. In case of confrontation, replacement will be easier and less costly.

b. Earrings should be small, a clip or post style, not hook type.

c. Your jewelry should reflect a conservative professional image.

7. Handbags/Purses

a. Years ago the rule was that handbags should always match your shoes. Most professional women now find that impractical and have opted to purchase one good bag (like a Coach or Dooney & Bourke) that blends with most outfits—like black, brown, taupe or tan. For evening wear they usually switch to a smaller bag—again, a classic leather style.

b. Maintain the appearance of your handbag and keep it in good shape.

c. Do not overstuff your handbag. Over-stuffed bags project an unorganized image.

d. Handbags with a shoulder strap are recommended, to leave hands free.

e. Handbags/purses should be chosen carefully to accommodate weapons.

8. Personal Hygiene

a. Minimize attention needed to maintain your hairdo. Do not fuss with your hair while on a detail.

b. Keep your choice of perfume or cologne light.

c. Makeup should enhance natural beauty and not overwhelm. Seek professional color analysis to determine which colors are best for you. This would also apply to clothing selections.

d. Nails should be manicured regularly. Polish should be conservative and compliment your outfit.

e. Physical fitness is mandatory in this profession. **Stay in shape.**

Although appearance and proper dress have been stressed in this chapter, a third and often overlooked component is comfort. If clothes don't fit well, or shoes are too tight, too high, or even too low, serious discomfort can result. Never sacrifice comfort for style; you cannot perform proficiently if you are in pain from leg cramps, a constricting waistband, or blisters. One good pair of black, practical mid-heel pumps, is a much better investment than three pairs of faddish sandals or spikes. The same can be said for classic well-tailored clothes.

If your assignment is going to require a lot of travel—remember: Don't wear tight or constricting clothes or shoes while flying. There is something about the pressurized cabin that causes swelling and water-retention. Clothes that were comfortable when you embarked can feel two sizes too small after a long flight.

Every woman needs to have her own look, style, color, etc.; however, if you are new in this type of work, or have questions about appropriate dress because you're in a new locale or climate, don't be afraid to ask questions of fellow team-members or business associates. Another trick is to watch for someone whose style and professionalism you admire and imitate their look, adjusting it to your particular needs.

Last, but not least, work at setting up a regular routine for clothes maintenance and haircuts, etc. This will save a lot of time in the long run and also ensure that you are always prepared and ready should an emergency arise. Another excellent idea is described in detail in Roch Brousseau's chapter on **Being Prepared**—keeping an emergency kit, including extra clothes, in the trunk of your car. You just might be surprised at how often it will be used to save you, your principal, or a fellow team-member from an embarrassing situation.

TWENTY-THREE

Communications Integrity: A Briefing on Electronic Surveillance and Audio Countermeasures

by Patrick L. Spatafore

A GREAT RISK IN TODAY'S WORLD of high-tech micro electronics is the threat of audio recovery of an individual's private conversations. The need for protection in this field is essential when a Protection Specialist takes into account his duties while providing protection services for his/her clients. There has been much written on the subject of Electronic Surveillance detection and Countermeasures, so this chapter will not deal with the engineering or design of devices. However, this chapter will help you, the Protection Specialist, to know what to look for when preparing protective measures for your client.

Governments throughout the world have introduced Audio Counter-measure (ACM) and Technical Security Countermeasure (TSCM) Programs for their leaders in order to provide a high degree of integrity in their security.

Simply put, if you take the time to advance a site, then you should utilize all security efforts including protecting your employer's private information.

All a person needs is a good imagination when it comes to surveillance, so it's up to you not to be compromised. Remember the following about transmitters:

1. Bugs (transmitters) come in all sizes and shapes.
2. They are widely available.
3. They are easily utilized.

In order to identify and explain what takes place, let's list some areas which must be secured:

1. Telephone systems
2. Office, residence, automobiles, aircraft and marine vessels
3. Power lines

4. Computer equipment
5. Furnishings
6. Cellular phones

TELEPHONE INSTRUMENTS

Telephone instruments along with speaker phones are a security hazard. Let's look at what they give an eavesdropper to use—wires, microphones and a connection block. These items are already in the location that you're trying to secure for your protectee. The simple installation of a radio transmitter or modification of the instrument to pass audio is all that is needed to intercept audio out of a location. Speaker phone systems many times radiate radio frequency energy and can broadcast audio conversations up to a distance of twenty-five (25) feet without even modifying the unit. All it takes to recover audio is knowing what type of system your protectee uses. Once that is established, the eavesdropper can begin his plan.

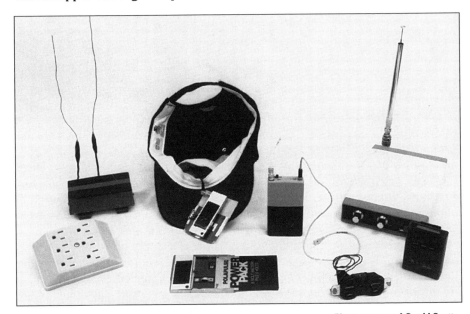

Photo courtesy of Gerald Spette
Radio & Video Transmitting Equipment

TRANSMITTERS

There are different types of radio transmitters that can be used as surveillance devices, such as, the Free Space Transmitter (the classic bug) and the Carrier Current Transmitter which can transmit audio on power lines.

Free Space Transmitters are usually miniature radio transmitters which can broadcast audio (voice conversations) from 10 feet to many miles away (with the use of repeaters). These units come in many varieties and price ranges and are available from electronic hobby shops and mail order catalogs. These devices can be remotely switched on/off in order to conserve battery life and detection. They can be installed in various types of items such as books, walls, pencil sharpeners, pen and pencil holders, etc. Again, it is up to the imagination of the installer.

In 1952, the Russians initiated electronic surveillance of the U.S. Embassy in Moscow with the use of a sophisticated transmitter called a Resonant Cavity. This type of device is unusual in that it contains no power supply or other electronic parts. The device was buried in the wood of the Great Seal of the United States in the Ambassador's office, which had been given to the Embassy by the Russian government. This device operated for a period of eleven years before it was discovered.

In short, a Resonant Cavity is a small metal cylinder, which has an antenna attached to a diaphragm enclosing one end of the cylinder. When the cavity is saturated by radio frequency energy (RF) from an area outside the target area, or when Room Audio strikes the diaphragm, it modulates RF energy which is radiated from the antenna and is intercepted at a Listening Post (LP). When the RF signal is removed the device no longer transmits intelligence.

Photo courtesy of Gerald Spette

Carrier Current Detector (Used to check AC power lines)

CARRIER CURRENT TRANSMITTERS

Below the AM broadcast portion of the radio spectrum is an area defined as Very Low Frequency (VLF). Audio transmitters are manufactured that operate within this region and utilize both power and telephone lines. These units, while operating at lower frequencies, radiate very little Radio Frequency (RF) into space, therefore making their detection difficult. However, their installation is simple.

Carrier current transmitters can also be packaged into lamps, appliances, wall outlets or multiple AC strips. Once again, it's up to the installer as to how to disguise these items. Remember, however, because the "CC" Transmitter uses power lines (AC) and telephone circuits, they have to be received in an area where the AC and telephone lines appear in order to intercept and receive the audio.

Example—your client decides to go on a trip and Remain Over Night (RON). He/she selects the hotel and you advance the sight. You proceed to do all of your advance procedures but you now have to be aware of what has been discussed about audio interception and therefore, must add the following:

1. See how the switchboard is utilized and who the operators are.
2. How many telephone instruments are there and do they contain speaker phones and/or intercom networks.
3. Do they work?
4. Visually inspect all telephone cables in the room and, if possible, AC outlets.
5. Open the drapes and look at the surrounding buildings to see if anyone can observe your site by the use of video or optical equipment.
6. Conduct a physical search of the area. Look for the obvious, and always use the "what if" principle.
7. Make your decision—do you need an audio countermeasures survey done by an ACM specialist?

Now you have gone over everything, but you weren't able to get into the other rooms located above, below and side to side. If a carrier current transmitter was utilized, it would be possible to simply plug a remote unit into the AC outlet from any of those rooms and monitor your sight. The point I'm tying to make is, just become aware of what *could* take place.

INFINITY TRANSMITTERS

One piece of equipment that is available to the public, and an excellent piece of monitoring equipment, is called the infinity transmitter. Usually advertised as a home monitoring unit, "that lets you listen to your residence when no one's home." The unit works this way: A unit is placed at the location that is to be monitored. Then from a remote telephone (at another location) you call the residence's telephone number and activate a code. The residence phone does not ring, but the telephone line is seized and allows you to listen in. The receiving unit can be set in any location and when it is dialed allows the caller to listen in without alerting anyone (say maybe a burglar). This unit is not advertised as a *bug* but simply as a home monitoring unit.

This is one of the items that you should look for during a physical search of telephone lines. *Use your imagination.*

MICROPHONES

Probably the oldest and most effective type of technical attack is the use of a microphone and hardwire. Many types of microphones are on the market ranging from carbon, electric, FET shotgun, to Parabolic. The use of a hardwire microphone, when installed correctly at the target site, assures the best audio quality possible back to the listening post.

Example 1: In your principal's office there are a number of spare wires that go to the telephone, computer, or intercom system. By selecting the right type of microphone all that would be required is to connect a microphone to any spare wire on the telephone block. (You would have to use a line tracer to locate where these spare wires terminate, which is usually in the frame room). By simply using an amplifier at the terminated ends audio (conversations) could be recovered.

Once again a physical search would aid in detecting the microphone. However, an installer could run his own cable wherever it would be convenient for him. *Remember the installer's imagination.*

Example 2: If an office area contains a public announcement or muzak system, it can be used as a microphone to pass room audio to another point. All that is necessary is to connect an amplifier to the speaker wires and audio can be recovered. Once again a complete eaves-dropping system is already in place.

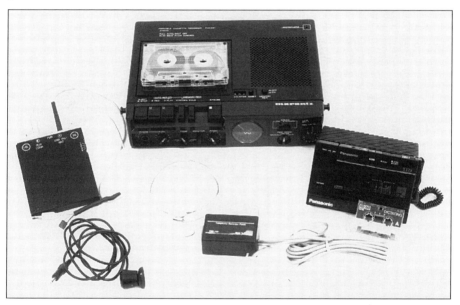

Photo courtesy of Gerald Spette

Telephone & Voice Recording Equipment
Note: The mini receiver to the left of the cassette recorder—this unit is ideal for close in monitoring.

CELLULAR TELEPHONES

It should come as no surprise to anyone that Cellular Telephones are vulnerable to audio interception. A portable hand held scanner or receiver is all that is required to retrieve information.

Example 3: You have conducted an advance for your principal and you now have to call the office with some critical information. You discuss arrival time, persons to be involved in the transportation, and other itinerary details.

Now you are doing this from your car because you are stuck in traffic, and of course, you are using your mobile phone. The one thing that you were not aware of is that you are under surveillance by other persons who want to get information or target your protectee. Guess what? They are monitoring your car phone with a portable receiver and you just gave them all the intelligence that they need, whether to assassinate your protectee or to just gain further information that could be used to discredit and embarrass him/her. Remember: if you do not want to read about it in the headlines, then do not discuss it on the telephone, regardless if it is a cellular or an in-house telephone network.

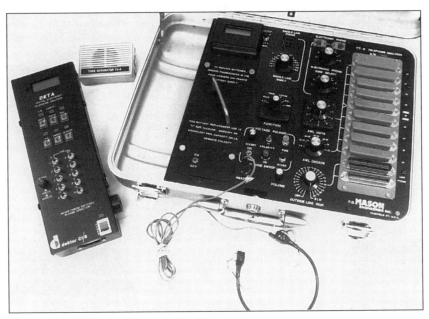

Photo courtesy of Gerald Spette

Telephone Analyzers & Line Testing Equipment

COMPUTER SYSTEM

Most computer systems are safe, provided they are not connected to a modem (via telephone lines). There are a number of security programs on the market which allow the user to secure his/her unit. A security program can provide a simple *password* accessibility to raise the level of security higher, based on national security standards.

Whatever your threat level may be, remember to always do the following:
a. Limit access to your PC.
b. Clear your video display unit (monitor) before leaving the terminal.
c. Secure your diskettes and label them.
d. Secure your printer.
e. Turn your personal computer off after using it.
f. Beware of borrowed software. It may contain a virus which could knock out your files.

Remember, computer systems generate radio frequency internally, and there are studies and reports establishing that the interception of these emissions and displaying of your information on another CRT (monitor) at another location is possible. So be aware!

It is important to consider your vulnerabilities when installing your units. Think about windows and access points in your area when setting up your system and do not forget about an optical/visual threat ranging from telephoto lens and binoculars to telescopes.

Remember:

1. Change your password often.
2. Use passwords that do not contain names of persons, places, or things that are close to you.
3. NEVER give out your password.
4. Check your files periodically.
5. Never leave an active terminal unattended.
6. "Secure your data."

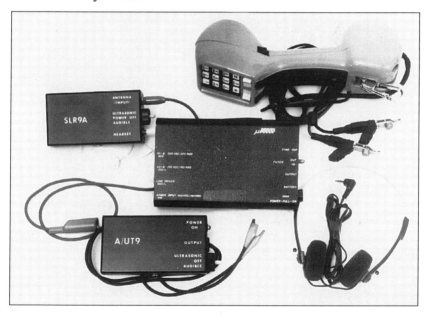

Photo courtesy of Gerald Spette

Line Tracing Equipment
(Used to verify all existing wiring not in use)

FAX MACHINES

A fax machine is a computer that transmits written material to a like unit. By simply attaching a unit to a phone line, a person's in business.

As a Protection Specialist a fax machine, along with a cellular phone, can make your mission a lot easier; however, a fax can be intercepted also. If you fax information from point "A" to point "B" a person utilizing a fax intercept machine simply has to connect his unit to your client's phone line and he will be

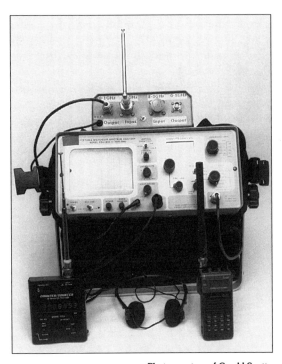

Photo courtesy of Gerald Spette
Spectrum Analysis Equipment
(Used for detecting clandestine transmitters)

able to intercept all communications coming or going to your client's fax without alerting anyone to what has taken place. **Remember:** If you don't want it to appear in the newspaper, then do not fax anything critical (like itineraries) or anything else that can be an embarrassment to your employer. Remember, there is no way to tell who may pick up a received fax and read it. In fact, it is more likely that an unintended party will read a fax, than listen in on a phone extension.

CELLULAR FAX

Cellular phone fax machines provide a great opportunity for intercepts! The fax signal can be received with an inexpensive scanner and recorded, and when utilized with additional equipment, the message can be intercepted. No physical connection is necessary; therefore, there is no risk of being detected.

PHYSICAL SEARCHES

The physical search is probably the most critical part of the audio countermeasure survey. It has been estimated that approximately 90% of all electronic finds have been located during the physical search.

Take a look at your site. Does anything look out of the norm? Look for any wires that are running from the building that may be used for a microphone

Various Types of Optical Surveillance Equipment
Note: The board camera on the lower left hand row.

and possibly be going to a Listen Post (LP). Is there any indication of someone trying to penetrate the roof area for the installation of antennas? Look at your surroundings and concentrate on other structures that could utilize an optical or visual attack. Stand back and look for <u>anything</u> <u>UNUSUAL</u> and out of the <u>NORM</u>.

ROOM SEARCHING

Now that you have a general idea of what types of threats to look for in an Audio Countermeasures Survey (ACM), we're ready to discuss room searching.

The greatest threats come from Radio Frequency (RF) transmitters, carrier current devices, and hard wire microphones. A good tool kit will help you facilitate your ACM and should contain basic hand tools, a metal detector, inspection mirrors, lamps, and meters. Keep in mind that you must examine everything in your area. If you have conducted an EOD (explosives search) sweep, the techniques are the same. Do the search thoroughly and the way you feel is best for you.

Pay attention to the following areas:
  a. Furniture—top, bottom, and cushions
  b. Baseboards
  c. False ceilings
  d. Books
  e. Recent construction or modifications. *Use an ultra violet light for this.*

f. Light switches and electrical outlets. *Again, remember the installer's imagination.*

g. Adhesive seals are available and are a good idea to use after you have searched specific items. These seals show "void" if an attempt to open them was made.

AUTOMOBILE SEARCHES

A good physical search of the automobile(s) should be conducted, again using the same techniques as an explosive (EOD) search. Be aware of vehicle locating transmitters that can be attached to the chassis of the vehicle and also voice activated tape recorders (VOX) and transmitters. These units can be wired into the ignition system and can run continuous. However, with a recorder a tape would have to be retrieved and reinstalled, therefore, a transmitter would be the more likely device to have been used. *Do not forget how vulnerable the cellular phone makes your client.*

RADIO FREQUENCY ANALYSIS

The radio frequency analysis deals strictly with searching for radio transmitters and carrier current transmitters. (Remember the difference in the two!) The most effective electronic equipment utilized for an RF Sweep is the radio receiver and spectrum analyzer. This equipment should be capable of tuning from 10 kilohertz (KHZ) thru 2 gigahertz (GHZ). These two units, utilized in conjunction with one another gives the user full capability in breaking out and analyzing the majority of any RF signals in the environment. There are different types of features which are needed to do this and they vary with each use, from sensitivity, selectivity and receiving modes to subcarrier detection (double demodulation) and the use of a panadapter (scope) signal strength and a headphone jack.

In order to understand transmitters and receivers, I would strongly recommend further study of the subject and, if possible, attending a seminar on this subject.

TELEPHONE ANALYSIS

When checking telephone systems, the Protection Specialist should try to ascertain the appearance of the telephones which are to be examined. This is where the inspection should begin. A physical search should be conducted in the areas of frame room, communications closets, etc. Look at the terminal points and look for the obvious, such as small boxes, recording devices, cable bridging points; stand back and just look around. After completing your examination in the above areas, proceed to the area where you would like to conduct your survey using a telephone analyzer (a test unit that measures voltage, resistance, capacitance, and high voltage when necessary), tone and all wire listen test. The unit should also be able to detect subcarrier transmitters on the telephone line.

NON-LINEAR JUNCTION DETECTOR

A non-linear junction detector is an excellent tool to use when conducting physical searches. The unit itself has a broom-type handle with a paddle at one end, which the operator passes over the area that he wants to examine. Simultaneously, the operator listens on headphones to a portable receiver, which is connected to the handle and paddle, for various responses, and watches a signal strength meter. Some units also contain signal strength lights.

The principle of operation is simple. The unit transmits an RF signal into a target area and produces reflections from the target. A non-linear junction between two pieces of metal is one where the impedance of a current flowing in one direction is different from the impedance of a current flowing in the opposite direction. Electronic components such as semi-conductors, which may be constructed and buried in walls, can be detected. However, false junctions are also detected such as nails and metal studs. If a non-linear junction detector is to be utilized, then consideration should also be given to using it in conjunction with an x-ray unit. (Your principal wouldn't appreciate holes in his walls because of a false hit.)

DISCOVERY PROCEDURES

If you discover a listening device or telephone modification, there are a number of procedures that should be observed. Keeping the find confidential is a must. Set up a surveillance post and try to observe someone returning either to change batteries or to retrieve tapes. Remember you also have the advantage of knowing that a device is there and active *(use your imagination)*.

Unauthorized use of an intercept device is a violation of federal law; therefore, a report of the discovery should be made to the Federal Bureau of Investigation. Keep in mind that you should treat the device as a piece of evidence. Don't handle it until the proper authorities have been contacted. If possible, photograph it in the condition that it was found and document how it was discovered. Make certain that you get a receipt and follow up reports from the investigating agency. *Remember, don't touch it.*

CONCLUSION

This chapter has been compiled to explain the basic types of intercept devices on the market today. This does not by any means cover all areas of technical intercept, but rather, is only to make you, "The Protection Specialist" aware of what is out there.

The science of electronic surveillance and countermeasures is a specialty in today's world and should be treated as such. The installation of any surveillance device can be made highly sophisticated, or very simple. Once again, this is up to the imagination of the installer so you must become aware of your environment. If you feel that you or your client is being, or has been compromised, then you should consider having an Audio Countermeasures Survey conducted, but make sure you know who you're employing. By trusting these persons to come into your domain, you are, in effect, exposing your employer to great vulnerability.

GLOSSARY

ACM — Audio Countermeasures
BUGS — Radio Frequency Transmitters
CC — Carrier Current
CRT — Cathode Ray Tube
EOD — Explosive Ordnance Disposal
GHZ — Gigahertz (Radio Frequency)
KHZ — Kilohertz (Radio Frequency)
LP — Listening Post
RF — Radio Frequency
RON — Remain Overnight
SCOPE — Video Monitor
TSCM — Technical Security Countermeasures
VLF — Very Low Frequency
VOX — Voice Activated Switch

TWENTY-FOUR

Medical Kit Considerations

by Michael Tucker

OVER-THE-COUNTER MEDICINES

As a Registered Pharmacist I am often asked to recommend over the counter medications. The same was true while attending a recent Personal Protection training program in Winchester, Virginia. Many of the participants would seek information about minor health problems and the recommendation of an appropriate over-the-counter medication. This chapter will try to touch on some of the more common ailments and the medications available to the Personal Protection Specialist.

As Personal Protection Specialists our primary concern has been that of the principal's health, safety and security. But what of those of the Specialist? Minor aches and pains, acid indigestion and gas, seasonal allergies, constipation, travelers' diarrhea, minor coughs and colds, and foot problems have affected everyone from time to time. While not life-threatening these symptoms can be unpleasant and affect both performance and appearance.

Minor aches and pains are a common occurrence. Headaches, bumps, bruises and even occasional dental discomfort can make a long day seem to go on forever. Aspirin and non-aspirin products are available. They provide analgesic relief, fever reduction, and decreased swelling and inflammation in joints and tissue. They alleviate the discomfort. Aspirin in still the most effective analgesic on the market and is found under a number of trade names (i.e., Bayer, Anacin, Excedrin). It is inexpensive and readily available at numerous outlets. For those unable to take aspirin the non-aspirin products, such as Tylenol, (acetaminophen) are available. While acetaminophen is good for analgesia and fever reduction it is not as effective in reducing inflammation. The newcomer to the market has been Ibuprofen (Advil, Nuprin, Motrin IB). Ibuprofen has many of the same characteristics as aspirin and is quite effective. Be aware that individuals who experience problems with aspirin will most likely have them with Ibuprofen.

Acid indigestion and gas follow close behind minor aches and pains as a source of discomfort and professional inconvenience. That chili dog with cheese and jalepeno peppers, which had to be eaten in 10 seconds or less, has an unpleasant way of coming back to haunt us. Liquid antacids work the most quickly but are bulky and best left in the room or command post. Tablets are much more convenient to carry and consume and are made by various manufacturers. Magnesium Hydroxide and Aluminum Hydroxide (Maalox, Mylanta) are the most common ingredients found in today's antacids. They are effective treatments but if overused can produce diarrhea. Calcium Carbonate (Tums, Rolaids), another effective agent, can produce constipation if used too often. Individuals should monitor their consumption of these agents and avoid becoming an antacid junkie.

Many manufacturers are adding Simethicone to their product line (Maalox plus, Mylanta plus, Riopan plus). It is safe and helps relieve bloating from gas trapped in the stomach and intestines. Persistent indigestion with a severe burning sensation or blood appearing in the stools could be signs of something more serious and a physician should be promptly consulted.

Spring and Fall, two of the most pleasant periods of the year, can be a nightmare for allergy sufferers. Pollen, ragweed, mold and fungus counts can reach high levels in many areas, giving rise to sniffling, sneezing, wheezing and other unpleasant symptoms. Red, irritated, puffy eyes, sinus drainage and difficulty breathing can severely detract from one's appearance and performance. Who wants a Personal Protection Specialist around that looks like that? For occasional occurrences many over-the-counter products are available. The Personal Protection Specialist will need to avoid medications which cause drowsiness or affect mental alertness. One of the better combination products contains Pseudoephedrine HC1 with Chlorphenaramine Maleate and is commonly recognized as Sudfed-Plus. This medication relieves the drainage and congestion while causing little or no drowsiness. Pseudeoephedrine also has comparatively little effect upon blood pressure and is the safest decongestant for individuals with hypertension. Products which primarily contain high doses of antihistamines (Dimetapp, Benadryl, Chlor-Trimeton, Teldrin) should be avoided because drowsiness is the primary side effect. Seldane, a prescription only product, is available through a physician's prescription and has been shown to control heyfever and allergy symptoms without causing drowsiness.

Travelers' diarrhea, popularly known to visitors to Mexico as Montezuma's Revenge, seems to occur when it is least expected and often under the least desirable of conditions. Food, water and medication can all cause this malady for many who travel regularly or in areas where proper sanitation and hygiene guidelines are not observed. Due to the loss of fluids involved many of those affected will quickly become fatigued and irritable. For mild cases, Pepto Bismol and Kaopectate work well. Imodium AD, once a prescription only product, is now available over-the-counter and is an antidiarrheal product which is effective and is easy to carry and administer.

Constipation is, in many ways, the opposite of diarrhea. High fiber diets, insufficient fluid intake and the use of some medications, can all cause this unpleasant condition. Many over-the-counter remedies are available. Some work more quickly than others but can have drawbacks that should be taken into account. M.O.M., milk of magnesia, is widely advertised and effective. It is gentle on the digestive tract and will generally work in one to six hours. Products containing Bisacodyl (Doxidan, Surfak, Dulcolax) are safe, but can take 12 hours or more to produce the desired results. Ex-Lax and Feen-a-Mint are the fastest acting available. Abdominal cramping is a common side effect and can be quite unpleasant. Nothing can be more embarrassing than to have these products do their job at an inappropriate moment.

With over 2000 bacteria and hundreds of viruses causing common cold symptoms it is no wonder physicians make out like bandits. There is such a wide range of products from which to choose. For head cold symptoms— headache, sinus congestion, etc., —I recommend some of the products discussed in the previous section on allergies.

Coughing can be a very annoying and embarrassing problem. Dextromethorphan is the most effective over-the-counter cough suppressant. Delsym, a liquid, which is alcohol free is a very effective product. HOLD cough lozenges are easily carried and effective when on the move. Robitussin, Novahistine, and Vicks as well as numerous manufacturers make multi-symptom liquids and tablets. Some are low in alcohol content and some are sugar-free. These are important considerations for those providing protective services. Nyquil, promoted as the do everything remedy, contains 25 percent alcohol and high levels of antihistamines and should be avoided unless the sufferer can count on being off duty for at least 12 hours.

Blisters and Athlete's Foot round out our brief list of common inconveniences. We spend so much time on our feet that it is well worth investing in a pair of shoes that are both comfortable and appropriate in style and dress for your particular protective detail. Blisters can arise from time to time for a variety of reasons and it is well worth investing in a portable blister repair kit. These can be found in the foot care section of drug stores or at specialty hiking and camping outlets. They are inexpensive and will protect the affected area from rubbing and irritation. Athlete's Foot, another greatly irritating condition, once started takes a long time to eradicate. Many prescription items are now available over-the-counter (Micatin, Tinactin, Lotrimin AF) for treating these fungal infections. The key to effective treatment is to use them daily as directed, up to four to six months in stubborn cases. Initially, creams are the most appropriate form of application and once under control sprays can be considered. These products are also excellent remedies for jock rash, a common condition familiar to those who live or travel in hot climates.

Entire books have been published on over-the-counter products and are available in local bookstores. They are a useful addition to the busy traveler's library. The products specifically mentioned here constitute but a small portion of a vast array of what is actually available. but are quite adequate for a travel kit. As always, be sure to follow label directions. Taking more than is necessary may produce the very side effects one would wish to avoid. If you are unsure of a product, the dosage, or whether it is suitable for you, consult a local pharmacist. These professionals can be a gold mine of free information and are often happy to suggest an appropriate and inexpensive product. Remember, too, many products are available generically. They contain the same ingredients as the trade name products and can be purchased at considerable savings.

A small, compact traveling kit could be put together for under twenty-five dollars and serve the needs of several team members.

The objective is to maintain the general health of those who perform this arduous work. When a button comes off your jacket during a busy detail, you do not rush off to a tailor. The job demands that you use the appropriate repair kit. These brief recommendations should be taken in a similar vein.

MOTION SICKNESS

"Not in a car, not in a plane, not on a boat and not on a train" so wrote Dr. Seuss. While we are not speaking of green eggs and ham, vertigo and motion sickness can quickly have one looking as green as those eggs in the story. Even for those with a cast iron stomach a choppy sea, a plane ride in turbulent skies or a winding road can trigger a nausea reaction which can lead to vomiting. Sight, smell, food, extreme temperature and pressure change, flu and colds can all induce or contribute to vertigo or motion sickness. For many this is an uncomfortable and sometimes embarrassing situation. For those providing personal protection services it can incapacitate one's ability to perform affectively or negate it completely.

Vertigo (dizziness) is a disturbance in which a person has a subjective impression of movement or of objects moving around them, usually with a loss of equilibrium. It results from a disturbance somewhere in the equilibratory apparatus of the ear, brain and eyes. Symptomatic relief may be obtained by bedrest and the use of a number of over-the-counter medications. Dimenhydrinate (Dramamine) 50mg or 100mg orally every 4 to 6 hours or Meclizine (Bonine, Dramamine II) 25mg orally three times a day are effective against both intermittent and continuous vertigo. These agents belong to the antihistamine class of drugs and in most individuals sedation is the adverse reaction most often encountered.

For these agents to be truly effective one should start taking the medication at least 24 hours prior to departure. This will not only give the drug a chance to exert its effect but will also give a time period in which the Personal Protection Specialist can adjust the dosage or duty schedule to avoid side effects.

Motion sickness is a disorder caused by repetitive side-to-side or straight line acceleration and deceleration and is characterized mainly by nausea and vomiting. Excessive stimulation of the inner ear apparatus is the primary cause and there is great individual variation in susceptibility. Visual stimulation (moving horizon), poor ventilation (fumes, smoke and carbon monoxide), and emotional factors (fear, anxiety) commonly act in concert with motion to trigger an attack.

Cyclic nausea and vomiting are characteristic of motion sickness. They may be preceded by yawning, hyperventilation, salivation, profuse cold sweating and somnolence. Once nausea and vomiting develop the individual is weak and unable to concentrate, which could become a serious complication in individuals who are already ill. With prolonged exposure to motion, individuals may adapt and gradually return to well being. However, symptoms may be reinitiated by more severe motion, or a recurrence of motion, after a short respite.

Prevention is easier than treatment. Susceptible individuals should minimize exposure by positioning themselves where there is the least motion (amidships, or in airplanes, over the wings). Lying down with the head braced is best. Reading should be avoided. Keeping your vision at an angle 45 degrees above the horizon will reduce the susceptibility to inner ear stimulation. Avoid visual fixation on waves or other moving objects. A well ventilated cabin or going for a fresh breath of air is helpful.

Alcoholic or dietary excesses before or during travel are not advised. Small amounts of fluids and simple foods should be taken during extended periods of exposure; if exposure is short, as in air travel, food and drink should be avoided.

Drugs to prevent the onset of motion sickness are those that are also used for vertigo. They should be started at least 24 hours prior to departure and continued for the duration of the detail. Remember that side effects may force you to alter your schedule and plan accordingly. Transderm-Scop, a prescription only item, may be obtained from a physician. This unique product contains a small amount of scopolamine sandwiched between the patch material. When the patch is placed behind one ear the drug is delivered through the skin to exert its effect. These patches are convenient and last 72 hours giving prolonged coverage from a single application.

The most common adverse reaction is dry mouth and occurs in about two thirds of the people. Less frequent is drowsiness (about one sixth). Transient impairment of eye accommodation, including blurred vision and dilating of the pupils, is also observed. These patches are effective in over 75 percent of the people that do receive relief of motion sickness using dimenhydrinate.

At no time should one wear more than one patch at a time as the incidence of serious side effects increases dramatically.

While for many vertigo and motion sickness are uncomfortable, in the case of the Personal Protection Specialist the consequences take on an even greater importance since appearance and performance can be seriously compromised.

SUNBURN AND INSECT BITES

Sunburn Protection

In our stress filled society, to relax means not just to get away but to get away to someplace warm and sunny. For the executive and his family as well as the Personal Protection Specialist skin care from sun exposure becomes a concern.

As our consciousness about the sun's damage to our skin increases, more people are interested in protecting themselves during prolonged exposure. That lobster red color should be reserved for the crustacean variety of marine animal. For the human variety it is not only painful but can be quite unsightly as the burned layers of skin start to peel away. Even for those fortunate enough to have a tan they must still be aware that proper skin care is essential to prevent premature aging of the skin as well as cancerous skin lesions which can develop from unprotected excessive exposure.

Ultraviolet B radiation is responsible for producing the red skin and sunburn. The tanning effects begin 2 to 3 days after sun exposure. It is also responsible for much of the skin-connective tissue destruction in the photoaging process. Ultraviolet A radiation is associated with the development of a slow, natural tan.

As a result of this increased awareness and knowledge the sunscreen business has boomed. There is a huge array of products to choose from. They can be purchased anywhere, from a posh boutique to the corner convenience store.

There are two types of typical sunscreens. The first type includes what are called physical sunscreens or sunblocks because they are usually opaque formulations. Zinc oxide, titanium oxide, and certain colored clays are common ingredients. These products are best used on localized areas most susceptible to sun exposure, such as the bridge of the nose, tops of the ears, lips and shoulders. They are not for overall body use because they need to be applied thickly and are messy to use. Plus they are not easy to wash off and can stain expensive clothing. The second type of topical sunscreens are the chemical sunscreens. They provide protection by absorbing various wavelengths of light, and preventing the skin from burning. Para-amino benzoic acid, Padimate A, Padimate O, dioxybenzone, and oxybenzone are ingredients found in modern sunscreens. Ingredients are important but proper use is critical. If your skin type always burns easily and never tans the recommended Sun Protection Factor (SPF) should be 15 or greater. The same is true with skin that burns easily with minimal tanning. Skin which burns minimally to moderately should use a product with an SPF of 6 or 15. Even those who rarely burn should still use a product with an SPF of 4 to 6 to help prevent excessively dry skin as a result of exposure.

Sun intensity will depend upon time of day, season, latitude, altitude, and atmospheric conditions (smoke, smog, cloudiness). These factors should be taken into account when selecting a sunscreen. Just as important is that the sunscreen be used properly. Apply the product to dry skin, indoors, at least an hour before exposure. Allow it to absorb into the skin for 10 to 15 minutes before applying makeup of clothing. Reapply every 2 to 3 hours or more, depending on the amount of swimming or sweating. Reapplication does not extend the time you can stay in the sun and be protected. Should itching or rash develop stop using the product and seek advice on an alternative product.

Some drug products and prescription medications can cause the skin to be more sensitive to the sun's rays. Tetracycline and Sulfa antibiotics are two of the most common offenders and are used quite frequently when traveling in Central and South America. If you are in doubt check with your local pharmacist, he or she can steer you in the right direction.

Who should use sunscreens? Anyone who wants to protect him/herself from the harmful short and long-term effects of the sun, or anyone using a drug known to cause sun sensitive reactions.

Personal Protection Specialists should pay special attention. Severe sunburn is not only painful and unsightly, but in a must-work situation your ability to perform quickly and efficiently can be severely impaired.

Sunburn Relief

It's too late, you overdid and now you feel like a french fry. A number of over-the-counter remedies are available. Please keep in mind that if the sunburn is severe and over a large body area a trip to a physician might be in order.

First off we want to try and reduce the body temperature. Aspirin or Tylenol work well and will also help to reduce some swelling associated with the burn site. A cool shower can help relieve some discomfort but avoid using too much soap as it may have a drying effect on the skin. Depending on the severity of the burn one will experience some discomfort and skin peeling, or areas of watery blisters and large scale peeling. Do not puncture the blisters. Some of the fluid may be reabsorbed or they will usually break as the skin begins to peel. Breaking the blisters early will only add to the discomfort. Clothing will stick to the burn area and irritate the site more.

Creams and gels are preferable to sprays unless the spray is alcohol free. That Solarcaine spray felt great initially but had a double edged effect. As the alcohol evaporated it created a cooling sensation but the alcohol dried out the skin thus accelerating the peeling process and causing one to use more spray and create a vicious circle. These sprays will usually contain a topical anesthetic (benzocaine, lidocaine) or a counter-irritant such as camphor or menthol which are useful in reducing the discomfort and itchiness of the peeling skin.

Aloe vera products are of tremendous value to sunburn victims. Not only do they help to desensitize the burn area but they help moisturize the skin and reduce the amount of skin damage. Benzocaine and lidocaine are being added to these products and provide an additional anesthetic effect; a welcomed addition when you have to be in a suit and tie the day after the over-exposure. Read the labels of the various products carefully to be sure you are getting a product with a high percentage of aloe vera from a plant source and that it contains a topical anesthetic if one is desired.

After a few days the pain will subside and the peeling process begins. Use of a skin moisturizer will be of benefit to condition the skin and prevent scaring in a bad case. One that is oil free is preferable as it is not as likely to stain the clothing. Also, one that has little or no fragrance would be a plus in warm and cramped space situations.

All of these products are readily available at numerous locations. If you have questions do not hesitate to consult a pharmacist for a product that will suit your needs and maintain your comfort and alertness as you provide personal protection services.

Insect Bites

As the weather grows warmer insects can present an irritating dilemma. For most people mosquitoes, bees, wasps and other biting or stinging insects are a nuisance and somewhat painful. For a small group of individuals their stings can be lethal. These people can respond to multiple or a single sting with a violent allergic (anaphalactic) reaction in which tissue swelling can lead to suffocation.

Antihistamines (Benadryl, Tavist, Chlor-Trimeton) are very effective in the general public but for the highly allergic individual prescription medication is a must. Two portable and highly effective prescription products contain epinephrine to counteract the allergic reaction resulting. Ana-Kit is a self contained unit containing a preloaded syringe containing 2 doses of epinephrine as well as antihistamine tablets. The kit is in a plastic container with a clip so that it can be worn on the belt if necessary. The other product is an Epi-pen auto injection device. The pen comes in a plastic tube resembling a large cigar tube for protection. Once the device is removed from the tube a plastic safety cap is removed and the pen is placed against the thigh and constant pressure applied until an audible snapping sound is made. While the Epi-pen is easier to use it has the limitation of a single dose. Depending on location of the nearest hospital one might wish to discuss the two choices with their personal physician. But either could be a life-saving device for a principal or a member of his personal protection team.

Summer can indeed be a relaxing and enjoyable period of the year. With proper planning and knowledge it can be safe as well.

MEDICATIONS AND TRAVEL ABROAD

The fall of the Berlin wall, the breakup of the former Soviet Union, and a decrease in hostile activities in parts of Central and South America have opened up vast new frontiers for corporations and entrepreneurs from the United States.

In the rush to exploit new commercial opportunities, however, many executives and the Personal Protection Specialists who have accompanied them into these new business areas have discovered one thing very quickly—*expect the unexpected.* If you're among those headed outside the U.S. you should take into account that health care, as you know it, is not likely to be accessible in many areas.

As you gather information during the advance detail, the location of medical and pharmaceutical services should be of paramount importance. Many of the health care services we take for granted in the United States are non-existent or very limited in parts of the Third World. For example, a drive to the doctor or local pharmacy could easily turn into a journey of days in remote areas, and when you arrive you'll find "Babushka Hubbard's" shelves are bare.

Before you start your journey, prepare as complete a medical profile as possible on the principal and members of his staff and protection team. Detailed information about medications and any special medical devices must be taken into account as well as the local health condition of the regions to be visited.

In Central and South American countries, such as Peru, Ecuador, and Colombia, the recent epidemics of cholera and hepatitis have given new meaning to the warning, "Don't Drink the Water." Whenever the water system is questionable, reliable bottled water must be considered a necessity, even when brushing teeth. Ice cubes can also be a vehicle for pathogens so, when in doubt, leave them out of beverages. If a refrigerator is available make your own ice using bottled water. Appetizing shellfish should be avoided. The lack of appropriate waste disposal and dumping of contaminated sewage into the areas in which shellfish dwell can result in exposure to the bacteria that causes cholera. The experience can be quite unpleasant, even dangerous, despite how delicious the crabs appeared or tasted at the time. While a cholera vaccine is available it provides only about 60% coverage and a booster shot must be given every six months. Tetracycline and Doxycycline, antibiotics, are highly effective in preventing and treating the disease as well as Furazolidone for tetracycline resistant strains.

In Central America, many of the U.S. pharmaceutical companies (Lilly, Dista, Searle) have set up manufacturing plants and prescription items are available over-the-counter for the asking. Many drugs will have the same proprietary names (trade names) as those found in the United States. As you move into South America similar items may still be found, but the manufacturers are of European origin (Swiss, French, German) and the proprietary names are unfamiliar. Some preparatory work is called for here.

When the boss's ulcer is at full tilt is not the time to discover his medication is nowhere to be found. Suppose he has an attack. Your checking of his medical profile, reveals that his medication is Zantac. You send out a member of the team who returns frustrated and empty handed because none of the English speaking pharmacists in Peru recognized the name. Had you known the generic name of the drug, ranitidine hydrochloride, the pharmacist would have provided the correct medication regardless of the proprietary name used. The point stressed here is that you must make a list of not only proprietary names, but generic names of the required prescription medications. This could be of vital importance in obtaining these items, not to mention saving face with the boss.

Prescription drug manuals, such as the Physicians Desk Reference (PDR), are available at better bookstores in the health section. They will list not only the proprietary names, but the generic names as well, plus valuable information about the drug itself. Your friendly local pharmacist can also be a valuable source of information when you are pressed for time.

One final note on identifying drugs. If you take a supply of prescription medications with you from the United States, you must keep them in the properly labeled prescription bottles in which they were dispensed. This will save you and your principal from having to answer embarrassing questions from more than just curious customs officials.

The opening of doors to the former Soviet Union has sent many U.S. corporations on expeditions to see what business opportunities exist there. While working on an assignment in Russia and Kazakhstan something became very clear to me. There are two kinds of people in the former Soviet Union; those who are pushing the system to the limit to make money, and those who are writing down the names of all the people in the first category. Some things never change. Also, business in Russia requires the capacity to work with a political, legal, and regulatory moving target.

While the world was not looking, the Soviet regime poisoned its environment in the name of progress. In Leningrad (St. Petersburg), the most westernized city in the regions, the water is, by Western standards, unfit for drinking and is to be avoided. The same is true in Moscow, so once again reliable bottled water is a necessity. It is readily available at kiosks, local shops and even in the hotel shops run by your friendly, former KGB, shopkeeper.

While some Western style shopping complexes exist in Moscow, they may not have adequate medical or prescription items on hand. Common over-the-counter items such as aspirin and antacids can be found, but specialty items, when finally found, are scarce and expensive. Some hospitals in the large cities can provide adequate health services, but they may seem poor by Western standards. Pharmacies, when available, are poorly stocked and many times can offer only home remedies of doubtful value.

In the remote areas of Kazakhstan, unsanitary living conditions, polluted water, unclean and inadequate medical facilities only spell trouble. Here you will be working in a republic five times the size of Texas with limited and sometimes unreliable transportation as well as a foreign language unfamiliar even to many native Russians.

Those anticipating extended stays should plan to have enough medical and pharmaceutical supplies for the trip plus a reserve of several days should delays result or something other than your dirty laundry travel back with you. The over-the-counter medications mentioned earlier in this chapter would provide an excellent travel kit. Prescription medications should be purchased in advance and kept in the original labeled bottles. All vital medications should be carried by the team leader and be easily accessible at all times, should an emergency arise.

With the varying health and political climate outside the U.S., all travelers should check with the United States Department of State for travel advisory information in advance of departure. Your local Public Health Service Center for Disease Control may also publish valuable travel information on your destination.

Yes, new frontiers are awaiting in Central and South America as well as the former Soviet Union. Proper advance work and complete medical profiles should make the trip safe, not only for the principal and his staff, but also for the Personal Protection Specialists traveling with them.

TWENTY-FIVE

Surveillance and Counter-surveillance as a Protective Function

by Raymond L. Mirabile

ALTHOUGH IT MAY BE OBVIOUS to some that counter-surveillance techniques have a place in the protection of persons, it may not be as clear regarding the value and function of a proactive surveillance operation within the framework of the overall protective program. Nevertheless, it can be an important and extremely valuable tool when properly and effectively deployed.

> **Surveillance:** The word derives from the French **Surveiller,**
> "To Watch Over". . . "Close Observation"

> **Stalk:** To move menacingly; to track; to move stealthily.

It should be obvious from the above definitions that there is a great deal of difference between a surveillance and a stalking; mainly it is the intent. For it should be apparent that the same techniques can be utilized for both purposes. Today stalkers seem to be everywhere. (If we are to believe news reports.) Anti-stalking laws are in effect in many states and are being proposed in others. The Los Angeles police department has instituted a "Threat Management" unit to deal with stalking cases. The unit keeps track of suspects by surveillance.

In reality this is not unlike the Federal agencies when they suspect a threat against the President or other government official. As stressed throughout the protective services profession, **PREVENTION** and **AVOIDANCE** are the keys to a successful operation. A well planned and professionally executed proactive surveillance operation can go a long way in aiding the protective detail in doing just that, by keeping the principal out of harm's way.

Police agencies have long recognized the benefits of such surveillance when dealing with organized crime figures and professional criminals. By instituting a "protective surveillance" on an individual that has threatened harm to your principal you will gather important and possibly lifesaving intelligence information about the subject. One caveat may be in order here. That is: Check with a responsible and knowledgeable attorney-at-law to ensure that you are acting within the legal limits of the jurisdiction in which you will be operating. Laws differ from state to state and, most certainly, in foreign countries. Once you have established that you may proceed with the surveillance, you will need intelligence information on the target subject.

This intelligence or background information is essential. It is essential first of all in selecting the location where you intend to set up the operation. It is also important in the event you lose the subject during the course of the operation that you know certain locations where the target subject may have gone, and thereby re-establish contact and continue the surveillance. If the subject is an employee of the principal, or a former employee, it would be wise to start with the personnel file. A very discreet background investigation should also be conducted. It you are not in a position to oversee this phase yourself or do not possess the means by which to accomplish this, you may wish to hire a reliable and competent private detective. I stress **reliable** and **competent.** I speak from the standpoint of over twenty-five years experience, and of a profession with which I have been associated for almost twenty of those years. There are charlatans in all professions of course, but an unscrupulous private detective or an incompetent bungler, whether on the detail itself or in the pre-surveillance planning stage, can spell disaster, serious injury, or death to you, your principal and your team. The upside would be embarrassment and litigation. All of which you have **BEEN HIRED TO AVOID.** Check out the person you are considering for the background phase of the operation. Ask other professionals who may know the individual or have used his/her services and are satisfied. And remember **you get what you pay for.** You shop for excellence—not bargains.

Once the background and intelligence phase of the operation are completed you are ready to pick the surveillance team. Let me state right here that a covert moving surveillance is one of the most difficult of operations. Murphy's law seems to thrive during moving surveillance operations. Murphy's law states that, "if anything can go wrong, it will; and it will go wrong at the worst possible time." Therefore you must choose individuals who can "think on their feet," persons who can make a judgement call, adapt to situations as they unfold and not be easily shaken. They must be intelligent and intuitive, educated and street smart, all at once. They should be able to read a map, articulate events, write a report, plan ahead, take orders and function for long hours without sleep. They must not become easily bored, and should be able to shift from a state of non-activity to high activity and back again with precision and professionalism. Members must not be afraid to get dirty, or perform menial tasks. There is **no room for egos on an assignment.** The team leader is in charge and he designates alternates and/or assistant leaders. Each member of the team must be fully briefed and have current photographs and all pertinent intelligence information available on the target subject. Pre-surveillance photos of the subject's residence, place of employment, etcetera, should be taken and discussed at the team briefing (the chalk talk). Questions and discussion of tactics, overall strategies, logistics or any other details, should be encouraged. Make sure that every member knows the assignment, their individual mission, and the overall objectives. There will not be time nor opportunity once things get under way.

The number of members on the surveillance team may vary. But it is of paramount importance that enough people are deployed to get the job done. While working narcotics cases it was not unusual to have five to ten vehicles each containing two operatives on a moving surveillance. A minimum of three (3) vehicles and six (6) persons (two to a car) is what I suggest. This would allow for the employment of the basic "A,B,C" method and a possible parallel deployment if feasible. All of these, and additional methods, will be explained later in this chapter. The reason for two person vehicles is due to the difficult nature of a moving surveillance and the unpredictability of the operation. From an observational standpoint, to do the job correctly the driver must pay close attention to what he/she is doing. The driver cannot be preoccupied with the concerns of addresses, street signs and note-taking if he or she is to stay on the "tail" and not get into an accident. In addition it must be realized that the target subject may leave their vehicle, walk or take a cab or public transportation, get into a second vehicle, go shopping, or a myriad of other things that would require an immediate change from a vehicular to a foot surveillance. Male/female teams are important to have in the group. They will be able to go into certain places that could bring suspicion if entered by one person or by a man or woman alone, i.e., dress shops, certain lounges or restaurants, picnic areas and so forth. When parked at night a man/woman team is less likely to draw suspicion when parked on a side street or parking lot. If possible, it would be wise to include at least one such team in the group.

Proper equipment is of the utmost necessity. Both for the team and on an individual level. When possible a team should be relieved at least every twelve hours. However, it is common for a surveillance team to be required for longer periods due to the target subject's activity or other reasons. Therefore pre-planning is, as with everything else in this business, essential. Good quality radios with portable chargers should be available and accessible to each two person team. Each team-leader (the number of cars assigned to him/her will vary) should have a mobile telephone. Each member of the team should have the number. Vehicles should be modified to include special on/off switches for headlights, tail lights, backup lights, brake lights and interior lights. When on night surveillance brake lights, etcetera, are a dead bang giveaway in a dark parking lot. You should be able to control all lights from a special control board, thus eliminating confusion and accidental flashing of these lights while maneuvering in certain areas. Each vehicle should have a full tank of gas, the engine in good running order and possibly an extra gas can of fuel for an emergency. Jumper cables should be in each team-leader's car along with flares and emergency equipment. Each vehicle should be equipped with a flashlight, notepads, pens, a 35mm camera, binoculars, maps of the area and surrounding locale, and all necessary information on the target subject. Personal items that should be carried by each member are small plastic portapotties of the type used by private pilots or those that can be found in certain medical sections of drug stores and so forth. Snacks, coffee, tea, soda, high energy bars, nodoz type tablets, candy bars, sandwiches and other items that each member may feel they need to keep going on an extended surveillance operation. More than one change of clothes both to disguise and to adapt to situations as they arise, for example, a dress shirt, tie and sport jacket for men, a skirt and blouse, or dress for women. Also, casual clothing, possibly shorts or bathing suits, or anything else that you may foresee that subject's activities including, would be the guideline for extra clothing. And don't forget plenty of change for tolls, pay phones, meters, etc.

Once these matters have been attended to, the target identified, intelligence gathered, surveillance team chosen and briefed and a plan established; we must then begin to consider a **surveillance command post.** This command post will be the central point of contact and coordination throughout the operation. All ancillary equipment along with extra rations, sleeping quarters for off duty personnel and a direct line of communication to field units will be within the control area of the command post. For local operations of relatively short duration, a command post might consist of a van or station wagon or even the team leaders vehicle. For longer, out of area and more intricate information gathering surveillance activity, or protective surveillance operations on a subject that has threatened your principal, more elaborate accommodations may be in order.

When operating outside of your immediate area of operations a relatively comfortable and convenient hotel or motel is usually appropriate. The team-leader should occupy a suite or double connecting room. This will be the main command center and will be manned when feasible twenty-four hours a day. However, this is not set in stone, there may be times when the team-leader and other units are deployed at the same time. However, twenty-four hour access is necessary. Other team members can share rooms at double occupancy rates to keep some of the expense down. However, cost must not become a major factor in these operations. There should be a restaurant on premises or nearby, within walking distance. All members of the team whether on or off duty **must let the team leader know where they are at all times.** If an off duty member is leaving the compound area they must check in and give an itinerary as well as calling in periodically to ascertain whether or not plans have changed and they are needed.

When relieving a team in the field, it should be done as expeditiously as possible. The relieving units will be briefed on the activities of the prior shift, ensure that they have all necessary equipment and newly charged batteries for their radios. Briefings should take place at least an hour before the relief is made. Field units being relieved should be informed by radio which team is relieving them and what vehicle they are in, they can then coordinate the change over among themselves. This changeover should be smooth and professional without drawing attention to the area. One unit moves into position and the unit relieved moves out of the area. Keep it simple and save the "war stories" for the command post when you're all off duty.

METHODS OF SURVEILLANCE AND FORMATIONS

There are several types of formations utilized in surveillance operations as well as different methods. I will first discuss methods. **First,** there is the direct *tail* or A, B, C method. This method as you can see requires three (3) persons or vehicles. It can also be utilized with only two (2) units. Second, there is the *parallel method*, although it can be done with one unit, it is risky and a minimum of two units should be deployed. Third, there is the *progressive* surveillance, one unit can be used for these types of operations but again a minimum of two (2) units is recommended. Fourth, the *Leap Frog*. This method is merely a redeployment of the A,B,C, formation. Fifth, the *box*. And sixth, the *front and rear Bracket* formation.

The following diagrams should assist you in understanding the principles involved and when each method and formation would be the most effective. All of the formations and methods depicted can be combined, modified or used in any sequence that fits a given situation. You may find that in one movement the team switches several times from one method and formation to another. Remember, a moving surveillance is dynamic and constantly changing; team members must be able to think on their feet and adapt.

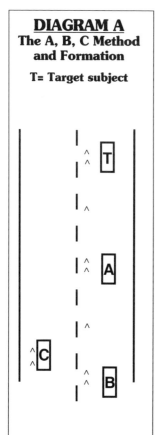

DIAGRAM A
The A, B, C Method
and Formation

T= Target subject

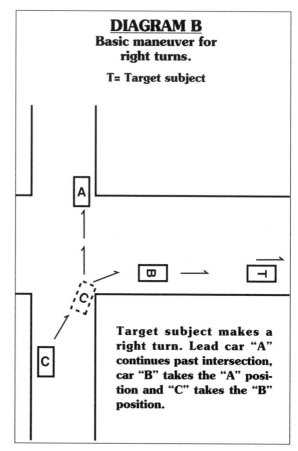

DIAGRAM B
Basic maneuver for
right turns.

T= Target subject

Target subject makes a right turn. Lead car "A" continues past intersection, car "B" takes the "A" position and "C" takes the "B" position.

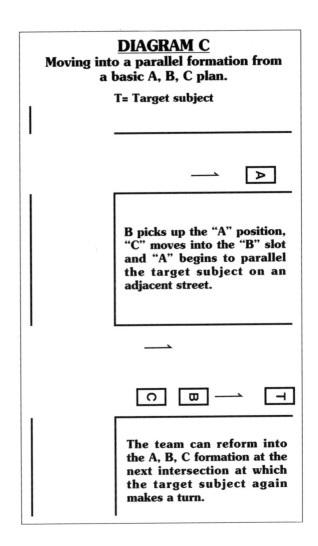

DIAGRAM C
Moving into a parallel formation from a basic A, B, C plan.

T= Target subject

B picks up the "A" position, "C" moves into the "B" slot and "A" begins to parallel the target subject on an adjacent street.

The team can reform into the A, B, C formation at the next intersection at which the target subject again makes a turn.

There are numerous personal tricks that each individual, having participated in several surveillances over a period of time, develop. These are as varied as the individuals and the surveillances themselves, and must be learned and developed 'on the job.' There is no substitute for "on the job training" in this area, or any area of the protective business for that matter. You can explain to a person how to swim but they must get into the water and experience it for themselves. It is the same here. I could list countless tricks used by myself and others during an operation, but that would only tend to limit the thought process and narrow the reader's vision to a few techniques. As with my chapter on defensive tactics, it is not technique, but reacting to a situation as it unfolds, that separates the pros from the amateurs. Common sense and good imagination go a long way in determining the successful outcome of an operation.

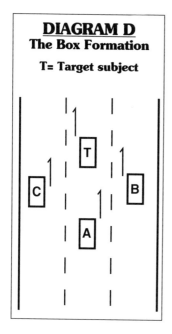

DIAGRAM D
The Box Formation

T= Target subject

DIAGRAM E
The Front and Rear "Bracket Formation."

T= Target subject

As easily seen in Diagram E, this is a difficult maneuver for the "A" unit. However, it can allow for "tail" units to fall back to a great degree and avoid being spotted on long trips.

STAKEOUTS OR STATIONARY SURVEILLANCE

Stationary surveillances better known as "Stakeouts" pose certain problems inherent to such activity. Mainly the arousal of suspicion on the part of the target subject, and/or the apprehension and curiosity of neighbors.

You must also consider that wary neighbors may call the local authorities. This could prove embarrassing, and even worse, expose the operation. All of these things must be taken into consideration. When feasible the team-leader should check in with the local police district or precinct. He should make sure that each shift will be notified that a stationary surveillance is under way in the area. It is not necessary to give details as to who or what you are watching. If you have proper credentials or notarized letters of authority, I have found that the police are quite cooperative. However, much depends on **YOUR** attitude. Be respectful and polite. Remember, they are the **police,** they are in **authority, not you!** You may have the right to conduct a surveillance but without police cooperation you are going to have a problem. If it is possible, it is not a bad idea to employ an off duty officer and put the officer with the stakeout team. By doing this you have a spokesperson who can speak on your behalf to assure the local commander or field officers that there is nothing illegal going on. This will also create the groundwork for good relations with the police, which is essential in this business.

Another caveat should be made here. Be sure that the off duty officers that you hire are legally allowed to work in the capacity for which you will employ them. Although most departments allow their officers to work off duty security or investigative assignments and even post lists of available off duty jobs, some do not. This can be essential, as I found out the hard way. Several years ago I was in charge of a surveillance team that numbered about twenty persons. We were out of our state of jurisdiction and had contacted a local security agency to assist us. We also requested that some local police officers be hired in an off duty capacity for the reasons cited above. All was taken care of and the operation set in motion. One evening I, along with my assistant, were checking on the team members assigned to the surveillance. They had followed the target subject to his residence and had set up for the long night ahead.

As we approached the area we noticed police cars cruising as if they were looking for something. We got out of our vehicle and proceeded on foot. As we approached, the grease hit the pan! Police came in from everywhere. We found ourselves "in the position" against cars and trying to explain ourselves. We were all taken to the police station and after a short time and much convincing we secured the cooperation of the district commander and were allowed to return to the area. The field officers were notified of our presence and in this case no harm was done. I was however, quite upset that this had happened as we had specifically hired two off duty officers to prevent just such an incident. Upon returning to the scene we found the two officers still on the stakeout. I furiously asked why they had not cleared the way for us and let the local officers know what was going on? They answered that they were not from that particular jurisdiction (although they did have concurrent jurisdiction in this case) and that their department did not allow them to work in an off duty security/investigative capacity. They therefore sat in their cars, merely showing their badges to the responding officers and said nothing. I relate this incident to emphasize the importance of having a **reliable** local agency and making sure that any off duty officers hired are acting within the scope of their individual departmental regulations. [I would like to make a special note here about personal equipment. When you feel that a stakeout may be necessary be sure to have a heavy blanket available for cold winter nights. Running the engine all night will surely invite unwanted attention.]

THE PROGRESSIVE SURVEILLANCE

A progressive surveillance can be done when the route of the target subject is known and this route is taken regularly, but the final destination is unknown.

A surveillance team can, for instance, pick up the surveillance each day at a different point along the route and eventually locate the final destination. This might be the case when you known where certain stops are regularly made as routine. For instance you may, through your intelligence gathering phase, have learned that the subject stops at a certain donut shop every day for breakfast, eats lunch at an unknown restaurant every Thursday at 1:00 p.m. and from there proceeds to a 3:00 p.m. meeting that lasts until 4:30 p.m., then proceeds to the final destination. You may need to know the final destination but the subject acts suspicious and seems to be "tail conscious." One way to solve this problem is the progressive surveillance.

Example: On Monday you begin your surveillance at the subject's residence and establish his/her departure time. You follow the target subject to the donut shop, noting all pertinent information and break off the surveillance. The following Thursday you pick up the surveillance activity at the donut shop. The team stays with the subject and establishes the location of the Thursday luncheons. The surveillance is terminated until the following Thursday. You begin the surveillance this time at the restaurant and after the subject has lunch, follow him/her to the meeting and terminate the surveillance. The next Thursday you begin the surveillance at the meeting site and follow the subject to the final destination.

A modification of this method is the **"leap frog."** In this case the target subject can be followed along a known route and units can pass the subject 'leap frogging' from location to location constantly changing "tail" vehicles and staying ahead of the subject, arriving and setting up stationary surveillances before the subject even arrives. 'Leap frogging' can be done in different combinations when you have a limited number of vehicles and personnel so that the same vehicles are not constantly in the 'follow' or 'tail' position.

The above methods can be very effective when it is necessary to keep a subject under surveillance for long periods of time and you have established patterns. These methods can also be utilized to simply "keep tabs" on an individual that is not considered a serious threat but nevertheless needs to be watched. Now that we have the basics of the proactive surveillance it is time to discuss "Counter-surveillance."

COUNTER-SURVEILLANCE

As discussed in Dr. Kobetz' first book on *Providing Executive Protection (P.E.P.)* (page 136, "Early Warning System") it is important. . . "that a close watch be kept for any abnormal activity. . . ."

This early warning system can take on many forms and they come under the heading of "Countermeasures and Counter-Surveillance." In this business we are paid to be somewhat paranoid, suspicious of anything and everything. As the saying goes, "Just because I *think* someone is watching *doesn't mean they're not!*" In other words we can start to get careless when nothing happens for long periods of time. We can let our guard down and begin to believe that we are really worried over nothing or being "too paranoid." Well, remember "Murphy's Law" because you can pretty well bet that this is the time that something will happen. One of the inherent and very annoying aspects of this work is that we are regularly accused of 'over reacting' or always seeing 'the dark side' of everything. Yes, that is true sometimes, but that is what we were hired for in the first place. It is what we do to protect others and to stay alive.

We must *never* make the mistake of thinking like those uninitiated individuals who believe that the world is really a nice place, and that no one would really want to harm them! After all, 'everyone just loves me'!

Let's not forget John Lennon! Remember that we are hired to counter or thwart the actions of the group known in the business as the three "C's" — Crusaders, Criminals and Crazies. It is not my intent here to categorize. I merely make the statement as a fact of life (and death) that we **cannot** allow ourselves the luxury of "rose-colored glasses." If we do, the consequences can be tragic indeed. So, what should we do as professionals on a daily basis that will allow us to protect our principal, and at the same time allow for the latitudes necessary for them to lead a comparatively normal lifestyle? For if we restrict and frighten those we are to protect, they will not cooperate and we may find that they will refuse security altogether. There is a thin wire that we must walk.

One thing is certain, and that is an assailant will attempt to gain the element of surprise. Even when warnings have been sent to frighten and upset the principal and his/her family, the attacker will try for surprise. Many times several targets may be initially selected and then as they are observed, eliminated due to heavy security precautions, poor locations or opportunities for an attack, etc. This information will most likely come from surveillance activity. It is up to us to spot this activity and thwart their intentions.

One of the most basic steps, of course, is that you change route and times of departure **OFTEN.** This in itself discourages the use of the progressive or leap frog method of surveillance. The opposition will have lost two surveillance tactics automatically. They will have to use one of the other methods, and they are much easier to spot and to counter. We must also consider that initially there may be only a **perception** that there is some abnormal activity. At first there is a low threat level and therefore the countermeasures would be minimal. If a driver feels that someone is following, he may simply make a series of three (3) consecutive right hand turns, keeping his or her eye on the rearview mirror. This will do two things. One; the driver will be able to determine whether or not a car always turns the corner when he/she does. It may not be the same car, but is there **always** a vehicle turning behind. Second; it will help to disrupt any parallel surveillance vehicles and possibly even lose one or more, at least temporarily.

If you suspect that you are being followed you may go the wrong way down a one-way street, go through an alley, use culs-de-sac, make "U" turns, stop at a green light and creep through the intersection as the light changes to red, stop in the middle of the street, back-up and park, then pull out again. There are many things that you can do in order to try to "spot a tail." If you suspect that an ambush is being attempted however, go to the nearest police station '**PRONTO.**'

Once you have reason to believe you are the target of surveillance activity you may want to initiate a 'convoy.' The 'convoy' is a method of counter-surveillance used by drug dealers and certain intelligence operations. It is simply a matter of putting your principal under a "loose" surveillance and observing whether or not anyone is following. I suggest that a minimum of three vehicles be used for this, so that you can utilize the "parallel" tactic in establishing the extent of the surveillance activity, if any in fact does exist. It might be added here that this 'convoy' method is a good way to check, in periodic fashion, whether your principal is being watched. This may be done with very little participation or inconvenience to him or her or even without their knowledge as a standard security procedure. Before leaving this subject of vehicular counter surveillance, I would like to add that; if you undertake any of the maneuvers described and find that you will be in violation of the traffic laws, you should be reasonably convinced that it is necessary to do so in order to protect. It is a trade off that should not be taken lightly as any professional should certainly realize. You will not be around in this business very long if you do these things as routine or to impress a client/principal. Not to mention the legal ramifications. **You must be able to justify your actions at all times.**

Awareness is a countermeasure. Is there unusual activity in the area lately? How about an increase in couples walking or picnicking, couples in cars, street crews working on sewers, or telephone lines? How about landscapers and window washers? Loiterers or young people on mopeds or bicycles? You as a professional should be aware of the environment and any changes within it. Pick up the telephone! Check with the agency in charge of the 'street crew'. Ask whether or not there is legitimate work being done in the area and is the crew supposed to be there at that particular time? How long will they be in the area?, etc. Place a loose surveillance on the suspicious individuals. Check them out quietly and with discretion. **Watch the watchers!**

Remember that we live in an age of gadgets and unbelievable technology. There are televisions that can **watch you!** There are video cameras made to look like telephone company equipment and 'splice boots,' optical equipment that will reverse the image in a door 'peep hole' and allow a room scan. Telephones can be tapped, micro-transmitters secreted almost anywhere! Mobile telephones are not immune either. Time lapse recorders can be concealed in brief cases, sprinkler heads, car antennae, clocks, headboards, bedposts, you name it and it can be "wired." I don't mean hard wire, those days are over. Wireless equipment of top quality can be purchased by anyone with the desire to find it and the money to pay for it. And usually with **no questions asked.** The only method of maintaining a security buffer from these items is to include in your standard security procedures, periodic "sweeps." I don't mean those done by someone who comes in, opens an impressive looking briefcase full of "bells and whistles;" I mean professional **physical** room examinations along with a professional electronic 'scan' of important areas. There is no substitute for a physical "eye search" coupled with a state of the art electronic scan. This will entail dismanteling sockets, sprinkler heads, vents, light fixtures, clocks, you name it. This is very time consuming and detailed but it is the only sure way. But *remember* as soon as you leave the room unsecured it is no longer "clear" from electronic eavesdropping. As soon as you leave, someone can set up again and be back in business in a very short time. And don't discount the old "spy in the sky,"—the fact is that given the right circumstances, anyone can watch anyone else at anytime! Our job is to make life so difficult for those who would do so that they will give up, foul up, or go elsewhere.

In reality, that is all we as professionals can do. We do our best to out-think the opposition. If we do this well we usually are successful. Many times as we have seen from the news reports, these individuals who would harm another human being for some twisted reason or cause, are not intellectual giants. Many times their actions would be comical if not for the tragic results. They may be clever and cunning but they are not the boogie man. Carlos Marighela wrote of urban guerrilla warfare and the advantage of, **surprise, superior knowledge of the terrain, greater mobility, superior information, and greater decisiveness.** There is no reason that this should be the case. If we do our jobs we rob the opposition of those necessary tools and defeat them before they even get started. In this chapter you have been given an overview of one of the tools that can assist in doing just that.

TWENTY-SIX

The Private Eye

by John I. Kostanoski

THE PRIMARY REASON for the success of terrorists, aside from the choreography they rehearse so well, is the element of surprise which has always been part of their repertoire. A new type of security surveillance, in comparison with which other techniques pale, is turning that highly successful tactic to the advantage of Personal Protection Specialists. Infrared illuminators, in combination with the infrared sensitive image sensor of a closed circuit television camera, constitutes a novel type of security searchlight system. This approach is a decisive improvement over the old searchlight technique in which a beam of light was cast across an area in periodic sweeps to, unwittingly, signal the intruder when to move and when to remain still. The only nice thing one can say about it was that it provided Hollywood script writers with a useful device to effect the successful attack against the inevitable fortified compound in the typical terrorist action-adventure movie. Far more subtle and much more effective is a video technique in which the intruder is kept in the dark as it were.

VIDEO SEARCHLIGHT SYSTEM

The system is composed of the following devices: CCD camera, motorized zoom lens, pan-and-tilt positioning device, narrow and wide beam infrared illuminators, and an environmental housing.

CCD Camera — The Charge Coupled Device (CCD) has transformed the CCTV camera from a vacuum tube to an infrared sensitive image sensor. It is more reliable, less troublesome, and smaller in size than predecessor devices. CCD is immune to image burn-in, free of shock and vibration problems because of its solid state design, less costly to maintain, with a short start-up time, and with the ability to operate indoors or outdoors from batteries and use less power when operating.

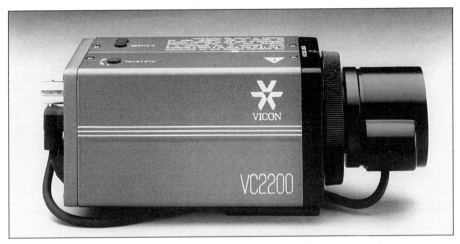

Courtesy of Vicon Industries, Inc., Melville, NY

Charge Coupled Device (CCD) Camera

Courtesy of Vicon Industries, Inc., Melville, NY

Motorized Zoom Lens

Motorized Zoom Lens — A standard lens views the size of a scene in much the same way as a person with normal vision. A wide angle lens captures a wider view than a standard lens but not without the loss of some scene detail. A telephoto lens enlarges the size of some detail in a scene at the expense of an overall diminution in scene size. A motorized zoom lens incorporates all three

Courtesy of Vicon
Industries, Inc., Melville, NY

Pan-And-Tilt Positioning Device

Courtesy of
Vicon Industries, Inc.,
Melville, NY

Infrared Illuminator

focal length settings with the capability to move uniformly across them at will.

Pan-And-Tilt Positioning Device — A device that traverses both horizontally and vertically and greatly increases the viewing range of a camera mounted to it by allowing the camera to sweep in a left to right motion (panning) and an up and down movement (tilting).

Infrared Illuminators — Lamps that are designed to illuminate a scene with infrared light invisible to the human eye but not to the artificial eye of the CCD camera. The illuminator enables the camera to "see" in the dark and is ideal for both indoor and outdoor applications. Narrow and wide beam models are available with an average lamp life of about 10,000 hours.

THE APPLICATION

Both narrow and wide beam infrared illuminators are mounted on both sides of a pan-and-tilt positioning device that supports a CCD camera with a motorized zoom lens fitted inside a protective housing. A range of illumination

Courtesy of Vicon Industries, Inc., Melville, NY

Environmental Housing

along a 350° degree arc is continuously maintained through pan-and-tilt sweeps. The intruder does not know what area is illuminated or what security sees at the viewing monitor even though at any given moment only about three percent of the total area is under observation. The intruder can no longer use the visible light conventional lamp sources provided as intelligence to plot a surreptitious course through a compound's dark areas to reach an executive's residence. Instead, intruder actions are under constant surveillance through remote control of camera operations and as a result the principal has the all important tactical advantage. The profession's most sophisticated *private eye* has provided a solution to one of our more troublesome spots by illuminating, yet preserving for counter-measures purposes, the shadows that lie within what was once a successful criminal *modus operandi.*

Dr. Richard W. Kobetz

DR. KOBETZ HAS BEEN AND CONTINUES to be a pioneer in the training of personnel engaged in protective services. With a background of service from police patrolman to Chief of Police and Security Officer to Director of Security, he joined the staff of the International Association of Chiefs of Police in Washington, D.C. in 1968 on a leave of absence as a commanding officer in the Chicago Police Department.

For the I.A.C.P. he created the first world-wide series of week-long training programs made available to law enforcement, military and security officers that were conducted on a tuition basis. His presentations became the influence for program offerings to this day by educational and non-profit institutions, corporations and trainers. With selected instructors he presented the first tuition programs in 1972 on Hostage Tactics and Negotiation Techniques, Counter-Terrorism and VIP/Dignitary Protection, featuring the most realistic actual training scenarios ever offered to attendees at any program.

While at the I.A.C.P. he traveled throughout the world on training programs and as a liaison to INTERPOL. He served on several national commissions involved in the development of doctrine and response standards for law enforcement and criminal justice personnel, authored seven books and contributed numerous articles for professional magazines and journals. His major projects included: Directing the U.S. Attorney General's International Conference on Narcotics, Smuggling Intelligence and Crime Prevention for over a decade; Developer of the U.S. Coast Guard Law Enforcement Manual (Maritime); Director of the D.E.A. Narcotics Investigators Manual (Enforcement); and Program Director for the National Crime Prevention Program for Senior Citizens.

After departure as an Assistant Director from the staff of I.A.C.P. in 1979, he formed Richard W. Kobetz and Associates, Ltd., and opened North Mountain Pines Training Center and the Executive Protection Institute. His training programs continue to be offered on an international basis with on-site training for corporations, universities, military personnel, and law enforcement academies. His concept of providing executive protection has become the standard of the personal protection career field.

Over the past two decades the professional contributions made by Dr. Kobetz in the field of private and public protective services have been and continue to be original, in-depth and thought provoking. He is regarded as the *"trainer's-trainer"* and received the first designation of Certified Security Trainer (C.S.T.) and is a Fellow of the prestigious Academy of Security Educators and Trainers (A.S.E.T.). He has served on committees of the American Society for Industrial Security (A.S.I.S.). He is presently serving as President and Board Member of A.S.E.T. and as the Executive Secretary of the Nine Lives Associates (N.L.A.), a fraternal organization of dedicated professionals in the field of personal protection.

Selected Bibliography

Albert, Frank. *One-Strike Stopping Power.* Boulder, Colorado: Paladin Press, 1993.

Albrecht, W. Steve, et.al. *How to Detect and Prevent Business Fraud.* Englewood Cliffs, New Jersey: Prentice-Hall, 1982.

Applegate, Rex. *Kill Or Get Killed.* Boulder, Colorado: Paladin Press, 1976.

Barefoot, Kirk J. and Maxwell, David A. *Corporate Security Administration and Management.* Boston, Massachusetts: Butterworths, 1987.

Baron, Anthony S. *Violence In The Workplace: A Prevention and Management Guide for Business.* Bakersfield, California: Pathfinder Publishing of California, 1994.

Barron, John. *K.G.B.* New York: Readers' Digest Press, 1974.

Bell, J. Bowyer. *Assassin.* New York: St. Martin's Press, 1979.

Blakey, G. Robert and Billings, Richard N. *The Plot to Kill the President.* New York: Times Books, 1981.

Coleman, John L. *Practical Legal Guidelines For the Private Security Officer.* Springfield, Illinois: Charles C. Thomas, Publisher, 1990.

Duet, Karen Freeman and George. *The Home and Family Protection Dog: Selection and Training.* New York: Macmillan Publishing Company, 1993.

Eells, Richard and Nehemkis, Peter. *Corporate Intelligence and Espionage: A Blueprint for Executive Decision Making.* New York: Macmillan and Company, 1984.

Fairbairn, W.E. *Get Tough! How to Win In Hand-to-Hand Fighting.* Boulder, Colorado: Paladin Press, 1979.

Fox, Michael. *Understanding Your Dog.* New York: Coward, McCann and Geoghegan, 1992.

Fugua, Paul O. and Wilson, Jerry V. *Terrorism: The Executive's Guide to Survival.* Houston: Gulf Publishing Company Book Division, 1978.

Gillen, Mollie. *Assassination of the Prime Minister.* New York: St. Martin's Press, 1972.

Gerahty, Tony. *The Bullet-Catchers, Bodyguards and The World of Close Protection.* London: Grafton Books, 1988.

Glazebrook, Jerry and Nicholson, Larry. *Executive Protection Specialist Handbook.* Shawnee Mission, Kansas: Varro Press, 1994.

Havens, Murray Clark, Leiden, Carl and Schmitt, Karl M. *The Politics of Assassination.* Englewood Cliffs, New Jersey: Prentice Hall, 1970.

Heims, Peter. *Countering Industrial Espionage.* Leatherhead, Surrey, England: 20th Century Security Education, Ltd., 1982.

Horowitz, Irving L. *Assassination.* New York: Harper and Row, 1973.

Hyams, Joe. *Zen In the Martial Arts*. New York: Bantam Books, 1982.

Irving, John. *Setting Free the Bears*. New York: Pocket Books, 1968.

Joll, James. *The Anarchists*. New York: Grosset and Dunlop, 1966.

Kinney, Joseph A. and Johnson, Dennis L. *Breaking Point*. Chicago, Illinois: National Safe Workplace Institute, 1993.

Kobetz, Richard W. *Providing Executive Protection*. Berryville, Virginia: The Executive Protection Institute, 1991.

Kraayveld, Jan H. *Pressure Point and Control Techniques*. Toronto: Superior Baton and Police Tactics Corp., 1989.

Kupperman, Robert and Trent, Darrell. *Terrorism: Threat, Reality, Response*. Stanford, California: Hoover Institutional Press, 1979.

Kyle, Thomas G. and Aldridge, James. *Security Closed Circuit Television Handbook: Applications and Technical*. Springfield, Illinois: Charles C. Thomas Publisher, 1992.

Lewis, Michael. *Liar's Poker*. New York: W.W. Norton, 1989.

Mantell, Michael with Albrecht, Steve. *Ticking Bombs: Defusing Violence In The Workplace*. New York: Irwin Publishing, Inc., 1994.

Meyer, Herbert E. *Real World Intelligence*. New York: Weidenfeld and Nicolson, 1987.

Molloy, John T. *Dress For Success*. New York: Warner Books, 1975.

Morgan, Forrest E. *Living the Martial Way*. Fort Lee, New Jersey: Barricade Books, 1992.

Mullen, W. C. *Terrorist Organizations In The United States*. Springfield, Illinois: Charles C. Thomas, 1988.

O'Toole, George. *The Private Sector*. New York: W. W. Norton and Company, Inc. 1978.

RoAne, Susan. *How to Work A Room: A Guide To Successfully Managing The Mingling*. New York: Shapolsky Publishers, Inc., 1994.

Shackley, Theodore. *The Third Option*. New York: Readers' Digest Press, 1981.

Siddle, Bruce K. *Spontaneous Knife Defense Instructor Manual*. Middlestat: P.P.C.T. Management Systems, Inc., 1991 (2nd Rev.).

Sprouse, Martin. *Sabotaging The American Workplace*. San Francisco, California: Presdure Drop Press, 1992.

Sterling, Claire. *The Terror Network: The Secret War of International Terrorism*. New York: Holt, Rinehart and Winston, 1981.

Stoll, Clifford. *The Cuckoo's Egg: Inside The World of Computer Espionage*. New York: Doubleday, 1989.

Strickland, Winifred. *Expert Obedience Training for Dogs*. New York: Macmillan Publishing Company, 1988.

Tannen, Deborah. *You Just Don't Understand: Women and Men in Conversation*. New York: Ballantine Books, 1990.

Varney, Michael. *Bodyguard to Charles*. London: Robert Hale, 1989.

Wykes, Alan. *Hitler's Bodyguards: Leibstandarte*. New York: Random House, Inc., 1974.

Yeager, Robert. *The Failure to Provide Security Handbook*. Columbia, Maryland: Hanrow Press, Inc., 1986.

Index